THE HUMAN RIGHTS OF CHILDREN

For Our Families

The Human Rights of Children
From Visions to Implementation

Edited by

ANTONELLA INVERNIZZI
JANE WILLIAMS
Swansea University, Wales, UK

Routledge
Taylor & Francis Group

LONDON AND NEW YORK

First published 2011 by Ashgate Publishing

Published 2016 by Routledge
2 Park Square, Milton Park, Abingdon, Oxfordshire OX14 4RN
711 Third Avenue, New York, NY 10017, USA

First issued in paperback 2016

Routledge is an imprint of the Taylor & Francis Group, an informa business

British Library Cataloguing in Publication Data
The human rights of children : from visions to
    implementation.
    1. Children's rights. 2. Convention on the Rights of the
    Child (1989) 3. International and municipal law.
    I. Invernizzi, Antonella. II. Williams, Jane M.
    346'.0135-dc22

Library of Congress Cataloging-in-Publication Data
The human rights of children : from visions to implementation / by Antonella Invernizzi and Jane Williams.
    p. cm.
    Includes bibliographical references and index.
    ISBN 978-1-4094-0531-3 (hardback)
    1. Children's rights. 2. Children--Legal status, laws, etc. 3. Convention on the Rights of the Child (1989) I. Invernizzi, Antonella. II. Williams, Jane M.
    K639.H86 2011
    323.3'52--dc22

                                                                    2010047887

ISBN 13: 978-1-138-25240-0 (pbk)
ISBN 13: 978-1-4094-0531-3 (hbk)

Contents

List of Figures

List of Tables

Notes on Contributors

Harriot Beazley, BA (Hons), London; PhD (ANU), is a Lecturer in the School of Social Sciences, at the University of the Sunshine Coast (Australia), where she teaches Human Geography. Dr Beazley's research interests are the geographies of children and young people in Southeast Asia and the Pacific, including street and working children in Indonesia, and rights based research with children and young people. Dr Beazley is Commissioning Editor (Australia and the Pacific) for the Journal *Children's Geographies* (Routledge).

Sharon Bessell is a Senior Lecturer at the Crawford School of Economics and Government, The Australian National University. Sharon's research focuses on the social policy and the human rights of children, particularly children's participation and citizenship, child labour, child protection, children without parental care, and the gendered and generational dimensions of poverty. She has published widely on these topics. Sharon has worked in Australia, Southeast Asia and the Pacific as a researcher, with non-government organisations and as a consultant.

Nigel Cantwell is a Geneva-based international consultant on child protection policies, with a main focus on safeguarding children's rights in alternative care and intercountry adoption, and juvenile justice. He founded the NGO Defence for Children International in 1979, and headed up the NGO Group for the Convention on the Rights of the Child throughout the drafting of the treaty. From 1998 to 2003, he was responsible for the 'Implementation of International Standards' unit at UNICEF's Innocenti Research Centre in Florence.

Rhian Croke is the UNCRC Monitoring Officer for Save the Children Wales and is a committed advocate for children's rights. She coordinates the work of the Wales UNCRC Monitoring Group, a national alliance of agencies tasked with monitoring and promoting the implementation of the UNCRC in Wales. She is co-editor of *Righting the Wrongs: The Reality of Children's Rights in Wales* and *Stop, Look, Listen: The Road to Realising Children's Rights in Wales*. She has previously worked as Assistant Director for Save the Children Wales and at the University of Cape Town Children's Institute as a Senior Researcher in the HIV/AIDS Programme.

Anne Crowley is a policy and research consultant and is currently studying for a PhD at Cardiff University. Anne has undertaken research with children and young people on a range of issues including youth crime, public care, advocacy services and child poverty. She is currently a member of the Welsh Assembly Government's Child Poverty Expert Group and the Wales Committee of the Equalities and Human Rights Commission. In 2008 Anne co-edited (with Rhian Croke) the 'alternative' report on progress in implementing the United Nations Convention on the Rights of the Child in Wales *Stop, Look, Listen: The Road to Realising Children's Rights in Wales*.

Jaap E. Doek is Emeritus Professor of Law (Family and Juvenile Law) at the Vrije Universiteit in Amsterdam. He was a member of the UN Committee on the Rights of the Child from 1999 to 2007 and a chairperson of that Committee from 2001 to 2007. He is an advisor/consultant involved in, among others, activities of the Special Representative of the Secretary General of the UN on Children and Armed Conflict, the regional office of UNICEF for East and Southern Africa, a number of UNICEF country offices and some governments of States Parties to the CRC.

Eleanor Drywood is a Lecturer at the Liverpool Law School, University of Liverpool. She has been engaged in research on immigrant and asylum-seeking children in EU law and policy for the past six years and has published on this topic in major European legal journals. She has a wider interest in the Union's fundamental rights regime and EU activity in relation to young people. She has also worked on an EU Fundamental Rights Agency project to develop a set of indicators to measure the impact of European law and policy on the rights of the child.

Judith Ennew is currently Visiting Senior Research Fellow (2009–2011) in the Gender Studies Programme, Faculty of Arts and Social Sciences, University of Malaya. She gained a PhD in social anthropology (1978) at the University of Cambridge and has been an activist and researcher in the human rights of children worldwide since 1979.

Michael Freeman is Professor of English Law at University College London where he has taught since 1969. His research interests are in child law and children's rights, medical law and medical ethics and jurisprudence. He has published extensively. His books include *The Rights and Wrongs of Children*, *The Moral Status of Children* and *Introduction to Jurisprudence*, now in its 8th edition. He is the editor of the *International Journal of Children's Rights*.

Funky Dragon is the Children and Young People's Assembly for Wales. It is a peer-led organisation supported by Welsh government and other funding. Funky Dragon gives 0–25 year olds the opportunity to get their voices heard on issues affecting them.

Jeffrey Goldhagen, MD, MPH, is Professor of Pediatrics at the University of Florida-Jacksonville and Chief of the Division of Community Pediatrics. He has extensive experience in domestic and international health; urban, community and maternal and child health; medical education; the core functions of public health; health care administration and in children's rights and advocacy. As a member of the academic faculty at the University of Minnesota, Case Western Reserve University (CWRU) and the University of Florida, he has been actively engaged in the delivery of health care to urban communities and in the training of health professionals.

Brian Gran is on the faculty of the Sociology Department and Law School of Case Western Reserve University. His research focuses on how law is used to designate public–private boundaries in social life. He currently directs the Children's Rights Index (CRI) project. He is completing a book on independent children's rights institutions.

Dr Antonella Invernizzi, until recently a Senior Lecturer at Swansea University, is an honorary research fellow in this institution as well as working as a research consultant. She has published books and academic journal articles in relation to children's work, children 'in' the street, family poverty and, with Jane Williams, on children and citizenship.

Ursula Kilkelly is a Senior Lecturer at the Faculty of Law, University College Cork. She has published widely on children's rights including *The Child and the ECHR* (1999), *Youth Justice in Ireland* (2006), and *Children's Rights in Ireland: Law, Policy and Practice* (2008). She has recently published in the *Child and Family Law Quarterly*, *Youth Justice: An International Journal* and the *Northern Ireland Law Quarterly* on various subjects relating to the implementation of children's rights. Her research includes major projects for the Northern Ireland Commissioner for Children and Young People (2004), the Ombudsman for Children's Office in Ireland (2007 and 2010) and the Council of Europe (2010) with whom she works on issues of child friendly justice, juvenile justice (with the Commissioner for Human Rights) and child friendly healthcare

Raúl Mercer, MD, MSc, works for the Program of Social Sciences and Health at the Latin American University of Social Sciences, Buenos Aires, Argentina. He is the coordinator of the Southern Cone Initiative on Child Rights and Health and coordinator of the Seminar on Gender and Childhood. He is academic coordinator of the Summer Program of Public Health and researcher at the Perinatal Network of the Metropolitan Area of Buenos Aires.

Helen Stalford is a Senior Lecturer at the Liverpool Law School. She has researched and published widely in the area of EU child and family law over the past decade and has worked as a consultant to UNICEF, the Fundamental Rights Agency and the European Commission on a range of EU children's rights issues.

John Tobin is an Associate Professor at Melbourne Law School where he teaches courses on International Law and Children's Rights. He has been a Visiting Professor at the American Academy of Human Rights and Humanitarian Law, Washington College of Law, American University and a Visiting Professor at New York University Law School. He works with numerous statutory, non-governmental and private sector bodies in connection with human rights issues. He is currently writing a Commentary to the Convention on the Rights of the Child with Professor Philip Alston.

Geraldine Van Bueren, one of the original drafters of the Convention on the Rights of the Child, is Professor of International Human Rights Law at Queen Mary, University of London and Visiting Fellow at Kellogg College, Oxford. She is a Commissioner on the Equality and Human Rights Commission.

Roxana Waterson is an Associate Professor in the Department of Sociology, National University of Singapore. She has a PhD in Social Anthropology from the University of Cambridge, and has done extensive fieldwork in Indonesia, particularly Sulawesi. Her publications include *The Living House: An Anthropology of Architecture in Southeast Asia* (4th edn, Tuttle, 2009), *Southeast Asian Lives: Personal Narratives and Historical Experience* (National University of Singapore Press/Ohio University Press, 2007) and *Paths and Rivers: Sa'dan Toraja Society in Transformation* (KITLV, 2009). Her main interest currently is in research with children, and she has collaborated with Dr Judith Ennew on projects for UNICEF and Save The Children Sweden, training Indonesian researchers in this area.

Elspeth Webb is a Reader in Child Health, Cardiff University. She grew up on a farm in Wales and trained in London. Her clinical work includes autism, child protection and improving services for marginalised communities. She has a long-standing commitment to the promotion of children's rights and to combating discrimination particularly against children who are socially marginalised, interests reflected in her publication record.

Jane Williams is a Senior Lecturer at the School of Law, Swansea University. She researches and has published on implementation of the human rights of children and on aspects of devolution within the UK. She is a member of the Wales NGO monitoring group for the CRC.

Preface and Acknowledgements

The origins of this compilation are to be found in a project for a seminar series and a small conference held at Swansea University in September 2008. A number of questions and thoughts were in our mind. In common with many people, we do ask ourselves in what ways the CRC has made a difference to children. Although this is probably the main question to be asked and is at the centre of the monitoring process, it is also a broad one, far too ambitious and even a pretentious ambition for the small conference at Swansea. The key question focused instead on what lies behind any action in favour of children. The key issue of the day was to examine what we today call the children's rights agenda and efforts for implementation in the light of what was intended at the time of the drafting and adoption of the CRC. More precisely the questions were: What were the original visions of the CRC held by those involved in the drafting or by those who have been in one way or another contributing to the CRC's success in its adoption and in subsequent signatures and ratifications? Are today's machinery, advocacy and actions of UN bodies and organisations, NGOs and government offices in line with it? What is the key dilemma or difficulty in its implementation? What are the state-of-the-art processes and machinery that have been created? And in what ways has there been development in the very much needed research necessary to promote children's rights? The one-day conference, titled *Children's Rights: From 20th Century Visions to 21st Century Implementation?*, involved leading experts including Nigel Cantwell, Jaap Doek, Judith Ennew and Geraldine Van Bueren in a discussion at the international level and a number of leading speakers who debated the situation in Wales at the time when the third and fourth periodic reporting round for the UK Government under the CRC was nearing its conclusion. The latter group of speakers presented different aspects of the situation in Wales and of the monitoring process during plenary presentations and workshops. Among them were Rhian Croke and Anne Crowley, Funky Dragon and Elspeth Webb (whose contributions are included in this book), Keith Towler (the Children's Commissioner for Wales), Eleri Thomas (then chairperson of the Wales NGOs' monitoring group for the CRC) and senior officials from the Welsh Assembly Government.

The excellence of the contributions and the amount of knowledge transmitted during the day made us regret having restricted the conference to one day and not having extended invitations to other experts, covering further topics. The edition of a compilation of the speakers' contributions has thus become an opportunity to expand the debate a little further to include a number of different perspectives and topics whilst separating the contributions into two different books: the present collection, and a second focusing exclusively on the CRC in Wales, delayed to enable account to be taken of the important developments towards a general legislative measure of implementation at the Wales-only level within the UK (of which some foretaste is provided in the chapters by Williams and Croke and Crowley in the present collection). Unless a later date is indicated in the text, the information in the book is correct as of September 2010.

A number of persons contributed to the conference and associated seminars and meetings which brought this book to fruition and whilst extending our thanks to all involved we would like to make particular mention of some of them. We extend special thanks for the support of Judith Ennew who, besides presenting a plenary paper and providing an outstanding contribution to the topic of research, gave great encouragement and counsel to us when organising the Swansea conference. Although he was not able to open the conference as expected, Per Miljeteig's support for our idea and his insights spanning the entire period of gestation, infancy and maturity of the CRC were invaluable in providing intellectual capital and stimulus for our main theme of 'visions to implementation'. All the speakers and facilitators on the day have our grateful thanks: likewise the most able and enthusiastic administrative support team led by Trish Rees at the School of Law, Swansea University. Lastly we extend our thanks to the contributors who stand ready to relate in more depth the experience and innovation of the CRC in Wales in the volume yet to come.

Antonella Invernizzi and Jane Williams
Swansea University

List of Abbreviations

ACRWC	African Charter on the Rights and Welfare of Children
BEM	Black Ethnic Minority
CRC	United Nations Convention on the Rights of the Child
CRC Committee	United Nations Committee on the Rights of the Child
CRPD	Convention on the Rights of Persons with Disabilities
ECHR	European Convention on Human Rights and Fundamental Freedoms
ECJ	European Court of Justice
ECOSOC	Economic and Social Council
EU	European Union
ENOC	European Network of Ombudspersons for Children
ICCPR	International Covenant on Civil and Political Rights
ICESCR	International Covenant on Economic, Social and Cultural Rights
ICJ	International Commission of Jurists
ICRI	Independent children's rights institution
IUCW	International Union for Child Welfare
IYC	International Year of the Child
JCHR	Joint Committee on Human Rights of the House of Lords and the House of Commons (UK)
NGO	Non-governmental organisation
NHRI	National human rights institution
OHCHR	Office of the High Commissioner for Human Rights
OP	Optional Protocol
OPAC	Optional Protocol on the Involvement of Children in Armed Conflict
OPSC	Optional Protocol on the Sale of Children, Child Prostitution and Child Pornography
TEU	Treaty on European Union
TFEU	Treaty on the Functioning of the European Union
UDHR	Universal Declaration of Human Rights
UN AIDS	United Nations Joint Programme on HIV/AIDS
UNICEF	United Nations International Children's Emergency Fund
WAG	Welsh Assembly Government
WHO	World Health Organization

Introduction
Human Rights of Children:
From Visions to Implementation?

The aim of this book is to examine aspects of contemporary approaches to the human rights of children. The conference in Swansea in 2008 that originally included some of the papers upon which the chapters published in this book are based set out to revisit the original visions behind the drafting and adoption of the UN Convention on the Rights of the Child (CRC) and focus on the mechanisms and strategies put in place for implementation, research and advocacy. Thus this book does not attempt to present an analysis of what has been achieved for children around the world during the period since the CRC was adopted, but rather more attempts to reflect on some significant developments at the international, State Party, regional or local level which have been stimulated or influenced by the CRC. The collection comprises a selection of experiences, reflections and critiques contributed by experts who in different roles and disciplines have been intensely involved in promoting and using the CRC. Some of them were, in fact, involved in drafting it. Whilst drawing on past or present experiences, research findings or practice, or reflecting on the context of development of the CRC as a legal and political instrument, thoughts about future directions and challenges are also proposed.

Why Revisiting Visions?

The CRC has promoted a new vision of the child as bearer of human rights, which is essentially influential in policy, legislation, research and programming worldwide as well as at regional, national and local levels. Yet, despite the near universality of adoption of the CRC and its success, as Michael Freeman points out in this collection, it seems necessary constantly to rehearse and re-affirm the case for human rights for children. Furthermore, despite the prevalence of focus in a good deal of literature on assessing the progress in (or lack of) implementation, 'mainstreaming' and impact on children's lives, we argue that that there is also a need to revisit the visions behind the drafting and adoption of the CRC. One might pause to reflect on the underlying assumptions and beliefs (and how these may have developed since the negotiation of the text) as a 'healthy' exercise for reconsidering present efforts to implement the CRC. This was at least our inclination at the time of the Swansea conference in 2008. By the same means we also wanted to explore possible reasons for the mixed and contradictory feelings that one perceives in the field, where assertions of strong commitment to the CRC go alongside high levels of frustration about resistance encountered and where confusion, sometimes enthusiasm and elsewhere discomfort arise from initiatives taken in the name of children's rights that are presented as a straightforward set of technicalities. When scrutinising the content of this collection, one could indeed argue that a better understanding of the philosophical foundations and visions expressed at the time of the drafting and adoption of the CRC is of considerable aid for making sense of the perhaps inevitably contested and differently interpreted claims made in the name of human rights of children as well as the resistance sometimes encountered.

Accounts on the history of the CRC (for instance Cantwell 1992, Freeman 2004, Alston and Tobin 2005, Milne 2008) often outline the role played by key figures such as Eglantyne Jebb, Janus Korczak or Adam Lopatka as well as illustrate examples of resistance marking the path to adoption by the UN General Assembly in 1989. Each step forward was an achievement in overcoming opposition expressed on one or another ground and some steps needed to be taken over a few decades. The 1924 Geneva Declaration did not bring about acceptance of the child as an independent individual as, for instance, the oeuvre and writing of Korczak may have inspired. During the preparation of the 1959 Declaration on the Rights of the Child there was still no such recognition as exemplified in the statement of the French delegate indicating that 'the child was not in a position to exercise his [or her] own rights. Adults exercised them for the child ...' (Freeman 2004: xiii). Freeman also reports the discussion on the need to protect 'the legitimate family' proposed by the representative of the Italian government in response to the expressed need to protect illegitimate children against discrimination. Whereas the 1959 Declaration introduced the principle of non-discrimination it still did not recognise the child as a subject and active agent: this was later incorporated in the CRC and today is often recognised as a foundation of the 'participation' articles. Those articles were included to reaffirm existing human rights and acknowledge justly that they apply to children. That said, Alston (1994) describes the role they had in the hands of US delegates whose emphasis on issues of freedom of expression or information was seemingly intended to point out the lack of those freedoms in the Soviet bloc. Aspects of those negotiations well illustrate the weight of ideological difference between East and West, still tangible during the drafting of the CRC, but also remind how issues enveloped in the CRC may be examined in terms of content as much as use individuals and organisations make of the Convention for many purposes. An example of the *how* mattering as much as the *what* can be found, for instance, in Nigel Cantwell's (1992) mention of resistance within the human rights arena towards the significant role NGOs took in drafting the CRC for the first time in the human rights field. It is valuable to remember various confrontations, some of which look perhaps trivial today, to give a sense of the context of progressive negotiation of the CRC over 10 years. As Cantwell stresses in this volume, the CRC reflects 'a hard-won consensus on the substance of the human rights of children'.

Following its overwhelming success of signatures and ratifications, accounts about the more recent history of children's rights have just started to be addressed. Alston and Tobin (2005) explicitly refer to two post-adoption stages. The first, at the end of the twentieth century, is identified as one of 'enthusiasm and optimism'. Coalitions developed and promoted the diffusion of initiatives to make the CRC known and procedures as well as a normative framework emerged which, as they argue, 'would have been unimaginable even a quarter of a century earlier' (2005: 7). The second and more challenging post-adoption stage starting in the twenty-first century is identified by them as one of 'consolidation and reaction' which would somehow end the 'honeymoon' with children's rights.

> Consolidation was called for on the part of the principal actors involved in the CRC process, as the relative euphoria of the third phase began to wear off and governments, NGOs and international agencies all began to realize the true enormity of the task they had set themselves. This has already given rise to a period of reaction in which governments seek to reclaim some of the ground that they fear was conceded in the 1990s and as they come under greater financial and other pressures ... which accord no particular priority to children. Many will also begin to resist either passively or actively some of the demands for greater accountability, which are an integral part of the philosophy of the CRC.
>
> The post-September 11 syndrome in many countries has focused attention on a phalanx of 'security' concerns, often at the expense of human rights. We can expect a diminution in human rights consciousness on the part of governments, an increased hesitance on the part of human rights groups to insist on the respect for human rights in the face of new threats, both real and imagined and what appears to be a growing public tolerance of measures to limit the enjoyment of human rights in the name of security and related objectives. (Alston and Tobin 2005: 7–8)

After the period when Alston and Tobin wrote, one has to consider the economic downturn, the impact of which is only beginning to be assessed[1] and is likely to be measured, among other indicators, by a dramatic increase in rates of child poverty, deprivation, malnutrition and health deficiencies and falling levels of education. This goes hand in hand with immense budgetary cuts in governments' expenditure that are inexorably changing the landscape in which a children's rights agenda is placed.

If these are rather gloomy times in the recent history of the CRC, they are essentially those in which human rights, including those of children, prove their

---

1   See for instance the social and economic policy section developed by UNICEF (http://www.unicef.org/socialpolicy/ [accessed 28 September 2010]).

value. What transpired in times of enthusiasm and optimism might need to be reassessed, and whilst further reinforcing the agenda to protect, promote and fulfil human rights of children, a closer look at the relatively recent history of the CRC might allow assessment of the rigour and viability of paths taken. Indeed a very superficial reading of some key texts written at the time of drafting and adoption of the CRC[2] provide much food for thought.

Inevitably, the notion originally proposed by Jebb, arguing that 'it is ... children who pay the heaviest price for our short-sighted economic policies, our political blunders, our wars' (cited in Hammarberg 1990: 98) was well represented in some of the early-1990s writing. Hammarberg's vision of the role of the CRC, whilst raising the question of allocating priorities, reminds inevitably of the enthusiasm and optimism of the post-adoption era described above:

> The time has come to work out a comprehensive strategy for the realisation of the Convention. It is a question of allocating priority. The rest of this century should be made a decade for children and their rights. The adoption of the Convention should be seen as the start of radically renewed effort to put right the wrongs we do to children with our short-sighted economic policies, political blunders and wars. (1990: 104)

Such concerns are very valid in today's socio-economic and political reality. Beside this, that statement endorses the specific aim of safeguarding and promoting the rights of categories of children who are particularly vulnerable to violation as a consequence of, among other things, economic policies, political blunders and wars. For the intents and purposes of this collection, that statement produces the question of assessing how far this aim reflects different fields and activities carried out in the name of children's rights and how far such activities actually focus on those who are more vulnerable to rights violations, often in many ways.

On a different level, texts around the time of adoption remind that the CRC was intended to collate a number of rights previously found in different human rights instruments, whilst developing and elaborating some of them to account for children's specific needs and interests (e.g. Miljeteig-Olson 1990: 149). Whilst being a human rights instrument, it needed to move from a traditional categorisation of rights and emphasise indivisibility, equal importance and mutual reinforcement of rights:

> The Convention is extraordinarily comprehensive in scope. It covers all the traditionally defined areas of human rights – civil, political, economic, social and cultural. In doing so, however it has shied away from distinguishing between these areas and, on the contrary, has happily tended to underscore the indivisibility, mutual reinforcement and equal importance of all rights. In order

---

2   These extracts were presented at a workshop given at the Conference 'Children's Rights: From Visions to Implementation', September 2008, Swansea University.

precisely to avoid that traditional categorisation, with its negative historical connotations, many commentators have preferred to describe and analyse the scope of the Convention in terms of rights relating to 'protection', 'provision' ... and 'participation' ... – the 3 Ps. (Cantwell 1992: 27)

Looking at that now, one can thus ask if '3Ps' has been a successful concept in promoting the application of the principle of indivisibility, equal importance and mutual reinforcement of all rights enshrined in the CRC. As the discussion on participation below indicates, one can ask how emphatic specialisation of programmes and advocacy handles this important principle. Are today's key issues systematically addressed in terms of indivisibility of rights and if not what priorities are proposed?

Further questions arise when considering the vision of the child. It is overwhelmingly recognised that the CRC has promoted a fundamentally new vision of children. The drafting process set out to draw together a set of human rights that were distinctly for children, whilst redefining them to account for their 'specific needs and interests'. Per Miljeteig regards this as 'a global consciousness-raising process ...' which '... in many ways changed the world's thinking about children' (Miljeteig-Olson 1990: 149). Whereas the CRC embraces an understanding of the child as an independent human being with rights, it is significant that what was written at that time is remarkably cautious. In contrast with today's mainstream writings on the rights of children, the outcome of the drafting process is phrased in terms of 'growing understanding', 'regional differences', 'careful development' and 'delicate balance':

> ... a growing understanding of the child as an independent individual with rights exercised by the child, not only by representatives from the adult world.

> ... we learned ... about regional differences and restrictions in the interpretation of the exercise of children's rights ...

> ... that the understanding of the child as an independent human being must be very carefully developed ...

> ... that there is a delicate balance between the rights of the parents and those of the child ... (Miljeteig-Olson 1990: 149 and 150)

Similarly to Miljeteig, Alston handled the discussion on culture, best interest and the competing or conflicting interests and rights of human beings with notable caution:

> The text of the Convention does not, and indeed realistically could not, reflect any set formula for accommodating the competing interests that arise in this regard. Rather it consists of a range of different principles, the balancing or

> reconciliation of which in any given situation will depend on a variety of considerations. This complexity needs, however, to be explored and illustrated in actual case studies. (Alston 1994: 5)

This careful consideration and acknowledgement of the complexity seems to contrast with some of today's predominant statements of certitude that populate guidelines, implementation handbooks, policy making or programming and advocacy in relation to the CRC. That point is also made by John Tobin in this book.

In 1994, Alston wondered how to avoid future misunderstandings in relation to the balance struck by the CRC and the complexity of the tasks. In the extract below that relates to the competing rights and interests of women and children, but is easily expandable to other settings, he examines the risk of this instrument being moulded to reflect particular value preferences. Case studies, he argues, would need to be carried out to provide illustration of the balance struck by the CRC:

> ... In the absence of the understanding that such case studies could generate, it is very likely in the years ahead that the balance struck in the Convention will be misunderstood or misrepresented whether by those wanting to argue that the Convention elevates children's rights at the expense of those of women, or vice-versa, by children's advocates who wish to present a one-sided picture of the implications flowing from the Convention, or by other parties who would wish to mould the text to reflect their own particular value preferences. (Alston 1994: 5)

More than any other text, Alston's quote begs questions of relevance today: has the CRC been misunderstood, has the text been moulded to reflect particular values? Have the rights of the child been elevated at the expense of rights of other human beings?

Interpretation ... and Appropriation?

Returning to the above mentioned mixed feelings encountered in the field, one thus wonders how much confusion, frustration and sometimes discomfort are precisely the outcome of the 'global-consciousness-raising process', to borrow Miljeteig's expression, sustained and amplified after the adoption of the CRC through the efforts of international organisations (IOs), NGOs, academics, experts and governmental agencies. It has lead to an enthusiastic 'appropriation' of the children's rights agenda by different instances and organisations, bringing about multiple interpretations as well as, as one can read in Nigel Cantwell's work, a distance from human rights instruments themselves and their foundations.

Literature generally makes reference to oppositions outside the children's rights or human rights arena. Thus, it might seem paradoxical that the increased distance from human rights instruments and procedures comes at least partly from professionals and organisations which intend to promote it. Yet this is what can be extrapolated from Cantwell's and Tobin's contributions, both expressing pleas for a more rigorous use of the CRC.

As Cantwell points out, the enthusiastic multiplication of interpretations at variance with the CRC brings about significant consequences. In his words

> The CRC reflects a hard-won consensus on the substance of the human rights of children, and it was indeed quickly heralded as the most widely ratified human rights instrument ever. Clearly the standard-setting, crucial in itself as an agreed basis for action, has also enabled progress to be made in many spheres of the ensuing year .... Children's issues have been significantly moved up the international and national agendas .... But, despite clear advances such as these, and the treaty's pedigree, a problem has gradually been surfacing: too often, these rights are not looked on as children's inalienable *human* rights but simply as ... *children's* rights. (Cantwell, Chapter 2, this volume)

However this begs the question of what constitutes the human rights basis and where shifts have taken place. Three contributions in this book focus specifically on the foundations and visions behind the agenda of children's human rights, themes surprisingly little developed when compared to existing literature in human rights. Other contributions, whilst providing examination of specific issues, equally introduce significant material for discussion.

In Chapter 1, Michael Freeman makes the case of needing to re-affirm the case of human rights for children. His starting point is acceptance of the basic Kantian perspective that human beings are ends in themselves, not just the means to ends and that rights are pre-eminently a key which opens doors for those human beings who are un-powerful, providing a method of reasoning and a basis for demanding basic human dignity. The fundamental significance of the CRC, he argues, is that it claims rights for children. That is a claim that needs to be made repeatedly as there remains far from universal acceptance even amongst those who endorse rights for adults. The CRC thus represented a 'paradigm shift' in thinking about children.

In a similar vein but in relation to the human rights based approach, John Tobin, in Chapter 3, expresses the concern that 'that advocates for children ... have been too active in their embrace of a rights based approach and insufficiently attentive to the need to develop a more reflective, internally coherent and sophisticated understanding of what this term should mean.' He particularly questions the basis for the routinely mentioned principles identified in the CRC such as non-discrimination, best interest of the child, right to survival and development and participation. He proposes discussion of issues regarding human dignity, interdependence and indivisibility, cultural sensitivity and the complementary principles of due deference (the requirement to respect parents and guardians in the exercise of their responsibilities toward children) and evolving capacity. One can argue that the key significance of due deference and cultural sensitivity is evident when looking at the poor outcomes of child focused approaches that ignore the context in which the young person lives. This debate well echoes some of the points made by Judith Ennew, Harriot Beazley, Sharon Bessell and Roxana Waterson. Their discussion on rights based research in the South puts considerable emphasis on examining the experiences and views of children as a heterogeneous category, addressing the multiple facets of their lives as well as the indivisibility and mutual reinforcement of their rights.

The reader might find in both Cantwell's and Tobin's chapters that there are a number of points in which discourse in the name of children's rights seems to have shifted away from the human rights normative framework, the acknowledged human rights based approach or the intention of those who drafted the CRC. Cantwell points out a particular interpretation of the best interest of the child that is analogous with the rights approach in a *'children first'* dictate. That position precisely undermines the possibilities for the careful examination of both the other rights of the children and young people involved and the rights of other human beings around them. What can be extrapolated from the content of both chapters is that the assessment Alston (above) claimed to be required to act in complex situations made of competing interests of different human beings, scarce resources and potential resistances might be too often overlooked.

Another aspect of the discourse Cantwell identifies as moving away from the human rights agenda may be seen as the 'infantilisation' of all under-18 rights holders under the CRC, whereby they all end up being regarded as children. This is illustrated by the emotionally charged labelling of young people as 'child soldiers', a category which, he indicates, ultimately includes for the most part persons who are strictly speaking neither children nor soldiers.

The explanation for these apparent shifts away from the normative content of the CRC may lie in part in the fact that much of the activity has taken place within a largely non-legal arena. The new vision of the child and a rights based approach have characterised work in development, emergency, national and international policy making, the political arena and the media – just to mention some key fields – and the efforts of a multiplicity of actors: non-governmental and international organisations, governmental agencies, researchers and experts. This, needless to say, has been an important part of the success of the CRC but it also raises questions about how the instrument has been understood. In the social welfare arena interpretations by 'non-legal' authorities in the form of administrative guidance, target-setting, regulation and inspection of services and indeed research and academic writing have tended to be the dominant modes of discourse about the CRC. There are obvious advantages to such channels as they offer potential for proactive decision making in contrast with the essentially reactive role of the courts. Judicial interpretation both at the international and domestic levels remains a relative rarity and is generally limited to discussion of how the CRC may add a new shade of meaning to other international or domestic legal obligations. As expounded by both Doek and Van Bueren in this collection, there remains no international judicial enforcement mechanism nor even any complaints or referral system, although a serious attempt has begun to develop such a mechanism within the UN. However, the downside of the dominance of social over legal interpretation of the CRC is a tendency both to mask the importance of the CRC as a legal text generating normative standards – the inalienable human rights of children – and to render those standards susceptible to being reinterpreted and even subverted to service pre-existing or supervening objectives.

As Cantwell notes, sentimentalism is part of the equation. Literature has for long pointed out that the idealised and emotionally charged image of the vulnerable child has mobilised actions of charitable nature. What Cantwell seems to suggest is that whereas the normative framework should have somehow reduced the power of those idealised images in determining the agenda in relation to the human rights of children, they have persisted, leading to partial reinterpretation of the CRC. This may well be the case where, using Alston's words above, claims have 'mould[ed] the text to reflect [particular] value preferences' or more simply to reflect actual approaches and work undertaken. Beside the image of the vulnerable child, one could argue that the more recent image of the disempowered child requiring increased 'participation' initially is an equally significant source of mobilisation in need of scrutiny.

Interestingly, the texts written around the drafting of the CRC contain some comments referring to specific values of some children's activists who 'perhaps … were unable to add realism to the idealistic position of not being satisfied with anything but the best solution … (Miljeteig-Olson 1990: 148).[3] 'Not being satisfied with anything but the best solution' indeed reminds us of a notion of the dominance of children's interests and an idealised view of what children should be entitled to. An analogous idealised position can easily be identified through efforts of experts and academics working on the topic as well as NGOs, international organisations or governmental agencies. Rather than being the matter of solely an individual attitude, the idealised position and emotionally charged image of the child is embedded in the public image of an organisation's work and inevitably part of its fundraising strategies, constructed to attract donors rather than reflect actual experiences. Uncritical use of these sentimentalised and idealised images of children as a standard for designing policy making and programming, however, inevitably leads to problems and imperfect outcomes. This echoes the case of the label 'child soldiers' which, whilst relying on the emotional impact of the image of the child, in practice contributes, among other things, to rendering the specific interests of adolescents invisible.

---

3 The texts refer to the significant and positive role played by NGOs in the drafting of the CRC: '… a number of non-governmental organisations have made a significant impact on the Convention as well as on its conceptual framework … [they] fought for children's interests during the drafting process … they injected an element of creativity and progress … they often seemed to be closer to the reality of the world's children than government representatives … perhaps they were unable to add realism to the idealistic position of not being satisfied with anything but the best solution' (Miljeteig-Olson 1990: 148).

It is unreasonable to expect a human rights instrument setting inalienable rights for all young persons under 18 and thus characterised by an indispensible level of vagueness to generate consensus in its interpretation, particularly when success, if not popularity, relies on a social platform without defined boundaries. Tobin and Cantwell's contributions clearly show how much some claims made for children in the name of the CRC are of a contested nature. Cantwell censures the rights' inflation, which proposes particular interpretations of rights far removed from what was intended in the CRC. If we follow Cantwell, it is not possible to naively welcome interpretations that go further than that enshrined in the CRC without assessing the danger rights inflation poses for consensus achieved in the past. Will States Parties be willing to subscribe to these new interpretations of CRC articles far removed from what they originally signed up to? Can the children's rights agenda be taken seriously in the field of human rights with a proliferation of claims at variance with the CRC?

The Contested Claims on Children's Participation

Among the most contested, confused and discussed claims in the name of the CRC are probably those made with regard to participation articles. In this collection, one will find several very different statements relating to participation which, whilst seeming contradictory at first, sufficiently describe some of the different levels of analysis needed to attain an overview in the field. For Cantwell, the present enlarged definition of participation inclusive of very different initiatives has led to claims at variance with the CRC. He argues that scrutiny is needed, for example, of claims for children to have a platform at all sorts of events without consideration of how the initiative concerned links to the human rights agenda, claims which emphasise decision-making and child-led processes going well beyond the right to be consulted included in the CRC and likewise activities regularly deployed for 'ticking boxes' to prove that participation was considered.

The enlargement of the definition of participation questioned by Cantwell is also visited in other chapters, although sometimes accompanied by warnings. An enlarged definition is proposed by Tobin in his discussion of a human rights based approach. Jaap Doek likewise considers the need for consolidating child participation within the monitoring activities of the CRC Committee. Beazley et al., whose rights based research is firmly rooted in participatory articles, also warn about frequently insufficiently thought out attempts to promote participation, often with poor outcomes, which do not always respect other rights of children. They also argue that some claims relating to child participation might better be framed in terms of citizenship. Geraldine Van Bueren, indeed, frames her discussion in terms of global or international citizenship and provides strong evidence in favour of participation beyond the potential mechanism of communication / complaint she examines.

Cantwell's call for a clear link between participatory initiatives and the human rights agenda clearly resonates with the examples of successful involvement of children described by Van Bueren. As for other historical processes that have considerably empowered human beings, Van Bueren argues that initial stages inevitably will not provide real empowerment. One may read her chapter as an invitation to promote a rigorous discussion of current difficulties and limitations in the field.

Despite efforts to conceptualise and develop a coherent approach, a structured overview capable of considering the very different approaches and paths taken by initiatives named as participation is still missing (van Beers et al. 2006). Furthermore, it can easily be observed how, despite efforts to develop guidance and standards for activists and organisations, confusion is very much present in the field. One easily finds evidence of young people not entirely clear about the role they can have in the specific event in which they are participating.[4] Also raised more than once are issues regarding conflicting rights of children involved in international events. Beazley et al. and Elspeth Webb provide examples of children's participation in health related issues that explicitly seem to coincide with the 'ticking boxes' exercises criticised by Cantwell. In the field of participation one can also identify the position of activists and experts 'not being satisfied with anything but the best solution'. While clear distinctions between consultation and child-led initiatives were made relatively early after the CRC's adoption (Hart 1992), the field often involves an unreservedly hierarchical approach whereby a maximal level of involvement is systematically sought, that is, the 'best solution'. In simple terms, young people seem never to be involved enough, not deciding enough or not involved in all aspects of the initiative taken. While child-led initiatives have indeed shown incredibly significant achievements, a number of other experiences show that confusion still dominates the field. The democratic nature of selection and issue of representativeness, whilst essential to avoid manipulation, is also sometimes geared toward a perfection that would not be conceived as such in the adult world.[5]

A critical approach might be seen as a threat to the child participation agenda. Development of participation is more than ever needed, among other things to ensure that children are treated with dignity and respect as well as providing

---

4 An example can be see in one of the points made by Nigel Cantwell in the documentation of the World Congress against Sexual Exploitation held in 2008 in Brazil. Clear indication of the confusion between child-lead initiatives and the consultation processes characterising events of this nature is evident as a young representative stated 'We need to urge the governments to join us in our decisions. We ask for their commitment here today, in their respective countries, to accept the decisions children have made here and follow up on them' (ECPAT et al. 2009: 35). On this basis questions about the preparation of representatives and delegates need to be raised.

5 As stated by Ennew in relation to models of children and young people's participation within the UN, should this ever be achieved, 'children's democratic representation in the UN could be argued to exceed by far that of adults' (Ennew 2008: 71).

invaluable information and to counteract overall processes of disempowerment. Yet, despite outstanding achievements made in some areas, the need for greater clarity and rigour in relation to the overall field of child participation is evident.

Human rights claims and conceptualisations might be contested and the reader might disagree with some arguments whilst also identifying contradictions and discrepancies between experts on more than one ground. Yet, assessing the evolution of children's rights discourses and reappraising current aims in the light of original views appears to be an indispensible task. Many of the views and positions presented in this book can certainly be used to examine the variety of claims and discourses made in the name of children's rights as well identifying different positions and views and criteria on which they are based. This should certainly be of assistance to any professional or expert wishing to work for the achievement of the human rights of children. Furthermore, criteria for measuring progress inevitably depend on the manner in which intentions are defined and need to be assessed in the light of that discourse. Finally, identifying idealised images and unrealistic expectations might reduce avoidable frustration and introduce some clarity.

Human Rights of Children within the UN

Beyond the debates considered thus far, a number of issues discussed in this compilation are likely to permit the reader to assess the remarkable progress made in two last decades.

The first area where progress is assessed in this book relates to structures and procedures to protect and promote rights enshrined in the CRC at the international level. Doek's contribution outlines the work of the UN Committee on the Rights of the Child (CRC Committee) in monitoring and fostering the CRC. It implicitly describes considerable advances where procedures have progressively been put in place to examine, respond to and follow up State Party, alternative and children's reports, with current discussion on addressing the subsequent workload of the Committee dealing with a considerable number of reports. Beside formal procedures, he describes a dynamic process generating awareness and discussion whilst promoting dialogue and collaboration between governments and civil society. Suggestions are made on how to increase feedback and collaborations in these communications and efforts to involve children, an area where he considers progress is still limited. In relation to the monitoring process, Judith Ennew's examination of data included in national reports provides complementary information. Comparative analysis of reports by States Parties between 1992/1993 and 2010 certainly shows progress, mainly because of the regrettable lack of focus characterising the first reporting round. She shows that greater clarity has been achieved, with the contribution the 2003 General Commentary made to more accurate reporting. However, the 2010 reports still present very significant gaps in knowledge. A lack of child focused and disaggregated data, permitting assessment of discrimination and information on key categories of children (e.g. children with disabilities, juvenile justice system, child poverty, in care or sexually abused children), inevitably limits the capacity to monitor the CRC.

It is perhaps in the activities aimed at fostering implementation of the CRC that Doek describes (Days of General Discussion, Recommendations, General Comments) that material can be found for assessing the enormous progress made. This includes contributions to the Optional Protocol on the Involvement of Children in Armed Conflicts adopted in 2000 or the UN studies on children and armed conflict and violence against children, in turn resulting in the appointment of Special Representatives on each topic. Efforts to provide guidance on the interpretation of the CRC through General Comments are also described, although the outcome of these documents remains to be evaluated. On a slightly different level, it is in Van Bueren's contribution that evidence is found of achievements in the international human rights arena. As she indicates in Chapter 5 in her discussion on the rationale and need for a complaint or communication procedure: 'if a gauge is necessary to measure how far the international social movement for children has progressed in its attitude towards child citizenship, a valuable one is the attitude of civil society around the world to developing a complaints mechanism, to be used by children, to protect violations of their rights under the CRC.' Objections expressed against the creation of a complaint mechanism at the time of the CRC drafting, she argues, are no longer sustainable today. Beside an examination of the content of objections made in the past she outlines the advantages of a mechanism allowing communication to be heard by the CRC Committee, not only at the state level but in the overall process of implementation worldwide and at the regional level. Particular consideration, she argues, needs to be given to promote child-sensitive procedures as well as make them accessible to the most vulnerable children.

The UN system has vigorously promoted the establishment of independent human rights bodies as a mechanism to help progress in the implementation of human rights obligations. The number of children's commissioner or ombudsperson offices established across the world since 1989 presents at first sight an indication of the CRC's success in this regard. Yet the situation begs careful investigation with particular attention to the question of appropriation discussed above. Examination of the statutory role and remit of these offices discloses highly variable (including no) emphasis on CRC monitoring and implementation. Examination of their practices may on the other hand show a high level of commitment to the CRC despite an inauspicious statutory base. The 'English' Commissioner (that is, the Children's Commissioner with UK-wide responsibility for non-devolved matters and England-wide responsibility for others) is a case in point (see Williams 2005). Brian Gran's chapter in this collection presents selected findings from a study of a number of independent children's rights institutions demonstrating both the range of approaches and also the distance in some cases and in some respects from the model promoted by the UN.

Progress in Rights Based Research

Three contributions in this book deal specifically with research: the chapters by Ennew, by Beazley, Bessell, Ennew and Waterson, and by Funky Dragon. Other chapters convey material reflecting progress and what needs to be achieved in research to support the human rights of children. Progress in terms of research cannot be assessed without referring to the debate on what a human rights based approach entails in relation to the CRC. Ennew argues that the mainstream of the new sociology of childhood, which has been broadly influential in the social sciences to recognise the child as a subject and active agent, has failed in responding to the needs of information to promote, protect and fulfil the rights of children enshrined in the CRC. One can read between the lines that there is a lack of commitment in relation to the human rights of children reflected in misinterpretations cited. Beyond what Ennew exposes, one may easily observe high levels of specialisation, in turn inevitably leading to reference to selected rights and articles. As for NGOs and other actors, one can point to the appropriation and re-interpretation of the CRC agenda by academics and researchers. While lack of space prevented Ennew providing detailed description of aspects of a rights based approach in research or examination of the relatively diverse field of child research, where some significant advances can be found, her analysis points to the need for thorough examination of what research can bring to the agenda of human rights of children which would be invaluable for professionals. Beazley et al. present advances in methodology and methods developed in the global South to research children and young people within a rights based approach that clearly stands in contrast with mainstream social research in industrialised countries. The methodology and examples employed indeed give, as indicated above, considerably attention to key principles and issues recognised in human rights instruments. Moving away from a charitable approach, it integrates the notion that children are entitled to the highest possible standard of services (CRC Art. 3) which includes high quality scientific research. This chapter certainly provides material for assessing advances made in research methodology and methods since the adoption of the CRC. Whilst considering overall advances in research by academics and organisations as well as information included in reports to the CRC Committee, Ennew nonetheless concludes by reporting limited progress. Rather than because of the lack of rigorous methodology or innovative methods, one wonders to what extent discipline and organisational resistance to change has limited the possibility of fully integrating the human rights based approach. The Child Health Equity model introduced by Goldhagen and Mercer stands as an example of the distance between what they argue is needed to fulfil the human rights of children and how traditional biomedical medicine thinks and operates in relation to child health.

On a very different level, and a rather welcome source of optimism, the chapter describing the work of Funky Dragon – The Children and Young People's Assembly for Wales – provides robust evidence of achievements in researching the commitment to report on the CRC implementation process by members of an organisation led by young people. This example of young people's involvement in reporting processes resonates with Doek's suggestion that this area needs to be promoted further by the CRC Committee. In terms of research, elements of Funky Dragon's project echo the good practice and choices presented by Beazley et al. It illustrates enormous progress in the capacity of a young people-led organisation to gain significant amounts of both skill and knowledge required to carry out good standard and child sensitive research and comply with the reporting and monitoring requirement and procedures set by the CRC Committee. The large sample and separate research with younger children reflect the vision of producing data and a report that, in contrast with previous reports submitted by young people, was legitimately representative of young people in a nation. Translation of the CRC, as well as all relevant material, into Welsh were components of activities undertaken, in itself showing how much careful consideration was paid to a number of issues too often dismissed in research.

The Impact of Multi-level Governance

The legal and political impact of the CRC encompasses institutional and procedural developments as well as instances of substantive change in law and policy. The conversations generated by the CRC system have produced a wealth of opinion, guidance and commentary in the form of General Comments and reports as well as Concluding Observations on individual State Party reports. This jurisprudence of the CRC has become a resource on which the legal and administrative systems of States Parties can draw, as demonstrated by Ursula Kilkelly, for example by means of litigation, audit and inspection or incorporation in designs for policy development. This effect is not confined to the States Parties, nor does the CRC's influence flow through a single channel: as discussed by Helen Stalford and Eleanor Drywood, the Convention has acquired an increased profile and influence on EU law and policy which took hold in the first decade of the twenty-first century and seems set to continue to grow in the second.[6] The European narrative is one of incremental steps towards protection of the rights of the child where relevant to specific fields of legal regulation (several examples of EU regulation are presented by Stalford and Drywood and beyond the EU, Council of Europe instruments, most obviously the Convention on the Exercise of Children's Rights 1996), coupled with the introduction of fulfilment of the rights of the child as one of the broad aims of the EU as a legal and political entity. This partial or piecemeal approach stands in contrast to the comprehensive re-statement of the rights of the child in the African Charter on the Rights and Welfare of the Child[7] but both the European and African developments

---

6   The EU Commission's 2006 Communication Towards an EU Strategy on the Rights of the Child (COM/2006/0367 final) provided the foundation for policy development which continues to be actively pursued at the time of publication.

7   OAU Doc. CAB/LEG/24.9/49 (1990), entered into force 29 November 1999.

represent a transformation of the law of the CRC within the law and institutions of a regional treaty system, opening up yet further channels of communication and influence. A picture then emerges of the normative standards of the CRC being conveyed in several ways not just that established by the Convention itself, to the legal and political systems of the States Parties. As Jane Williams' contribution to this collection shows, the impact may also be differentially absorbed within States Parties in those cases where competence in CRC-relevant fields is allocated to internal levels such as regions or provinces. This permeability of membranes dividing the several levels of governance, being not limited to the impact of the CRC, necessitates a working out of the relationship between and relative status of the normative standards of the Convention and those of other binding international instruments and domestic laws.

A further feature of the development of layers of government within the States Parties since the adoption of the CRC, discussed here by Williams, is that it throws a particular focus on different routes to accountability for CRC implementation. In many cases responsibility for social welfare, health, education and other areas of obvious importance to CRC implementation is allocated to internal regions, whilst overall responsibility for compliance with international human rights obligations, and often also for legal remedies through the courts, remains at the State Party level. Williams demonstrates that this raises the significance of administrative and parliamentary mechanisms of accountability and offers opportunities for closer engagement between NGO and governmental bodies but at the same time produces challenges of coordination that have been noted by the CRC Committee. If multi-level governance is, as she suggests, on an ascendant trajectory, this issue will merit closer and comparative study as part of ongoing assessment of progress in CRC implementation in the years ahead.

Rethinking Implementation

The rationale for 'rethinking' implementation is simple. In the time that has passed since the adoption of the CRC, many things have changed – in political and institutional structures as much as in the social and economic environment. And, as Gran points out in the specific context of the work of the independent children's rights institutions, no change has occurred in isolation. 'Everything' is a resource, every body, institution or activist operates in a context that includes every other. This in itself generates a certain 'dynamic' surrounding the dynamics of the CRC itself discussed by Doek. Several chapters in this collection examine through selected case studies efforts to apply the CRC in particular ways and in particular fields. This examination produces food for thought about further progression in implementation as well as echoes of some of the concerns articulated in other chapters.

Kilkelly gives examples of the use of the CRC in policy implementation, audit and inspection and points to the ways in which it has been and can be used strategically in litigation. She concludes by remarking that while each of these mechanisms offers discrete possibilities, they are also inter-related and share a crucial dependence on rigorous attention to the various legal texts that now underpin the case for the human rights of children. This point echoes Tobin's exposition of the challenges to be faced in developing a sufficiently detailed yet universally applicable conceptual foundation for implementation. In the absence of such a foundation much (too much) may be left to the interpretation and imagination of the protagonists in specialist fields of policy and practice. This can be seen as positive in terms of using rights as a tool in the way put forward by Freeman but can also easily become caught up in the 'old' ways of thinking and travel along the road identified by Cantwell.

Rhian Croke and Anne Crowley's account of the development of rights-based approaches in Wales compared with the rest of the UK provides evidence of both of these pathways. A false dichotomy between 'rights' and 'outcomes' lay behind statements made by the UK Government at the time of the legislative passage of the Children Act 2004, where it was claimed, with misplaced virtue, that the government was concerned with outcomes rather than rights.[8] The Welsh approach described by Croke and Crowley can be seen as closer to the interpretation suggested by Freeman and by Tobin, wherein States Parties take rights-based action in the form of policies and programmes geared towards improvement in outcomes that are themselves defined by reference to rights.

Contributions from Elspeth Webb and from Jeffrey Goldhagen and Raul Mercer both bring a focus on complementary issues of child health. Webb brings to the forefront an overall overview of the mechanism of discrimination well beyond health, illustrating how, beside overt discrimination, childism, marginalisation, age blindness, victim blaming and stereotyping function to generate as well as justify choking inequalities in health. She furthermore addresses more indirect forms of discrimination in which children and young people are disadvantaged as a result of other forms of discrimination such as gender, ethnicity, socio-economic conditions, disability or homelessness. Her review includes powerful examples of multiple disadvantages generated by very diverse mechanisms. Her argument is that it is necessary to 'identify not just the fact of disadvantage but why and how children are disadvantaged'. Her argument connects with the notion put forward by Freeman of rights demanding that discrimination be justified. In relation to health, her contribution shows how in a CRC-sensitive analysis, many disadvantages to both the overall category of children or sections of them become unjustifiable forms of discrimination.

Goldhagen and Mercer present an attempt to import CRC values and principles into paediatric medicine through the new discipline of Child Health Equity. This

---

8   This position stands in contrast to that taken by the UK Government in relation to international development aid, where it has insisted that human rights and achievement of development objectives go hand in hand. Interestingly, a similar fallacy has been identified in the wider sphere of EU human rights policy (see Williams, A. 2005).

can be seen as an illustration of the CRC galvanising and informing development in thinking about professional practice with children and, wider than that, also about the broad approach to public health, planning and service delivery with an ultimate focus on outcomes that explicitly support the realisation of rights. They show how the case for social and environmental 'root causes' of health outcomes is thoroughly made but how challenges remain regarding how to create an impact of these demonstrable truths in terms of action that can hope to produce improved health outcomes. They take the CRC as one of the core elements of Child Health Equity, a model which they argue can help to bridge this gap. Thus the CRC is promoted as 'an effective tool to guide and support the expanded involvement of child-serving professionals in clinical care, child advocacy, community development and public policy formulation'. The expansion in role and influence of the medical professional in this model is ambitious and no doubt controversial, demanding that they move beyond medical specialisation to become advocates for those lacking formal or real capacity, using the CRC as 'a template for community advocacy and policy formulation'. Child Health Equity, with other social movements, the authors conclude, is built on 'a foundation of human rights and social justice'.

The chapter written by Funky Dragon provides encouraging reading to close this compilation, with material that permits optimism. It provides evidence of significant advance in research, in this case carried out by a child-led organisation (see above) and enabling them to carry out a broad study of the views of young people in Wales on which Funky Dragon's reports to the CRC Committee were based. The sustainability of the work done is an important aspect of this project. Funky Dragon's initiatives, including translation of the CRC and the acquisition of essential skills and knowledge in research and on human rights, have generated invaluable capital for the future work of the organisation in Wales and possibly even outside. The history of the organisation they present conveys evidence to support Van Bueren's point about the need to take a long view in attempting to assess any initiative. It took some years of efforts for Funky Dragon to gain the legal status of a charity involving trustees under the age of 18, opening the way to other organisations to legally involve young trustees. Their redefinitions of organisational structures, for instance avoiding labelling and stigmatisation of the young people from different backgrounds, also illustrate well the potential for transformation in approaches where young people are included in an organisation's management. Readers inclined to hope and work for progressive implementation in the twenty-first century of the visions of the human rights of children that started with the negotiation of the CRC in the twentieth century may take some reassurance and perhaps some further inspiration from the last chapter of this book.

References

Alston, P. 1994. *The Best Interest of the Child: Reconciling Culture and Human Rights*. Oxford: Clarendon.

Alston, P. and Tobin, J. 2005. *Laying the Foundations for Children's Rights*. Florence: UNICEF/Innocenti. Available at: http://www.unicef-irc.org/ publications/pdf/ii_layingthefoundations.pdf [accessed 5 January 2011].

Cantwell, N. 1992. The origins, development and significance of the United Nations Convention on the Rights of the Child, in S. Detrick, *The United Nations Convention on the Rights of the Child: A guide to the 'Travaux préparatoires'*. Dordrecht: Martinus Nijhoff, pp. 19–30.

ECPAT, IIDAC, Plan International, Save the Children, UNICEF, Viração, World Vision. 2009. *Pulling a Face at Sexual Exploitation. World Congress III against Sexual Exploitation of Children and Adolescents. Report on Children and Adolescent Participation, 2008.*

Ennew, J. 2008. Children as 'citizens' of the United Nations (UN), in A. Invernizzi and J. Williams (eds), *Children and Citizenship*. London: Sage, pp. 67–78.

Freeman, M. 2004. Introduction, in M. Freeman (ed.), *Children's Rights*, Volume I. Aldershot and Burlington, VA: Ashgate and Dartmouth, pp. xi–xlii.

Hammarberg, T. 1990. The UN Convention on the Rights of the Child: and how to make it work. *Human Rights Quarterly*, 12(1), 97–105.

Hart, R. 1992. *Children's Participation: From Tokenism to Citizenship*, Innocenti Essays no. 4. Florence: UNICEF.

Miljeteig-Olssen, P. 1990. Advocacy of children's rights: The Convention as more than a legal document. *Human Rights Quarterly*, 12, 148–55.

Milne, B. 2008. From chattels to citizens? Eighty years of Eglantyne Jebb's legacy to children and beyond, in A. Invernizzi and J. Williams (eds), *Children and Citizenship*. London: Sage, pp. 44–54.

van Beers, H., Invernizzi A. and Milne B. (eds). 2006. *Beyond Article 12: Essential Readings in Children's Participation*. Bangkok: Black on White.

Williams, A. 2005. *EU Human Rights Policies: A Study in Irony*. Oxford, Oxford University Press.

Williams, J. 2005. Effective government structures for children? The UK's four Children's Commissioners. *Child and Family Law Quarterly*, 17, 37–53.

Chapter 1

The Value and Values of Children's Rights

Michael Freeman

'Each time we let in a new excluded group, each time we listen to a new way of knowing, we learn more about our current way of seeing.' This was written by Carrie Menkel-Meadow in 1987, and it was not written about children, or their rights. But it is a useful point to make at the beginning of a chapter on children's rights. The language of rights can make visible what has too long been suppressed. And children's rights, their values were for most of history not discussed, indeed they were denigrated.

Why Rights are Important

It is worth asking first why rights are important, not rights for children, but rights generally. And there are a number of reasons.

They are universal, available to all members of the human family. They do not depend on gender or race or class or competence. Of course, in the past there were attempts to so confine them. Women were non-persons, and people of colour were kept in subservience by policies which justified so-called 'separate but equal' practices or worse by slavery and similar regimes. But just as concepts of gender inequality have been key to understanding womanhood and women's social status, so the 'concept of generation is key to understanding childhood' (Mayall 2002). It has always been to the advantage of the powerful to keep others out: it is not therefore surprising that adults should want to do this to children – that they should wish to keep them in an often imposed and prolonged dependence which history and culture show to be neither inevitable nor necessary. It is worth always thinking of the other side of inclusion – of exclusion and what this generates both on the part of the excluders and their victims, the socially excluded. We can note the way the powerful regulate space (social, political, geographical), define participation, marginalise significance and frustrate development.

Rights too are indivisible and inter-dependent. Rights include the whole range of civil, political, social, economic and cultural rights. The denial of one right can impact upon, even totally undermine, other rights. Rights work best where all have rights. A society which denies women rights, for example freedom from domestic violence, is unlikely to protect children from abuse. The same applies the other way round too.

Rights are important because they recognise the respect the bearers of rights are owed. To accord rights is to respect dignity. To deny rights is to cast doubt on humanity and integrity. Rights affirm the principle which we tend to associate with Immanuel Kant that we are ends in ourselves, and not means to the ends of others.

It is, therefore, important that, as Ronald Dworkin so eloquently reminded us, we see rights as 'trumps' (Dworkin 1977). As such, they cannot be knocked off their pedestal because this would be better for others, even for society as a whole, were these rights not to exist. We grant the right not to be tortured – and we should – even to those who would dismantle our liberal rights-based values. Of course, for the powerful – and for children adults are always powerful – rights are an inconvenience, just as they are for those battling against the threat of terror. The powerful would always find it easier if those below them lacked rights. It is easier to rule, decision-making is swifter, cheaper, more efficient, more certain when the rights of others do not get in the way. It is hardly surprising that we have had to fight for the rights we have and often to fight to keep them.

Rights are important because those who have them can exercise agency. Agents are decision-makers. They are persons who can negotiate with others, who can alter relationships and decisions, who can shift social assumptions and constraints. And there is now clear evidence that even the youngest amongst us can do this (Alderson, Hawthorne and Killen 2005). That we don't believe this is in part because we don't want to do so. As agents, rights-bearers can participate. They can make their own lives, rather than having their lives made for them. And participation is itself a fundamental human right. It enables us to demand rights. We are better able to do so where there is freedom of speech and orthodoxies can be challenged (this was recognised by John Stuart Mill), as well as freedom of association, and freedom of information.

Rights are an important advocacy tool (see also Veerman 1991), a weapon to use in the battle to secure recognition. Giving people rights without access to those who can present those rights, without the right of representation, is thus of little value. That is one of the reasons why the cutback in access to legal aid and advice is so sad. The emphasis on the importance of advocacy points also to the rather obvious fact that we must get beyond rhetoric. Rights without remedies are of symbolic importance, nothing more. And remedies themselves require the injection of resources, a commitment on behalf of all of us that we respect the institution of rights, that we want them to have an input on the lives of all people, and not just on the lives of the powerful and the privileged.

And so rights offer legitimacy to campaigns, to pressure groups, to NGOs, to lobbies, to direct and indirect action, in particular to those who are disadvantaged or excluded. They offer a way in; they open doors. The silenced may rediscover their voices. Rights are 'a militant concept', part of an ideology in a campaign for social change (Cohen 1980: 52).

Rights are also a resource; they offer the opportunity to make reasoned argument. They can put a moral case. And too often opponents of rights have little to offer in response. A glance at history reveals this all too tellingly. Think of the opposition to the extension of the suffrage. Think of the kind of arguments adduced to counter gay rights, for example to gay marriage. I am always reminded of Lord Devlin's invocation of 'widespread intolerance, indignation and disgust' (Devlin 1965: 17) as the basis for decision-making. Or, in relation to children, the response to the demand that violence should not be used against children in the name of punishment, the incantation 'it never did me any harm' (to which it is difficult to resist adding *sed quaere!*)

Rights offer fora for action. Without rights the excluded can appeal to the charitable nature of others, they can request, they can beg, rely on *noblesse oblige*, hope that others will be benevolent or co-operative, or even sensible and foresighted. But they cannot demand: they lack the entitlement to do so.

And yet what the excluded must lack is a right one rarely finds articulated. This is the right to possess rights. Few have postulated this better than Hannah Arendt. She observed, *à propos* the *Shoah* (the Holocaust), that 'a condition of complete rightlessness was created before the right to live was challenged' (Arendt 1986: 296). She explains: before the Nazis robbed the Jews of their lives, they robbed them of their humanity, just as generations had done, and continue to do so, with slaves. To quote Arendt again: 'Slavery's fundamental offense against human rights was not that it took liberty away ... but that it excluded a certain category of people even from the possibility of fighting for freedom – a fight possible under tyranny, and even under the desperate conditions of modern terror (but not under any condition of concentration-camp life)' (Arendt 1986: 297).

So Why Has it Been Thought Unimportant to Give Rights to Children?

Many of today's critics of children's rights are passionate defenders of the rights of others. Martin Guggenheim, for example, who is so convinced of the evils of recognising children's rights that he calls his book *What's Wrong With Children's Rights* and unashamedly omits a question mark, talks of parents' rights as 'sacred' (Guggenheim 2005: 71). And there are legal disputes which, though they centre self-evidently on the rights of children, are fought as if the children do not count. The *Williamson* case is a prominent example. This revolved about whether parents (as well as teachers) could exercise their right, as they saw it, to continue the practice of beating children in their Christian fundamentalist schools. Throughout this dispute was conceived as one between the state (it had by then banned corporal punishment from schools) and parents and teachers. Children were just objects, whose bottoms were to be fought over, not subjects in their own right. They were not represented: their views were not sought or known. The courts found against the parents and teachers. But it is significant that the state did not argue that corporal punishment necessarily involved an infringement of any of the rights of children. It is, of course, a clear breach of the UN Convention on the Rights of the Child. At least Arden LJ recognised that the common law 'effectively treats the child as the property of the parent', and she realised the inevitable, that the courts would one day have to consider whether this is 'the right approach'. More significantly, children's rights were afforded a ringing endorsement by Baroness Hale in the House of Lords, and this is not the only occasion when she has put her head above the parapet in this way. Her judgment begins:

> This is, and always has been, a case about children, their rights and the rights of their parents and teachers. Yet there has been no one here to speak on behalf of the children. The battle has been fought on ground selected by the adults.[1]

Her speech is, she says, 'for the sake of the children'.

Children's rights have been neglected for a number of reasons. The shadow of children as property, rather than as persons, still hangs over debates about children. But there are more significant explanations today. I discussed some of these in an article I wrote nearly 20 years ago, and I will do no more than state those again here. There is the argument that the importance of rights and rights language is exaggerated. There are two versions of this. One, with veritable vintage, attacks rights themselves. It is, however, significant that even among radical thinkers today the importance of rights to the less powerful is not denied (Crenshaw 1988, Williams 1991). The second strand of this argument emphasises that there are other morally significant values like love, friendship, compassion, altruism, and that these raise relationships to a higher plain than one which relies on rights (and duties). The problem with this is that it is not the experience of many children.

The second argument is related to the first. It assumes that adults already relate to children in terms of love, care and altruism, so that the case for children's rights is otiose. But this idealises adult–child relations. There is a tendency for those who postulate such an argument to adopt a *laissez-faire* attitude towards the family. A good example is the philosophy of Goldstein, Freud and Solnit (1979) that minimum coercive intervention into the family – of course very much the ideology of the Children Act 1989 – accords with their firm belief in 'individual freedom and human dignity'. The trouble is that this overlooks *whose* freedom and *what* dignity this upholds.

The third argument equally rests on a myth. It sees childhood as the best years of our life, a golden age, a time when we are spared the rigours of adult life, a time for joy and play. But for many this image of, what John Holt (1975) called, 'happy, safe, protected, innocent childhood' is just a distortion of the truth. Children are still subjected to abuse, exploitation and the worst form of labour, including slavery.

But there are other reasons why rights for children have been neglected. I will mention two.

The first explores the implication of the public–private dualism for children (see further Freeman 2011). Much has been written of this in relation to women,

---

1   *Williamson v Secretary of State for Education and Employment* [2005] 2 A C 246 at para. 71.

but curiously little in the case of children. So, what is the impact on children of 'relegating' them to the 'private' realm? Rights are largely public coinage: it is thought they are not as important in the private sphere. But the curtain of privacy cloaks all manner of evils – the many 'wrongs' inflicted on children. It also stifles the opportunities children might have to participate in the public arena, to communicate their views to decision-makers. And when they do communicate their opinions in public, they are deemed 'out of place', and met with patronisation or simply ignored. This is not, of course, to say that the position of the child is any stronger in the private sphere – the power imbalance ensures this. The public/private divide is a social construction, and it is problematic. Where does the school fit? As far as children are concerned, the school may well be experienced as private, rather than public. Certainly, in so far as the language of rights has any meaning in the school setting, the rights inhere in parents rather than children. Not all children are in school. Many – at least 20 per cent of the world's children – work, many in 'hazardous forms of labour'. Many more are engaged in low-status work in the home environment. This work is largely hidden within a private economy of care: it is not paid employment and there are few if any employment rights. For such children the 'heartless world' has been installed in the so-called 'haven' (Lasch 1977). Also hidden are the many 'young carers', perhaps as many as 50,000 in Britain.

But, perhaps the most interesting group of children to test the public/private binary are street children. They are not a category recognised as such by the CRC Committee, though as children many of the articles of the Convention address their situation. The street is 'a metaphor' for the public sphere. Street children are 'out of place', they don't belong in the street, which is adult territory. They should be at home, in the family, in the private world. Instead, they are doing things on the street, like sleeping and eating which should be done in the privacy of the family. Thus, they are an anomaly. They are not really children, and not quite 'human'. Is it any surprise that there are parts of the world where state authorities have pursued policies of 'cleansing'? Dickens describes street children, though he does not use this label. We don't perceive of our children on the street as 'street children'. But we see them as truants, as gangs, as nuisances, and perceive them as a threat. They are not 'street children', because they are found in Rio, Bangkok and Nairobi. However, because we perceive them as a threat, we control more and more the public space of children, confirming that they are supposed to be in the private space of the family or quasi-private space of the school, but not roaming in adult territory. And so we use group dispersal powers and employ the 'mosquito'. The former are incompatible with the CRC (most obviously Article 15). The latter – an ultrasonic device which disturbs young ears – is an outrage. The practice has been condemned by the CRC Committee (CRC/ C/GBR/CO/4. paras 34 and 35), but its demise is not expected in the near future.

Rights for children have been undermined for a second reason. It was Onora O' Neill who wrote that 'a child's "main" remedy is to grow up' (O'Neill, 1988). She articulated more thoughtfully what many believe. Adults have duties to children, but children don't have rights. For Harry Brighouse, it is indeed, 'strange' to think of children as having rights (Brighouse 2002: 31). Why? Because on this analysis a child is an adult in the making. S/he is a future adult, rather than a young human being. The child lacks skills – is incompetent – whereas the adult is the finished product with full competency. So, we are expected to understand childhood through adulthood. Children's lives and activities are envisaged as 'preparation for the future'. On this view children undertake a journey that ends with adulthood. This of course assumes, as Lee points out (2001), that adults are stable and complete. This is a view of childhood nurtured by many disciplines: developmental psychology (the works of Piaget [1929] being prominent), social anthropology (for example, the work of Margaret Mead), and sociology (including Talcott Parsons [1951]). Together, these disciplines constructed children as dependent, incomplete, inadequate. Such a model left little scope for any notion of the child as 'agent'. The talk was all of children as 'becomings'. But now we recognise that they are 'beings', and some of us recognise that they are both beings and becomings. A new sociology of childhood has emerged. Lawyers joined in. By the late 1980s it was recognised that children were 'beings', social actors, agents. This was reflected in the *Gillick* case. In this, Lord Scarman expressed the view that a child's capacity to make her own decisions depended upon her having 'sufficient' knowledge and 'intelligence to make the decision', and not on 'any politically fixed age limit'.[2] This was articulated by two leading sociologists of childhood thus:

> ... children are and must be seen as active in the construction of their own lives, the lives of those around them and of the societies in which they live. Children are not just passive subjects of social structures and processes. (James and Prout 1997: 8)

It is important to recognise that children are more than pre-adult 'becomings'. But it is equally important to understand that appreciating that they are 'beings' does not preclude their being also 'becomings' (see also Uprichard 2008). It is all too easy to assume children have to be one thing or the other. We like to dichotomise. We like clear categories. This may be one of the reasons why we struggle with adolescence (Scott 2000–2001). But we accept laws which permit children to do different things at different ages: marry at 16, but not vote until 18. And, rather perversely, be criminally responsible at 10, even, as we saw in 2010, for rape (Atkinson 2010).

The Value of Rights of Children

The world now accepts that children have rights. All states, except Somalia and the United States (see Fineman and Worthington 2009), have ratified a convention (the

---

2   *Gillick v West Norfolk and Wisbech Area Health Authority* [1986] A C 12.

CRC) which endorses a major package of rights for children, rights of protection, of provision and of participation. Of course, there are rights which are missing, there is vagueness; there is cultural compromise; certain categories of children are neglected, for example the gay child, the girl child, the street child. It is but a beginning, a foundation on which to build. The CRC offers us a measuring rod. It provides criteria for an audit. The mechanism of enforcement is weak, but at least the obligation to put in a periodic review to a committee of experts and the critiques which follow can keep states on their toes. There is at worst some vigilance.

The Convention is about 'the child'. It sets a global standard, thus ignoring the obvious fact that many different childhoods exist in the world. To be a child in Africa or India is not the same as to be one in the United Kingdom or Germany. It is early to criticise the Convention as 'eurocentric', and many, particularly I suspect sociologists of childhood, do (for example, Wells 2009). But the African Charter on the Rights and Welfare of Children is strikingly similar to the CRC. This is not the place to debate culture – I have done so several times, elsewhere anyway (Freeman 1995, 2000a.). But on the whole I am happy that the world collectively has offered all children the same package.

In a sense, the Convention is international law's response to the paradigm shift in thinking about children largely engineered by modern sociological thinking. And so it recognises the child both as 'beings' and as 'becomings'. If children were only 'becomings', the Convention would have emphasised the importance of their best interests (as it does in Article 3), and concentrated on provision and protection rights exclusively: rights to life, survival and development, to protection from violence, injury, abuse and neglect, to the highest possible standard of health, to education and to much else besides.

But, because it accepts children are also 'beings', it gives them also a 'voice'. It recognises the dangers of enveloping them in silence. Thus, children are given the right to express views freely in all matters affecting them, and the opportunity to be heard in judicial and administrative proceedings in which they are involved. Other important participation rights include freedom of expression, thought, conscience and religion, as well as freedom of association and peaceful assembly. And one of the aims of education, as articulated in the Convention (in Article 29) is the development of the child's personality, talents and abilities to their fullest potential.

The Values of Children's Rights

The institution of rights upholds certain values. We have been recommended by Ronald Dworkin to 'take rights seriously' (Dworkin 1977). For Dworkin anyone who proposes to take rights seriously must accept the ideas of human dignity and potential equality. He argues in favour of a fundamental right to equal concern and respect, and against any general right to liberty. The advantage in so arguing, as John Mackie acknowledged in an important article in 1984, is that the right to equal concern and respect is a final and not merely 'a prima facie right', in the sense that one person's possession or enjoyment of it does not conflict with another's (Mackie 1984). Dworkin put this forward as a 'postulate of political morality' (Dworkin 1977: 272) that is a fundamental political right, namely governments must treat citizens with equal concern and respect.

But why do we have the rights we have? Is this sufficient by itself to explain a right-based moral theory? The question is still left open as to where rights come from: why do we have the rights we do? I am not talking here of legal rights. The answer to why we have these can be sought within the legal framework itself (the statute/convention says …), or historically by depicting the struggles (for the vote, trade union rights, to rid schools of the cane) that were ultimately successful (or largely so).

What is there then when there 'are' rights? As Jan Narveson put it: there 'must be certain features or properties of those who "have" them such that we have good reason to acknowledge the obligation to refrain from interfering with, or possibly sometimes to help other bearers to do the things they are said to have the right to do, or have those things they are said to have a right to have' (Narveson 1985: 164). Rights, then, are dependent on reasoned argument, though this is not always clear. Thus, Robert Nozick can merely assert peremptorily that 'individuals have rights' (Nozick 1974: ix) and leave it at that. Justifying principles can, and have, been sought. One common answer links rights with interests. This takes us part of the way, but not, I would suggest, far enough. Thus, as an example, Joel Feinberg tells us that the 'sort of beings who can have rights are precisely those who have (or can have) interests' (Feinberg 1966). There is much that is in my interests but to which I can in no way make a justifiable claim. The same applies to other adults and to children too. This is rather different from Onora O' Neill's objection to finding rights where there are imperfect and non-institutionalised obligations only, but it creates a caveat at least against the indiscriminate use of the 'manifesto' sense in which rights are sometimes used.

Another argument often put forward is purely formal. It is that all persons ought to be treated alike unless there is a good reason for treating them differently. Dworkin, for one, accepts this. He envisages the right to treatment as an equal as a morally fundamental idea (Dworkin 1977: 226–9). It is that which requires that each person be accorded the same degree of concern and respect as every other person. Though an attractive argument, this reasoning alone is not without its difficulties. A problem lies in deciding what constitutes a 'good reason' for treating people differently. Gender and race are now almost universally accepted to be indefensible distinctions, and sexual orientation is close to achieving this status – though on all three examples I am speaking of the liberal developed world. Whether discrimination on grounds of age is justifiable is still controversial. But what of children? The United Kingdom has just passed the Equality Act 2010: this bans discrimination on more or less every conceivable ground, except discrimination against those under 18 years of age (see further Freeman 2011).

We cannot but accept that children, particularly young children, have needs, and recognise also their vulnerability. These needs cannot be met by recognising that they have rights on a par with adults. Vulnerability may justify granting rights to children over and above those which adults have. An appealing argument has been advanced by William Frankena. He argues that humans are 'capable of enjoying a good life in the sense in which other animals are not'. And he continues: 'it is the fact that all men are similarly capable of enjoying a good life in the sense that justifies the prima-facie requirement that they be treated as equals' (Frankena 1962). Superficially, this is an attractive argument. But it question begs. Are all persons, even all adults, capable of enjoying a good life? All children are capable of so doing, even if their capacities during childhood are limited. But there are dangers in using an argument like this: it can backfire. It can lead to the deprivation of rights on the ground that it is meaningless to the person in question. For example, the decision to allow the sterilisation of learning disabled women has been so justified in England and elsewhere. (for example in *Re B*, 1988,[3] and see Freeman 1988). So has withdrawing artificial nutrition and hydration from permanently vegetative patients (as in *Airedale NHS Trust v Bland*, 1993[4]). It can also be argued that, without more, it fails to show how factual similarity can be said to ground the obligation claimed by Frankena. Nor is it entirely clear how factual similarity should lead to egalitarian treatment, since it would be possible to argue that two reasons were similar, and at the same time support useful treatment on the ground that the value of one person's happiness is greater than that of other persons. Dworkin himself attempts to identify the existence of a moral right against the state when, for 'some' reason, the state would 'do wrong' to treat a person in a certain way, 'even though it would be in the general interest to do so'. It is, however, clear that what is 'wrong' for the state to do is what the state has an obligation not to do. Dworkin, in other words, seems to be defining rights in terms of duties. But, why is it 'wrong' for the state to act in a particular way? It is because the individual has a 'right' in which state action of a particular sort would illegitimately trample. This suggests the argument is inherently circular.

Thus, Dworkin's arguments take us so far, but not far enough. Equality by itself cannot explain what Dworkin is trying to explain: namely that rights as such 'trump' countervailing utilitarian considerations. Something more is needed. I believe this additional concept/value is autonomy. A plausible theory of rights – and this most emphatically includes rights for children – needs to take account not just of equality but also of the normative value of autonomy. It is important to recognise that persons as such have a set of capacities that enables them to make independent decisions regarding appropriate life choices. The deep structure of the rights thesis is this equality and autonomy. Kant recognised this, and it is also at the root of the Rawlsian contractarian conception (Rawls 1971). To see persons as both equal and autonomous is to repudiate the moral claim of those who would allow utilitarian calculations of

---

3 *Re B* [1988] A C 199.
4 *Airedale NHS Trust v Bland* [1993] A C 789.

the greatest happiness of the greatest number to prevail over the range of significant life choices which the rights thesis both facilitates and enhances. Utilitarianism, by contrast, demands that the pattern of individual life choices be overridden if others are in this way made better off. The result of this is that life choices become in effect the judgement of one person, the sympathetic onlooker whose pleasure is maximised only when the utilitarian principle is upheld. But such an assimilation contradicts the central thesis of equality and autonomy – the fundamental tenet of ethics that people are equal and have the capacity to live as separate and independent beings. To treat persons as utilitarianism requires is to focus almost obsessively on aggregated pleasure as the only ethically significant goal, and to ignore the critical fact that persons experience pleasure and that pleasure has human and moral significance only in the context of a life a person chooses to lead.

It is the rights thesis that protects the integrity of the person in leading his or her life. One of Dworkin's insights was to link Rawlsian contractarian theory to the language of rights. One of his failings was not to appreciate that both values at the root of Kantian moral theory (equality and autonomy) were equally morally significant. When we take both equality and autonomy seriously, we are back to the contractarian thinking which we find in Kant and in the contemporary constructivism of John Rawls. Equality is, I would argue, best expressed as an original position of equal beings, and autonomy is best understood as the putative choice of those beings under a 'veil of ignorance'.

To believe in autonomy is to believe that anyone's autonomy is as morally significant as anyone else's. And autonomy does not depend on the stage of life that a person has reached. Only human beings are 'persons'. A legal system may attribute 'personhood' to other entities, corporations or animals, for example, but these do not become 'persons' in the sense used here. What is it, then, about human beings that makes them 'persons'? A possible answer is critical competence or the capacity for reasoning. It is interesting that such a test is close to that posited by Lord Scarman in his groundbreaking judgment in the *Gillick* case in 1985. Lord Scarman offered no guidelines as to when a child reached '*Gillick*-competence' and, in terms of age, legal commentators have since assumed this was reached during adolescence, at perhaps 14 or 15. However, there is clear and increasing evidence that it is achieved much earlier. Once criteria for personhood are examined this conclusion is supported. A good account of the criteria of personhood is found in Richard Lindley's account of autonomy. He argues:

> Certainly consciousness is a requirement. More specifically a person is a creature which has beliefs and desires, and acts on its desires in the light of its beliefs. However, this is insufficient for personhood. What is required in addition is the capacity to evaluate and structure one's beliefs and desires, and to act on the basis of these evaluations. (Lindley 1986)

To respect a child's autonomy is to treat that child as a person and as a rights-holder. It is clear that we can do so for a much greater extent than has been assumed hitherto. But it is also clear that the exercising of autonomy by a child can harm that child's life chances. It is true that adults make mistakes too. And it is undoubtedly the case that they make mistakes when interfering with a child's autonomy. But having rights means being allowed to take risks and make choices. There is a reluctance to interfere with an adult's project. This is exemplified by the law's attitude to a competent adult's decision to refuse medical treatment. Such a person may do this for a reason that is quite irrational or indeed for no reason at all. And the legal system has come out at last to recognise the institution of the advance directive. But this reluctance is tempered when the project pursuer is a child because of a belief that choice now may undermine the exercise of choice later. Lomasky puts this thus: 'what counts as damage ... is determined by what will likely further or diminish its eventual success in living as a project pursuer' (Lomasky 1987).

This is to recognise that children are different. Many of them have lesser abilities and capacities. They are more vulnerable. They need protection. Without welfare rights – protection – they will not be in a position to exercise autonomy, to participate in decision-making. Of course, all of this is true, but it is not as true as we have come to believe. Children are different, but they are not all that different. Age is often a suspect classification. If we are to use a double standard, it needs to be justified. The onus lies on those who wish to discriminate. Hitherto, it has to be said that they have not discharged this burden very convincingly. How many of the structures, institutions and practices established to 'protect' children actually do so? It is much easier to assume abilities and capacities are absent than to take cognizance of children's choices. A recent example in the United Kingdom is the peremptory way in which the argument to include children within the remit of the recent Equality Act 2010 was dismissed.

If we are to make progress we have to recognise the moral integrity of children. We have to treat them as persons entitled to equal concern and equal respect, entitled to have both their present autonomy recognised and their capacity for future autonomy safeguarded. This is to recognise that children, particularly younger children, need nurture, care and protection. In other words, children have rights that adults do not have – additional rights.

In seeking to develop a children's rights prospective we must thus recognise the integrity of the child and his/her decision-making capacities, but at the same time note the dangers of complete liberation. The child liberation writers of the 1970s enlivened the debate, but they went too far. The writings of John Holt (1975), Richard Farson (1974), Howard Cohen (1980) and others – interestingly all Americans, since the United States has obstinately refused to ratify the CRC (but see Woodhouse 2008 and Fineman and Worthington 2009) – need to be rediscovered and reassessed, but I doubt if the message they preached, in effect an adulthood for every child, would command respect today. When they wrote – to take just one example – sexual abuse of children had not been discovered.

Nevertheless, too often writers on children's rights have dichotomised: thus there is either salvation or liberation, nurturance or self-determination – in Richard

Farson's pithy phrase, the one protects children, the other their rights. But both are necessary. Thus, for example, we will be better able to tackle child abuse if we recognise that children have rights. To take children's rights more seriously requires us to take more seriously the protection of children and recognition of their autonomy, both actual and potential. This recognises that there is a need to respect both individual autonomy and to treat persons as equals. Actual autonomy is important, but it is as much the capacity for autonomy that is at the root of this thinking. The constructivism of John Rawls's theory of justice (Rawls 1971) is useful to this argument. It is the normative value of equality and autonomy which forms the substructure of the Rawlsian conception of the social contract. The principles of justice which Rawls believes we would choose in the 'original position' are equal liberty and opportunity, and an arrangement of social and economic inequalities is that they are both to the greatest benefit of the least advantaged, and attached to offices and positions open to all under conditions of fair equality and opportunity.

These principles confine paternalism – the philosophy at the root of protection – without totally eliminating it. Those who participate in a hypothetical social contract would know that some human beings are less capable than others. They would in turn know about variations in intelligence and strength, and they would know of the very limited capacities of small children and the rather fuller, if incomplete, capacities of adolescents. They would employ the insights of psychology. They would also bear in mind how the actions of those with limited capacities might thwart their autonomy at a future time when their capacities were no longer as limited.

These considerations would lead to an acceptance of interventions in children's lives to protect them against irrational actions. But what is to be regarded as 'irrational' must be carefully monitored. It is, of course, both vague and value-laden. Is it irrational to refuse a clinically-indicated blood transfusion, and does the reason for the refusal matter? Is it irrational to want to work rather than go to school? Does this depend on age, on the work involved, on the reasons for wanting to work? Is it irrational to want gender reassignment? (Spain, I note, has just allowed this to a 16-year-old boy: *The Guardian*, 13 January 2010) The examples are legion. What is to be regarded as 'irrational' must be strictly confined. The subjective values of the would-be protector must not be allowed to intrude. But this is easier said than done. What is 'irrational' must be defined in terms of a neutral theory capable of accommodating pluralistic visions of the 'good'. We should not see an action as irrational unless it is manifestly so because it is obvious that it would undermine future life choices, impair interests in an irreversible way. And, we must tolerate mistakes: Dworkin notes 'someone may have the right to something that is wrong for him to do' (Dworkin 1977: 188–9). He writes, of course, only about adults – nowhere does he consider the application of this argument to children. However, we cannot treat persons as equals without also respecting their capacity to take risks and make mistakes. We would not be taking rights seriously if we only respected autonomy when we considered the agent was doing the right thing. But we would also be failing to recognise a child's integrity if we allowed her to choose an action which could seriously and irreparably impair the attainment of a full personality and development subsequently. The test of 'irrationality' must also be confined so that it justifies intervention only to the extent necessary to obviate the immediate harm, or to develop the capacities of rational choice by which the individual may have a reasonable chance of avoiding such harms.

It is not difficult to present a case for protecting children against actions which may lead to their death or serious injury. A straightforward example today is the use of dangerous drugs such as heroin. Another is protecting children from the worst forms of labour. We did this in the nineteenth century when we stopped children going down coal mines and up chimneys. Of course, we cannot really believe that children were exercising any autonomy in undertaking these tasks. We would also wish to protect children from sexual exploitation and abuse and from trafficking.

What should legitimise such interferences with autonomy is, what Gerald Dworkin has called, 'future-orientated' consent (Dworkin 1972). The question is: can the restrictions be justified in terms that the child would eventually come to appreciate? Looking back, would the child appreciate and accept the reason for the restriction imposed on him/her, given what s/he now understands as a rationally autonomous and mature person? This is far from an easy test to apply. It involves something akin to what Derek Parfit has called 'ideal deliberation' (1984). He explains it thus: 'What each of us has most to do is what would best achieve, not what he *actually* wants, but what he *would* want, at the time of acting, if he had undergone a process of "ideal deliberation" – if he knew the relevant facts, was thinking clearly, and was free from distorting influences.' But what are 'relevant facts'? And how are hypothetical preferences to be considered? Can the distortion of values be eliminated? These are very real problems. We must recognise these before we can begin to disentangle them. The effort to do so is, I believe, worthwhile.

The dichotomy drawn between autonomy and protection is thus to a large extent a false divide. It should not divert us from the proposition that the true protection of children does also protect their rights. Thus, it is not a question of whether child-savers or liberationists are right. They have both grasped an essential truth in that they each emphasise part of what needs to be recognised. But both have also failed in that they do not address the claim of the other side.

Conclusion

Rights are important moral coinage. Without them we are impoverished. Benevolence is no substitute. This can be seen strikingly in the case of children. Children's rights thus becomes an interesting test-case for rights generally. In examining the case for children's rights and the values such rights uphold we are thus engaged in a wider enterprise of exploring rights, their rationale and their role. We are also finding a way of evaluating society. I first started writing about children's rights 30 years ago (Freeman 1980), the CRC was then 10 years away. The child's voice was silent, or least silenced. We hadn't yet awakened to sexual abuse or child slavery. We have come a long way since, but more progress needs to be made (Freeman 2000b). There is always a concern that we may go backwards, that we may have witnessed a false dawn. Part of the way forward lies in reiterating the case for children's rights and exploring the values such rights embody. This chapter is part of, what I hope will continue to be, a healthy debate.

References

Alderson, P. Hawthorne, J. and Killen, M. 2005. The participation rights of premature babies. *Int. J. of Children's Rights*, 13, 31–50.

Arendt, H. 1986. *The Origins of Totalitarianism*. London: Andre Deutsch.

Atkinson, M. 2010. The children's rape trial shows we need an urgent review of the system. *The Guardian* [online, 27 May 2010]. Available at: http://www.guardian.co.uk/commentisfree/2010/may/27/children-rape-trial-urgent-review [accessed 21 September 2010].

Brighouse, H. 2002. What rights (if any) do children have, in D. Archard and C. Macleod (eds), *The Moral and Political Status of Children*. Oxford: Oxford University Press, pp. 31–51.

Cohen, H. 1980. *Equal Rights for Children*. Totowa, NJ: Littlefield, Adams.

Crenshaw, K. 1988. Race, reform and retrenchment. *Harvard Law Review*, 101, 1331.

Devlin, P. 1965. *The Enforcement of Morals*. Oxford: Clarendon Press.

Dworkin, G. 1972. Paternalism, in R. Wasserstrom (ed.), *Morality and the Law*. Belmont, CA: Wadsworth, pp. 107–26.

——. 1977. *Taking Rights Seriously*. London: Duckworth.

Farson, R. 1974. *Birthrights*. Harmondsworth: Penguin.

Feinberg, J. 1966. Duties, rights and claims. *American Philosophical Quarterly*, 3, 137.

Fineman, M. and Worthington, K. 2009. *What is Right for Children?* Farnham: Ashgate.

Frankena, W. 1962. The concept of social justice, in R. Brandt (ed.), *Social Justice*. Englewood Cliffs, NJ: Prentice Hall, pp. 1–29.

Freeman, M. 1980. The rights of children in the International Year of the Child. *Current Legal Problems*, 33, 1.

——. 1988. Sterilizing the mentally handicapped, in M. Freeman (ed.), *Medicine, Ethics and Law*. London: Stevens, pp. 55–84.

——. 1995. The morality of cultural pluralism. *Int. J. of Children's Rights*, 3, 1–17.

——. 2000a. Children and cultural diversity, in D. Fottrell (ed.), *Revisiting Children's Rights*. The Hague: Kluwer Law International, pp. 15–30.

——. 2000b. The future of children's rights. *Children and Society*, 14, 277–93.

——. 2011. The human rights of children. *Current Legal Problems* (forthcoming).

Goldstein, J., Freud, A. and Solnit, A. 1979. *Before the Best Interests of the Child*. New York: Free Press.

Guardian, The. 13 January 2010. Sixteen-year-old becomes Spain's youngest transsexual [online]. Available at: http://www.guardian.co.uk/world/2010/jan/12/spanish-teenager-transsexual-operation [accessed 21 September 2010].

Guggenheim, M. 2005. *What's Wrong with Children's Rights*. Cambridge, MA: Harvard University Press.

Holt, J. 1975. *Escape from Childhood*. Harmondsworth: Penguin.

James, A. and Prout, A. 1997. Hierarchy, boundary and agency: towards a theoretical perspective on childhood, *Sociological Studies of Children*, 7, 77–99.

Lasch, C. 1977. *Haven in a Heartless World: The Family Besieged*. New York: Basic Books.

Lee, N. 2001. *Childhood and Society: Growing Up in an Age of Uncertainty*. Buckingham: Open University Press.

Lindley, R. 1986. *Autonomy*. London: Macmillan.

Lomasky, L. 1987. *Persons, Rights and the Moral Community*. New York: Oxford University Press.

Mackie, J. 1984. Can there be a rights-based moral theory? In J. Waldron (ed.), *Theories of Rights*. Oxford: Oxford University Press, pp. 168–81.

Mayall, B. 2002. *Towards a Sociology of Childhood*. London: Routledge, Falmer.

Menkel-Meadow, C. 1987. Excluded voices: new voices in the legal profession making new voices in the law. *Univ. of Miami L.R.*, 42, 29–53.

Mill, J.S. 1989. *On Liberty*. Cambridge: Cambridge University Press (originally published in 1859).

Narveson, J. 1985. Contractarian rights, in R. Frey (ed.), *Utility and Rights*. Oxford: Blackwell, pp. 161–74.

Nozick, R. 1974. *Anarchy, State and Utopia*. Oxford: Blackwell.

O'Neill, O. 1988. Children's rights and children's lives. *Ethics*, 98, 445–63.

Parfit, D. 1984. *Reasons and Persons*. Oxford: Oxford University Press.

Parsons, T. 1951. *The Social System*. London: Routledge, Kegan Paul.

Piaget, J. 1929. *The Child's Conception of the World*. London: Routledge, Kegan Paul.

Rawls, J. 1971. *A Theory of Justice*. Cambridge, MA: Harvard University Press.

Scott, E. 2000–2001. The legal construction of adolescents. *Hofstra L.R.*, 29, 547–98.

Uprichard, E. 2008. Children as being and becomings. *Children and Society*, 22, 303–313.

Wells, K. 2009. *Childhood in a Global Perspective*. Cambridge: Polity Press.

Williams, P. 1991. *The Alchemy of Race and Rights*. Cambridge, MA: Harvard University Press.

Woodhouse, B.B. 2008. *Hidden in Plain Sight: The Tragedy of Children's Rights from Ben Franklin to Lionel Tate*. Princeton, NJ: Princeton University Press.
Veerman, P. 1991. *The Rights of the Child and the Changing Image of Childhood*. Dordrecht: Martinus Nijhoff.

Chapter 2

Are Children's Rights still Human?

Nigel Cantwell

Introduction

When Poland presented its proposal for a convention on the rights of the child in 1978, it did so to the then UN Commission on Human Rights. In response to the Polish initiative, and after a round of initial consultations with UN member states and international organisations, the Commission decided the following year to set up a Working Group 'on the question of *a* convention on the rights of the child'. Today, two decades after the entry into force of *the* Convention on the Rights of the Child (CRC), there is a general acceptance of the fact that children 'have' the rights it contains. During the 30 years since drafting began, what many would call the 'international children's rights movement' was born and has grown exponentially, not only globally but also at national level.

On the face of it, this is undoubtedly a highly positive development for work to improve the status and situation of children. There is indeed a vast range of examples of initiatives taken that have substantially advanced the children's agenda, as well as of increasing recognition of the rights perspective in drawing up policies and programmes.

At the same time, there are grounds for concern that this development is too often founded on, or results in, approaches and actions that are at variance with the human rights context in which the CRC was formulated and in which, therefore, efforts to optimise its implementation were expected to take place. This has led to increasing discomfort in some quarters over certain ways in which 'children's rights' are being taken forward. Has the mindset on tackling children's issues really changed since the advent of the CRC? Do the bases used for determining orientations, priorities and policy in this field tally with those that characterise established and well-proven work in favour of human rights?

Without denying the progress achieved, this chapter points to a number of approaches and initiatives that could usefully be reviewed and remedied in order to optimise work to implement the CRC and that, taken together, would seem to justify asking the logical follow-up question: are children's rights still human?

Securing a Human Rights Treaty on Children's Issues

Despite the UN General Assembly's 1959 Declaration on the Rights of the Child, children's rights were not 'human': it is clear that the general perception in the run-up to the drafting of the CRC was that children's issues did not fall within the scope of human rights. This section is a brief reminder of how the vital link between them was forged.

Children's Rights in the 1970s

In terms of child-focused work, the pre-CRC era was characterised by *ad hoc* charity to children – and particularly to young children – who were seen as the most vulnerable and deserving members of society. On the relatively rare occasions that 'children's rights' were mentioned, reference was usually not being made to the 1959 Declaration on the Rights of the Child. The 'rights' being promoted – in a number of industrialised countries at least – concerned more particularly older children and were very much grounded in the post-1968 mindset of pitting young people against parents and other authority figures such as teachers: 'Kid Lib', for instance, or 'Pupil Power'. These 'rights' were invariably expressed, and therefore perceived, as a series of aggressive, disparate demands. They were invariably grounded in self-determination and anti-paternalism – the 'rights' to 'divorce' parents as of a certain age, to financial autonomy, to control over education, to the use of drugs and to sexual freedom, for example – rather than in the civil, political, economic, social and cultural rights contained in the Universal Declaration of Human Rights and the two Covenants it inspired.[1] The concept of protection was notably absent from their claims. Although sometimes made by young people themselves, they were far more frequently put forward by adults, nominally on their behalf. Indeed, and perhaps unavoidably at a time when adults alone had a voice and children's issues were not in the spotlight, in the 1970s there was considerable manipulation by self-styled advocates over what children and young people were – or 'should be' – demanding.[2]

Somewhat unsurprisingly in that climate, the term 'rights' was to all intents and purposes absent from the vocabulary of child-focused organisations, which were invariably welfare-based and assistance-oriented at that time. Thus, UNICEF's view was that its development work in health, nutrition and education had the secondary effect of contributing to the realisation of certain rights, but that its role

---

1   The major exception was the claim to children's enfranchisement that was key to their demands.

2   For a detailed review of these developments as of the early 1970s, see Veerman (1992: 133–52). Veerman makes a valid distinction between the children's *rights* movement and the children's *liberation* movement. It was nonetheless the latter's reference to 'rights' that vastly overshadowed use of the term in relation to children by those in the human rights sphere at that time.

was not to promote or protect rights as such. The largest international NGO in the field, the now-defunct International Union for Child Welfare (IUCW), had a policy that it dubbed 'active neutrality' whereby it notably refused to take stands on rights violations. This was all the more ironic in that the IUCW's very existence was due in good part to Eglantyne Jebb,[3] who had authored the first Geneva Declaration on the Rights of the Child in 1924 which was to be a major inspiration for the 1959 Declaration.

For their part, existing human rights organisations such as Amnesty International and the International Commission of Jurists (ICJ) had mandates and priorities that essentially sidelined any special concern for children's issues. The major exception was the Anti-Slavery Society (now Anti-Slavery International), which gave quite considerable attention to the exploitation of child labour.

In other words, children's issues and human rights were, to all intents and purposes, two rather different worlds.

The Impact of the International Year of the Child

The nascent concept of children's rights in the 1970s was thus surrounded by considerable confusion. Hillary Rodham Clinton summed this up neatly in 1973, in her now well-known comment that 'the phrase children's rights is a slogan in search of definition' (in Rodham 1973). But the necessary subsequent quest for such definition certainly did not take place in an auspicious context for developing consensus on 'the human rights of children'.

The confusion was compounded by a narrow focus on children's issues and a distinct lack of data in their regard. The fundamental importance of hard data for monitoring, effective advocacy and implementing the CRC is now recognised, but at that point there was very little information – and consequently very little effective action – on anything bar 'traditional' subjects such as health and education.

The International Year of the Child (IYC) in 1979 played a remarkable role in turning this situation around. IYC sparked the expression of concerns regarding a range of children's issues that had previously received very little publicity, such as children in prison, 'street children', sexual exploitation and child labour. Wider knowledge of the existence of such problems led to attempts to quantify them. Indeed, the International Labour Organisation (ILO) already went that extra step in 1979 itself when it came out with probably the most striking figure of the year: that there were an estimated 52 million working children worldwide. It was, literally, headline news.

And IYC also, of course, instigated Poland to propose its initiative to draw up the Convention.

---

3   The IUCW was established in 1946 as a merger between the International Association for the Promotion of Child Welfare and the International Save the Children Union, founded by Jebb.

Drafting the Human Rights of Children

The drafting of the CRC marked the first time that a child-specific international instrument was developed from start to finish under the auspices of a human rights body – the then UN Commission on Human Rights.[4] This 'environment' brought together interested international NGOs as participating observers at the Working Group over the lengthy 10-year period of negotiating the content of the treaty. It was an unprecedented encounter between human rights NGOs, well-versed in that kind of exercise and in operating in the UN context, and other NGOs that had specialist knowledge on a wide range of children's issues but little or no experience of working with human rights bodies and at the intergovernmental level. It was the ever-developing cooperation among these different sectors of civil society, made possible by the nature of the exercise and the lengthy time-frame, that produced the global 'children's rights movement'. It also gave rise to the concept that might best be described as 'the human rights of children'.

Within the unprecedented impact that civil society had on this treaty, human rights organisations such as Amnesty International, the Anti-Slavery Society and the ICJ were as active in shaping the draft and pushing it forward as the NGOs specialising in children's affairs – and, indeed, more so than many of them.

In addition, largely as a result of this unprecedented contact with their child-focused peers, these human rights organisations began to pay more attention in their own work to the violations of children's rights. The 1980s saw the creation of Working Groups for Children within Amnesty International national sections, for example, and the ICJ also devoted unprecedented energy to issues and cases involving children.

Child-focused organisations and associations of professionals working with children, for their part, increasingly began to understand the true potential of the future CRC (not just as a legal instrument but also as an educational tool) and how they could most effectively contribute to its formulation. By the half-way mark in drafting, once it had become clear that governments were taking the exercise seriously, UNICEF decided that it too should be directly involved despite its previous reticence towards any linkage with the 'rights' field. This brought the organisation, for the very first time in its then 40-year history, into cooperation with its sister body, the UN Centre for Human Rights.

---

4   The non-binding 1959 Declaration also went through the UN Commission on Human Rights but had been first mooted at the UN Social Commission in 1948. The latter then passed it to the Economic and Social Council (ECOSOC) which delegated the issue to its Social Committee in 1950. This Committee drew up a 'concept-declaration' and the UN Commission on Human Rights was asked to consider this and to report back to ECOSOC. Although the Commission put the issue on the back burner until 1957, it finally developed and approved its own text for the Declaration, and this was the one that was accepted without a vote by the UN General Assembly in 1959. For a more detailed account of this process, see Veerman (1992: 161–6).

Thus the drafting of the CRC not only produced a human rights text on children but also set the stage for innovative collaboration for children both in civil society and at the intergovernmental level, as well as between the two.

Human Rights Standards and Children's Issues

At that time, there was a kind of paradox underlying the 'human rights of children'. On the one hand, there were relatively few clearly-recognised child-focused standards, in terms of 'hard law' in particular.[5] On the other, general human rights instruments – notably the Covenants that were adopted in 1966 and came into force in 1976 – contained many provisions that concerned under-18s: through explicit reference, implicitly by their subject-matter, or simply because no age-limit applies to the beneficiaries.[6]

Not only did the launching of the CRC drafting process put children's issues squarely into a human rights context, but also the final text adopted took its inspiration as much from existing human rights texts as from purely child-centred concerns.[7] Indeed, one of the aims of drawing up the CRC, especially in the eyes of the NGOs, very quickly became that of bringing together the rights that were scattered throughout a range of instruments that was so wide as to render them almost inoperative as a basis for coherent, comprehensive advocacy and meaningful responses to violations. This had been one of the many factors militating against a rights-based approach to children's issues, moreover.

The importance of this human rights base is underscored by the struggle that was necessary to secure the inclusion of certain 'human rights' in the text of the CRC. A number of governmental delegates in the Working Group questioned the need for reaffirming 'fundamental rights and freedoms', expressing a preference for limiting the treaty to those rights specific to children. However, it became clear during the debates that the drafters of the two Covenants – and, more to the point, many of the states that had ratified them – had by no means considered that children might automatically be beneficiaries, alongside adults, of the rights they

---

5 Those that existed dealt more especially with exploitation, such as the Supplementary Convention on the Abolition of Slavery, the Slave Trade, and Institutions and Practices Similar to Slavery (1956), Convention on Consent to Marriage, Minimum Age for Marriage and Registration of Marriages (1962) and ILO Convention 138 on Minimum Age of Employment (1973).

6 Examples of these are: International Covenant on Civil and Political Rights (ICCPR) Art. 10.3 which reads: '... Juvenile offenders shall be segregated from adults and be accorded treatment appropriate to their age and legal status'; International Covenant on Economic, Social and Cultural Rights (ICESCR) Art 13.2 (b) provides that 'Primary education shall be compulsory and available free to all'; and there is no age barrier to the 'fundamental freedoms' set out in the ICCPR.

7 Among the general human rights issues taken on board in the CRC, in addition to those mentioned in the preceding footnote, are discrimination, right to life, protection from torture, social security, health care, exploitation and trafficking.

contain.[8] Most delegations thus came out in favour of incorporation, and it finally proved possible to reach agreement on their explicit mention in the CRC. This cemented even more firmly the human rights foundations of the Convention.

The CRC thus reflects a hard-won consensus on the substance of the human rights of children, and it was indeed quickly heralded as the most widely ratified human rights instrument ever. Clearly the standard-setting, crucial in itself as an agreed basis for action, has also enabled progress to be made in many spheres over the ensuing years, from the increased attention to rights areas that had previously been considered out of bounds or too sensitive for general take-up (such as juvenile justice and harmful traditional practices) to the CRC Committee's reporting process which has stimulated the involvement and cooperation of NGOs throughout the world in the monitoring exercise. The Committee itself, moreover, has revised its initial reporting guidelines so that they are now far more appropriate from a rights standpoint (in the first version, the key issues were drowned in a mass of unrealistic demands for peripherally-important information from states). Children's issues have been significantly moved up the international and national agendas, and children and young people are gradually becoming consulted more systematically on problems affecting them and how they might best be tackled.

But, despite clear advances such as these and the treaty's pedigree, a problem has gradually been surfacing: too often, these rights are not looked on as children's inalienable *human* rights, but simply as … *children's* rights. Since the CRC's adoption, and as implementation initiatives and efforts ostensibly intended to maximise its impact have taken their course, a number of disturbing features of the overall response have emerged. On several important counts, we seem to be sliding rapidly backwards, often unwittingly, to a situation reminiscent of the pre-CRC era of 'children's rights' rather than moving forward by building on the essential 'human rights of children'.

Symptoms of the Move away from Human Rights

Three inter-related phenomena can be highlighted as being indicative of this unfortunate trend. First is the persistent sentimentalism over 'children' that does not sit well in a human rights frame. Second, organisations are often failing to respect some fundamentals of the human rights approach. Finally, pronouncements on, and interpretations of, certain provisions risk jeopardising the human rights consensus.

---

8   See, for example, the record of debates during the drafting contained in UN documents E/CN.4/1983/62, paras 53–5 (on freedom of thought, conscience and religion) and E/CN.4/1987/25, paras 112–17 (on freedom of association and peaceful assembly), quoted in Detrick (1992), at respectively 239–40 and 250–51.

Continued Acceptance of Sentimentalism

The 'charity approach' is founded in large part on sentimentalism: arousing sympathy for individuals or groups who involuntarily find themselves in difficult situations and who, because of their perceived vulnerability and helplessness, are deemed to deserve assistance. Not unnaturally, the children's sphere has been notoriously exploitable from this sentimentalist standpoint. Regrettably, even in the 'rights' era, this exploitation continues in far too many instances.

In the beginning was 'the child' ...   One way of maintaining – consciously or not – a maximum level of supportive sentimentality is thus to infantilise older CRC rights-holders. An illustration of this is the frequent statement that the CRC 'defines a child' as anyone under the age of 18. It does no such thing, though even the UN itself sometimes gets it wrong.[9] It is very important to recognise the difference between the supposed 'definition' and what the CRC really says: that when the word 'child' is used in the text of this treaty, it is to be interpreted as meaning anyone under the age of 18. Indeed, there was no little discussion, during the drafting, of the most appropriate term or terms to use, including consideration of 'minors' and 'children and young persons'. The final choice of 'child' in English was made essentially on the grounds of simplicity and common usage. Similar debates took place in other languages, with Francophone and Hispanophone delegates in particular concerned that the scope or connotation of the equivalent of 'child' in their respective languages would not extend to adolescence (and, in Italian, also down to toddlers).

Consequently, with the advent of the CRC, there seems to have come a mistaken belief that it was both politically correct and almost legally necessary to refer to anyone under 18 solely as 'a child', and that terms such as 'young people' and 'adolescents' were suddenly *non gratae* in the human rights field. Indeed, young people of 16 and 17 were – and still are – feeling forced to refer to themselves, often rather sheepishly, as 'children' when speaking in public debate, for fear of somehow compromising their status under the CRC. And their embarrassment at doing so is often as palpable as it is justified:

> The United Nations, *for statistical purposes*, defines 'youth' as those persons between the ages of 15 and 24 years, without prejudice to other definitions by Member States. This definition was made during preparations for the International Youth Year (1985) ... *By that definition, therefore, children are those persons under the age of 14 ...*[10]

---

9   See, for example, the UN website at http://www.un.org/esa/socdev/unyin/qanda. htm#4 [accessed 28 July 2008]: 'Article 1 of the United Nations Convention on the Rights of the Child defines "children" as persons up to the age of 18.'

10   See http://www.un.org/esa/socdev/unyin/qanda.htm#4 [accessed 28 July 2008] (emphasis added).

The emergence of this terminology problem was picked up quite rapidly by one commentator who wrote in the mid-1990s:

> The Convention started out to be only about children's rights but later in the negotiations a decision was made to extend coverage to 18.[11] This created a discrepancy: draft article 1 was extended to cover minors ('18 years unless … majority is attained earlier') but the rights were still defined in the rest of the draft articles in terms of 'child'. Rather than change 'child' to 'minor' or use other words, the discrepancy was resolved by using legalistic language to create an artificial definition of 'child'. The objective of Article 1 is to identify the class of persons who get CRC rights, not to change language … [Its intention] is to give CRC rights to minors, not to get governments and the public to call all minors 'children'. (Abramson 1996: 393–402)

This does not mean that the word 'child' has to be avoided, of course. But the stubborn determination that has been displayed by many in referring solely to 'children' unfortunately, and whether deliberately or not, prolongs the sentimentalist view rather than, for example, helping to promote the CRC rights of adolescents at the same time.

… then 'child soldiers' …   A good example of this problem lies in the term 'child soldiers'. The Coalition to Stop the Use of Child Soldiers, set up in 1998, 'considers a child soldier any person under the age of 18 who is a member of or attached to government armed forces or any other regular or irregular armed force or armed political group, whether or not an armed conflict exists'.[12] While children aged 10 and even younger have been identified as 'soldiers', clearly most are between the ages of 15 and 18 years (UN 1996, IRIN 2003). Their higher age of course does not give them any less right to the full protections of the CRC and its Optional

---

11   This terse statement tends to mask important aspects of how agreement on age 18 was reached, however. Certainly, Poland's initial proposal, like the 1959 Declaration, gave no indication of the age-group that the term 'child' was intended to cover, so could be said to be 'only about children's rights'. However, draft Article 1 of its revised proposal of 1979 already stipulated that '[a]ccording to the present Convention, a child is every human being from the moment of his birth to the age of 18 years unless, under the laws of his state, he has attained his age of majority earlier.' During the UN Working Group's debate on this proposal (1980), concerns were expressed by several delegations that the age of 18 was too high. They proposed age 15, on the grounds that, *inter alia*, this was the upper age set by the UN General Assembly when proclaiming the International Year of the Child. Some even suggested 14 as the cut-off age, partly because this would 'establish a clear distinction between the concept of minor and that of child …' (UN Doc E/CN.4/L.1542, para. 32). However consensus was finally reached at that same 1980 meeting on maintaining the age of 18 as proposed by Poland.

12   'Who are child soldiers?' Frequently Asked Questions, http://www.child-soldiers. org/childsoldiers/questions-and-answers [accessed 31 July 2008].

Protocol, but applying the term 'child' to a 17-year-old may not give an accurate image of the young person concerned.

This confusion is of course further compounded by the use of the word 'soldier'. One of the earlier efforts to codify the approach to children and adolescents involved in armed conflict took place in 1997, at the Cape Town consultation organised by UNICEF and the NGO Group for the CRC. It came up with the following definition, which held for many years thereafter:

> A child soldier is any person under 18 years of age who is part of any kind of regular or irregular armed force or armed group in any capacity, including but not limited to cooks, porters, messengers and anyone accompanying such groups, other than family members. The definition includes girls recruited for sexual purposes and for forced marriage. It does not, therefore, only refer to a child who is carrying or has carried arms. (UNICEF 1997)

By using this term and definition, it was therefore possible to cover a far larger number of young people than just those directly engaged in hostilities – so that the substantial figure of 300,000 could be quoted rather than, perhaps, 'only' tens of thousands – and, to boot, retain the emotive word 'child'. It might be said that in this way, maximum advantage is taken of the sentimentalist view of children in order to arouse support for the cause, rather than rigorous reference to the violation of their human rights in different ways.

It was nonetheless recognised, over time, that including such a wide range of activities under the term 'soldier' might be somewhat misleading. This led to the development of the term 'children associated with armed forces and groups' and its uninspiring acronym CAAFG. At the 2007 ministerial meeting hosted by the French Government to adopt a revised version of the Cape Town Principles, the agreed re-definition of the target-group thus read as follows:

> A child associated with an armed force or armed group refers to any person below 18 years of age who is or who has been recruited or used by an armed force or armed group in any capacity, including but not limited to children, boys and girls, used as fighters, cooks, porters, messengers, spies or for sexual purposes. It does not only refer to a child who is taking or has taken a direct part in hostilities.[13]

To all intents and purposes, therefore, the definition is the same and the term 'child' is retained, but reference to the 'soldier' misnomer has been dropped. Nonetheless, 'child soldiers' remains a widely-used term – including of course by the eponymous Coalition. Rather like 'child' in the CRC, 'child soldier' has been given a special meaning 'for the purposes of' those who use it – but in this case it

---

13　Principles and Guidelines on Children Associated With Armed Forces or Armed Groups (The Paris Principles), February 2007.

is arguably even less apt since a sizeable majority of the group it purports to cover would be, by common perception, neither children nor soldiers.

Of course there are, among others, historical reasons for the choice of the term 'child soldiers'. The use of boys as young as 12 in direct combat during Iran's war against Iraq in the early 1980s was well-documented and publicised at the time, and this situation was certainly a major factor in arousing concern about the issue of 'child soldiers' in general. The subsequent discovery of the extent to which children and young people were also used by armed groups (such as the LRA as of the early 1990s) in other capacities, and the fact that they may become 'attached' to armed forces (as in the case of Rwanda in 1994) demonstrated the additional non-combatant 'duties' they fulfilled, but these were nonetheless subsumed under the 'child soldier' terminology. In contrast, while the term 'comfort women' is a patent euphemism, at least we understand exactly to whom and to what phenomenon it refers. Masking the egregious sexual exploitation of girls by talking of 'child soldiers' simply contributes to their invisibility as an unmentioned sub-group of non-combatants. This, it might be argued, does little to highlight their situation in terms of the specific human rights violations to which they fall victim, and which in addition are to be addressed in ways that may differ considerably from those employed in response, for example, to boys forced, persuaded or allowed to bear arms in combat.

... and adolescence lost   This kind of invisibility in the human rights and other fields used to apply to all minors, and this was something that the CRC set out to tackle. But subsequent over-zealous use of the word 'child' when referring to CRC rights-holders has in turn created invisibility for adolescents as a whole. This may seem all the more paradoxical in that the CRC – notably, though not only, through its Article 5 that recognises the child's evolving capacities – very clearly sought to empower the rights-holders it covers increasingly as they mature.

It could be said that this reinforces the lack of attention often paid to older children in programme responses, moreover. Illustrative of this is the situation of adolescents in refugee and internally displaced persons (IDP) camps. While we readily recognise the particular types of vulnerability experienced by adolescents in general, 'child protection' in these circumstances tends to focus on younger children (and their mothers). Adolescents are seemingly expected to need less support.[14] Yet spontaneous fostering by the local community is common in regard to young children without parental care, while even those above the age of seven will often find it harder to benefit from such arrangements. Older children and adolescents are also generally more affected – and for a longer period – by traumatic experiences. Until the age of seven or eight, for example, death is usually perceived as a reversible event and witnessing it is therefore a somewhat less traumatising experience than for older children; and as of age 11, boys have

---

14   See, for example, UN (1996), para. 170: 'Adolescents, during or after wars, seldom receive any special attention or assistance.'

a high propensity to re-enact violence and traumas in an aggressive manner if not provided with appropriate support.[15]

Insisting, come what may, on using the word 'child' simply contributes to the specificities of adolescence continuing to be overlooked.

Ignoring Some Fundamentals of Human Rights

Even accepting that it may take a generation to change attitudes, that time is now up for those seeking to work for children's human rights on the basis of the CRC.

This section looks at some of the ways in which many advocates are still at variance with the human rights community in the messages that they put over and how they choose to work. Some seek to prioritise children's issues — or certain among them — unduly; others twist the meaning of CRC provisions to their own ends; and yet others seem intent on reinventing the human rights wheel almost as if decades of experience of advocacy and protection activities in the sphere would count for little as far as children are concerned.

Making children more equal than others　Many efforts have justifiably been directed to securing a higher place for children's issues on the international (and national) agenda. Unfortunately, these have often translated into attempts to ensure an enhanced status for children's issues among all human rights concerns. Slogans such as 'children first' and initiatives to secure priority for children's issues above all others are surely well-intentioned but, taken at face value, they express a goal that runs completely counter to human rights ideals. Once more, they reflect the surviving legacy of a charitable approach in which sentimentalism based on the special vulnerability and defencelessness of children trumps securing their rights in common, and on an equal basis, with those of all other human beings.

The Preamble to the CRC certainly recalls – taking inspiration from the UDHR and the 1959 Declaration – that 'childhood is entitled to special care and assistance', that 'particular care' needs to be extended to the child, and that the child 'needs special safeguards and care', but neither there nor elsewhere in the text is the idea of 'priority' to children articulated.[16]

Indeed, essential to the idea of human rights is of course the fact that each and every individual is to benefit from them, automatically and inalienably, without

---

15　Interview with Dr Leila Gupta, Psycho-social Trauma Programme, UNICEF Rwanda, October 1996, noted in Cantwell (1997: 47).

16　It might be argued that treatment of children in emergency situations does not correspond fully to this general rule. Principle 3 of the 1924 Declaration of Geneva states. 'The child must *be first* to receive relief in times of distress' (emphasis added), and this was echoed in the 1948 draft version. However, it was modified in the 1959 Declaration to read: 'The child shall in all circumstances be *among the first* to receive protection and relief' (emphasis added). This wording also figured in the initial Polish proposal (Art. VIII) but, tellingly, all reference to such prioritisation had already disappeared completely from the revised proposal presented by Poland in 1979 (UN Doc E/CN.4/1349).

discrimination or distinction, by the very fact that he or she exists. The problem that children faced was, precisely, that due account had never previously been taken of them or of their specific situation in human rights instruments – and at that time the same problem confronted, for example, persons with disabilities, indigenous peoples, and many other groups. When drawing up the CRC, the aim was therefore to ensure that children received full recognition as 'human beings' by their explicit inclusion in human rights law and by consideration therein of the particular requirements that their age demanded.

Lack of rigour when referring to the substance of CRC rights   Advocacy on children's issues often demonstrates a distinct lack of rigour in setting out the exact rights that can be defended on the basis of the CRC. Among many possible examples, those relating to 'the child and the family' and to 'best interests' are illustrative of the problems encountered to date.

<u>Family</u>   In human rights, the term 'right to a family life' is understood essentially to include the right to found a family (as the 'natural and fundamental group unit of society') and to have that family protected from arbitrary or illegal interference (ICCPR, Articles 17 and 23) together with an obligation on the state to protect and assist the family, materially and otherwise, especially with a view to enabling it to carry out its child-caring role (ICESCR, Articles 10 and 11).

The CRC has not only reiterated these rights (save the one relating to founding a family) but has also built on them by adding details such as 'as far as possible, the right to know and be cared for by his or her parents' (Article 7.1) and the right to 'maintain personal relations and direct contact with both parents' (Article 9.3), as well as specifying the obligation to ensure protection from arbitrary separation (Article 9.1) and to facilitate family reunification (Article 10). It has also introduced the concept of 'family environment' which – on the important condition that it be characterised by 'an atmosphere of happiness, love and understanding' – is qualified in the Preamble as being the ideal context for the child's upbringing. And it is when the child is deprived of his or her own family environment that the state's obligation to provide alternative care steps in (Article 20.1).

Implicitly distancing themselves from the human rights approach to family-related rights, many organisations (not to mention individuals) that should know better now talk blithely about a child's 'right to a family' in the sense that any child without a family must be given one. Indeed, such has been the pressure in favour of this erroneous affirmation that now we even see 'Every human being, especially every boy and girl, has the right to a family ...' in nothing less than an OAS Declaration.[17]

Of course, few would disagree that the overall policy goal to be pursued is that of maintaining children in their own 'family environment' and, if this is not

---

17   Inter-American Declaration on the Family, Organization of American States, 2003, doc. AG/RES. 678 (XIII-O/83).

possible, finding an alternative family setting in which they can be cared for, in line with the CRC Preamble. But neither the CRC nor any other treaty affords anything like a 'right' in this respect. Indeed, as is the case for similarly desirable objectives that are unrealisable 'rights' – to be loved or to live in a peaceful society, for instance – it is difficult to imagine how a State Party might be willing to make, let alone be able to fulfil, an uncompromising formal commitment to ensure that every child has a family.

Furthermore, the experiences of many children and adolescents mean that they themselves express a preference for group care rather than dealing with the intimacy of a family setting, at least at certain points in their lives, or cannot function in such a setting. A refusal, on principle, to recognise this can easily result in destructive serial foster placements.

But whether or not there could or should be such a right is in the end immaterial at present: no such human right exists in hard law, and the children's rights community should resist attempts, within its midst and elsewhere, to infer that it does.

Best interests   Another frequent advocacy thrust is the oft-stated demand that, 'in conformity' with the CRC, the best interests of the child be systematically the determining factor in decision-making that affects the child, whereas the general obligation on states is of course to look on these interests as simply one of the primary considerations.

There was lengthy and in-depth debate in the UN Working Group before the term 'a primary consideration' was settled on. This choice reflected a realistic assessment that many other important factors might need to be taken into account when coming to decisions regarding children, such as upholding the rule of law, protecting the rights of others and reviewing material (including financial) issues. Thus, the drafters were very clear, for example, about the distinction to be made between the above-mentioned wording of the general obligation in Article 3 and the specific reference in Article 21 to best interests as 'the paramount consideration' solely as regards adoption. In the latter case, and in that case alone, the child's best interests 'must take precedence over any other interests, in particular those of his/ her birth parents, prospective adoptive parents, accredited adoption bodies or the States concerned' (Vité and Boéchat 2008: 24).

Too many advocates seek to use 'best interests' as a kind of general trump card that can override rights that they deem dispensable in the circumstances, or that eliminates the need to take account of external factors. Wilfully or not, they are misreading the CRC and, as a result, they not only undermine the credibility of their own advocacy but also risk diminishing the perceived value of the 'best interests' principle. The right of the child concerns the state's obligation to take his or her best interests into account, not to come to a decision solely on the basis of those interests. In that sense, it constitutes one among all the rights of the child. It is this fact, moreover, that serves as a safeguard in decision-making: no outcome where considerations other than the best interests of the child are also brought into play should jeopardise or violate other CRC rights.

The welcome and relatively recent advent of 'best interests determination' (BID) exercises clearly highlights the complexities of decision-making on this question. BID involves the review of a wide range of factors in the overall context of a comprehensive rights-based child protection system before coming to a decision on what constitutes the best interests of a given child. At that point, the preferred outcome for the child may have to be reviewed in the light of any conflicting rights-based interests of others, which must also be considered a 'primary consideration' within the human rights framework.[18]

Ignoring human rights experience   Traditional human rights strategies seem to be frequently eschewed by those working in the field of children's rights. Much advocacy is still based more on rhetoric and generalisation than on documenting facts and setting them against the background of rigorous interpretation of human rights law.

Even when information has been collected and painstakingly verified and cross-checked, it is not enough simply to disseminate it or to pursue the course of aggressive condemnation. There must be a commitment and capacity to strategise: to determine and then to pursue the potentially most effective paths to obtain redress or resolution. As yet, this necessary combination is often lacking in the children's rights sphere.

Furthermore, of the two essential pillars of human rights work – promotion and protection – the former often tends to eclipse the latter as regards efforts in favour of children.

As a result, there is in particular a perceived unwillingness to tackle the most egregious violations of children's human rights. Thus, while considerable resources may be mobilised to ensure that children are given the floor to express their views at various meetings and conferences, efforts by the children's rights community to secure the release of children detained simply for having expressed their views – such as several Kurdish children in Turkey whose cases have been highlighted more especially by Amnesty International[19] and certain other human rights NGOs – have generally been feeble.[20] Similarly, the promotion of 'restorative' rather than punitive forms of juvenile justice is to be applauded – but all the more so if there is also a will to systematically call to account those thankfully few countries who

---

18   See for example: UNHCR Guidelines on Determining the Best Interests of the Child, Geneva, May 2008. As one example of conflicting best interests, this publication cites the *a priori* preferred option of a foster placement for a girl with a contagious illness, but which would endanger the health of the foster family.

19   See for example, Amnesty document EUR/44/011/2008.

20   The Children's Rights Information Network (CRIN) notes that '[f]reedom of expression is rarely a part of children's rights advocacy – at least as a stand-alone issue – yet it is critical for the realisation of all children's rights ...'. See www.crin.org/resources/infodetail.asp?id=22487 [accessed 30 June 2010].

continue to apply the death penalty or life imprisonment without possibility of parole for crimes committed when the offender was aged under 18.

Defending the human rights of children involves a willingness to tackle the problems from both the bottom and the top, i.e. identifying effective ways of promoting good practice as well as of countering violations. If the children's rights community allows the worst violations to go with only meagre response, this will inevitably be seen as reflecting insufficient commitment to the human rights cause.

Surprising priorities   From a human rights standpoint, some of the 'issues' that have captured most attention within the children's rights movement cause, at the very least, eyebrows to be raised. Clearly, for example, there is every justification for efforts to eliminate the parental 'right' to physically chastise their children, in those countries where it has not yet been prohibited. But when, as has often been the case to date, this issue becomes the major element on the overall 'violence against children' agenda, questions are bound to be asked. In the human rights field, domestic violence is certainly not neglected, especially against women and all the more so in its most serious forms such as honour killings and other fatal or harmful 'traditional' practices. At the same time, this does not overshadow the concern about, and efforts to combat, the various forms and contexts of violence and torture perpetrated directly by states and state actors.

On a different plane, the human rights community is also often sceptical, to say the least, about the degree to which their children's rights counterparts devote efforts to securing certain forms of what is commonly termed 'child participation'. In so doing, they are not questioning the validity of involving and consulting with children and young people. What does intrigue them, however, is the amount of 'rights-fuelled' energy that is diverted into exercises of little or no proven efficacy that are apparently designed simply to demonstrate that so-called 'participation rights' are somehow being respected. In many such instances, the young people concerned are often placed in virtually the same situation as those who, in pre-CRC days, used to be brought on stage to sing and dance at the opening of meetings on children's issues. And not unnaturally, therefore, the reaction of the audience is usually broadly similar as well: 'Weren't the children wonderful!' As noted below, there is reason to encourage the children's rights community to take a close look at how it has approached at least some aspects of 'participation' and why is has devoted such attention to them.

Demanding the impossible   There is often a lack of realism in the demands that children's rights organisations make of states. Sometimes the unrealistic nature of what is being called for is founded on questionable interpretations of state obligations, such as those related to the status and meaning of 'best interests' referred to above. In other cases, it seems to stem from a desire to be perceived as resolutely 'progressive' in the interpretation of rights, leading to objectively exaggerated claims (see below). Lack of realism also results from a 'jurist-purist' approach that sticks, come what may, to a principle and refuses to take a more pragmatic view of the issue at hand.[21] And it may also quite simply be the consequence of calls for a state to act while being unable oneself to come up with a constructive, 'do-able' strategy to achieve the advocated change: how to reduce reliance on residential placements in a cash-strapped country where care provision is virtually exclusively in the hands of foreign-funded private entities, for example.

One of the most militant and impressive international human rights lawyers of our time was the late Katarina Tomasevski. As well as her general human rights work, as of the 1980s she also devoted considerable attention to children's issues, including imprisonment and detention, and was UN Special Rapporteur on the Right to Education from 1998 to 2004. But despite her consistently uncompromising analyses and outspoken condemnation of state action and inaction, she realistically held that 'No government can be legally obliged to do the impossible' (Tomasevski 2006: 36). Such impossibility may exist for a variety of reasons: inadequate or conflicting demands on resources, of course, but also opposition within the legislature, lack of societal acceptance, etc. Some of the demands made in the name of children's rights, and the 'strategies' adopted in an attempt to achieve them, might usefully take this into account.

Putting the Human Rights Consensus at Risk

To be sure, although the *Travaux Préparatoires* and the Preamble provide vital guidance on the spirit of the CRC and the intentions of its drafters, the interpretative base cannot be limited to these two sources alone. Jurisprudence in the form of decisions from the European Court of Human Rights, for example, as well as advice formulated in General Comments from the CRC Committee and other treaty bodies provide additional grounds for justifying interpretations of given rights. Moreover, certain formulations in CRC provisions beg questions because of their vagueness or ambiguity[22] and, as time goes by, new phenomena appear that are not clearly covered by the treaty.[23] In some cases, even incoherencies in

---

21   A frequently debated issue in this vein is whether or not the general obligation to accommodate juvenile and adult detainees separately should extend to providing a dedicated facility for juvenile offenders even in relatively remote areas where the need for recourse to deprivation of liberty is so infrequent that it would rarely be in use.

22   For example, the obligation to resort to 'arrest, detention or imprisonment' only as a 'last resort and for the shortest appropriate period of time' (Article 37.b) and lack of guidance on setting 'a minimum age below which children shall be presumed not to have the capacity to infringe the penal law' (Article 40.3.b).

23   Such as child-headed households and unaccompanied or separated children outside their country of habitual residence. Also, for example, CRC Article 21 calls for inter-country adoption to be subject to 'safeguards and standards equivalent to those existing in the case of national adoption', whereas the advent of the 1993 Hague Convention now means that

its provisions are coming to light.[24] In other words, it is eminently reasonable to look on the CRC as both a landmark treaty and a 'living document', and not as the definitive word on children's rights.

But this outlook is far removed from espousing an ideal of pushing ever outwards the interpretative boundaries of the CRC's provisions as if that would somehow correspond more adequately to optimising rights protection or advancement for children. This kind of strategic aim is rather infrequent in general human rights work but has become an all-too-common feature of the children's rights movement. Unfortunately, it carries with it a number of dangers that can have several negative ramifications for the human rights of children.

The risk of undermining the fragile consensual foundations of many rights   In large part due to the skilful chairmanship of the Working Group by Adam Lopatka, the entire text of the CRC was adopted by consensus, save the provision on how the work of the Committee should be financed. Achieving this consensus was a phenomenal task, as attested by the fact that the drafting process took a full decade. The inclusion of many words and terms, let alone whole provisions, required lengthy negotiation and compromise.

The fragility of the foundations of that consensus, however, shows in the fact that so many states notified reservations, of varying scope and appositeness, on ratifying or acceding to the CRC. Over time, a number of these reservations – and sometimes quite significant ones – have been withdrawn. On that score, it can be said that we are moving ever-closer (or back) to the original consensus achieved. This can only strengthen the latent force of the treaty that can be put to good effect.

It is therefore important to keep intact the common understanding of the substance and intent of the CRC rights by which States Parties have agreed to be bound: it is this that provides the fundamental legitimacy of CRC-based demands that are made. If due weight is not given to this, progress made towards achieving their recognition could be jeopardised.

Rights inflation: the 'participation' example   When pressure to have an ever-increasing number of interpretations and claims considered as 'rights' results in their *de facto* elevation to this status, the intrinsic value of established rights is whittled away, just as the value of money falls when too much is put into circulation. Hence the term 'rights inflation' to describe the dangerous ramifications of meeting constant demands for ever-wider interpretation.

---

national adoption is in fact carried out to lower standards than its inter-country counterpart in many countries.

24   One example is that reference is made variously to 'parents', 'parents or legal guardians', 'parents or others responsible for the child', 'other persons legally responsible', 'family', 'family environment', 'relatives' and 'extended family', where the differentiations or terms chosen do not always seem warranted by the context.

To prevent this erosion of the value of recognised rights – and thus of the acknowledged CRC basis on which they can be defended – it is vital that reference to 'rights' never be confused with unilateral interpretations, claims (however valid they might be), or means or objectives.

Unfortunately, one of the prime examples of this confusion being fostered would seem to lie in activities to promote what have come to be known as 'participation rights'.

In her opening remarks at the official meeting at the Palais Wilson in Geneva to mark International Children's Rights Day 2004, the representative of the Office of the High Commissioner on Human Rights (OHCHR), without questioning the concept of 'child participation' *per se*, nonetheless noted that it was still very open not only to resistance, but also to 'misinterpretation and manipulation'.[25]

The concept of the child's right to participate appears explicitly in just three provisions of the CRC. Under Article 9, concerning the removal of children from parental care, 'all interested parties' have the right 'to participate in the proceedings'; Article 23 recognises the need to facilitate the disabled child's 'active participation in the community'; and Article 31 sets out 'the right of the child to participate fully in cultural and artistic life'. But these are not the main articles that are usually being referred to when 'participation rights' are mentioned.

During the CRC drafting process, the notion of the 3 'Ps' – provision, protection and participation – was adopted by the NGOs concerned as a snappy way of describing the coverage of the future convention. Articles 12 through 16 were not unnaturally assigned to 'participation' as being the most pertinent category of the three. Unfortunately, this link has since been taken well beyond a convenient public-awareness slogan.

Four of the five provisions in question (i.e. Articles 13–16) were, as noted previously, included in the CRC in order to reaffirm existing human rights, by explicitly stipulating for the first time that children are to benefit from them as well. The original thinking behind these civil human rights, or 'fundamental freedoms', was of course to prevent states imposing undue or arbitrary restrictions and punishment in relation to the actions in question.

There is nothing in the *Travaux Préparatoires* to indicate that the 'intentions of the legislator' were any different concerning the corresponding rights for minors. Thus, a child – like an adult – henceforth has the right to receive and impart information, to freedom of expression, to manifestation of religion or beliefs, to freedom of association and peaceful assembly, and to protection of privacy. These rights are – for adults and children alike – subject to certain limitations, which are somewhat more restrictive in the CRC only on the question of freedom of religion.

Grave violations of these rights involving children persist, sometimes resulting in incarceration, torture and worse. They can be addressed, preventively and reactively, with all the more confidence in light of those provisions in the CRC. But in some 'children's rights' quarters, this is deemed far from enough. They go

---

25   Author's notes.

as far as to claim, for example, that the right to 'freedom of expression' as it applies to children and young people includes or implies an obligation to systematically provide, or at least not to deny on request, a platform for that expression, regardless of the appropriateness of the forum and, therefore, of the foreseeable impact of the intervention. This is the kind of claim that can fuel counter-productive 'rights inflation' in the children's rights sphere. A similar demand, on behalf of other groups, made on human rights grounds, would surely not be countenanced, moreover. And indeed, it is yet another cause of concern in human rights circles about the way 'children's rights' are too often being tackled.

In addition to those reaffirmed 'fundamental freedoms', Article 12 was adopted – and rightly so – to remedy the scant attention that had previously been paid to children's opinions 'on matters affecting them', particularly when administrative and judicial decisions were being made about their lives. It therefore set out the obligation to consult them on such issues and to take due account of the views they express. A look at the drafting history of Article 12 brings to light a number of important elements regarding the intent of this provision.

First, although Article 12 refers to 'the right to express [his or her own] views freely', this is not a restatement of the general right to 'freedom of expression' but is directly linked to the context and requirement of consultation with the child. In other words, the child is to be given the opportunity to state his or her point of view on the matter at hand without pressure, influence or threat, and under conditions that enable him or her to do so. This implies as well that the child is provided with all necessary information on which to found his or her opinion. Thus, the notion here is analogous to that of 'free and informed consent'.

Second, the 'matters' it seeks to refer to are clearly meant to be those that are directly pertinent to the life of the child concerned, not general issues that may have ramifications for children – these would no doubt be better dealt with from the pure 'freedom of expression' perspective, moreover.

Third, as intimated by the previous consideration, the right-holder is the individual child, since the questions to be covered are foreseen as those that relate to his or her specific personal situation.[26]

This interpretation, relying on the combined background of human rights law and the spirit of the CRC, is worlds apart from what many advocates deem to constitute 'advancing child participation rights' today on the basis of Article 12 –

---

26   Initially, the proposed wording was 'matters concerning his own person', with a non-exclusive list of such matters (marriage, choice of occupation, medical treatment, education and recreation). This proposed list was then substantially extended to include questions such as place of residence and matters of conscience. When the opportuneness of such a lengthy list was questioned, it was suggested simply to refer to 'all matters', but since this was seen as too broad, the qualifying phrase 'affecting the child' (not 'children') was added with a view to reflecting better the original intention of the provision without resorting to a nominative list of the matters concerned.

and hence, surely, a major element in the above-mentioned expression of concern by the OHCHR representative.

The CRC Committee was initially borne along rather too easily on the 'participation wave' without always looking to the justification for its positions and statements. The theme chosen for its 2006 Day of General Discussion, for example, was 'Speak, Participate and Decide – The Child's Right to be Heard'. This incongruous and wholly misleading reference to 'decide' was downplayed in the body of the final report, where the definitely more apt term of 'have their views taken into account' was preferred. The report is nonetheless studded with statements that arguably bear little relation to the letter and spirit of the CRC, and especially those of its Article 12, for example, 'Particular attention was given to the implications of [Article 12] for child participation – both as individuals and a collective constituency – in all aspects of society'; 'the right of the child to participate fully [in society] in accordance with article 12' (Committee on the Rights of the Child 2006: para. 3). But the CRC Committee went even further, contending in that same report that 'the new and deeper meaning of this right [to participate] is that it should establish *a new social contract*' (Committee on the Rights of the Child 2006: Recommendations, Preamble) This is arguably quite a leap. One wonders what other CRC rights may suddenly be deemed to have 'new and deeper' meanings, what those meanings might allegedly imply, and whether States Parties to the treaty are prepared to accept that they knowingly signed up to them. Clearly, if this kind of rights inflation is accepted, it will be almost impossible to avoid substantially sapping the strength of the original right in question and to engage states through credible advocacy.

It was surely symptomatic of the push into uncharted waters that was taking place that the development and finalisation of the CRC Committee's General Comment on Article 12 proved particularly difficult. Already well under way at the time of the Day of General Discussion in 2006, it was to take a further three years before agreement was reached on a final text (Committee on the Rights of the Child 2009). Despite successive redrafts being proposed and considered, many Committee members continued to have serious concerns about the rights-based justifications for the approaches suggested and the implications of how the provision in question was being interpreted. There seems to have been realisation that matters were getting out of hand. In the end, the Committee successfully resisted an 'inflationary' mindset and settled on a text that is, overall, realistic and well-founded. This is one of the more encouraging steps in favour of the human rights of children in recent years.

The undeniably positive effect of the inclusion of Articles 12–16 in the CRC is that it stimulated widespread reflection on how children and adolescents might become better prepared and more actively involved in identifying and tackling problems related to respect for CRC rights, and that it has inspired a wide range of initiatives designed to achieve that highly desirable end.

So the issue at hand is not whether 'child participation' should be promoted or not. It is one of making certain that initiatives that go beyond the precise rights set out in the CRC are not dubbed 'participation rights' but are looked on – and assessed – as one potential means of improving the realisation of CRC rights in general. Thus, for example, in the same report but in a far wiser moment, the CRC Committee itself has noted 'the importance of encouraging opportunities for child participation *as a tool* to stimulate the evolving capacities of the child' (Committee on the Rights of the Child 2006: para. 11). Looked at in that way, the justification of how, when and why 'participation' takes place can be objectively assessed, as can its outcomes, in the same way as would apply to adults.

If, in contrast, pressure is exerted to regard all 'child participation' automatically as grounded in a right, when it is not, we are inexorably moving back to the disparate claims and counter-productive disharmony of the pre-CRC era. If being 'progressive' in that way is deemed to be more important than being rigorous, work for the human rights of children will surely be endangered.

Conclusion: The Spectre of the 1970s ...

It no doubt needs to be stressed again at this point that much has been achieved for, with and by children since the CRC came into force. This chapter deliberately focuses only on what may be seen as problem areas in the way the human rights of children have been taken forward.

The combination of the various factors reviewed in the chapter has marginalised a growing number of child-focused organisations from the human rights mainstream and, consequently, children's rights from human rights. Too much emphasis has been placed on trying to obtain 'more' from the CRC, at the expense of securing everything possible on the basis of what the CRC clearly sets out as obligations. This distracts attention and diverts considerable energy away from undertaking the significant work constantly required just to promote and protect the basic and vital rights that the CRC intended to grant.

As a symptomatic consequence, the long-standing human rights community seems to have become increasingly leery of children's organisations. There is now remarkably less cooperation between 'human' and 'children's' rights bodies than during the 1980s. In some spheres it has quite simply died out completely. Some human rights NGOs have virtually given up on children's issues, others are undertaking children's rights work on their own, unconvinced that reference to children's organisations will be of benefit from a human rights standpoint. Child-focused NGOs have generally failed to capitalise on the new and highly productive relationship created with their human rights peers during the drafting of the CRC. In other words, just as in the pre-CRC 1970s, it is sadly tempting to describe children's issues and human rights as once again, in too many instances, two rather different worlds.

This is of course exactly the opposite of what was intended when the CRC was being drawn up. If it is allowed to continue, it does not augur well for making the most effective use of the CRC as a international legal instrument to improve respect for the human rights of children.

References

Abramson, B. 1996. The invisibility of children and adolescents, in E. Verhellen (ed.), *Monitoring Children's Rights.* The Hague, Boston, MA and London: Martinus Nijhoff, pp. 393–402.

Cantwell, N. 1997. *Starting from Zero: the Promotion and Protection of Children's Rights in Post-Genocide Rwanda, July 1994–December 1996.* Florence: UNICEF International Child Development Centre.

Committee on the Rights of the Child. 2006. *Report on the Day of General Discussion on the Right of the Child to Be Heard.* 43rd Session, Geneva, 11–29 September 2006. Available at: http://www2.ohchr.org/english/bodies/ crc/docs/discussion/Final_Recommendations_after_DGD.doc [accessed 8 September 2010].

——. 2009. *General Comment No. 12. The Right of the Child to Be Heard.* 51st Session, Geneva, 25 May–12 June 2009. CRC/C/GC/12. Available at: http:// www2.ohchr.org/english/bodies/crc/docs/AdvanceVersions/CRC-C-GC-12.doc [accessed 8 September 2010].

Detrick, S. (ed.). 1992. *The United Nations Convention on the Rights of the Child: A Guide to the Travaux Préparatoires.* Dordrecht: Martinus Nijhoff.

IRIN. 2003. Too small to be fighting in anyone's war. *IRIN Humanitarian News and Analysis* [online, December 2003]. Available at: http://www. irinnews.org/IndepthMain.aspx?IndepthId=24&ReportId=66280 [accessed 8 September 2010].

Rodham, H. 1973. Children under the law. *Harvard Educational Review*, 43, 487–514.

Tomasevski, K. 2006. *Human Rights Obligations in Education.* Nijmegen: Wolf Legal.

UNICEF. 1997. *Cape Town Principles and Best Practices Adopted at the Symposium on the Recruitment of Children into the Armed Forces and on Demobilization and Social Reintegration of Child Soldiers in Africa (Cape Town, 27–30 April 1997).* Available at : http://www.unicef.org/emerg/files/ Cape_Town_Principles(1).pdf [accessed 8 September 2010].

United Nations. 1996. *Impact of Armed Conflict on Children.* Report of the expert of the Secretary-General, Ms. Graça Machel, submitted pursuant to General Assembly resolution 48/157, UN Doc. A/51/306, 1996. Available at: http://www.unhchr.ch/huridocda/huridoca.nsf/(Symbol)/A.51.306. En?Opendocument [accessed 8 September 2010].

Veerman, P. 1992. *The Rights of the Child and the Changing Image of Childhood.* Dordrecht: Martinus Nijhoff.

Vité, S. and Boéchat, H. 2008. Article 21, adoption, in A. Alen, J. van de Lannotte, E. Verhellen, F. Ang, E. Berghmans and M. Verheyde (eds), *A Commentary on the United Nations Convention on the Rights of the Child*. Leiden: Martinus Nijhoff.

Chapter 3

Understanding a Human Rights Based Approach to Matters Involving Children: Conceptual Foundations and Strategic Considerations

John Tobin[1]

Introduction

It has been suggested that 'children's rights have ... become perhaps the dominant programme within a social system which makes sense of the adult/child relationship' (King 2004: 275) and that advocacy for international children's rights is 'one of the most powerful social movements of the twentieth century' (Fernando 2001: 10). It is debateable whether the status and influence of children's rights has reached such heights. However, it is fair to say that the idea of children as rights bearers is occupying an increasing space within contemporary social and policy debates concerning the treatment of children.

One manifestation of this development is the emergence of what is often referred to as 'a rights based approach to children' or 'child rights programming'. Although there are an abundance of reports and manuals that seek to illustrate how this approach is to be applied in practice (Save the Children UK 2002, Save the Children Denmark 2005, Theis 2004, Jonsson 2003, CARE undated, United Nations Philippines 2002, UNFPA 2010), its conceptual foundations have largely escaped any detailed attention. So while some commentators believe that rights based approaches 'are here to stay' (Theis 2004: 12), others have argued that the 'continued credibility of rights based approaches demands a higher degree of conceptual rigour and clarity than has prevailed in the past' (Darrow and Tomas 2005: 537).

This chapter seeks to respond to this challenge by identifying the principles upon which a coherent and persuasive account of the conceptual foundations of a rights based approach to matters involving children can be constructed. It remains wary of the risk that a discussion as to the abstract or theoretical basis of a rights based approach is particularly unhelpful in the absence of any guidance as to the

---

1   I would like to thank Mac Darrow and Dan Seymour for their thoughtful and helpful comments on earlier drafts of this chapter. Any errors and omissions remain my own.

operational methodologies required for the implementation of such an approach. Fortunately there is already an impressive supply of manuals and guidebooks that seek to address this question. However, my concern and interest lies in the failure of these 'how to' publications to demonstrate an awareness of the social, political, institutional and disciplinary obstacles to the implementation of such an approach. As a consequence the secondary aim of this chapter is to identify several strategic considerations that must accompany and inform attempts to advocate for and operationalise a principled yet pragmatic human rights based approach to matters involving children.

The Emergence of the Rights Based Approach: Moving Beyond Development

During the later part of the twentieth century a number of events took place that paved the way for the evolution of the so-called rights based approach to development. For example, in 1986 the United Nations General Assembly adopted the Declaration on the Right to Development which provides that development is 'an inalienable human right by virtue of which every person and all peoples are entitled to participate in, contribute to and enjoy economic, social, cultural and political development in which all human rights ... can be fully realised' (Article 1). This was followed by the adoption of the Vienna Declaration and Programme of Action at the 1993 World Conference on Human Rights which recognised that development and respect for human rights were interdependent and mutually reinforcing (Vienna Declaration 1993: para. 8).

This synergy between the previously discrete discourses of development and human rights was the result of two key factors. First, there was an increasing recognition within the development sector that the existing models of development, which had a narrow focus on economic development, had been inadequate in alleviating poverty (Darrow and Tomas 2005, Theis 2004, Uvin 2007). There was also a realisation that 'good governance, participation and accountability had human rights dimensions that would not be promoted without addressing those dimensions' (Steiner, Alston and Goodman 2008: 1434). At the same time there was a growing strategic awareness among human rights advocates of the need to expand their agenda beyond the narrow window of human rights doctrine and formalism (Koskenniemi 2006). Thus for practical and political reasons, an alliance of sorts between the two discourses began to form and the concept of a rights based approach to development emerged.

This tentative relationship was deepened as a result of several developments at the institutional level in the late 1990s and early twenty-first century (Frankovits 2005, Alston 2005). In 1997, for example, Kofi Annan as Secretary-General of the United Nations issued his directive that human rights should be mainstreamed into the activities of all UN agencies (UN Secretary-General 1997) – an approach that was endorsed and expanded by Mary Robinson as UN High Commissioner

(Robinson 2002). Significantly for the purposes of this chapter, the first agency to embrace this directive was UNICEF which issued Guidelines on Rights Based Programming in 1998 (UNICEF 1998). Other UN agencies followed soon after. For example, the UNDP adopted the policy document, *Integrating Human Rights with Sustainable Development*, in 1998 and its annual report of 2000 was devoted to an examination of the nexus between human rights and development (UNDP 2000). UNESCO adopted a Strategy on Human Rights in 2003 (UNESCO 2003) and in the same year, a number of UN agencies adopted what is known as the 'Stamford Common Understanding' in an attempt to reflect an understanding as to the common elements of a rights based approach to development (UNDG 2003).

It is important to note that the development of this relationship between human rights and development was given the academic imprimatur of Amartya Sen, one of the world's leading development economists, is his text *Development as Freedom* (1999). This is not the place to examine Sen's work in detail and it is sufficient to note that he rejected the traditional economic models of development in favour of an approach that placed the individual at the centre of the development enterprise. Moreover he argued that respect for human rights and individuals' freedoms was critical to economic progress. I will return to the significance of Sen's work later but at this juncture it is important to note that his contribution reduced the level of discipline resistance, scepticism and ambivalence with respect to the adoption of a rights based approach by the development sector.

Today much of the literature on rights based approaches is concerned with the model that applies within the global development context (Alston and Robinson 2005, Alston 2005, Darrow and Tomas 2005, Olowu 2004, Oppong 2006, Schmidt-Traub 2009, Nyamu-Musembi and Cornwall 2004, Frankovits 2005, McInerney-Lankford 2009, Hickey and Mitlin 2009). This is certainly the context in which this model was originally conceived and it remains the primary context in which organisations working with children make recourse to this model. But it is by no means the only context in which the rhetoric of a rights based approach has been or can be employed. For example, academic commentators have invoked a rights based approach in a range of contexts including the protection of migrant workers (Hainsfurther 2009), the protection of religious cultural property (Mose 1996), education (Anderson 2006), food insecurity (Chilton and Rose 2009, Sarelin 2007), health (Yamin 2008, Durojaye and Ayankogbe 2005, Tobin 2006, Bright 2007), public space (Copeland 2004), indigenous affairs (Pounder 2008) and urban planning and early childhood (Smith and MacNaughton 2010). Moreover there is evidence of an increasing recourse to the idea of a rights based approach within domestic human rights institutions. For example, the Victorian Human Rights Commission in Australia promotes the use of a rights based approach for all public authorities (Victorian HR Commission 2008) which includes activities in sectors such as policing, public education, public health and public housing. And commentators have used the phrase to evaluate the decision making process of judges (Tobin 2009b) and the development of parliamentary processes to protect rights (Evans 2005).

These developments indicate a proliferation in the use of a rights based approach across a range of discrete areas well beyond the international development agenda at both the international and domestic level. Moreover, this model is being invoked to address matters that are of concern to individuals generally *and* those that are of concern to specific groups such as children. These trends give rise to two central questions. First, what is the meaning of a rights based approach and second, how, if at all, does a general human rights based approach differ from a children's rights based approach?

Part I – The Meaning of a Rights Based Approach for Children: A Slogan in Search of a Definition or a Coherent Concept?

Overview

Commentators almost universally agree that there is no single definition of a rights based approach (Sarelin 2007, Nyamu-Musembi and Cornwall 2004) and many caution against reducing it to a fixed or determinate concept (Darrow and Tomas 2005). Indeed a flexible approach to the implementation of a rights based approach is seen as being its greatest virtue enabling its application to adapt to the particular circumstances of any issue or environment (Theis 2004, Lansdown 2005a). But there are dangers if the meaning of such an approach is so vague and flexible that any individual or organisation can claim they are adopting a rights based approach and there is no means by which to assess whether the use of such an approach is authentic. In such circumstances it becomes impossible to distinguish a human rights approach from other policy approaches (Koskenniemi 2006).

As a consequence a number of commentators have sought to place boundaries around the parameters of what they believe can be legitimately described as a rights based approach. Darrow and Tomas have provided a list of what they believe are the key 'principles' and 'values' of a rights based approach (Darrow and Tomas 2005: 482); Jonsson has identified 11 'elements' (Jonsson 2003); while the 'Stamford Common Understanding' (see above) lists four 'necessary elements' and 13 'other elements of good programming practices'. However as Philip Alston explains, the problem with this approach is that the criteria identified by commentators as being fundamental to a rights based approach 'are often expressed at a level of abstraction and generality that ... is likely to seem abstract, untargeted and untested' by the communities in which this approach is to be deployed (Alston 2005: 802). Take, for example, the following 'other elements' listed in the 'Stamford Common Understanding' the meaning of which could not be said to be readily apparent – 'the development process is locally owned'; 'strategic partnerships are developed and sustained'; 'analysis involves all stakeholders'.

Thus while a flexible approach to the meaning of a rights based approach has been encouraged, this carries the risk that the term will become an empty rhetorical vessel into which the subjective preferences of whichever group or individual that chooses to use the term can be poured. It risks becoming, to borrow the words of Hillary Rhodam Clinton and Martin Guggenheim, 'a slogan in search of a definition' (Rodham 1973: 487) that has made 'very little progress in developing a cogent conceptual position' (Guggenheim 2005: 12). In an attempt to address these concerns, I intend to identify and explore the conceptual foundations of what it means to adopt a rights based approach. Instead of simply reciting or compiling a list of features commonly associated with a rights based approach, an approach I myself have adopted in the past (Tobin 2006), I intend to assess and critique the legitimacy of these features as elements of a rights based approach. My concern is that advocates for children, including myself, have been too active in their embrace of a rights based approach and insufficiently attentive to the need to develop a more reflective, internally coherent and sophisticated understanding of what this term should mean.

Take, for example, UNICEF's attempt to identify the 'key guiding principles' of a rights based approach in its guidelines on rights based programming in 1998 (UNICEF 1998). These 'key guiding principles' were classified into six different categories: 'obligations', 'special characteristics of the CRC', 'the four general principles of the CRC', 'characteristics of the CRC that are especially important', 'implementation' and 'the relationship between the CRC and CEDAW'.[2] However, this taxonomy was unaccompanied by any explanation as to why, for example, the 'special characteristics of the CRC' were distinct from the 'characteristics of the CRC that are especially important'; or why 'obligations' should be considered distinct from 'special characteristics' or 'general principles'; or the basis upon which the 'four general principles' were identified. In other words this model was not informed by any cogent conceptual analysis that could generate an internally consistent and coherent understanding of a rights based approach.

In an attempt to provide a sense of the logic and reasoning that underpins the conceptual foundations of a rights based approach I have developed the following taxonomy for the elements of this approach. This taxonomy consists of three levels:

- the core principle of a rights based approach
- the express principles of a rights based approach
- the implied principles of a rights based approach

It is acknowledged that this taxonomy is rudimentary and no doubt in need of refinement, but its underlying rationale is to offer a conceptual framework for a rights based approach that is internally consistent in the sense that it has a normative basis and a nexus can be shown to exist between one level of the taxonomy and the next. As such it seeks to avoid, or at least minimise, the potential for subjective preferences to inform the understanding of a rights based approach and offer a coherent analytical structure around which the meaning of a rights based approach

---

2 Convention on the Elimination of All Forms of Discrimination against Women.

can be constructed. It resiles from the view that 'every organisation will necessarily have its own unique framework for rights based programming' (Lansdown 2005b: 2). It accepts that the measures required for the *implementation* of a rights based approach will undoubtedly vary. But if no consideration is given to first identifying and then maintaining the integrity of the principles that underlie this approach, it will simply become a hollow and meaningless slogan that can be massaged to suit individual or organisational preferences.

Level 1: The Core Principle of a Rights Based Approach

Although much of the literature on the meaning of a rights based approach adopts differing formulations, the central and recurring theme is the requirement to integrate *rights* into the resolution of the issue that is the subject of analysis and consideration. In the international context this is often referred to as mainstreaming *human* rights, a process described by UN Secretary-General Kofi Anan as 'the process of assessing the human rights implications of any planned action including legislation, policies or programs, in all areas and at all levels. It is a strategy for making human rights an integral dimension of the design, implementation, monitoring and evaluation of policies and programs in political, economic and social spheres' (UN Secretary-General 1997, paras 78–9). This idea of integrating rights standards into every aspect of decision making is the core (fundamental, basic or central) principle of a rights based approach and provides the foundation from which all other principles of a rights based approach are derived.

It demands that the impact of issues and decisions upon individuals must be seen and examined through the lens of rights with its predilection for envisioning the entitlements of individuals and the duties of states, as opposed to alternative paradigms such as a needs based approach (Robinson 2002, Darrow and Tomas 2005, Jonsson 2003) or, as is commonly the case with children, a welfare based approach (Santos Pais 1999, Eekelaar 2006). Moreover, the adoption of a rights based approach need not be confined to issues such as programme and policy design and there is an increasing awareness of the benefit of extending a rights based approach to matters such as service delivery (Lynch 2004, UK Department of Health 2008) and judicial decision making (Tobin 2009b).

Importantly the mainstreaming of rights is a proactive process that is designed 'to be anticipatory rather than essentially remedial' (McCrudden undated: 6). It therefore differs from the traditional compliance model of human rights in which the focus is placed on an inquiry as to whether a particular standard had been protected. This approach invariably manifests itself in court room litigation or official investigations. These are important processes and necessary for the effective protection of human rights. However, a focus on the normative value of human rights is unnecessarily restrictive and fails to appreciate the instrumental role of human rights in shaping the means and process by which policies are developed to achieve the protection of human rights. This broader role and value of human rights is a critical feature of a rights based approach. It requires a vision of human rights that extends beyond recognition of their legal status to an understanding that such standards embody a particular system of ethical demands that are designed to inform, assist, constrain and direct the actions of those actors who have the capacity to impact on the rights of other actors (Sen 2004).

Within the international context it is invariably assumed (and in some cases expressly asserted) that the human rights at the core of a rights based approach are those rights contained in *international human* rights treaties. There are sound reasons for such an approach. For example, in contrast to individual theories of rights, or even constitutive models of rights that are found in domestic or regional legal instruments, international human rights treaties 'embody a core set of values about the pre-requisites for a dignified human life that *do* enjoy widespread if not universal acceptance' (Darrow and Arbour 2009: 498). Certainly in the case of the CRC, 193 states have voluntarily assumed an international legal obligation to fulfil their duties under this treaty in good faith (Vienna Convention on the Law of Treaties Article 26). But it is important to stress that there is no logical impediment to a rights based approach embracing alternative sources of human rights standards which could be drawn from regional or domestic human rights instruments (or indeed a moral or political theory of rights that has not been transformed into law) (Sen 2004, Eekelaar 2006, Griffin 2008). I make this point because whenever the phrase 'rights based approach' is invoked the question must be asked, which rights?

The fact that the rights in question may be drawn from a source other than international law does not *necessarily* make that particular approach illegitimate, just different. International human rights law does not have an exclusive right of possession over the meaning of the term 'rights' within a rights based approach (cf. Alston 2005: 800). There may be an argument to say that it represents a more appropriate source of rights relative to other models of rights. But this chapter is not the place to resolve this debate and the key point to stress here is that it remains important to clarify the source of the rights that underlie a particular rights based approach because this source will inform and determine the express and implied principles of that particular approach. This chapter is only concerned with the features of an international human rights based approach. This is partly for reasons of space but also because the international human rights standards are international and thus, at least in theory, represent standards that have been widely accepted by states (a contentious claim that will be addressed in part III). However, the methodology adopted for the identification of the features underlying a rights based approach that is founded on international standards could be just as easily applied to approaches that are based on domestic or regional human rights instruments.

In terms of children they are *prima facie* the beneficiaries of the human rights articulated under *all* the international human rights treaties by virtue of their status as human beings. Moreover the International Covenant on Civil and Political

Rights (ICCPR),[3] International Covenant on Economic Social and Cultural Rights (ICESCR)[4] and Convention on the Rights of Persons with Disabilities (CRPD),[5] each have provisions that deal explicitly with children. As such, the principles of a rights based approach for children will be drawn from all these international human rights treaties. However, the CRC represents an international treaty that was designed specifically to protect and promote the rights of children, and 'has become the international standard against which to measure legislation and policies'[6] in relation to matters which affect children. The CRC therefore represents the primary, but not exclusive, instrument from which the principles of an international human rights based approach to matters involving children are to be derived.

Level 2: The Express Principles of a Rights Based Approach

Most of the literature about the elements of a rights based approach tends to provide a list of what are considered to be the standard features of a human rights based approach. At the international level these lists typically include features such as accountability, universality, indivisibility and interdependence, international co-operation, participation and non discrimination. But such lists are rarely, if ever, accompanied by any explanation as to the normative foundation for these concepts under international human rights law. This is to not suggest that these features are not features of a rights based approach, rather that the justification of their place within this model has been given insufficient attention. So instead of simply repeating this orthodox list, a coherent account of the conceptual foundations of a rights based approach demands that more consideration be given to the basis upon which features can be said to be integral to a rights based approach. The identification of what are termed the express principles of a rights based approach represents an attempt to provide this understanding.

Although this label is somewhat awkward (alternatives could include derivative, primary, explicit, direct), the concept of express principles of a rights based approach is designed to identify those principles that are *explicitly derived* and necessarily follow from the core principle of a rights based approach. Such principles must be expressly included in the instruments that form the basis of the particular model of rights used to inform the core principle of a rights based approach. Thus in the case of an international human rights based approach, the express principles are those overarching principles that are specifically included within international treaties. For example, the right to non discrimination is a separate and express provision under the ICCPR that is of general application

---

3   See Articles 10(3), 14(4), 23(4) and 24 of the ICCPR.

4   See Article 10 of the ICESCR.

5   See Articles 3(h), 4(3), 7, 8(2)(b), 16(5), 18(2), 23, 24(2), 24(3) and 25(b) of the CRPD.

6   Sachs J, *M* v *The State* Case CCT 53/06 (26 September 2007) para. 16.

and relevance to specific rights such as privacy and the right to a fair trial. It is therefore an express principle of a rights based approach. Express principles can be further classified as general and specific express principles – general principles being those that are derived from generic human rights treaties such as the ICCPR and ICESCR and specific principles being those derived from a treaty that aims to protect the rights of a specific group such as children under the CRC.

General express principles

Accountability   The concept of accountability is said to be the *sine qua non*, or key element, of a rights based approach (Alston 2005: 813). From a philosophical or political understanding of human rights, it arises by virtue of the fact the recognition of a human right entails the imposition of a duty on the state, for which it is accountable, to protect and secure that right. From a legal perspective this relationship of rights bearer and duty holder is reflected in the operative provisions of international human rights treaties that impose a legal obligation on states to realise the rights under the relevant treaty. Thus, for example, in the case of the CRC, Article 4 provides that:

> States Parties shall undertake all appropriate legislative, administrative, and other measures for the implementation of the rights recognized in the present Convention. With regard to economic, social and cultural rights, States Parties shall undertake such measures to the maximum extent of their available resources and, where needed, within the framework of international co-operation.

The text of this provision also reveals the scope and nature of a state's accountability for the protection of children's rights under the Convention. More specifically the obligation with respect to economic social and cultural rights is progressive and subject to available resources. And by implication the obligation of states with respect to civil and political rights is immediate – a position that is consistent with the provisions of the ICCPR.

Article 4 of the CRC also indicates that the notion of accountability with respect to children's rights is not confined to the state in which a child resides. On the contrary the requirement to secure economic social and cultural rights 'within the framework of international co-operation' is consistent with the obligation under other international instruments that the realisation of human rights demands international co-operation. Although the precise nature of this obligation is contentious, it is clear that the notion of accountability under a human rights based approach has consequences for both the state in which a child is residing and the broader community of nations.

Moreover, the adoption of a rights based approach with respect to children involves the imposition of accountability upon a third entity, namely parents or the guardians of children. Article 18(1) of the CRC states that, 'Parents or, as the case may be, legal guardians, have the primary responsibility for the upbringing and development of the child' while Article 27(2) provides that 'The parent(s) or others responsible for the child have the primary responsibility to secure, within their abilities and financial capacities, the conditions of living necessary for the child's development.' Importantly these provisions are not to be interpreted as creating strict lines of demarcation with respect to the level of accountability allocated between parents and states with respect to the realisation of children's rights. Indeed the text of Articles 18 and 27 specifically require that states must provide assistance to parents in the performance of their duties. As such the notion of accountability under the CRC should be seen as a tripartite system in which parents, states and the international community co-operate for the purpose of realising children's rights.

Non discrimination and equality   It has been said that 'Non discrimination, together with equality before the law and equal protection of the law without any discrimination, constitute a basic and general principle relating to the protection of human rights' (United Nations Human Rights Committee 1989: para. 1). Importantly this statement finds support in the text of the ICCPR (Articles 2 and 26). Moreover, Article 2 of the ICESCR demands that the rights under this treaty must be enjoyed without discrimination whereas the right to equality law is considered to be an autonomous right of general application. As such these interrelated principles, the prohibition against discrimination and equality before the law, are considered to be general express principles of a rights based approach because they are of general application.

Most of the literature with respect to the meaning of a child rights based approach lists non discrimination in a category of principles that is *separate* to the general principles of a rights based approach. Conceptually this approach is difficult to justify as non discrimination is a basic principle of any rights based approach and is not specific or peculiar to a child rights based approach. At the same time it is important to note that the understanding of discrimination is slightly modified in the context of children. This is because Article 2(2) of the CRC requires that States Parties must 'ensure that the child is protected against all forms of discrimination or punishment on the basis of the status, activities, expressed opinions, or beliefs of the child's parents, legal guardians, or family members'.

Participation   Within the literature the concept of participation is always identified as a key feature of a general rights based approach. But rarely, if ever, is there any explanation as to the normative basis for this assertion. The text of the ICCPR does, however, provide such a foundation, principally Article 25 which declares that every individual has a right and opportunity to take part in the conduct of public affairs directly or through freely chosen representatives. This right of participation is complemented by the rights to freedom of expression (Article 19), freedom of association (Article 22) and freedom of peaceful assembly (Article 22).

With respect to the meaning of a rights based approach for children, the orthodox position within the literature is to list participation as a special feature of such an approach. But as with the treatment of non discrimination, conceptually, this classification is difficult to sustain. A more accurate and internally coherent account of a rights based approach is to explain that the express principle of participation remains a general principle that is modified with respect to children. The normative foundation for this modification can be found in Article 12 which provides that:

> States shall assure to the child who is capable of forming his or her own views the right to express those views freely in all matters affecting the child, the views of the child being given due weight in accordance with the age and maturity of the child.

Under both this model of participation, and indeed the general principle of participation, the views of individuals are never considered to be determinative. However, the principle of participation for children differs from adults to the extent that the value accorded to the views of a child is to be determined in light of his or her age and level of maturity.

Despite this caveat, the emphasis on the participatory rights of a child has still been described as 'the lynchpin' of the CRC (Freeman 1994: 319) and is considered to lie 'at the roots of any elaboration of children's rights' (Eekelaar 1992: 228). It therefore serves to distinguish a rights based approach to matters concerning children from traditional welfare approaches where children's voices remained, if not completely silent and marginalised, then subject to interpretation by the 'experts' (Tobin 2009b).

Specific express principles   Four principles are typically identified as being 'foundational' or specific to a **child** rights based approach: non discrimination, the best interests principle, the right to survival and development, and participation. This is the orthodox vision that UNICEF (1998), the Committee on the Rights of the Child (CRC Committee 2003, para. 12) NGOs and commentators (Save the Children Denmark 2005, Jonsson 2003) including myself (Tobin 2006) routinely cite without hesitation. But there has been no real scrutiny as to the basis upon which these principles can be said to form the foundation of a child rights based approach. It is true that each of these principles is expressly derived from a provision under the CRC and thus can be classified as an express principle. But as discussed above, two of them – non discrimination and participation – are not specific to the CRC and remain general features of any international human rights based approach. Although the CRC modifies the application of these principles with respect to children, for the purposes of the model outlined in this chapter, it is misleading to sever these principles from a general human rights based approach.

Moreover little attention has been given as to whether there are other express and overarching principles under the CRC that could be classified as specific express principles by virtue of their potential impact and relevance to the implementation of all the rights in the CRC. It is suggested here that there are at least two such principles, both of which are to be found in the text of Article 5 of the CRC which states:

> States Parties shall respect the responsibilities, rights and duties of parents or, where applicable, the members of the extended family or community as provided for by local custom, legal guardians or other persons legally responsible for the child, to provide, in a manner consistent with the evolving capacities of the child, appropriate direction and guidance in the exercise by the child of the rights recognized in the present Convention.

The first of these principles is a requirement to respect parents and guardians in the exercise of their responsibilities for the care of a child – what I have classified as the principle of due deference – the meaning of which I have explored elsewhere (Tobin 2005, Tobin 2009b).[7] The second is the principle of evolving capacities – a principle that has also been the subject of significant commentary (Lansdown 2005b).

Both of these principles inform the implementation of the rights under the CRC and thus satisfy the definition of an express principle of a rights based approach. They are also specific to the CRC and are therefore classified as specific express principles of a human rights based approach to children. No other international human rights treaty includes provisions that recognise the legitimate influence, indeed right, of third parties on the exercise of another individual's rights or the limited capacity of individuals to exercise their rights. For some commentators children's lack of capacity to exercise autonomy is seen as being grounds for denying them any entitlement to rights (Purdy 1992, 1994). International law does not adopt such an approach and reflects what is known as an interest theory as opposed to a will theory of rights (Eekelaar 1986, Archard 2006). Thus under the model outlined in this chapter, the specific express principles peculiar to a child rights based approach are: the best interests principle, the right to survival and development, the principle of due deference and the principle of evolving capacities.

---

7   The model of children's rights offered under the CRC does not represent a total severing of their interests from their parents or a complete abandonment of children to their autonomy. On the contrary there is a strong presumption that the realisation of children's rights will occur within the context of the family unit in a manner which accommodates a child's evolving capacities. This model is reflected in the text of Article 5 of the CRC. Importantly the deference given to parents is far from absolute and remains conditional on the exercise of parental responsibility being directed and undertaken in a manner that is consistent with the realisation of a child's rights including the recognition of his or her evolving capacity.

Level 3: The Implied Principles of a Rights Based Approach

The third category of principles under the model of the rights based approach advanced in this chapter, are called implied principles.[8] Again I recognise that this is an awkward expression and alternative labels could include underlying or foundational principles. But my primary concern is the meaning of this concept which is designed to capture those principles that are not expressly included in treaties, yet are considered to be principles of a rights based approach because they represent the fundamental values upon which the international human rights systems is said to be based. Evidence as to the acceptance of their underlying importance is often manifest by their inclusion in the preamble of human rights treaties and the text of resolutions and declarations concerning international human rights. Unlike express principles, which are identified by reference to the text of human rights treaties and are thus fixed and determinate, there is the potential for greater disagreement with respect to those principles that are considered to be implied. Despite this caveat, there is sufficient evidence to support the inclusion of at least three such principles within the category of implied principles – universal dignity, interdependence and indivisibility, and cultural sensitivity.

Universal dignity   The notion of universality is always cited in the literature as a discrete element of a rights based approach. But the idea of universality, that all children are entitled to human rights, is linked to the concept of non discrimination and equality, which is an express principle of a rights based approach. Given the overlap between these concepts, it is difficult to defend the assertion that universality and non discrimination remain discrete and separate features of a rights based approach. This distinction can, however, be maintained if the principle of universalism is conceived of as the principle of universal dignity. By this I mean that international human rights seek to offer a model of children's rights that contains those standards that are universally recognised as being necessary for a child to lead a life of dignity.

This idea that universal dignity is an underlying principle of an international human rights based approach finds support in Article 1 of the Universal Declaration on Human Rights that 'all human beings are born free and equal in dignity and rights' and is also affirmed in the preamble to the CRC which recognises the inherent dignity of every individual. This concept of dignity is linked to the 'Kantian moral philosophy that affirms the inherent worth of human beings' (Liebenberg 2005: 6) and requires that children are never to be seen simply as a means to an end but an end in themselves. Importantly such an approach rejects the exclusive construction of children as social capital which is often used to justify

---

8   This concept of implied principles is to be distinguished from the idea of an implied right which some commentators have used to describe rights which although not explicit within the text of human rights treaties are considered to have an implied foundation and can be derived from the formulation of other rights.

investment and action to assist children in various contexts such as early childhood intervention and the provision of education. For example, an early formulation of the Conceptual Framework for the World Bank's investment in children and young people (which has since been amended) rested on the argument that 'it is economically efficient to invest in the early years' (World Bank 2006, 2005: 11). In contrast, a rights based approach demands the provision of early childhood services and educational opportunities for children because they have a right to such entitlements irrespective of any prospective economic benefits.

The principle of universal dignity also stresses the need to secure the individual rights of every individual child and not simply children as a class. As Santos Pais explains:

> ... while it important to improve the situation of children as a group, it is essential to go beyond good averages of a high rate of progress ... [and] ... consider the specific reality of those children who have not been affected by the wave of general progress, who have remained invisible or forgotten and who are becoming increasingly vulnerable and marginalised. (Santos Pais 1999: 8–9)

The challenge therefore is to recognise the need to identify and respond to the individual needs of every child rather than become preoccupied with generalist approaches that simply set targets or indicators with respect to treatment of children as a class.

Interdependence and indivisibility The notion of the interdependence and indivisibility of all human rights is drawn from the Vienna Declaration and Programme of Action adopted at the World Conference on Human Rights in 1993. These terms are invariably used interchangeably, to assert that the realisation of a specific right cannot be divorced from the realisation of the other rights to which children are entitled. In the context of juvenile justice, for example, there is limited value in the provision of a system that complies with the requirements of Article 40 of the CRC with respect to children who are subject to criminal justice proceedings if these children are only to be denied the right to an effective education, appropriate health care and an adequate standard of living which is free from abuse and violence. In the context of the education of indigenous children or children from minority groups, the value of such education is diminished if it is unaccompanied by measures to protect the cultural and linguistic traditions of such children.

The principle that all rights are interdependent and indivisible therefore acts to dilute the artificiality of the distinction and historical antagonism between civil and political rights on the one hand and economic, social and cultural rights on the other. To say that rights are indivisible not only provides recognition of their interdependence but also dismantles any claims to there being a fixed hierarchy of rights. It thus affirms the equal status of all human rights and the need to adopt a holistic or whole-of-child response to ensure their realisation – a vision which is affirmed by the inclusion of economic, social and cultural rights alongside civil and political rights in the CRC.

Cultural sensitivity International human rights are invariably subject to the criticism that they seek to impose universal standards that reflect and prioritise Western values at the expense of non-Western values (Mutua 2001, Steiner, Alston and Goodman 2008, Merry 2006). Children's rights are certainly not immune from such accusations (Pupavac 1998, Harris-Short 2001). A discussion of the cultural relativist debate is not necessary here and it is sufficient to make the following observations. First, there is always the risk that human rights and indeed children's rights can be used to impose agendas and values that are inappropriate and ineffective in responding to the specific cultural needs of children. However, the preamble to the CRC emphasises the need to take 'due account of the importance of the traditions and cultural values of each people for the protection and harmonious development of the child'. This requirement to pay due deference to the culture of a child is an underlying theme of a rights based approach which is supported by the right of children under Article 30 of the CRC to enjoy their own culture. It is therefore considered to be an implied principle of a rights based approach.

The impact of this principle is that, although human rights are universal, a degree of flexibility must be granted to states in the implementation of measures to secure children's rights in recognition of the need to accommodate cultural differences (Donnelly 2007). A global one-size-fits-all approach is therefore not appropriate. At the same time, this does not allow for cultural or traditional practices to be invoked as a defence to violations of children's rights. Indeed the CRC demands, under Article 24(3), that 'States parties shall take all effective and appropriate measures with a view to abolishing traditional practices prejudicial to the health of children'. However, the process and measures required for the elimination of such practices are not to be imposed or defined exclusively by reference to the values and expectations of those in a position of power. On the contrary, a rights based approach with its emphasis on participation requires collaboration and consultation rather than the imposition of hegemonic strategies to address the violations of children's rights (Tobin 2009a).

Part II – Operationalising a Rights Based Approach: Strategic Considerations

The preceding discussion sought to detail the conceptual foundations of a rights based approach by identifying those principles that are considered to be fundamental to such an approach. Instead of simply restating an orthodox list of features commonly associated with a rights based approach, greater attention was given to the normative basis for those principles considered to be fundamental to such an approach. My intention was to identify the source of such principles and not simply rely on an unsubstantiated assertion that they were fundamental to a rights based approach. Recourse to the text of international human rights instruments was undertaken to perform this task and authenticate the relevance and place of the principles within an *international human* rights based approach. The intended result was to produce an internally coherent model of a rights based approach that has a sound conceptual basis.

The problem, however, is that the basis of this model – international human rights – is anything but stable. There is an increasing literature, primarily in the context of development, being generated by NGOs, UN bodies and to a lesser extent academics that tends to glean over this reality in preference for the production of manuals, guides and charts that detail the steps required for the practical implementation of a rights based approach. These 'how to' guides provide a significant contribution to the debate about how to develop appropriate operational methodologies for the implementation of a rights based approach. But they are often produced and packaged without any acknowledgement of the social, political, economic and cultural context in which a rights based approach is to be implemented. The danger with this approach is that it risks creating the impression that by offering a guide or manual, it is possible to infuse the abstract idea of a rights based approach with some practical measures that *will* facilitate its effective implementation.

The reality of course is that that the adoption of a rights based approach is not thwarted merely by the absence of a good guidebook or manual. On the contrary a more complex understanding is required of those factors that inhibit the capacity of actors to adopt a rights based approach in their work with children. It is not the place to undertake a detailed examination of compliance with human rights here (Koh 1999, Goodman and Jinks 2004, 2008, Simmons 2009: 112–58). Instead, a brief and rather idiosyncratic list of pragmatic considerations deemed relevant to the implementation of a rights based approach is offered in the hope that it will motivate a more reflective and strategic approach to this issue. I have identified at least seven considerations of which any advocate seeking to promote and engage with a rights based approach to children must be aware:

- the contested nature of human rights especially children's rights
- the contested content of human rights
- the competing nature of rights claims
- the marginalised status of a rights based approach
- the inevitability of political resistance or irrelevance
- the potential for disciplinary resistance
- the need to navigate institutional and organisational culture

The list is far from complete and many of these factors are already well known and interrelated. But my intention is clear: any attempt to engage with a rights based approach must not be limited to its conceptual foundations or the development of manuals to translate this model into practice. It must also consider the socio-political context in which the implementation of this model is sought.

The Contested Concept of Human Rights, Especially Children's Rights

The guide prepared by Save the Children on child rights programming explains that:

> The international system of human rights encompasses values that can be found in all cultures and all religious, moral and ethical traditions. They provide an international guide for common standards of conduct, which can be expected from all governments and societies. (Save the Children 2005: 12)

Recourse to such rhetoric may be reassuring to advocates of human rights and fortify their commitment to a rights based approach. But it ignores the reality that the idea of human rights and indeed the international human rights system and its purported universality is deeply contested on a number of levels: the political (Darrow and Arbour 2009: 498), theoretical (Douzinas 2000, Griffin 2008) and cultural (Mutua 2001) to name just a few. These concerns are only amplified with respect to children (Freeman 2007). The standard retort is that states have ratified treaties such as the CRC and are therefore bound by the provisions of such instruments as a matter of international law. But as John Eekelaar has warned, the legitimacy of this model within any given society may not be very secure (Eekelaar 2006).

Objections to the idea of children as rights bearers come on many fronts, one of the most persistent being the suggestion that it undermines the structure and foundations of the family unit (Hafen and Hafen 1996, Guggenheim 2005). But there is a strong theoretical and practical case to be made in support of the importance of rights for children and commentators such as Michael Freeman have made this case both in this collection of essays and elsewhere (Freeman 1987, 1992, 2007). I too have sought to address concerns about the impact of the CRC on parental rights and the structure of the family (Tobin 2005). But to date the literature on rights based approaches for children has largely failed to address this issue and indeed the broader debates as to the legitimacy of recognising children as rights bearers. This is despite the fact that the recognition and acceptance of a rights based approach for children remains conditional on there being acceptance that children have human rights especially among parents who, according to the CRC, are to play a primary role in securing such rights.

The Contested Content of Human Rights

Another oversight within the literature on rights based approaches is a failure to acknowledge or recognise the contested content of human rights standards. Although these standards are said to be the foundation of a rights based approach, very little effort has been dedicated to the task of ascribing meaning to what are often vague and ambiguous standards. For example, the orthodox position, which is outlined in the 'Stamford Common Understanding' simply states that a rights based approach requires the identification of the human rights claims of rights holders and the corresponding human rights obligations of duty bearers. (UNDG 2003, 2). But such an approach underestimates the complexity that is associated with defining the content of human rights and the corresponding obligations of states. Even the meaning of standards such as the prohibition against torture remain unsettled while economic and social rights such as the right to health are regularly derided due to their level of obfuscation (Tobin 2010). Moreover the actual meaning of those principles that are considered to be central to a rights based approach involving children often escapes attention. For example, the best interests principle and the principle of children's participation are routinely cited in guidebooks on rights based programming without any recognition that the meaning of these terms is deeply contested and accompanied by conceptual confusion as to the balance to be struck between the protection and autonomy rights under a child rights based approach.

This is not to say that the identification of the relevant rights of a child and the obligations of a state to secure such rights is not a relevant element of a rights based approach. This process is fundamental if the issues under consideration are to be seen through a human rights lens. But to date there has been insufficient acknowledgement as to the difficulties associated with achieving consensus or some form of resolution with respect to the content of human rights. The 'Stamford Common Understanding' demands that this discussion 'is informed by the recommendations of international human rights bodies' (UNDG 2003: 2) and some commentators have argued that the work of such bodies is authoritative (Blake 2008). But such an approach neglects the reality that the work of these bodies, although valuable, is hotly contested, invariably marginalised and rarely accepted by states (Alston 2005).

This is not to suggest that a common understanding as to nature and content of human rights standards is unattainable, or that the work of the human rights treaty bodies should be ignored. Indeed I have argued elsewhere that there is the potential to offer a robust and persuasive interpretation of the various human rights standards (Tobin 2010) including those standards that are particular to children such as the best interests principle (Tobin 2009b, Alston and Gilmour Walsh 1996, Lansdown 2005b). Moreover commentators are increasingly producing a more sophisticated understanding of what is required for effective participation by children that move beyond processes that are merely tokenistic or manipulative (Thomas 2007, MacNaughton Hughes and Smith 2008). My concern, however, lies with the failure to acknowledge that, for the most part, the meaning of a human right is not self evident and the work of the treaty bodies is unlikely to resolve disputes in relation to the meaning of rights.

With respect to this issue of interpretation, McCrudden has identified a tendency for human rights professionals – what he calls an 'epistemic community' – to take control of this process and forge an interpretation of a right that reflects their own preferences and biases (McCrudden undated: 9). Such an approach may be persuasive within a particular epistemic community, but it is unlikely to persuade the broader community of individuals, organisations and states whose cooperation is required to secure the effective implementation of human rights. As a consequence greater attention must be given to a process by which to generate a meaning of a human right that will persuade this broader interpretative community (Tobin 2010). McCrudden makes the point that any expansion of the interpretative function to include, for example, public administration professionals, carries a risk that values which are exogenous to the human rights professional will have a dominant position in the final interpretation of a right (McCrudden undated). This in turn, can lead to the bureaucratisation of human rights (Koskenniemi 1999, 2006) in which these standards are 'stripped of their radical promise' to transform lives (McCrudden undated: 9) – their meaning being informed, influenced and potentially constrained by the interests of state officials. This risk, however, would appear to be unavoidable because the alternative is to insist upon maintaining an interpretation of a right that is unable to persuade any of the actors required for its implementation as to its legitimacy.

The Potential for and Need to Resolve Competing Rights Claims

As detailed above, a rights based approach requires the identification of the human rights claims of rights holders. But the demand for such an inquiry within the literature on rights based approaches, is seldom accompanied by any recognition that the claim of one rights holder may be in conflict with the claims of another rights holder – a potential conflict that is repeatedly raised in the context of children's rights concerning matters such as corporal punishment and religious education (Tobin 2009b) let alone the competing claims that arise in relation to the allocation of scarce resources (Munro 2009). As a consequence the literature rarely provides any guidance on the process by which these competing claims to rights should be resolved.

In responding to this gap, the first point to stress is that, as a general rule, human rights and as a consequence children's rights are not without limits. Indeed the text of international human rights treaties includes the potential for limitations to be imposed on rights provided the scope of any interference is necessary in the interests of a democratic society and the measures adopted to achieved the legitimate purpose are reasonable and proportionate (Siracusa Principles 1985). Under this model, the state carries the onus to demonstrate, by reference to objective evidence and on the balance of probabilities, that any interference with the rights of a child was necessary and proportionate to protect the rights of another individual or indeed the broader community (Siracusa Principles 1985: para. 10). As a consequence a rights based approach actually offers a relatively sophisticated model for the balancing of competing interests within a society by demanding an approach that is informed by cogent and persuasive evidence as opposed to mere assertions and the subjective preferences of a decision maker (Tobin and McNair 2009, Tobin 2009b). To date however, discussions about the implementation of a rights based approach have largely failed to recognise the potential for competing rights claims and given insufficient attention as to the process by which human rights law seeks to reconcile these claims.

This deficiency is particularly acute in the context of the allocation of scarce resources at the macro level – a point well illustrated by the recent work of Lauchlan Munro in which he examined the impact of this dilemma within the work of UNICEF (Munro 2009). He argued that the insistence of 'emphasizing the sacred equality of all rights is not merely unhelpful [in the selection of priorities and allocation of scarce resources] it leads to organisational paralysis via a morass of relativism' (Munro 2009: 201). In other words, the notion of indivisibility, if taken to preclude the creation of a hierarchy of rights, means that no action can ever be taken because no decisions can ever be made as to where the priority for action should lie. But if prioritisation is a necessary and inevitable task in any decision-making process that involves the allocation of scarce resources, a question must be asked as to whether the principle of indivisibility and indeed a rights based approach has a pragmatic role to play?

Space does not allow for a detailed consideration of this question but there at least three factors that should feature in such a discussion. First, as Peter Rosenblum has explained, it is important to understand the strategic purpose that underlies the idea of indivisibility as this will inform its meaning and practical significance (Rosenblum 2002). When this perspective is taken, it becomes clear that the commitment to the indivisibility of human rights was 'an effort to raise one set of subordinated rights [economic, social and cultural rights] to the level of the other more hallowed ones [civil and political rights]' (Rosenblum 2002: 305). It was never intended to prohibit the prioritisation of individual human rights within particular jurisdictions and contexts. Second, and in the context of the need to decide how to allocate scarce resources, human rights become a *framework* by which to inform this process. In other words, if a decision must be made between funding something that is connected to the realisation of a human right, such as adequate assistance to homeless children, and something that is unconnected to a human right such as the installation of decorative lights on a bridge (an initiative recently undertaken in Victoria), then a rights based approach would demand that priority be given to housing homeless children. This of course does not resolve the question of how to allocate scarce resources *between competing rights* such as health care and education for children. A rights based approach cannot provide an explicit answer to this question but it can guide the process of determination to the extent that the principle of participation must be employed to inform how scarce resources are to be allocated (Sen 1981). It does not simply seek to identify the values and principles that must inform the decision making process, it seeks to transform this process by the creation of rights respecting governance structures and systems for civic engagement (more on this later).

The Marginalised Status of a Rights Based Approach

A report prepared by the United Nations Development Group claims that 'important progress has been made in many agencies and areas of work across the UN system from integration of human rights into policies and guidelines to strengthening the capacity of UN country teams' (UNDG Interagency Workshop 2008: para. 7, Frankovits 2005: 19–33). Numerous NGOs have embraced the idea of a rights based approach in policy and programming with respect to children and some governments have expressly acknowledged their shift to this model in the context of development assistance (New Zealand Agency for International Development 2002, United Kingdom DFID 2000). The reality, however, is that the idea of a rights based approach and indeed a child rights based approach remains marginalised in the design and delivery of policies and programmes at both the international and domestic level.

For example, in 2009 a number of leading international organisations working on matters relevant to children such as UNICEF, Save the Children, and the World Bank, adopted a joint statement on Advancing Child Sensitive Social Protection (UK DFID et al. 2008). The principles listed to guide this agenda make no mention of any specific rights to which children are entitled let alone the need to adopt a rights based approach. Some leading international agencies (beyond UNICEF) have at least engaged with the idea and relevance of human rights to their work with children. For example, the UNHCR has identified the need to adopt a rights based approach in its work with children who are to be treated as 'active subjects with rights' (UNHCR 2007 para. (b)(x)(viii), cf. Verdiname and Harrell-Bond 2005). But there is limited evidence that a rights based approach has become mainstreamed in the sense anticipated by Kofi Anan (Alston and Robinson 2005). Thus, for example, the United Nations has struggled to make this transition (Darrow and Arbour 2009); the World Bank still resists such a cultural shift (Sarfaty 2009); and the WHO is still to adopt its much anticipated Health and Human Rights Strategy.

Moreover at the domestic level there is limited evidence to suggest that governments are even aware of a rights based approach let alone embracing such an approach in the design of policies (Frankovits 2005). For example, in Australia, there are a number of major policy initiatives being undertaken by the Federal Government in areas such as public housing, education, child protection and health care that impact directly on children. None of these initiatives adopt a rights based approach or even identify the relevance of human rights to the development of these policies (Australian Government 2010, Commonwealth of Australia 2008, Australian Ministerial Council 2008). Nor is there any compelling evidence to suggest that other actors that impact on the realisation of children's rights, such as the courts, are embracing a rights based approach (Tobin 2009a, Fortin 2006, cf. Sloth-Nielsen and Mezmur 2008).

This failure to adopt a rights based approach cannot be explained simply on the basis that there is insufficient guidance about the meaning of a rights based approach and the practical measures required for its implementation. A more complex explanation is required part of which involves an understanding that a rights based approach is what Koskenniemi has described as a 'project of power' (Koskenniemi 2006). Ultimately the fundamental aim of a rights based approach is to transform the way in which states (and indeed all the other actors that impact on the enjoyment of children's rights) perform their role by demanding that every issue is examined and responded to through a human rights lens. It is therefore deeply concerned with and complicit in attempts to redistribute power within any society. As the Task Force for the Millennium Project on Child Health and Maternal Health has observed:

> Power comes in many guises. Among them is the power to set the terms of the debate, to structure the patterns of thought and language, the fundamental taken for granted assumptions that shape our approaches to problems and solutions. (Freedman et al. 2005: 19)

This is precisely what a rights based approach seeks to achieve. It seeks to challenge, dismantle and reconfigure existing power relations and structures both within states and between states (Hughes, Wheeler and Eyben 2005) by orientating the terms of policy debates towards the language of rights. The principle of participation also seeks to transform the process by which these debates are undertaken. As such a rights based approach is not a benign product that can simply be taken from the shelf of policy options and implemented without resistance. Careful consideration and reflection is therefore required to assess the socio-political context in which advocates seek to implement a rights based approach. Space does not permit a comprehensive examination of this context and I have confined my discussion to three key considerations that must be taken into account when seeking to implement a rights based approach:

- the inevitability of political resistance or irrelevance
- the potential for disciplinary resistance
- the impact of institutional or organisational culture

The Inevitability of Political Resistance or Irrelevance

To date proponents of a rights based approach do not appear to have given sufficient consideration to what Lanse Minkler has described as the 'policymaker's decision problem' (Minkler 2009: 369). Understanding the nature of this problem is complex and will vary within states according to the individual preferences of political decision makers and the broader history, culture, institutions and level of development of the state in which they make their decisions (Minkler 2009). Minkler, who is an economist, seeks to reduce this complexity to a formula such that 'the policymaker's problem is to choose x and z to maximize $U(Q(x),z)$, subject to the budget constraint $px+\mu z <T+A$'

(Minkler 2009: 372) where x = policies, z = personal perks, U = utility and p = price. In lay persons terms this means that a policy maker's decision will be influenced by a complex and multifaceted set of factors in which personal preferences and budgetary constraints will be significant factors.

Significantly Minkler's empirical studies indicate that a *domestic* human rights regime, such as a bill of rights, can actually be used to inform and constrain the policy maker's decision problem (Minkler 2008). But the relevance of *international* law to the policy maker's problem is more questionable. An appeal can be made to the binding nature of international law as a basis to advance the merit of a rights based approach. The reality, however, is that international human rights law does not always exert a significant impact on decision making at the local level. Part of the reason is that, unlike domestic systems for the protection of rights, international human rights treaties are unenforceable and voluntary compliance with them rarely delivers domestic political perks.

This should not be taken to mean that a rights based approach based on international human rights standards is destined to be an irrelevant consideration in the resolution of the policy maker's decision problem. It simply means that more consideration must be given to the strategies used to shape and influence the policy maker's decision problem. In this respect elements of the work of Derek Jinks and Ryan Goodman may prove helpful (Goodman and Jinks 2004, 2008). They have identified three processes by which human rights can be implemented – coercion, persuasion and acculturation. Coercion, which is based on material rewards and punishment for compliance and non-compliance, is of limited use with respect to the international human rights system given the absence of a compulsory adjudicatory system; persuasion refers to the process in which a decision maker's preferences are changed as a result of being convinced as to the truth, validity or appropriateness of a norm, belief or practice; acculturation is a process whereby actors adopt the beliefs and behavioural patterns of the surrounding culture without actively assessing the merits of those beliefs and behaviours (Goodman and Jinks 2004).

Acculturation may represent an alluring process for some human rights advocates because of its links with the development of a perceived culture of rights protection. Indeed in many respects the rush to actively embrace a rights based approach by organisations within the development sector or child rights sector could be characterised as a form of acculturation. Certainly this would be the case in those instances where the decision to adopt such an approach was not informed by a careful and detailed examination as to the merits of this approach. For some this may be inconsequential because organisations are still forced to engage with the discourse of human rights. Indeed Goodman and Jinks take the view that despite the risk of a shallow and formal commitment to human rights initially, the process of acculturation can lead to deeper cultural reforms over time (Goodman and Jinks 2008). But for others the empirical basis of their model is yet to be substantiated (Mushkat 2008) and there remains the risk of an ostensible commitment to a rights based approach being in name only – an outcome described as a 'decoupling of general values from practical action' (Meyer et al. 1997: 155).

In contrast the process of persuasion involves the internalisation of the values that promote behaviours that are informed by the principles of a rights based approach. It thus offers a more enduring means by which to develop a rights based culture that is based on robust conceptual foundations. The challenge, however, is to develop techniques and strategies that will persuade decision makers to adopt this approach. Space does not permit a detailed discussion of what these strategies might look like and techniques that rely on coercion and acculturation are likely to remain relevant. In this chapter, however, I intend to focus on the process of persuasion which requires what is known as 'framing', that is, the structuring of a message to resonate with already accepted norms and 'cuing' – the prompting of actors to 'engage in a high intensity process of cognition, reflection and argument' (Johnston 2001: 496).

In the past advocates of human and children's rights have understandably tended to frame their claims by reference to the universality and legally binding nature of human rights treaties or their claims to being a universal set of moral or ethical standards. But these appeals often fail to resonate with and address the policy maker's decision problem which is more likely to be informed by the discourses of risk management (Murphy and Whitty 2009) and economic utility (Minkler 2009).

This presents a real challenge for the advocate of a rights based approach because to frame rights in the language of risk or economic utility raises the prospect that a rights based approach will be reduced to an instrumentalist vision. For example, under such a vision the allocation of scarce resources to eliminate child labour or invest in early childhood is justified not because children have a right to be free from exploitative labour or a right to survival and development but because this investment will yield economic dividends (Hageman et al. 2006).

Rights become seen 'as a means to an end, using a functionalist, economics driven rationale to determine whether, and how, human rights have value in any given case' (Murphy and Whitty 2009: 242). Such an approach threatens the intrinsic or normative value of human rights for children – there is the risk that the notion of rights as an end in themselves becomes not only marginalised but potentially invisible. At the same time to insist on an intrinsic vision of human rights and ignore the reality that this is unlikely to resonate with the policy maker's decision problem is unlikely to be persuasive. As a consequence, as Murphy and Whitty explain, the challenge becomes to develop 'a mixture of human rights agendas, including – and this is the key point – human rights advocates adopting *instrumentalist* strategies and language [in addition to intrinsic or normative strategies] … in order to promote human rights protection' (Murphy and Whitty 2009: 242). Moreover, there must be a realisation that the onus for proving the case for a rights based approach rests on advocates of such an approach (Alston 2005: 808) because recourse to the universal and legally binding status of international human rights treaties have proven to be an insufficient strategy to persuade policy makers to change their behaviours.

The Potential for Disciplinary Resistance

In his much cited critique of the human rights movement, 'The International Human Rights Movement: Part of the Problem?', David Kennedy alleged that 'human rights occupies the field of emancipatory possibility' (Kennedy 2002: 108). By this he meant that the human rights movement has a tendency to devalue and displace other alternative strategies for emancipation. Putting to one side the merits of this claim, the fact remains that a rights based approach, with its foundations in law, offers a model to address issues concerning children that are already the subject of attention within a vast range of disciplines in areas such as development, public health, education, social work, economics, criminology, behavioural psychology, urban planning, advertising, marketing, media, architecture and early childhood. Within each of these disciplines, complex and sophisticated models based on empirical evidence have invariably been developed about how best to secure (and in some cases such as advertising, exploit) the needs and interests of children that are relevant to the discipline in question. Moreover, with the exception of development, an examination of the leading academic journals for these disciplines indicates that the idea of a rights based approach has had at best minimal impact and in many cases none at all on these disciplines. So far from occupying the field of emancipatory possibility, as Kennedy would suggest, a rights based approach has struggled to find even a place on the field. Despite this reality, the literature on rights based approaches provides little indication that other disciplines are likely to be unaware of, resistant to or suspicious of the value of adopting a rights based approach in their work.

The challenge therefore is to demonstrate the utility of this approach and the value it can add to the resolution of the problems confronting another discipline (Darrow and Tomas 2005). It is at this point that my promised return to the work of Amartya Sen becomes relevant. As one of the leading scholars in the field of development economics, Sen's embrace of rights became a critical factor in opening up the potential to develop what I have termed the disciplinary legitimacy of a rights based approach. By this I mean the acceptance of a rights based approach as a legitimate model to inform the development of research and the delivery of services within a particular discipline. Few commentators would suggest that this process has led to the colonisation of the development agenda by the rights agenda (another alleged concern of Kennedy). Indeed commentators are more likely to lament the failure to properly integrate a rights based approach into the development agenda (Alston 2005, Schmidt-Traub 2009, McInerney Lankford 2009).

Of relevance to this chapter, however, is the complementary nature of relationship between rights and development. It is this emphasis on the potential complementarity or mutual reinforcement of human rights and other disciplines that must be the focus of those who seek to advance a rights based approach to matters concerning children (Seymour and Pincus 2008, Alston and Robinson 2005, Gauri 2005). Such an approach cannot be achieved simply by an appeal to the moral force or legal significance of rights – an all too common approach used by human rights advocates (Hannum 2006). Instead a respectful conversation must take place in which the limits and potential opportunities of a rights based approach to a particular discipline are identified and discussed. The aim is to ensure that engagement with a rights based approach within a discipline is ultimately a collaborative enterprise. This is why Sen's work was so significant because it paved the way for the legitimacy of a rights based approach to emerge within the development sector. The challenge now is for advocates of the rights based approach to create the relationships with colleagues from other disciplines –education, health, urban planning, child protection – that will facilitate opportunities to expand opportunities to achieve the disciplinary legitimacy of a rights based approach in a much broader range of fields.

The Need to Navigate Institutional or Organisational Culture

Related to the potential for discipline resistance is the potential barrier of institutional or organisational culture (McCrudden undated) where culture is defined as the dominant values and practices of an organisation as reflected in its operational procedures, incentive systems and management structures (Sarfaty 2009). The significance of organisational culture to the implementation of a rights based approach is highlighted by two recent studies. The first by Galit Sarfaty on the status of human rights within the institutional culture of the World Bank and the second by Hurst Hannum on the perception of members of the Office of the High Commissioner for Human Rights by members of the UN Department of Political Affairs (Hannum 2006).

A significant volume of literature has been dedicated to the task of providing a legal basis to integrate human rights into the work of the World Bank (Darrow 2003, Ghazi 2005, Skogly 2001). In contrast Sarfaty's research focused on the organisational culture of the World Bank in order to gain an understanding as to why the Bank has failed to adopt or internalise human rights despite external and internal pressure to do so over the last 20 years. Although his research revealed a complex set of factors provided this explanation, the most significant was a clash of expertise:

> The theoretically orientated people (who emphasized the indivisibility of human rights) clashed with the more pragmatically minded, who were mainly concerned with operational issues and the need to make trade offs between different rights in projects with limited budgets. (Sarfaty 2009: 662)

The result of this 'turf war', as one Bank member described it (Sarfaty 2009: 662), was that those advocating a rights based agenda were unable to bring about internalisation of their model because they failed to frame their case in a way that could be adapted or incorporated into the existing cultural values and practices of the Bank.

The lesson in this experience for advocates of a rights based approach for children is to recognise that the culture of an organisation of an institution may be embedded in values other than human rights. However, organisational culture is not a fixed or static concept and remains amenable to change (Merry 2006). Of course the process of facilitating cultural change within any organisation is complex and requires various strategies in areas such as leadership and the development of appropriate incentive structures (Darrow and Arbour 2009, Frankovits 2005). And the adoption of a rights based approach by an organisation can be, as Peter Uvin explains,

> a radical affair ... demanding profound changes in choices of partners, the range of activities undertaken and the rationale for them, internal management systems and funding procedures, and the types of relationships established with partners in the public and non government sectors. (Uvin 2004: 166 cited in Alston and Robinson 2005)

The key point to be made here is that, as demonstrated by Sarfaty's research, internalisation of a rights based approach within the culture of an organisation will depend heavily on the extent to which this approach is framed in a way that resonates with the underlying mission of that organisation. This in turn requires a capacity to adapt human rights norms to local meanings and existing cultural values and practices (Sarfaty 2009).

This capacity to undertake adaptive persuasive strategies has not always been a hallmark of human rights advocacy. Indeed as Hurst Hannum explains, 'The traditional or stereotypical view of human rights advocates is that they are confrontational and norm-based (if not moralistic) and that they tend to practice their craft through "naming and shaming" rather than through persuasion or consensus-building' (Hannum 2006: 16). Moreover his study as to the perceptions of staff within the Office of the High Commissioner for Human Rights held by staff within the UN Department of Political Affairs confirmed this stereotype. He found that:

> Most of those interviewed believed that OHCHR had different values than DPA, that they 'speak a different language' than those engaged in traditional diplomacy. Many also believe that the human rights perspective 'lacks sophistication,' that OHCHR is overly technical or legalistic, or that Geneva-based OHCHR staff live in an 'ivory tower' insufficiently related to the realpolitik concerns of headquarters in New York. (Hannum 2006: 16)

Of course these findings should not automatically be extrapolated to apply to all human rights advocates. But they do indicate the real danger if rights based organisations or advocates assume a particular culture with respect to the strategies adopted for the promotion of human rights. As such a level of introspection is required to ensure that the organisational culture of a body advocating for children's rights is not itself an obstacle to the implementation of these rights in other institutions and organisations whose work impacts on children.

Conclusion: The Need for a Principled yet Pragmatic Approach

Recourse to the rhetoric of a rights based approach to matters concerning children has become increasingly fashionable in a range of contexts – indeed an 'ideological fortress' according to Nigel Cantwell, a long time advocate of children's rights (2004: 1). This trend has led to the development of diverse and differing understandings of what this term means and requires in practice. However, there has been a lack of attention to the conceptual foundations of this approach. This is potentially dangerous because an individual or organisation can invoke or co-opt the term to serve whatever subjective interests or objectives are being pursued. In this respect, a fluid and unfettered understanding of a rights based approach risks becoming a slogan in search of a definition or worse still a slogan for which no definition is sought because this would only serve to constrain the way in which this slogan could be deployed.

Aware of these dangers I set out to identify a coherent and consistent conceptual foundation for this approach. My aim was to provide a definition of a rights based approach that was bounded (to the extent that any concept can be) rather than indeterminate – to offer a conceptual model that could in the words of Amartya Sen, 'command reasoned loyalty' and 'establish a secure intellectual standing' (Sen 2004: 317). At the centre of this model was the idea of the core principle of a rights based approach, namely that rights provide the lens by which all issues which impact on children should be reviewed and resolved. But whenever the term rights is raised, the inevitable question to be asked is which rights – moral rights, collective rights, regional rights, domestic rights, international rights? The focus in this chapter was on the rights to which children are entitled under international law. This led to the identification of two further principles that provide the conceptual foundation for an *international human* rights based approach – express principles and implied principles – both of which are derived from the source of the rights that inform the core principle, namely international human rights instruments.

Of course the development of a sound conceptual framework is only one component in the implementation of a rights based approach. Appropriate operational methodologies must also be developed in order to translate the theory into practice. Numerous manuals and 'how to' guides have been produced on rights based programming for children for this purpose leading to the creation of an entire lexicon in which phrases such as 'situation analysis', 'causality analysis', 'capacity building', 'the triple A approach' and 'impact monitoring' have emerged. Although necessary, these publications are not sufficient to ensure the effective implementation of a rights based approach. Ultimately this task requires shifts and modifications, often of significant proportion, to the way in which the multitude of actors who impact on children undertake their work (Alston 2005).

Commentators such as Martii Koskenniemi have complained that when mainstreamed human rights lose their specificity and demand nothing more from a decision maker than that he or she adopt a 'reasonable and intelligent adjustment of conflicting considerations – something they were surely expected to do anyway' (Koskenniemi 2006: 7). But such an understanding profoundly underestimates the potential impact of human rights generally and even more so the notion of children's rights. The very idea that children have rights is a transformative concept that reconceptualises the power relationship between children, adults and the state. Instead of being seen as chattels of their parents or objects in need of benevolent guidance and protection, children become active subjects with individual entitlements which they are entitled to claim.

Under a rights based approach the place of children and their voice within the political economy can no longer be ignored, devalued or marginalised on the assumption that decision makers whether they be parents, teachers, doctors, judges, institutions or government officials will automatically know what is in their best interests. As the Committee on the Rights of the Child has recognised, the right of a child to speak, to participate to have views taken into account, *represents a new social contract* and requires long term changes in political, social, institutional and cultural structures (CRC Committee 2009: para. 4, emphasis added). A rights based approach is not simply about including children in existing decision-making processes but *modifying* those systems to accommodate children's perspectives and the different ways they express themselves (Thomas 2007). Thus far from being empty and 'profoundly ambivalent in its political significance', as Koskenniemi would suggest (Koskenniemi 2006: 1), the mainstreaming of children's rights is a deeply political project with potentially transformative consequences for the way in which children are viewed *and* engaged with by all actors within society.

It is this potential that inspires and motivates advocates for children to actively embrace the rights based approach as a means of making the invisible visible, giving the silenced a voice, redirecting scarce resources to meet children's health, educational, housing, nutritional and development needs and holding the state, and indeed the international community, accountable when they fail to meet the standards set in these and other areas that are covered by the rights under the CRC. But with the enthusiasm to embrace this approach there has been a failure to acknowledge that its greatest strength – its political economy and capacity to offer a new way of engaging with, thinking about and dealing with children – is potentially its greatest limitation for it demands that individuals, cultures, organisations, institutions and states must change the way they have been dealing with children often for hundreds if not thousands of years.

With this challenge in mind, I have called for a more critical and reflective approach to any attempts to persuade others as to the merits of adopting a rights based approach. The central theme underlying the various strategic factors I identified was the need to anticipate and understand the reasons why resistance to the adoption of a rights based approach might occur from within various sections of any society. I also stressed the need to frame advocacy of a rights based approach in ways that will resonate with the interests of these actors – the potential value add of human rights. This requires a more modest conception of human rights in which this discourse may be forced to adopt a complementary role alongside other disciplines or strategies that seek to offer insights into how best to address children's needs and interests.

It requires a retreat from the moralising and legalism that has characterised human rights advocacy in preference for a more sensitive, reflective and collaborative dialogue with the diverse range of actors whose actions (or inactions) affect the capacity of children to realise their rights. It requires recognition as to the limits of human rights discourse and it demands that advocates of a rights based approach for children must bear the burden of demonstrating the merit and relevance of this approach. It also requires an awareness of the risk and need to take measures to ensure that this collaborative model does not descend into the co-option or appropriation of a rights based approach by existing power structures. As Sally Merry has warned, if human rights 'are translated so fully that they blend into existing power relationships completely, they lose their potential for social change' (Merry 2006: 135–6).

The task of securing the implementation of a rights based approach for children is, therefore, a complex and ambitious one. Moreover if progress is to be achieved it will be incremental rather than seismic. But while an active embrace of a rights based approach for children should be tempered by a dose of realism, there remains scope for cautious optimism because within the space of just over 20 years, the idea of children as rights bearers and the development of rights based programming for children has already travelled a significant distance. What will become of a rights based approach in the future we do not yet know (Kennedy 2002), but it seems reasonable to assume that a robust conceptual foundation when accompanied by some critical assessment and pragmatic calculations as to the means by which to implement such an approach is likely to serve it well.

References

Alston, P. 2005. Ships passing in the night: the current state of the human rights and development debate seen through the lens of the Millennium Development Goals. *Human Rights Quarterly*, 27(3), 755–829.

Alston, P. and Gilmour-Walsh, B. 1996. *The Best Interests of the Child: Towards a Synthesis of Children's Rights and Cultural Values*. Florence: UNICEF ICDC.

Alston, P. and Robinson, M. 2005. *Human Rights and Development: Towards Mutual Reinforcement*. Oxford: Oxford University Press.

Anderson, K. 2006. How can a rights-based approach to development programming help to achieve quality education? Evaluating the Education Guarantee Scheme in Madhya Pradesh. *Asia-Pacific Journal on Human Rights and the Law*, 7(2), 75–109.

Archard, D. 2006. *Children's Rights* [online: Stanford Encyclopaedia of Philosophy]. Available at: http://plato.stanford.edu/entries/rightd-children/ [accessed 26 July 2010].

Australian Government. 2010. *A Stronger, Fairer Australia*. Available at: http://www.socialinclusion.gov.au/Resources/Documents/ReportAStrongerFairerAustralia.pdf [accessed 26 July 2010].

Australian Ministerial Council on Education, Employment, Training and Youth Affairs. December 2008. *Melbourne Declaration on Educational Goals for Young Australians*.

Blake, C. 2008. *Normative Instruments in International Law: Locating the General Comment*. Center for Human Rights and Global Justice Working Paper Number 17, 2008. Available at: http://www.chrgj.org/publications/docs/wp/blake.pdf [accessed 26 July 2010].

Bright, L. 2007. Human rights in action: Les Bright says a human rights based approach can improve health outcomes. *Nursing Older People*, 19(6), 11.

Cantwell, N. 2004. *Is the Rights Based Approach the Right Approach?* Paper to the Defence for Children International, International Symposium 25th Anniversary, Geneva, 22 November 2004 (copy on file with author).

CARE Human Rights Initiative. Undated. *Basic Introduction to Human Rights and Rights Based Programming*.

Chilton, M. and Rose, D. 2009. A rights-based approach to food insecurity in the United States. *American Journal of Public Health*, 99(7), 1203–11.

Committee on the Rights of the Child. 2003. *General Comment No 5: General Measures of Implementation for the Convention on the Rights of the Child*. CRC/GC/2003/5.

——. 2009. *General Comment No 12: The Right of the Child to Be Heard*. CRC/C/GC/12 (20 July 2009).

Commonwealth of Australia. 2008. *The Road Home: A National Approach to Reducing Homelessness*. Canberra: Department of Families, Housing, Community Services and Indigenous Affairs.

Copeland, A. 2004. Public space: a rights-based approach. *Youth Studies Australia*, 23(3), 40–45.

Darrow, M. 2003. *Between Light and Shadow: The World Bank, The International Monetary Fund and International Human Rights Law*. Oxford: Hart.

Darrow, M. and Arbour, L. 2009. The pillar of glass: human rights in the development operations of the United Nations. *American Journal of International Law*, 103(3), 446–501.

Darrow, M. and Tomas, A. 2005. Power, capture, and conflict: a call for human rights accountability in development cooperation. *Human Rights Quarterly*, 27(2), 471–538.

Donnelly, J. 2007. The relative universality of human rights. *Human Rights Quarterly*, 29(2), 281–306.

Douzinas, C. 2000. *The End of Human Rights*. Oxford: Hart.

Durojaye, E. and Ayankogbe, O. 2005. A rights-based approach to access to HIV treatment in Nigeria. *African Human Rights Law Journal*, 5(2), 287–307.

Eekelaar, J. 1986. The emergence of children's rights. *Oxford Journal of Legal Studies*, 6(2), 161–82.

——. 1992. The importance of thinking that children have rights, in P. Alston, S. Parker and J. Seymour (eds), *Children, Rights and the Law*. Oxford: Oxford University Press, pp. 221–35.

——. 2006. *Family Law and Personal Life*. Oxford: Oxford University Press.

Evans, S. 2005. Improving human rights analysis in the policy and legislative process. *Melbourne University Law Review*, 29(3), 665–703.

Fernando, J.L. 2001. Children's rights: beyond the impasse. *The Annals of the American Academy of Political and Social Science*, 575, 8–24.

Fortin, J. 2006. Accommodating children's rights in a post Human Rights Act era. *Modern Law Review*, 69(3), 299–326.

Frankovits, A. 2005. *Mainstreaming Human Rights: The Human Rights Based Approach and the United Nations System – Desk Study Prepared for UNESCO March– April 2005*. Human Rights Council of Australia.

Freedman, L.P., Waldman, R.J., de Pinho, H. and Wirth, M.E. 2005. *Who's Got the Power? Transforming Health Systems for Women and Children*. Millennium Project Task Force on Child Health and Maternal Health.

Freeman, M. 1987. Taking children's rights seriously. *Children and Society*, 1(4), 299–319.

——. 1992. Taking children's rights more seriously. *International Journal of Law, Policy and the Family*, 6(1), 52–71.

——. 1994. Whither children: protection, participation, autonomy? *Manitoba Law Journal*, 22(3), 307–27.

——. 2007. Why it remains important to take children's rights seriously. *International Journal of Children's Rights*, 15(1), 5–23.

Gauri, V. 2005. Social rights and economics: claims to health care and education in developing countries, in P. Alston and M. Robinson (eds), *Human Rights and Development: Towards Mutual Reinforcement*. Oxford: Oxford University Press, pp. 65–86.

Ghazi, B. 2005. *The IMF, the World Bank Group and the Question of Human Rights*. Ardsley, NY: Transnational Publishers.

Goodman, R. and Jinks, D. 2004. How to influence states: socialization and international human rights law. *Duke Law Journal*, 54(3), 621–704.

——. 2008. Incomplete internalization and compliance with human rights law. *European Journal of International Law*, 19(4), 725–48.

Griffin, J. 2008. *On Human Rights*. New York: Oxford University Press.

Guggenheim, M. 2005. *What's Wrong with Children's Rights*. Cambridge, MA: Harvard University Press.

Hafen, B. and Hafen, B. 1996. Abandoning children to their autonomy: the United Nations Convention on the Rights of the Child. *Harvard International Law Journal*, 37(2), 449–91.

Hageman, F., Diallo, Y., Etienne, A. and Mehran, F. 2006. *Global Child Labour Trends 2000–2004*. Geneva: International Labour Organisation.

Hainsfurther, J.S. 2009. A rights based approach: using CEDAW to protect the human rights of migrant workers. *American University International Law Review*, 24(5), 843–95.

Hannum, H. 2006. Human rights in conflict resolution: the role of the Office of the High Commissioner for Human Rights in peacemaking and peacebuilding. *Human Rights Quarterly*, 28(1), 1–85.

Harris-Short, S. 2001. Listening to 'the other'? The Convention on the Rights of the Child. *Melbourne Journal of International Law*, 2(2), 304–51.

Hickey, S. and Mitlin, D. 2009. *Rights-Based Approaches to Development: Exploring the Potential and Pitfalls*. Sterling, VA: Kumarian Press.

Hughes, A., Wheeler, J. and Eyben, R. 2005. Rights and power: the challenge for international development agencies. *IDS Bulletin*, 36(1), 63–72.

Johnston, A.I. 2001. Treating international institutions as social environments. *International Studies Quarterly*, 45(4), 487–516.

Jonsson, U. 2003. *Human Rights Approach to Development Programming*. Nairobi: UNICEF.

Kennedy, D. 2002. The international human rights movement: part of the problem? *Harvard Human Rights Journal*, 15(1), 101–26.

King, M. 2004. The child, childhood and children's rights within sociology. *King's College Law Journal*, 15(2), 273–99.

Koh, H.H. 1999. How is international human rights law enforced? *Indiana Law Journal*, 74(4), 1397–417.

Koskenniemi, M. 1999. The effect of rights on political culture, in P. Alston, M. Bustelo and J. Heenan (eds), *The EU and Human Rights*. New York: Oxford University Press, pp. 99–116.

——. 2006. Human Rights Mainstreaming as a Project of Power. Unpublished paper 5 February 2006 (copy on file with author).

Lansdown, G. 2005a. *The Evolving Capacities of the Child*. Florence: UNICEF Innocenti Research Centre/Save the Children.

——. 2005b. *What's the Difference? Implications of a Child Focus in Rights Based Programming*. Discussion Paper prepared for Save the Children, UK, March 2005.

Liebenberg, S. 2005. The value of human dignity in interpreting socio-economic rights. *South African Journal of Human Rights*, 21(1), 1–31.

Lynch, P. 2004. Human rights lawyering for people experiencing homelessness. *Australian Journal of Human Rights*, 10(1), 4.

M v The State Centre of Child Law (CCT 53/06) [2007] ZACC 18.

MacNaughton, G., Hughes, P. and Smith, K. 2008. *Young Children as Active Citizens: Principles, Policies and Pedagogies*. Newcastle: Cambridge Scholars Publishing.

McCrudden, C. Undated. Mainstreaming human rights. *University of Michigan School of Law, Public Law and Legal Theory Research Paper Series*, Research Paper No. 47.

McInerney-Lankford, S. 2009. Human rights and development: a comment on challenges and opportunities from a legal perspective. *Journal of Human Rights Practice*, 1(1), 51–82.

Merry, S.E. 2006. *Human Rights and Gender Violence: Translating International Law into Local Justice*. Chicago, IL: University of Chicago Press.

Meyer, J.W., Boli, J., Thomas, G.M. and Ramirez, F.O. 1997. World society and the nation-state. *American Journal of Sociology*, 103(1), 144–81.

Minkler, L. 2008. *Integrity and Agreement: Economics When Principles also Matter* (Ann Arbor, MI: University of Michigan Press).

——. 2009. Economic rights and political decision making. *Human Rights Quarterly*, 31(2), 368–93.

Mose, G.M. 1996. The destruction of churches and mosques in Bosnia-Herzegovina: seeking a rights-based approach to the protection of religious cultural property. *Buffalo Journal of International Law*, 3(1), 180–208.

Munro, L.T. 2009. The 'human rights-based approach to programming': a contradiction in terms?, in S. Hickey and D. Mitlin (eds), *Rights Based Approaches to Development: Exploring the Potential and Pitfalls*. Sterling, VA: Kumarian Press, pp. 187–205.

Murphy, T. and Whitty, N. 2009. Is human rights prepared? Risk, rights and public health emergencies. *Medical Law Review*, 17(2), 219–44.

Mushkat, R. 2008. Incomplete internalisation and compliance with human rights law: a reply to Ryan Goodman and Derek Jinks. *European Journal of International Law*, 20(2), 437–42.

Mutua, M. 2001. Savages, victims, and saviours: the metaphor of human rights. *Harvard International Law Journal*, 42(1), 201–45.

New Zealand Agency for International Development. 2002. *Human Rights Policy Statement*. Wellington: New Zealand Agency for International Development.

Nyamu-Musembi, C. and Cornwall, A. 2004. *What is the Rights Based Approach All About? Perspectives from International Development Agencies*. Institute of Development Studies, Working Paper 234.

Olowu, D. 2004. Human development challenges in Africa: a rights-based approach. *San Diego International Law Journal*, 5(1), 179–224.

Oppong, R.F. 2006. Trade and human rights: a perspective for agents of trade policy using a rights-based approach to development. *African Human Rights Law Journal*, 6(1), 123–45.

Pounder, L. 2008. Never mind human rights, let's save the children: the Australian Government's emergency intervention in the Northern Territory. *Australian Indigenous Law Review*, 12(2), 2–21.

Pupavac, V. 1998. The infantilisation of the South and the UN Convention on the rights of the child. *Human Rights Law Review*, 3(2) 1–6.

Purdy, L.M. 1992. *In Their Best Interest? The Case Against Equal Rights for Children*. New York: Cornell University Press.

——. 1994. Why children shouldn't have equal rights. *International Journal of Children's Rights*, 2(3), 223–41.

Robinson, M. 2002. *Address to World Summit on Sustainable Development*. Johannesburg, 30 August 2002 (copy on file with author).

Rodham, H. 1973. Children under the law. *Harvard Educational Review*, 43(4), 487–514.

Rosenblum, P. 2002. Teaching human rights: ambivalent activism, multiple discourses and lingering dilemmas. *Harvard Human Rights Journal*, 15(1), 301–16.

Santos-Pais, M. 1999. A human rights conceptual framework for UNICEF. *Innocenti Essays No. 9*, UNICEF-ICDC.

Sarelin, A.L. 2007. Human rights based approach to development cooperation, HIV/AIDS and food security. *Human Rights Quarterly*, 29(2), 460–88.

Sarfaty, G. 2009. Why culture matters in international institutions: the marginality of human rights at the World Bank. *American Journal of International Law*, 103(4), 647–83.

Save the Children. 2002. *Child Rights Programming: How to Apply Rights-Based Approaches in Programming*. Stockholm: Save the Children.

——. 2005. *Child Rights Programming: How to Apply Rights-Based Approaches in Programming*, 2nd edition [online: Child's Rights Information Network]. Available at: www.crin.org/docs/PDN%20Ingles%20Final.pdf [accessed 28 July 2010].

Save the Children Denmark. 2005. *A Toolkit on Child Rights Programming* [online: Child's Rights Information Network]. Available at: www.crin.org/docs/resources/publications/hrbap/SC_Denmark_CRP_toolkit.pdf. [accessed 28 July 2010].

Schmidt-Traub, G. 2009. The millennium development goals and human rights-based approaches: moving towards a shared approach. *International Journal of Human Rights*, 13(1), 72–85.

Sen, A. 1981. *Poverty and Famines: An Essay on Entitlement and Deprivation*. Oxford: Oxford University Press.

——. 1999. *Development as Freedom*. New York: Oxford University Press.

——. 2004. Elements of a theory of human rights. *Philosophy and Public Affairs*, 32(4), 315–56.

Seymour, D. and Pincus J. 2008. Human rights and economics: the conceptual basis for their complementarity. *Development Policy Review*, 26(4), 387–405.

Simmons, B.A. 2009. *Mobilizing for Human Rights: International Law in Domestic Politics*. Cambridge: Cambridge University Press.

Siracusa. 1985. The Siracusa principles of the limitation and derogation provisions in the International Covenant on Civil and Political Rights. *Human Rights Quarterly*, 7(1), 3–14.

Skogly, S. 2001. *The Human Rights Obligations of the World Bank and the International Monetary Fund*. London: Cavendish.

Sloth-Nielsen, J. and Mezmur, B.D. 2008. 2 + 2 = 5? Exploring the domestication of the CRC in South African jurisprudence (2002–2006). *International Journal of Children's Rights*, 16(1), 1–28.

Smith, K. and MacNaughton, G. 2010. *City of Melbourne: A Liveable City for Children is a Liveable City for All* (Centre for Equity and Innovation in Early Childhood, University of Melbourne 2010) (internal use only – copy on file with author).

Steiner, H.J., Alston, P. and Goodman, R. 2008. *International Human Rights in Context: Law Politics and Morals*, 3rd edition. New York: Oxford University Press.

Theis, J. and Radda barnen (Society). 2004. *Promoting Rights Based Approaches: Experiences and Ideas from Asia and the Pacific*. Stockholm: Save the Children Sweden.

Thomas, N. 2007. Towards a theory of children's participation. *International Journal of Children's Rights*, 15(2), 199–218.

Tobin, J. 2005. Parents and children's rights under the Convention on the Rights of the Child: finding reconciliation in a misunderstood relationship. *Australian Journal of Professional and Applied Ethics*, 7(2), 31–46.

——. 2006. Beyond the supermarket shelf: using a rights based approach to address children's health needs. *International Journal of Children's Rights*, 14(3), 275–306.

——. 2009a. The international obligation to abolish traditional practices harmful to children's health: what does it mean and require of states? *Human Rights Law Review*, 9(3), 373–96.

——. 2009b. Judging the judges: are they adopting the rights approach with respect to matters concerning children? *Melbourne University Law Review*, 33(2), 579–625.

——. 2010. Seeking to persuade: a constructive approach to treaty interpretation. *Harvard Human Rights Review* 23(1).

Tobin, J. and McNair, R. 2009. Public international law and the regulation of private spaces: does the Convention on the Rights of the Child impose an obligation on states to allow gay and lesbian couples to adopt? *International Journal of Law, Policy and the Family*, 23(1), 110–31.

UK DFID, Help Age International, Hope and Homes for Children, Institute of Development Studies, International Labour Organisation, Overseas Development Institute, Save the Children UK, UNDP, UNICEF and the World Bank. 2008. *Advancing Child-Sensitive Social Protection* [online: Department for International Development]. Available at: http://webarchive.

nationalarchives.gov.uk/+/http://www.dfid.gov.uk/Documents/publications/
CSSP-joint-statement.pdf [accessed 28 July 2010].

United Kingdom Department of Health. 2008. *Human Rights in Healthcare
Evaluation: Final Evaluation Report* [online: UK Department of Health].
Available at: www.dh.gov.uk/prod_consum_dh/groups/dh_digitalassets/@
dh/@en/documents/digitalasset/dh_088980.pdf. [accessed 28 July 2010].

United Kingdom DFID. 2000. *Human Rights for Poor People: Target Strategy
Paper*. London: DFID.

United Nations Declaration on the Right to Development (adopted by the
UN General Assembly at its 97th Plenary Meeting, 4 December 1986 A/
RES/41/128) [online: UN]. Available at: http://www.un.org/documents/ga/
res/41/a41r128.htm [accessed 28 July 2010].

United Nations Development Group (UNDG). 2003. *UN Interagency Statement of
Common Understanding on Human Rights-Based Approaches to Development
Cooperation and Programming* [online: UNDG]. Available at: www.undg.org/
archive_docs/6959-The_Human_Rights_Based_Approach_to_Development_
Cooperation_Towards_a_Common_Understanding_among_UN.pdf [accessed
28 July 2010].

——. 2008. *Third Interagency Workshop on Implementing a Human Rights-Based
Approach, Background Paper, Human Rights Mainstreaming with the United
Nations* [online: UNDG]. Available at: http://www.undg.org/docs/9405/IAW3_
background_paper_(HR_mainstreaming).doc [accessed 28 July 2010].

United Nations Development Programme (UNDP). 1998. *Integrating Human
Rights with Sustainable Human Development: An UNDP Policy Document*
[online: Children's Rights Information Network]. Available at: www.crin.
org/docs/resources/publications/hrbap/UNDP_integrating_hr.pdf [accessed 28
July 2010].

——. 2000. *Human Development Report: Human Rights and Human
Development*. New York: Oxford University Press.

United Nations Educational, Scientific and Cultural Organization (UNESCO).
2003. *Strategy of Human Rights*, adopted by the 32nd UNESCO General
Conference 2003 (Document 32 C/57) [online: UNESCO]. Available at:
http://unesdoc.unesco.org/images/0014/001457/145734e.pdf [accessed 28
July 2010].

United Nations High Commissioner for Refugees (UNHCR). 2007. *Conclusion
on Children at Risk* [online: UNHCR]. Available at: http://www.unhcr.org/
refworld/docid/471897232.html [accessed 28 July 2010].

United Nations Human Rights Committee. 1989. *General Comment 18. Non-
Discrimination (Thirty-seventh session, 1989), Compilation of General
Comments and General Recommendations Adopted by Human Rights Treaty
Bodies*, U.N. Doc. HRI/GEN/1/Rev.6 at 146 (2003).

United Nations International Children's Emergency Fund (UNICEF). 1998. *A
Human Rights Approach to UNICEF Programming for Children and Women:
What It Is, and Some Changes It Will Bring* (CF/EXD/1998-04) [online: FAO].

Available at: http://www.fao.org/righttofood/kc/downloads/vl/docs/212951. pdf [accessed 28 July 2010].

United Nations Philippines. 2002. *Rights Based Approach to Development Planning: Training Manual*. Philippines: United Nations Philippines.

United Nations Population Fund (UNFPA). 2010. *A Human Rights Based Approach to Programming: Practical Information and Training Materials* [online: United Nations Population Fund]. Available at: www.unfpa.org/webdav/site/global/ shared/documents/publications/2010/hrba/table_of_contents.pdf [accessed 28 July 2010].

United Nations Secretary-General. 1997. *Renewing the United Nations: A Programme for Reform* (A/51/950) [online: UN]. Available at: http:// daccess-dds-ny.un.org/doc/UNDOC/GEN/N97/189/79/IMG/N9718979. pdf?OpenElement [accessed 28 July 2010].

Uvin, P. 2004. *Human Rights and Development*. Bloomfield, NJ: Kumarian Press.

——. 2007. From the right to development to the rights-based approach: how 'human rights' entered development. *Development in Practice*, 17(4), 597–606.

Verdiname, G. and Harrell-Bond, B.E. 2005. *Rights in Exile: Janus Faced Humanitarianism*. New York: Berghahn Books.

Victorian Equal Opportunity and Human Rights Commission. 2008. *The 2008 Report on the Operation of the Charter of Rights and Responsibilities: Emerging Change* [online: VEOHRC]. Available at: http://www. equalopportunitycommission.vic.gov.au/publications/annual%20reports/ 2008charterreport.asp [accessed 28 July 2010].

Vienna Declaration and Programme of Action, adopted at the World Conference on Human Rights, Vienna, 12 July 1993 A/CONF.157/23 [online: UNHCHR]. Available at: http://www.unhchr.ch/huridocda/huridoca.nsf/(symbol)/ a.conf.157.23.en [accessed 28 July 2010].

World Bank. 2005. *Children and Youth: A Framework for Action* [online: World Bank]. Available at: http://www-wds.worldbank.org/external/default/ WDSContentServer/WDSP/IB/2005/07/11/000160016_20050711153817/ Rendered/PDF/32934a0Y0framework0HDNCYno101public1.pdf [accessed 28 July 2010].

——. 2006. *Conceptual Framework for the Investment in Children and Youth* [online: World Bank]. Available at: http://web.worldbank.org/WEBSITE/EXTERNAL/ TOPICS/EXCTY/O,printY:-isCURL.. [accessed 7 February 2006].

Yamin, A. 2008. Will we take suffering seriously? Reflections on what applying a human rights framework to health means and why we should care. *Health and Human Rights*, 10(1), 45–63.

Chapter 4

The CRC:
Dynamics and Directions of
Monitoring its Implementation

Jaap E. Doek

Introduction

More than 20 years ago, on 20 November 1989, the UN General Assembly adopted the CRC in Resolution 44/25. With unprecedented speed it became the most – and almost universally – ratified international human rights instrument. It also became a driving force behind many and different legislative, social and other measures in the 193 States Parties aiming at the implementation of the rights of the child as enshrined in the CRC. In this implementation process civil society, in particular NGOs, UN agencies, notably UNICEF, and many other groups and individuals played an important role.

A Committee on the Rights of the Child has been established (Article 43 CRC) for the purpose of examining the progress made by States Parties. This examination is done on the basis of reports that States Parties have to submit to the Committee (Article 44 CRC) and on the basis of other information such as reports from NGOs, UNICEF and other UN agencies.

This monitoring of the implementation of the CRC can be considered the core activity of the CRC Committee. Other activities, with a view to fostering effective implementation of the CRC and international cooperation, include making recommendations for UN studies or issuing general recommendations (Article 45 CRC). Another activity, not mentioned in Article 45 but certainly aimed at fostering the effective implementation of the CRC, is the annual Day of General Discussion (which usually takes place on the first Friday of the September session).

The purpose of this chapter is briefly to describe and analyse the dynamics of this monitoring and fostering role of the CRC Committee, the directions this role may take in the coming years and the challenges the Committee may face.

In this regard it should be noted that the literature on the monitoring and fostering role of the CRC Committee is very limited. Apart from a rather comprehensive work on monitoring children's rights (Verhellen 1996) and one single analytical publication on activities of the CRC Committee (Gras 2001) there are some articles which analyse the Committee's interpretation of some of the articles of the CRC (e.g. Vandenhole 2005, Langlaude 2008). But except for some detailed information on the reporting by States Parties and NGOs to the CRC Committee, published more than 10 years ago (Santos Pais 1997, Karp 2000, Lansdown 2000), there is very little on the more substantive aspects of the Committee's monitoring and fostering role, their dynamics and future directions.

While this chapter focuses on the monitoring of the implementation of the CRC, it should be noted that the CRC Committee also monitors the implementation of two Optional Protocols to the CRC: on the Involvement of Children in Armed Conflict (OPAC) and on the Sale of Children, Child Prostitution and Child Pornography (OPSC). A separate discussion of the monitoring of the Optional Protocols may be interesting, but in this context such discussion is not necessary for two reasons. First, the dynamics of these monitoring processes are quite similar to those of monitoring the CRC. Second, after the examination of a separate initial report of States Parties on the implementation of the Optional Protocols, the CRC Committee monitors progress made in this regard as part of its monitoring of the CRC.[1]

Finally, and to avoid misunderstandings, it should be noted that the CRC Committee is not the only body in charge of monitoring the implementation of the rights of the child. First and foremost, this monitoring is to be given full attention at the national level, via systematic evaluation and research and via national independent monitoring bodies such as children's ombudspersons in each and every State Party to the CRC.

In addition there are other instruments that monitor explicitly or implicitly the implementation of the human rights of children such as the Special Representatives of the Secretary General on Children and Armed Conflict and on Violence against Children or the special mandate holders of the Human Rights Council such as the rapporteurs on the Sale of Children, Child Prostitution and Child Pornography and on Torture and specific country rapporteurs. Although there is some interaction and exchange of information between all these monitoring instruments (see below), it is rather haphazard.

Dynamics of Monitoring and Fostering the Implementation of the CRC

It may be somewhat artificial to make a distinction between monitoring and fostering the implementation of the CRC because it is arguable that monitoring itself implies (or even is a means of) fostering. However, the distinction can be found in the CRC itself: while Articles 43 and 44 focus on the monitoring role of the CRC Committee and the related reporting obligations of the States Parties, Article 45 deals with various other activities of the Committee aimed at fostering the effective implementation of the CRC. The advantage of using this distinction is (among others) that it allows clustering of the activities of the CRC Committee

---

1   Second and further periodic reports on the implementation of the Optional Protocols should be included in the regular reports on the implementation of the CRC (Article 12, para. 2 OPSC and Article 8, para. 2 OPAC).

and the (possible) encouragement of international cooperation (Article 45). The distinction is adopted in this chapter, resulting in first, a discussion of the different aspects of monitoring, second, observations on the fostering role of the Committee (Days of General Discussion, General Comments) and finally, some remarks about international cooperation. Throughout, the focus in on the dynamics and (potential) directions.

Monitoring the Implementation of the CRC

In the monitoring process three different activities can be differentiated: the reporting, the examination and the follow up.

The reporting[2]   The experience so far has shown that in most States Parties reporting to the CRC Committee is a dynamic process. First, the production of a report requires, given the comprehensive nature of the CRC, the involvement of a wide range of governmental ministries and departments, such as the ministries of health, education, justice, labour and social affairs, finance and defence. They all have to answer the question: what have we done and/or should have been doing to implement the provisions of the CRC? States Parties often establish an interdepartmental working group to coordinate the input from the different ministries. This process can result in an increasing awareness of the various aspects of the implementation of the CRC via exchange of information and discussions on achievements and remaining shortcomings.

Second, and as recommended by the CRC Committee, the government is expected to involve civil society, in particular NGOs and children, in the preparation of the report. This involvement, although not well developed in many States Parties, is important because it can contribute to the awareness that the implementation of the CRC is a common responsibility of the state and the civil society. It can promote a sense of partnership, with mutual respect for the differences in responsibilities. This means, among other things, that NGOs should respect that the content of the report is the state's responsibility; it is not a joint state–NGO report. It also means that the state should respect and accept that NGOs may have a different and critical assessment of the state's performance in implementing the CRC. The state should accept and respect the fact that NGOs submit their own report to the CRC Committee. But it is important, in the light of the sense of partnership, that the state and NGOs share each other's reports. Openness and transparency are important elements in a culture of partnership in implementing the CRC. It is therefore unacceptable that a state takes measures to hinder the work of an NGO as a form of punishment for its critical attitude. There are reasons to believe that sometimes this unfortunately happens. As a consequence the CRC

---

2   For details on what is expected from States Parties in meeting their reporting obligations I refer to Article 44 CRC and the reporting guidelines of the CRC Committee: CRC/C/58/Rev.1 29/11/1995.

Committee has recommended some States Parties end or refrain from taking such negative measures. The reporting process should be a catalyst for strengthening state–NGO partnership.

Third, increased awareness often results in the speeding up of legislative or other measures by States Parties. It is remarkable how often States Parties report – sometimes in response to a list of issues[3] – that they have recently enacted new legislative provisions or developed a new plan of action for, for example, the prevention of violence against children, and the trafficking and/ or sexual exploitation of children. This is an interesting and welcome dynamic element of the reporting process.

Finally, the CRC Committee encourages NGOs not only to submit supplementary reports, but also to produce, as far as possible, one national NGO report. This often results, with the important guidance and support of the NGO group on the Convention on the Rights of the Child, in the creation of a national platform or alliance of NGOs. Thus, the reporting process leads to cooperation between national NGOs in producing a national NGO report. This cooperation includes discussions about not only the progress made, but also the major shortcomings in the government's efforts to implement the CRC and the possible, necessary measures needed to address them. In addition these national alliances, coalitions or platforms are not limited to the production of a joint report. Experience shows that they continue their cooperation in the follow-up to the recommendations of the CRC Committee.

It should be noted that the input of children in the reporting process is *de facto* very limited. Moreover, very few states undertake efforts to involve children in the production of their reports. The performance of NGOs and UN agencies is better in this regard. However, many NGO and UN reports lack information on the way children have been involved in the preparation of the report. Nonetheless, there are some rare examples of separate reports produced and submitted to the CRC Committee by children and young people. Sometimes children do participate in the pre-sessional meetings of the CRC Committee. But the overall picture of child participation is rather bleak. This is considered further below in relation to the examination of State Party reports.

Concluding observations   The reporting process is not only a dynamic tool in generating awareness, inter-departmental discussions, consultations and NGO cooperation, but is also set up to allow the CRC Committee to examine progress made and to present to the State Party concerned targeted and concrete recommendations for further actions in the so-called Concluding Observations.

---

3   The list of issues is a set of questions for additional information. This list is sent to the State Party after the so-called pre-sessional meeting. In this meeting the CRC Committee has a dialogue with representatives of NGOs and UN agencies about the reports they submitted to the Committee.

The key actors in the production of this document are the secretariat and the country rapporteur.[4] The secretariat prepares in consultation with the rapporteur a first draft known as the country brief. This is a draft reflecting the information received in the State Party's report, NGOs' reports and other available information, for example reports of the Special Representatives of the UN Secretary-General and the thematic and country rapporteurs of the UN Human Rights Council. The CRC Committee, however, does not have the power (or the resources) to conduct separate country investigations, which means that the content of the Concluding Observations is dependent on the information received. Well-documented and concrete information contributes to useful, that is, targeted and concrete, recommendations for further action.

The final version of the Concluding Observations is drafted after dialogue with the State Party's delegation during a session of the CRC Committee. Members of the Committee submit their amendments to the first draft to the country rapporteur. The final draft is discussed in a private meeting of the Committee and formally adopted.[5] It should be noted that the Committee develops its opinions on the interpretation of the CRC provisions during this discussion. But there is very little time for in-depth discussions because of the pressure to adopt at least 10, and during a two-chamber session about 16, sets of Concluding Observations. The high level of consensus among members of the Committee makes it possible to achieve this goal. More in-depth discussions take place during the discussions about the General Comments (see below). A study of the first and the final draft will show that often the pre-sessional discussion with NGO and UN agencies and the dialogue have considerable impact on the content of the final Concluding Observations.

The dynamics of this process of reporting and examination is that the input (reporting) results in an output (examination/concluding observations) that in turn provides an input for the development of an agenda for the implementation of the CRC in the following five years. This brings us to the third element of the monitoring process: the follow-up.

Follow-up   One of the major concerns in the human rights monitoring system is the follow-up to the Concluding Observations of the treaty bodies like the CRC Committee. This follow-up is left to the governments, the NGOs, UN agencies and others. Some governments do take this follow-up seriously, for example a delegation that meets with the CRC Committee (or a national Children's Rights Committee), discusses the recommendations made in the Concluding Observations, and makes suggestions or proposals for their implementation. Furthermore NGO

---

4   The country rapporteur is a member of the Committee with responsibility to ensure as much as possible and with the support of the secretariat that the Concluding Observations do reflect the information received and are translated into concrete recommendations.

5   When the Committee operates in two chambers (as is the case in 2010) each chamber prepares the final draft that is then discussed in and approved by the full committee.

coalitions or platforms may undertake follow-up actions, for example raising public awareness regarding the recommendations of the CRC Committee, lobbying for their implementation and/or using them in (the planning of) their own activities. Unfortunately these activities are too often limited to a rather short period after the publication of the Concluding Observations and are not sustained throughout the full period up to the next report and examination.

With the support of the OHCHR, UNICEF, Plan International and Save the Children, the CRC Committee has undertaken regional follow-up meetings. The purpose of these meetings was to raise awareness regarding the need to follow-up the Concluding Observations. Presentations and discussions took place around topics common to the countries in the region. These meetings were held in Syria, Thailand, Costa Rica, Qatar and Burkina Faso in the period 2002–2007.[6]

In addition some individual members have conducted their own follow-up by visiting countries within the year after Concluding Observations were issued. This has only been possible thanks to support from, *inter alia*, UNICEF and Save the Children (the Committee does not have a budget for these activities) and is only for members who can and who are willing to devote the required time to these efforts (over and above the three months they are required to be in Geneva every year). Experience shows that these activities are an important contribution to the process of following-up the Committee's Concluding Observations.

Although the Committee and its individual members undertake efforts to maintain the dynamics of the reporting and examination well into the follow-up process, much more is needed in this regard.

Fostering the Implementation of the CRC

In addition to the monitoring, examination and follow-up processes the Committee fosters the implementation of the CRC through two activities: Days of General Discussion and General Comments.

Days of general discussion   Since 1992 the CRC Committee has organised an annual Day of General Discussion (DGD). The purpose of this event is to discuss a specified theme or topic of importance for the implementation of the CRC. It also creates an opportunity for the CRC Committee to engage in a dialogue with representatives of States Parties, NGOs, UN agencies and children. Examples of engagement with children include the active involvement of children in the 1999 Day of General Discussion commemorating the 10th anniversary of the CRC and the one in 2005 on Child Participation.

In choosing the theme for a Day of General Discussion the Committee often follows proposals made by NGOs, e.g. Early Childhood (2003) and Indigenous Children (2004). The Days of General Discussion are well prepared and

---

6   In the period 1992–1995 four informal regional meetings took place; see for more information Gras (2001: 78–80).

information about registration and submission of background papers can be found on the website of the CRC Committee.[7]

Discussions during the Day of General Discussion result in Recommendations approved by the CRC Committee. These Recommendations are meant to guide States Parties, NGOs, UN agencies and others with the implementation of the CRC. But they are also used as an input and basis for the production of General Comments. This was the case with, for example, the General Comments on Early Childhood, on Indigenous Children and on Article 12.

In addition, Days of General Discussion were the starting point for two important UN Studies recommended by the CRC Committee: the UN Study on Children and Armed Conflict and the UN study on Violence against Children. These Studies resulted in the appointment of Special Representatives by the UN Secretary-General for both topics and continue to contribute to international awareness and national actions for the protection of children in armed conflicts and child victims of violence. Moreover, the Day of General Discussion on children and armed conflicts contributed to elaboration of an Optional Protocol for which the CRC Committee submitted a preliminary draft. It took the Working Group of the UN Commission on Human Rights six years (1994–2000) to agree by consensus on the final text. The Optional Protocol was adopted by the General Assembly of the UN in May 2000 and by February 2010 had been ratified by 130 states. Hence, the Days of General Discussion have proven to be dynamic sources for activities well beyond the event as such with significant international impact.

General comments   The issuing of General Comments (or General Observations) has become a traditional part of the activities of human rights treaty bodies. As it goes beyond the scope of this chapter to elaborate on various aspects of these documents (see e.g. Steiner and Alston 2000: 731), it will suffice here to make the follow remarks:

- The authority of the CRC Committee to issue General Comments is based on Article 45d of the CRC;
- General Comments are distinct juridical instruments enabling the Committee to announce its interpretation of different provisions of the CRC;
- General Comments are relied upon by the Committee in evaluating the compliance of States Parties with their obligations under the CRC;
- General Comments are important guides for States Parties in their efforts to implement the CRC and the Committee therefore refers systematically to the General Comments, where applicable, in its Concluding Observations.

---

7   http://www2.ohchr.org/english/bodies/crc/ [accessed 6 January 2011]. The Committee decided not to have a DGD in 2010 due to an overwhelming workload addressed via two chamber meetings throughout 2010 in order to reduce the backlog.

The CRC Committee issued its first General Comment in 2001 on the Aims of Education (CRC/GC/2001/1, 17 April 2001) focusing on the interpretation of Article 29 of the CRC.[8] In the next six years the Committee adopted another nine General Comments including on HIV/AIDS and the rights of the child (CRC/GC/2003/3, 17 March 2003), adolescent health and development (CTC/GC/2003/4, 1 July 2003), implementing child rights in early childhood (CRC/GC/2005/7/Rev. 1, 20 September 2006), the rights of children with disabilities (CRC/C/GC/9, 27 February 2007) and children's rights in juvenile justice (CRC/C/GC/10, 25 April 2007). In 2009, General Comments on the rights of indigenous children and on Article 12 were adopted (nos 11 and 12).

As can be noted, the CRC Committee has a distinct preference for thematic General Comments. Only two (nos 1 and 12) focus on the interpretation of a single article. This policy reflects the Committee's holistic approach to the interpretation of the CRC and of its desire to pay special attention to vulnerable groups of children (for instance children affected by HIV/AIDS, children with disabilities, indigenous children, unaccompanied and separated children outside of their country of origin) and to highlight the importance of implementing the CRC for adolescents and young children.

Some of the General Comments have been prepared by members of the Committee, but more often the Committee benefits from the preparatory work of experts made available thanks to the support of UN agencies (UNICEF, WHO, OHCHR and UN AIDS) or NGOs. Drafts of General Comments have been made available to the NGO and UN partners for comments.

Altogether these comprise an impressive body of interpretation of the CRC and of guidance and recommendations for all States Parties. However, very little is known about the use of these General Comments by States Parties in their efforts to implement the CRC. There is no systematic follow-up and/or method to ensure that the General Comments are taken into account.

The only specific action taken to promote the implementation of a General Comment was a pilot project in Jamaica, regarding the General Comment on implementing child rights in early childhood, thanks to the support of the Bernard van Leer Foundation. A manual/handbook for the implementation of the General Comment on Article 12 with a view to make it a dynamic instrument in implementing the CRC will be published by UNICEF in 2011.

---

8   There are different reasons why the Committee did not issue General Comments in the first eight years of its activities (see Gras 2001: 72).

Directions in Monitoring and Fostering the CRC

General Remarks/Observations

This section focuses on possible directions in further developing an effective monitoring and fostering role for the CRC Committee. However, some attention first has to be given to the wider context of efforts made by the various treaty bodies over the past 10 years to reform the practice of monitoring human rights implementation.[9]

This practice suffers some chronic problems such as non-reporting and very late reporting, partly due to the growing number of international human rights treaties increasing the reporting burden on the states that take these treaties seriously enough to ratify them,[10] the overlap between these treaties resulting in information being repeated in different reports and in the recommendations of treaty bodies overlapping or being repetitive. Furthermore there are differences in each treaty body's reporting guidelines and in their practice of examining States Parties reports.[11]

The OHCHR presented two radical solutions to these (and other) problems: first, allow States Parties to submit regularly (e.g. every four years) one consolidated report on the implementation of all the human rights treaties they have ratified; second, dissolve all existing monitoring committees and in their place establish one standing committee to monitor all human rights treaties. These proposals were discussed in meetings with States Parties, treaty bodies, NGOs and other stakeholders and rejected out of hand. While the legal and practical implications of these proposals are huge, the key concern was that the specificity of the protection

---

9   Efforts to reform the treaty bodies system started seriously with reports by Philip Alston in 1989 (UN Doc. A/44/668), revised in 1993 (UN Doc. A/CONF.157/PC/62/Add.11?Rev.1) and in 1997 (UN Doc. E.CN.4/1997/74). This was followed by the Report of the UN Secretary-General: Strengthening the United Nations: An Agenda for Further Change (UN Doc. A/57/387). The proposal for a Standing Committee can be found in the Concept Paper on the High Commissioner's proposal for a unified standing treaty body (UN Doc. HRI/MC/2006/2) and comments of the author in a note to the CRC Committee (July 2006): Some Comments and an Alternative. For a critical and detailed analysis of the problems see also Bayefsky (2001).

10   In December 2006 two new human rights treaties were adopted by the UN General Assembly; one on The Rights of Persons with Disabilities and one on the Protection of All Persons from Forced Disappearances. The first treaty entered into force on 3 May 2008 (81 States Parties) together with the Optional Protocol on individual complaints (51 States Parties); a monitoring committee has been established. The second has not yet entered into force. There are now a total of nine international human rights treaties that require States Parties to submit regular reports, and nine different monitoring committees, eight of which are operational.

11   The practice of involving NGOs in the reporting and examination process also differs per treaty body.

of human rights provided by the different treaties – e.g. for women, children, migrants and their families, and persons with disabilities – would be lost in a system with only one report and/or one monitoring committee.

Consequently, these chronic problems still exist and the discussion on possible improvements continues. For example, at a meeting in Dublin in November 2009, members of various treaty bodies and other experts made efforts to suggest further steps for improving the monitoring system. The result was the Dublin Statement on the Process of Strengthening of the United Nations Human Rights Treaty Body System. This Statement contains observations/recommendations on the requirements and goals of treaty body reform efforts. Its aim is to revitalise the reform efforts and it concludes with an invitation to the High Commissioner on Human Rights 'to facilitate consultation among all stakeholders with a view to devising a process to develop specific proposals for the strengthening of the treaty body system'.

It is recommended that in the meantime the CRC Committee not wait for the outcome of these efforts but undertake measures to address the problems it is facing in its role as the monitoring body for the CRC. Below, some suggestions are offered in this regard.

Monitoring/Examination of Reports

In the coming years the CRC Committee will continue to struggle with a backlog of reports to examine and hence needs to find a way to deal with them, first and foremost because this serious problem can undermine the credibility of the Committee's monitoring role. The fact that a State Party submitting its report on the implementation of the CRC in February 2010 has to be informed that its report will be (at best) considered in May 2012 (or even later) is not an incentive for timely reporting. Moreover, by 2012 some of the information in the report may be outdated.

Furthermore, the situation could become worse as while there are currently 193 States Parties submitting regular reports on the CRC to the Committee and about 130 States Parties to each of the two Optional Protocols also submitting separate initial reports on the implementation of these Protocols, the number of States Parties to these Protocols will increase.

The conclusion of a lengthy discussion within the Committee was that the only way to address the backlog while maintaining a good standard of monitoring is to operate from time to time in two chambers.[12] This working method was successful in 2006 and is being repeated in 2010. This has required the allocation of additional financial and human resources, so far approved by the UN General Assembly. However, there are indications that the allocation of extra resources for 2010 may be the last. Nevertheless, the CRC Committee still has to insist on receiving

---

12   Introducing extra sessions (extending the three months members meet every year) was not an option as the reduction of the backlog would be limited to about 10 reports.

extra resources when needed to address the backlog. Arguments to support such insistence include that it is in the interest of States Parties and also that it honours compliance with reporting obligations if reports are examined within a reasonable period of time (within 12 months of the date of submission). Examination without undue delay also reflects the importance of monitoring the implementation of the rights of the child and is in the interest of children, as the primary stake holders, in respect for and protection of their rights.

Examination of Periodic Reports

Once States Parties have submitted their initial reports on the Optional Protocols, further reports have to be included in their regular CRC reports. This means that the CRC Committee needs to revise the current guidelines for CRC reporting. It needs to advise the States Parties on how to integrate reporting on the Optional Protocols into their reports on the CRC and what is expected in terms of information (e.g. on how they are following-up on previous recommendations on the implementation of the Protocols). The challenge is to keep the reporting burden as limited as possible while maintaining the quality of the reports. At the same time, the Committee needs to consider whether the existing reporting guidelines should continue to be applicable for all periodic reports to come. For instance, the number of States Parties that submit their fifth or further periodic report will increase. A continuation of the existing practice may result in the repetition of information and/or of recommendations in the Concluding Observations, e.g. on paying more attention to the best interest of the child, to non-discrimination or to the implementation of Article 12 of the CRC. The Committee could initiate a study on how it might develop reporting guidelines and examination practices with a focus on the remaining obstacles/problems in a State Party e.g. starting with the submission by that State Party of its fifth report. This could contribute to lessening the reporting burden and facilitate the production of a focused (and shorter) set of recommendations, avoiding too much repetition of standard recommendations.

Participation of Children/Follow-up

The CRC Committee adopted a General Comment on Article 12 of the CRC (CRC/C/GC/12, May 2009), which contains many recommendations for creating opportunities for children to express their views, have them taken into account and to actively participate in matters that concern them. In trying to integrate these recommendations into the activities of the CRC Committee the challenge for the coming years will be to strengthen the meaningful participation of children in the processes of reporting on and monitoring the implementation of the CRC, including in activities that follow-up on the recommendations of the Committee.

Such participation will give the CRC Committee the opportunity to receive first hand (and first rate) information about the views of children on their enjoyment (or lack thereof) of the rights in the CRC, information that can become a useful and important tool in presenting governments with well targeted recommendations.

It is recommended that such measures be taken by governments, for example by providing children with meaningful opportunities to contribute to the State Party's report, and by NGOs and UN agencies at the national level, for example by actively involving children in the production of their alternative reports and/or encouraging them to produce their own reports. Finally, and equally important, all the entities mentioned should encourage and support children to play an active role in finding the best possible ways in which to follow up on the recommendations of the CRC Committee.

However, all these efforts will most likely not result in more direct communication between children and the body that plays a crucial role in the monitoring of the CRC. The reality so far is that even in cases where children submitted their own reports, only two to four children have (in Geneva) an opportunity to communicate directly with the CRC Committee.

The following recommended actions could result in a significant improvement in the participation of children in the monitoring and follow-up processes mentioned. Firstly, as soon as the Committee receives the periodic report of a State Party, it would initiate, with the support of the NGO group on the CRC in Geneva, national NGOs, UNICEF and others (e.g. international NGOs), a meeting between a representative group of children/young persons and the member of the Committee who is the country rapporteur. The purpose of this meeting would be to obtain direct information from the children about their concerns/problems and possible solutions. In addition the country rapporteur could visit a couple of schools and/or institutions in remote/rural areas of the country (such meetings usually take place in a city). This would not be a fact-finding mission but is meant to give children first-hand information about the process of reporting and monitoring and their possible role in that respect and to bring them closer to the CRC and its implementation. The information the country rapporteur gleans from her/his visit will be used in the further deliberations of the Committee.

Secondly, another meeting of the country rapporteur with the same group of children would take place within a maximum of six to 12 months of the CRC Committee sending its Concluding Observations (with recommendations) to the government. During this meeting the country rapporteur will inform the children about the recommendations to the government, explain them and answer questions put by the children. In this discussion, attention would be given to the possibility of children playing an active role in promoting the implementation of the Committee's recommendations, actions needed to get them implemented and to the question of who is going to do what and in what order (priorities).

Experiences so far have shown that having a meeting on how to follow up on the Committee's recommendations, with participation of one of its members (preferably the country rapporteur), within about six to 12 months is a very effective way of raising awareness regarding the recommendations and supporting (or even initiating) actions for their implementation.

The development of this process to increase the participation of children in the monitoring of the implementation of the CRC will face various obstacles. Not every member of the Committee has the time for this kind of activity. Moreover, such activity requires financial and human resources (travel and lodging, support in the preparation of the visits) which the Committee does not have. Support from States Parties, UNICEF and other UN agencies and NGOs is necessary. Nonetheless, it is highly recommended that efforts in this regard be taken because it can contribute considerably to making the CRC a living instrument in the life of children.

Fostering CRC Implementation

In 2010 the CRC Committee was considering the addition of General Comments on the best interests of the child (Article 3), on violence against children in care settings (Article 19) and on the right to play (Article 31). Possible other topics for a General Comment were the role of parents in the implementation of the CRC (Articles 5, 18 and 27), national and international adoption (Article 21), an effective child protection system (procedural provisions, Article 9, the necessary services, Article 20, and the periodic review, Article 25) and one or more of the civil rights provisions (e.g. Articles 14, 15 or 16). The burden of the regular reviewing of States Parties' reports limits the capacity of the Committee to produce General Comments, but General Comments are a very important guidance for States Parties and all other stakeholders in their efforts to implement the CRC. If the regular sessions of the Committee do not provide enough time to give consideration to draft General Comments the Committee could explore the possibility of meeting an extra week before or after the sessions (or at another appropriate time) to discuss, for example, two or three draft texts.

The major challenge remains the follow-up and use of General Comments. More action in this regard is necessary. One possibility is to promote and support pilots for the implementation of a General Comment, for example on indigenous children or on children with disabilities (an example is the pilot in Jamaica on the General Comment on implementing children's rights in early childhood). Another possible action is the production of a manual for the implementation of a General Comment such as that prepared by UNICEF on the right of the child to be heard (General Comment No. 12), to be published in 2011. Similar manuals could be developed on, for example, the implementation of the General Comment on children's rights in juvenile justice. Many States Parties are in the process of reform of juvenile justice and a manual based on this General Comment could be very helpful.

Finally it is recommended that the CRC Committee systematically require States Parties (if necessary in the List of Issues) to present specific information on their use of the General Comments.

Remedies, a New Optional Protocol and Urgent Actions?

The CRC does not contain a provision explicitly providing the child with the right to remedies in case his or her rights are violated. But it is by now a rule of international customary law that everyone has the right to an effective remedy in case of violation of their fundamental human rights, in line with Article 8 of the UDHR. The ICCPR provides in Article 2 specific rules for the right to an effective remedy including the obligation of States Parties to ensure enforcement of remedies if granted. It should be noted that this right to remedies is elaborated only for actions at the national level. It does not require the establishment of remedy procedures before, for example, a treaty body such as the UN Committee on Civil and Political Rights. But currently the filing of an individual complaint on violations of human rights is possible under all existing human rights treaties except the CRC.[13] All this produces a number of implications for the protection of the rights of the child.

Firstly, States Parties need to introduce (or when necessary strengthen) special procedures for children allowing them, directly or via their legal representative, to file complaints about the violation of their rights before a competent judicial, administrative or legislative authority, and to develop the possibilities of judicial remedies (Article 2, ICCPR). In reviewing the States Parties' reports the CRC Committee does pay attention to this matter of national remedies. Indeed, in paragraph 24 of General Comment No. 5 (2003) on General Measures of Implementation, the CRC Committee elaborates on and underscores the importance of remedies at the national level. It is recommended, therefore that the Committee systematically request from all States Parties specific information on the provisions

---

13   Currently eight human rights treaties or their optional protocols (the International Convention on the Elimination of all Forms of Racial Discrimination [art. 14], the International Covenant on Civil and Political Rights, the Convention against Torture and Other Cruel, Inhuman or Degrading Treatment or Punishment [art. 22], the Convention on the Elimination of All Forms of Discrimination against Women, the Convention on the Protection of All Migrant Workers and Members of their Families [art. 77], the International Covenant on Economic, Social and Cultural Rights, the Convention on the Protection of the Rights of Persons with Disabilities and the Convention on the Protection of All Persons from Forced Disappearances [entered into force on 23 December 2010]) contain provisions which allow the submission of complaints (also known as: communications) from individuals to the respective treaty bodies (committees) about a violation of their rights. The provision in the treaty on the protection of all migrant workers allowing submission of individual complaints has not yet received the necessary 10 ratifications. The Optional Protocol to the International Covenant on Economic, Social and Cultural Rights regarding the possibility to submit individual complaints to the Committee on Economic, Social and Cultural Rights was adopted by the UN General Assembly on 10 December 2008, but has not yet entered into force (so far only three states have ratified this OP). The CRC is the only human rights treaty without a provision or optional protocol allowing submission of individual complaints.

for children to file complaints about the violation of their rights, the remedies that are available and data on the use of these provisions. If children's rights are to be taken seriously, and states state and show that they intend to, serious and effective procedures to remedy violations of these rights need to be established. A General Comment on this matter could help States Parties in this regard.

Secondly, at the international level there are regional human rights courts that can consider individual complaints on the violation of rights (European Court, Inter-American Court and the African Court; for more see Shelton 1999). Children can use these as well as the provision (only for children in Africa) under the African Charter on the Rights and Welfare of Children.

At the same time, however, children – as the most important stakeholders in the CRC – should be provided with the facility to file complaints (in addition to the national provisions) on violations of their rights enshrined in the CRC with the Committee in charge of monitoring the implementation of these rights. This is not only because that possibility exists under all the other human rights treaties but also – and more importantly – because it will give children the possibility to have their complaints considered by a body of experts in the field of their rights in a child-sensitive manner.

The lack of provisions for children to file complaints with the CRC Committee has been recognised by the UN Human Rights Council. It has consequently established an open-ended working group to explore the possibility of elaborating an optional protocol to the CRC to create a communications procedure. The task of the working group, to 'explore the possibility', suggests that the Council does not yet consider this protocol a matter of urgency and that support for this protocol is not yet very strong. Otherwise, why might it be thought that creating such a protocol is not possible? Otherwise, why would the group not be given the mandate to draft a protocol for communications procedure?

The open-ended working group met in December 2009 and discussed various aspects of a communications procedure for children with the participation of members of the CRC Committee, UNICEF and NGOs. The report of the three-day meeting (UN 2010) contains interesting information but no firm recommendations or conclusion, e.g. recommendation to the Human Rights Council to adapt the mandate of the working group charging it with the production of a draft text of an optional protocol to the CRC on a communications procedure. This reflects reluctance to engage in a drafting process and it was left to the Human Rights Council (meeting in March 2010) to decide on the next step. (For more on this process see Van Bueren in this volume.) It would be realistic to assume that it may take five years to produce an agreed upon text for the optional protocol. Whether children can benefit from the communications procedure established by the protocol will depend on the ratification by their governments.

Quite likely the text of the new protocol will follow, more or less, provisions laid out in existing communications procedure protocols. However, it is important to make the process as child-sensitive as possible. This means, among other points, that it should not always and without exception be an exercise on paper. The CRC

Committee should have the freedom to conduct oral hearings when it is considered necessary. It should also be possible to apply some flexibility to the principle that all national remedies have first to be exhausted. Such remedies may not exist for the child or may not be accessible due to financial or other obstacles. Finally it should be possible for NGOs, under specific conditions, to file a complaint on behalf of a child or a group of children.[14]

There is a long way to go before provisions for filing complaints with the CRC Committee are established. In the meantime States Parties should increase their investment in the establishment of effective remedies for children at the national level.

The Committee may (again) consider the possibility of engaging in urgent actions. Serious and large-scale violations of children's rights may take place in a State Party. However, the Committee traditionally will not respond to these violations until it considers a periodic report of the state concerned. That might be several years after the violations took place, and the violations may even continue. Thus it is recommended that the Committee consider ways and means to respond more directly to such situations. Although establishing clear guidelines or criteria for such cases is far from easy, by way of example the Committee might request the appropriate thematic or country rapporteur of the Human Rights Council to ensure full compliance with the CRC when considering a specific problematic situation, as happened during the Bosnia and Herzegovina conflict in 1993 (Flaherty 2000: 452). Another example is the letter issued jointly by the Special Rapporteur on Torture and the CRC Committee to the government of Iran on the execution of death penalties imposed on children.

Respect for and protection of the rights of the child requires in the first place all the necessary legislative, social and other measures (Article 4 of the CRC) but it is equally necessary to establish effective provisions to remedy violations of these rights.

Conclusion

Effective monitoring of the implementation of the CRC is a multi-level process in which the CRC Committee can and must play an important guiding and inspiring role. The dynamics of this monitoring process needs further strengthening, especially in the area of States Parties following-up on the Concluding Observations and the General Comments of the CRC Committee. Furthermore,

---

14   The open-ended working group has prepared a draft text which was discussed in a meeting on 6–10 December 2010. Further discussion will take place on 10–16 February 2011 and the hope is that the Human Rights Council will approve the final text, which will then be submitted to the General Assembly of the UN for adoption: see for updates, *inter alia*, http://www2.ohchr.org/english/bodies/hrcouncil/OEWG/index.htm [accessed 7 January 2011].

more and ongoing attention must be given to the establishment and/or further strengthening of an effective system of remedies, both at the national and at the international level. This is only possible with full support given to the States Parties, UNICEF and other UN agencies, national and international NGOs and children themselves. Full implementation of the CRC remains a huge challenge for everybody.

References

Bayefsky, A.F. (ed.). 2001. *The UN Human Rights System: Universality at Crossroads*. Ardsley, NY: Transnational.

Flaherty, M. 2000. Treaty bodies responding to states of emergency: the case of Bosnia and Herzegovina, in P. Alston and J. Crawford (eds), *The Future of UN Human Rights Treaty Monitoring*. Cambridge, New York and Melbourne: Cambridge University Press, pp. 439–60.

Gras, J. 2001. *Monitoring the Convention on the Rights of the Child*. Helsinki: The Eric Castren Institute of International law and Human Rights, Research Reports 8/2001.

Karp, J. 2000. Reporting and the Committee on the Rights of the Child, in A.F. Bayefsky (ed.), *The UN Human Rights Treaty System in the 21st Century*. The Hague: Kluwer Law International, pp. 35–44.

Langlaude, S. 2008. Children and religion under Article 14 CRC: a critical analysis. *International Journal of Children's Rights*, 16, 475–504.

Lansdown, G. 2000. The reporting process under the Convention on the Rights of the Child, in P. Alston and J. Crawford (eds), *The Future of UN Human Rights Treaty Monitoring*. Cambridge, New York and Melbourne: Cambridge University Press, pp. 113–28.

Santos Pais, M. 1997. The Convention on the Rights of the Child, in *Manual on Human Rights Reporting Under Six Major International Human Rights Instruments*, UN Office of the High Commissioner for Human Rights Geneva (HR/PUB/91/1 (Rev. 1), pp. 393–504.

Shelton, D. 1999. *Remedies in International Human Rights Law*. Oxford and New York: Oxford University Press.

Steiner, H.J. and Alston, P. 2000. *International Human Rights in Context: Law, Politics, Morals*, 2nd edition. Oxford and New York: Oxford University Press.

United Nations. 2010. *Report of the Open-ended Working Group to Explore the Possibility of Elaborating an Optional Protocol to the Convention on the Rights of the Child to Provide a Communications Procedure*. Geneva: UN Human Rights Council Doc. A/HRC/13/43. Available at: http://www2.ohchr.org/english/bodies/hrcouncil/docs/13session/A.HRC.13.43_AEV.pdf [accessed 8 September 2010].

Vandenhole, W. 2005. *Non-Discrimination and Equality in the View of the UN Human Rights Bodies, CRC Committee*. Antwerp and Oxford: Intersentia, pp. 79–82, 157–82 and 272–85.

Verhellen, E. (ed.). 1996. *Monitoring Children's Rights*. The Hague, Boston, MA and London: Martinus Nijhoff.

Chapter 5

Acknowledging Children as International Citizens: A Child-sensitive Communication Mechanism for the Convention on the Rights of the Child

Geraldine Van Bueren

The Emergence of the Child as a Citizen of the World

This chapter examines the recent developments in the move towards establishing a complaints mechanism under the CRC and argues that this is an important element of international child citizenship, because international child citizenship is a concept which offers much potential for children, not only for children who, in breach of the CRC, remain stateless, but for all children, regardless of nationality. International citizenship for children implies both that the protection of all children's rights are the legitimate concern of all nation-states and that children themselves are a global community, also actively responsible for helping protect, as in the case of *Minors Oposa*,[1] the rights of other children.

Historically, the embryonic development of children not merely as citizens, but as active citizens of the world, participating in helping develop global legislation regarding their own autonomy, began with the drafting of the CRC. The Convention was the first global human rights treaty in which children participated in some of the drafting. Thus for the first time the global community, as represented by the United Nations, acknowledged the value not only of children speaking on their own behalf but also, as citizens of the world, speaking on behalf of their fellow children globally. The work of children ranged from speaking directly to the Open-Ended Working Group of the Commission of Human Rights entrusted with drafting the CRC, to lobbying against the death penalty and to signing an international petition seeking to exclude child participation in armed conflict.

---

1   Although the case of *Minors Oposa* concerned deforestation within a national state, it recognised the principle that children have the locus standi to litigate on behalf of other children and children yet unborn. Republic of the Philippines, Supreme Court, G.R. No. 101083 July 30, 1993. See further below.

Although child participation was more *ad hoc* than structured, and occasional rather than comprehensive, the majority of the children's interventions were successful. The speeches of eloquent indigenous children from Canada were acknowledged by Australia as being the catalyst for Australia dropping its opposition to the inclusion of children's indigenous rights in the Convention.[2] Amnesty International worked with American schoolchildren successfully to urge delegates to include the prohibition of the death penalty (see further, Van Bueren 1995). It was only in the area of armed conflict that children's views were disregarded, although some of these concerns were later incorporated in the Optional Protocol to the CRC on the Involvement of Children in Armed Conflict 2000.

Citizenship has a political dimension, because citizens have the capacity to determine the law (Audigier 1998). However, progress towards active child world citizenship in part has been impeded by a lack of opportunities for children to engage with political systems and processes in their own nation-states. If it was reasoned that children could not contribute to domestic public policy, the possibility of children contributing to global policy appeared remote.

Nationally children have helped protect other children's rights. In *Minor Oposa* a group of children successfully sought legal standing to bring a case against deforestation not only for themselves but for generations yet unborn.[3] However, such contributions, although increasing, particularly before regional human rights courts, are still perceived as relatively infrequent.

There has also been a slow evolution toward child democratic citizenship in the creation of child parliaments. Hence an increasing number of states have established children's parliaments, even in states which have poorer infrastructures. In West and Central Africa children's parliaments have been established in states including Benin, Burkina Faso, Cameroon, Cote d'Ivoire, Gambia, Guinea, Liberia, Mali, Niger, Senegal and Togo. In addition, in Sierra Leone there is also the National Children's Forum. They are woven into the national political structure, with the majority falling under the Ministries of Social Affairs or the Ministry for Women and Children. Their electoral processes are mostly organised in partnership with decentralised ministry offices and with civil society (Plan International 2009).

These are still relatively new ideas, and to dismiss such initiatives as tokenism or without effective power is to ignore the historical evolution of nascent parliaments, such as those in England before the English Civil War, which began with very weak powers.

Children's parliaments can be important spaces to allow children to practise democracy and political participation, and thus also to develop their skills and contribute at an international level. However, there needs to be more strategic thinking to secure a wider pool from which to elect child parliamentarians,[4]

---

2   Author's notes taken during the drafting of the Convention.

3   For a discussion of this case see Van Bueren (2008a).

4   As Plan International observe, although there is no standard practice for their elections in most countries, elections appear to depend heavily on schools to reach young

and more innovative ways of creating more child initiated policies to avoid the risk of children merely following an adults' political agenda. In addition, even though children's parliaments can act as consultative bodies for governmental decision-making or actively influence governmental policy and practice, much more needs to be done to formalise their political contribution. Several countries have acknowledged high levels of influence of children's parliaments on national policy debates concerning children. The governments of Guinea and Liberia, for example, have adopted a national children's code, which owes much to the effective advocacy of their children's parliaments. In Cameroon, the children's parliament argued successfully for the eradication of compulsory fees for primary education, and for a raise of salary for government employees (Plan International 2009).

These successes ought to be stressed, as all too often the focus is on the dangers of children implementing their political rights as citizens. As Hart recognises, children are a readily available 'army' of concern that can be easily seduced into involvement in a movement which is really not 'their own' (Hart 1997). However, education for democratic citizenship minimises such risks.

In 2010 the Council of Europe adopted a Recommendation on the Council of Europe Charter on Education for Democratic Citizenship and Human Rights Education (Council of Europe 2010). The Recommendation defines education for democratic citizenship as

> education, training, awareness-raising, information, practices and activities which aim, by equipping learners with knowledge, skills and understanding and developing their attitudes and behaviour, to empower them to exercise and defend their democratic rights and responsibilities in society, to value diversity and to play an active part in democratic life, with a view to the promotion and protection of democracy and the rule of law.

The Recommendation has no minimum age limit, which means that it can be interpreted to apply to all children of any age, and indeed it specifically focuses on the role of states to support youth organisations in providing such education (para. 10). Although the focus of the Recommendation is on national citizenship it clearly has implications for children as citizens of the world.

---

voters, which excludes out-of-school children. There are also varying practices with regards to voter eligibility, often drawing on children's school performance. Age ranges for active and passive rights to vote in children's parliaments also vary significantly, though an active right to vote seems to be mostly determined by age 16 and above. Efforts have been made in most countries in West Africa to ensure that an equal number of boys and girls are elected into office. In Senegal, for example, the participation criteria for the children's parliament require a broad representation of all categories of children, including children in and out of school, with disability, affected by HIV, etc. However, this appears to be the exception to the rule, as few parliaments in the region have children with disabilities as members.

Overcoming the Obstacles to Children as Active Global Citizens

There are two obstacles which impede children's development as active global citizens. The first is the absence of a General Comment on Adolescents Rights and the second is the lack of a communication procedure under the CRC.

Although the international human rights law on the rights of women has adopted two separate treaties for general women's rights and political rights,[5] such an approach is not necessary for children. There is sufficient space within the CRC to permit a child's right to political participation, in the broadest sense, in accordance with their maturity and evolving capacities. However, guidance is needed for governments from the CRC Committee and the most appropriate form of guidance would be in the nature of a General Comment.

Although the CRC Committee has issued a valuable General Comment on Implementing Child Rights in Earlier Childhood (Committee on the Rights of the Child 2005), there is not a complementary General Comment on Adolescents' Rights in Childhood. Children in many states are beginning to engage in self-advocacy, establishing child-led organisations, or child sections within NGOs working on children's rights issues,[6] however this clearly will not apply to babies and very young children. Such a General Comment would be valuable, as it could focus attention on the ability of children to contribute to public policies and on the obstacles which prevent them from so doing. Feeding into such a General Comment ought to be a Day of Discussion on children's participation in national and international policy processes.

In addition, although several treaty bodies have the jurisdiction to receive complaints from children, their respective mandates remain limited[7] and such a scattered and non-child focused approach has limited the potential for developing a coherent and comprehensive approach to child citizenship. The CRC has a significant lacuna in relation to the concept of children as international citizens. The Convention omits procedures whereby children can challenge their own governments' violations if they fail to receive an effective national remedy. The Convention therefore, perhaps unwittingly, helps perpetuate a lesser image of the child as international citizen. The majority of original drafters, in even refusing to consider an inter-state complaints mechanism (Van Bueren 1995), unwittingly limited the concept of children as world citizens and therefore of equal concern to the world.

---

5 The Convention on the Political Rights of Women, 193 U.N.T.S. 135, entered into force 7 July 1954, since superseded, in effect, by the Convention on the Elimination of All Forms of Discrimination against Women 1979.

6 See for example the children's advisory board of Save the Children; see also Article 12 of the CRC.

7 Hence within the United Nations treaty bodies only 2 to 2.5 per cent of the complaints considered by the treaty bodies related to situations involving children.

However, if a gauge is necessary to measure how far the international social movement for children has progressed in its attitude towards child citizenship, a valuable one is the attitude of civil society around the world to developing a complaints mechanism, to be used by children, to protect violations of their rights under the CRC.[8]

During the 1980s not only were states against such a mechanism but, and this is not very well known, so were the majority of NGOs. A draft joint proposal by Amnesty International, which I had the privilege of representing, and the International Commission of Jurists, was opposed by the majority of states and NGOs on four grounds.

The first objection was that a petitioning or complaints mechanism would damage children's rights, because it would introduce an element of complaint when so much more had been achieved in the drafting procedure based on consensus. It was believed that incorporating state self-reporting and the CRC's scrutiny of states' reports, with technical advice and assistance into the treaty were sufficient.[9] Although never stated expressly, such an objection harked back to the era when it was believed that children's objections to a particular law or policy would be better represented indirectly and mediated through adults exercising citizenship on children's behalf. Although the CRC Committee has considerably expanded the role of child participation in the reporting process, the lack of direct access through a communications procedure has impeded the progress of moving towards an image of active child citizenship.

The second objection, which was more understandable in the historical context of the 1980s, was that the CRC not only enshrined civil and political rights but also economic, social and cultural rights. The latter, it was argued, were inherently non-justiciable and therefore inappropriate for any complaints mechanism.[10] Such objectors could point to the absence of petitioning mechanisms in global treaties protecting socio-economic rights, and the very few states which allowed their citizens access to the courts to litigate socio-economic rights violations. In the twenty-first century, however, the jurisprudence has significantly progressed. In addition to regional treaties, procedures allowing for individual complaints are permitted for all the core international human rights treaties, with the exception of the CRC and these treaties include the International Covenant on Economic, Social and Cultural Rights, the International Convention on the Elimination of All Forms of Racial Discrimination, the Convention on the Elimination of All Forms of Discrimination against Women, the International Convention on the Protection

---

8   By 8 December 2009, 601 organisations had signed the petition: see http://www.crin.org/petitions/petition.asp?petID=1007 [accessed 30 August 2010].

9   Articles 43, 44 and 45, CRC.

10   That civil and political rights do permit such communications is evidenced by the fact that, at the time of writing this chapter, only two more ratifications were needed for the entry into force of the International Convention for the Protection of All Persons from Enforced Disappearance, which also includes a procedure for individual communications.

of the Rights of All Migrant Workers and Members of Their Families, and the Convention on the Rights of Persons with Disabilities. These allow petitioning of socio-economic rights, so the non-justiciability issue disappears, at least on the international level.

Children, however, suffer from a double disadvantage, caused by the operation of two distinct ideologies: not only the resistance of law to take its capacity for the strategic alleviation of poverty as a legal cause of action seriously, but also the capacity of children as evolving citizens and rights holders in the economic and social sphere. The economic facets of citizenship are frequently conceptualised as exclusively adult. This common but erroneous perception fails to consider that economic and social rights are not only commodities, but are also essential for the right to live as citizens in security and dignity: a right which is as pertinent for children as for adults.

Child citizens are legally entitled to share in the resources of their own states and this has received constitutional protection in a growing number of states including Brazil, Chile, India, the Philippines and South Africa. Children have won socio-economic rights cases on the rights to nutrition,[11] the right to housing,[12] to a sustainable environment[13] and on the exploitation of child labour.[14] This evolution of national child citizenship conceptualises economic-socio entitlement as an equal facet to civil entitlement, and has impacted on the development of international child citizenship.

Relying on government political promises, or reliance only on governments fully to implement the Concluding Observations of the CRC Committee, has so far not proven successful, with child poverty increasing in the majority of OECD states since the adoption of the CRC (Van Bueren 2008a). This is evidence of the fact that political target-setting, without the safety net of an international child complaints mechanism, risks the continuing image of children being regarded as the means to a fairer society in the future. Child citizenship, in contrast, conceptualises that children have sufficient legal capacity to ensure their entitlement to a socially just society, to be enjoyed whilst they are still children, and the incorporation of a communication procedure to the CRC ought to, if properly drafted, make such a concept more realisable.

The third and fourth objections which were raised are inter-connected. It was considered impossible to incorporate a procedure by which children could petition the CRC Committee for a remedy for a violation of all of their Convention rights, as the Convention protects children's rights in armed conflicts, and complaints mechanisms had never before been extended to victims of armed conflicts. These

---

11 *People's Union for Civil Liberties v Union of India & Ors*, in the Supreme Court of India, Civil Original Jurisdiction, Writ Petition (Civil) No.196 of 2001.

12 *Government of South Africa v Grootboom*, Judgment of the Constitutional Court of South Africa, 4 October 2000.

13 *Minors Oposa*, op cit.

14 *M.C. Mehta v State of Tamil Nadu and others*, AIR 1997, SC 699.

objections imply that there is an acceptance that citizenship rights are, as a matter of law, lost in situations of armed conflict. Although it is often the case that *de facto* citizenship rights are lost in situations of conflict, this is very different from accepting a *de jure* loss of citizenship.

It was also argued that complaints mechanisms were Western, and not part of a universal tradition. States, it was erroneously argued, particularly in Africa, had a long tradition of improvement through the building of consensus, rather than the formal taking of complaints. However, within a year of the United Nations adopting the CRC, the Organisation of African Unity, as it was then known, adopted its own general regional treaty on children's rights, the African Charter on the Rights and Welfare of the Child, adopted in 1990. This not only enshrines a petitioning mechanism, allowing children to petition on civil, political, economic, social and cultural rights, but also creates a petitioning mechanism which allows children to petition the African Committee on violations of children's rights in peacetime and in times of armed conflicts.[15] Hence by clinging to old conceptions of Africa, armed conflicts and of child citizenship, at least on a *de jure* level, the majority of Convention drafters have created the arbitrary situation in which children in Africa have better *de jure* protection of their citizenship rights than those in other parts of the world.

Since the entry into force of the CRC additional objections have been raised to proposals for drafting a communication or complaints procedure. The first objection has been that because of the vulnerable status of children, there is a risk that children may be manipulated when submitting a complaint. However, there is not any evidence of this becoming a problem with applications submitted by children to the European or Inter-American Court of Human Rights, both of which have a substantial history of considering complaints from children. Nor is there any evidence of such manipulation before any of the United Nations human rights bodies, including the Human Rights Committee or the Committee on the Elimination of All Forms of Discrimination against Women.

There is a serious issue concerning the length of proceedings and the consequences for an application if a child reaches majority and adulthood before a communication is finally decided by the CRC Committee. However, in relation to the latter the problem is overstressed. The issue to be decided is the one which is the subject matter of the communication at the time of receipt of the child's

---

15   Under Article 44 of the African Charter on the Rights and Welfare of Children, the Committee of Experts may receive communications from any individual or group – including children, or from a NGO recognised 'by the Organisation of African Unity, by a Member State or by the United Nations' and investigate. A communication may be presented on behalf of a victim without his/her agreement on condition that the author is able to prove that his/her action is taken in the supreme interest of the child. The Committee adopted Guidelines for the Consideration of Communications in 2006 and communications have been submitted, but as at the time of writing no decisions have been adopted by the Committee.

complaint, and as it concerns a matter of public policy or national legislation, it will still be relevant to children living in the applicant's state after the child submitting the application reaches majority.

Two objections have also been raised which are common to all human rights treaties. The first concern is the risk of forum shopping by child complainants. However, this can be easily avoided, as the majority of States Parties to the European Convention on Human Rights, for example, have lodged a reservation to Article 5, para. 2 (a), of the Optional Protocol to the International Covenant on Civil and Political Rights, which limits the Human Rights Committee's competence to examine complaints which have already been examined by the European Court of Human Rights. Other treaty bodies are prohibited by the terms of the treaty itself from examining communications which have already been decided by relevant international organs.

The second objection is that of delay due to an overburdening of workload for the CRC. However, as this is an issue raised in relation to all human rights bodies, it is not a reason for denying one group in the global community access to a communications procedure, particularly as pending cases vary from treaty to treaty, with some having little delay.[16]

The Consequences of Recognising Children as International Citizens

One of the major consequences of recognising that children are both citizens of a nation-state and of the global community is that it helps to justify the need for an international remedy to be enshrined in the CRC. This is particularly important for children who live in parts of the world where such mechanisms do not exist, not even for violations of the civil and political rights of adults and children. Asia, where the majority of children live, has no regional human rights machinery to which children or adults can petition. Neither the Council of Europe[17] nor the Organisation of American States has a single general children's rights equivalent to the African Union's Charter on the Rights and Welfare of the Child. This produces the arbitrary and irrational result that whether a child has recourse to a remedy on an international level depends upon whether a child is within the African Union

---

16　In December 2009, in regard to the Human Rights Committee, the Secretariat indicated that approximately 430 cases were pending. Approximately 100 cases are registered each year and an equal number of final decisions are adopted each year. The Committee against Torture has 85 cases pending before it, and a total of approximately 400 cases had been registered under the Committee's procedure since the early 1990s. The Committee on the Elimination of Racial Discrimination and the Committee on the Elimination of All Forms of Discrimination against Women had very few cases registered (UN 2010: para. 77). At the time of writing, the newly created Committee on the Rights of Persons with Disabilities does not yet have any registered individual communication.

17　See further Van Bueren (2008b).

or living elsewhere. This lack of universal equity in procedural access hinders the development of children as citizens of the world.

Even for children living in states within the Council of Europe, the European Convention on Human Rights (ECHR) was not designed to protect children as a group, and this lack of child focus is reflected in both the language of the ECHR and in a number of unsatisfactory judgements. The ECHR does not even expressly enshrine the general principle of the best interests of the child, and ironically, the first express reference to children in the ECHR is to a provision which provides a ground for depriving children of their liberty, rather than protecting their liberty (Van Bueren 2008b). This is not to argue that the concept of child citizenship has been wholly neglected under the ECHR, this is clearly not the case, but to assert that the European Convention was never intended to be a child-focused treaty, and therefore it would be unrealistic to expect the European Court of Human Rights to go beyond its jurisdiction in order better to protect child citizenship.

Although the status of decisions made by the CRC Committee will be that of recommendation and not, as with the European Court of Human Rights, binding judgement, a communications procedure will assist in the development of international citizenship for children. The advantage of having communications heard by the CRC is that complaints will be judged by those with a direct experience of children's rights and whose focus is the development of child citizenship. A successful complaint against one state would not only benefit children living in that state, but would set the standard which other states would have to meet to avoid similar complaints brought against them. In this way the complaints procedure would serve both as a deterrent and as a catalyst for implementing, at the very least, minimal standards in child citizenship.

The decisions of the CRC Committee will also have a persuasive value for similar cases raised before national courts and regional fora. In this way there would be a circular process of increasing the implementation of the rights of children. Similarly, decisions of the CRC Committee, although recommendatory only, will provide a catalyst for changes through legislatures.

A communications procedure will also provide an opportunity for the CRC to provide fuller and better reasoned opinions, and therefore for the concept of child citizenship to gain more respect amongst states. There have been cases, for example concerning the physical punishment of children in schools in the United Kingdom, where the European Court of Human Rights found the United Kingdom not to be in violation while the CRC Committee found the United Kingdom to be in breach (Van Bueren 2008b). It is difficult to persuade a state to adopt a more progressive approach when it has two conflicting opinions from different international bodies, one of which, the recommendation from the CRC Committee, provided very little reasoning even though it contradicted the earlier decision of the European Court of Human Rights and extended the prohibition on physical punishment to intra-familial physical punishment. A more fully reasoned opinion would be more persuasive, opening the door to more reasoned arguments comparing the prohibition of physical punishment on adult citizens and questioning the reason for retaining such punishment for child citizens.

The actual negotiations over the procedures to be included in any communications mechanism will also impact upon the development of child citizenship as it operates on a formal level. It would be a loss of opportunity if the complaints mechanism for the CRC were simply to replicate the communications mechanisms of other treaties without taking into account the special needs of child citizenship. Neither the International Covenant on Civil and Political Rights nor the UN Convention on the Elimination of All Forms of Discrimination against Women offers appropriate models. At the time of writing, no girl under the age of 18 has won her case under the Convention on the Elimination of All Forms of Discrimination against Women, although there are decisions which have been helpful to children. The procedures of the International Covenant on Civil and Political Rights Covenant take insufficient account of a child's best interests (Van Bueren 1995).

Creating a complaints mechanism would also focus attention on the issue of children as citizens of the world and the degree to which others share an interdependent responsibility to protect child citizen rights. Although the communication procedure will be international, if it is sufficiently flexible and child-focused, it will help focus attention on how to make child citizenship more relevant to vulnerable children, who often are allowed to fall through the safety net of child citizenship protection. One issue which will require constructive and novel approaches is how an international complaints mechanism can be accessible to the world's most vulnerable child citizens, including the most impoverished children and children living and working in the streets and beyond the normal reach of formal structures. This is particularly challenging for children living and working at the margins of communities, as in common with all other international legal tribunals, children will not have access to an international communication procedure until all effective domestic remedies have been exhausted. Existing national children and human rights institutions, including national commissions and ombuds offices, will need to develop innovative approaches to securing access and the trust of the most vulnerable of children and, in so doing, comparative best practice will be invaluable.

One of the reasons for the success of the South African Bill of Rights is that there is a broad standing – non-governmental organisations, individuals and groups of individuals are able to bring cases[18] creating a network of support for the most vulnerable in the community. Allowing civil society, as well as states, to bring actions against states is essential for the full development of child citizenship.

The formal details of citizenship are usually accessible only in adult accessible form, although the CRC and other international laws on children place a duty on states to make their provisions available in child-friendly versions. Judgements and rulings, even when considering aspects of child citizenship, rarely appear in

---

18   Section 38 of the Constitution of South Africa.

a child-friendly format. The development of child citizenship requires that the decisions of the CRC on a child complaint be published in a form which would be child-sensitive. This is not only so that the child or child victims can understand, but also, in this era of international child citizenship, so that children globally are able to understand judgments concerning their own rights and status. The test for measuring progress in the development of international child citizenship will be the extent to which children participate in the formulation of a child complaints mechanism, *ad hoc* as with the drafting of the original Convention, or in a truly representative manner.

The Open-Ended Working Group and a Child-sensitive Communication Mechanism

Anniversary celebrations have often been used strategically to progress children's rights. Indeed the original proposal to draft a binding treaty on children's rights was accepted in 1979, the International Year of the Child. Diplomatically a rejection of the proposal in such a year would have been very difficult. The CRC Committee recognised in General Comment No. 5 (Committee on the Rights of the Child 2003), that children's special and dependent status creates substantive difficulties for them in pursuing remedies for breaches of their rights. This was further developed by the Chairperson of the Committee, expressing in her oral report to the General Assembly that the development of a communications procedure for the CRC would significantly contribute to the overall protection of children's rights. The CRC Committee has endorsed the idea on a number of occasions, including at the tenth anniversary of the Convention (for instance, Committee on the Rights of the Child 1999: para. 291) and more recently in the build-up to the twentieth anniversary. Hence the occasion of the twentieth anniversary of the CRC made it possible for a resolution to be adopted without a vote at the Human Rights Council, the successor body to the Commission on Human Rights, to establish an Open-Ended Working Group of the Human Rights Council to explore the possibility of elaborating an optional protocol to the CRC to provide a communications procedure complementary to the reporting procedure under the Convention.[19] The Council recognised that in many states national remedies are inadequate, but even where national remedies are effective children still have the same overwhelming case for gaining an international communications mechanism, alongside those created for the other international human rights treaties for the other groups traditionally subjected to discrimination.

It is too soon to assess what weight will be given to active child participation. The General Assembly has recognised, *inter alia*, that the full enjoyment of the right of the child to be heard and to participate requires adults to adopt an appropriate child-centred attitude, listening to children and respecting their

---

19   UN Doc. A/HRC/11/L.3 on 12 June 2009.

rights and individual points of view, and this would include the drafting of a communications procedure.[20] At its first meeting, on 16 December 2009, the working group elected Drahoslav Štefánek, from Slovakia, as its Chairperson-Rapporteur. The chairperson was nominated by a core group of member states, including Chile, Egypt, Finland, France, Kenya, Maldives, Slovakia, Slovenia, Thailand and Uruguay, which have supported the initiative for a new optional protocol on a communications procedure under the CRC.[21]

It is, however, clear that an opportunity was lost when states rejected the opportunity to incorporate a communications procedure into the main body of the Convention, making it part of the CRC rather than an additional and optional protocol. This would have meant that the communication procedure would not have been optional and would be similar to the approach used by the amended European Convention on Human Rights.[22] However, despite being optional, many advantages will follow. The development of an effective and accessible international procedure will, where necessary, highlight the need for, and may

---

20   General Assembly Resolution 64/146 para. 32.

21   UN Doc. A/HRC/13/43. Representatives of the following states members of the Human Rights Council attended the working group's meetings: Argentina, Bahrain, Bangladesh, Belgium, Bosnia and Herzegovina, Brazil, Burkina Faso, Chile, China, Djibouti, Egypt, France, Ghana, Hungary, India, Indonesia, Italy, Japan, Mauritius, Mexico, Netherlands, Nigeria, Norway, Pakistan, Philippines, Qatar, Republic of Korea, Russian Federation, Saudi Arabia, Senegal, Slovakia, Slovenia, South Africa, Ukraine, United Kingdom of Great Britain and Northern Ireland, United States of America and Uruguay. The following non-member states of the Human Rights Council also participated in the working group's meetings: Algeria, Armenia, Azerbaijan, Australia, Austria, Belarus, Bulgaria, Canada, Colombia, Costa Rica, Democratic Republic of the Congo, Croatia, Cyprus, Czech Republic, Denmark, Finland, Germany, Greece, Guatemala, Haiti, Iceland, Israel, Iran (Islamic Republic of), Kazakhstan, Kuwait, Lao People's Democratic Republic, Libyan Arab Jamahiriya, Lithuania, Malaysia, Maldives, Morocco, New Zealand, Oman, Panama, Paraguay, Peru, Poland, Portugal, Republic of Moldova, Romania, Serbia, Singapore, Spain, Sri Lanka, Sudan, Sweden, Switzerland, Syrian Arab Republic, Thailand, Tunisia, Turkey, Uganda, Venezuela (Bolivarian Republic of), Viet Nam and Zimbabwe. The Holy See and the Occupied Palestinian Territory were also represented by observers. The following intergovernmental organisations were represented at the meetings of the working group: African Union, European Union and the International Organization of la Francophonie. The United Nations Children's Fund (UNICEF) participated in the session as well. The following non-governmental organisations (NGOs) in consultative status with the Economic and Social Council were represented by observers: Good Neighbors International, International Commission of Jurists, International Federation Terre des Hommes, International Save the Children Alliance, Save the Children–Japan, International Service for Human Rights, Kindernothilfe, Norwegian Centre for Human Rights, Plan International, Inc., SOS Children's Villages International, World Organization against Torture, World Vision International.

22   The ECHR now has the communication procedure as an integral part of the treaty; originally states could have been party to the Convention without having to recognise the right of individual petition.

stimulate the development of, effective remedies for violations of the rights of the child at local, national and regional levels. Similarly the decisions by the CRC Committee on individual and group child cases ought to mean that the body of jurisprudence which it develops will assist in the interpretation of children's rights by national and regional courts and tribunals. Even the process of drafting and adopting an international communications procedure for the Convention may encourage the development of appropriate national remedies for children.

At present not all Ombudspersons for Children have the power to investigate complaints, nor do the majority of Ombudspersons in Europe have the jurisdiction to take legal action on behalf of children, either nationally or before regional human rights bodies. A communications procedure under the CRC may offer opportunities to strengthen the powers of national child ombudsmen.

The lack of a communications procedure in the Convention has, on occasion, resulted in national and regional courts interpreting children's rights in a limited way.[23] However, for the jurisprudence of the CRC Committee to maximise its potential as a dynamic catalyst for the development of children's rights, it is necessary that the procedures of the Committee are child sensitive. The UN Guidelines on Justice in Matters involving Child Victims and Witnesses of Crime define child-sensitive as 'an approach that balances the child's right to protection and that takes into account the child's individual needs and views'.[24] It is also clear that for a complaint mechanism to be child sensitive it should be designed so that its procedures are tailored both in line with the Convention and with the General Comments of the CRC Committee, particularly with its most recent General Comment on the right to be heard. General Comment No. 12 ranges from an analysis of how states give due weight to a child's maturity, to the necessity of having complaint procedures which should ensure that children are confident that using them will not expose them to risk of violence or punishment.[25]

A child-sensitive international complaint mechanism will also require a range of methods of submitting a communication. The Inter-American Commission on Human Rights, for instance, can receive online petition forms. Such an approach could be extended to allow for the possibility of sending audio or audio-visual materials. Child-sensitive procedures are being developed by a number of international bodies and offices. The Special Rapporteur on the Sale of Children, Child Prostitution and Child Pornography, for example, is developing a child-friendly version of the letter of allegation form, and the International Criminal Court has accepted over 400 drawings from children from Darfur, which it may use as evidence. This is consistent with the Convention which provides that a key element of the child's right to freedom of expression is the child's choice of medium of expression.

---

23 See above in relation to child physical punishment.
24 UN Doc. ECOSOC Res 2005/20, July 22 2005.
25 UN Doc. CRC/C/GC/12, paras 46 and 47.

A key element of child-sensitive communications procedures is that they take account of a child's sense of time and are processed accordingly. Since the CRC was born there has, however, been a rapid development of best practices concerning children's access to child-sensitive justice and to effective remedies. This means that the drafting of a child-sensitive communications procedure could be accomplished within a short period of time. There is no longer any reason for children to be denied Englantyne Jebb's promise that 'mankind owes the best it has to give'.[26]

References

Audigier, F. 1998. *Basic Concepts and Core Competencies of Education for Democratic Citizenship: An Initial Consolidated Report, 1998.* Strasbourg: Council of Europe.

Committee on the Rights of the Child. 1999. *Report on the 22nd Session of the Committee on the Rights of the Child on the 10th Anniversary of the Convention on the Rights of the Child*, UN Doc. CRC/C/90, 7.

——. 2003. *General Comment No 5 on General Measures of Implementation of the Convention on the Rights of the Child*, UN Doc. CRC/GC/2003/5.

——. 2005. *General Comment No. 7 on Implementing Child Rights in Early Childhood*, UN Doc. CRC/C/GC/7/Rev.1.

Council of Europe. 2010. *Recommendation of the Committee of Ministers to Member States on the Council of Europe Charter on Education for Democratic Citizenship and Human Rights Education.* CM/Rec(2010)7, adopted by the Committee of Ministers on 11 May 2010 at the 120th Session.

Hart, R. 1997. *Children's Participation: From Tokenism to Citizenship.* Innocenti Research Centre, UNICEF.

Plan International. 2009. *Children as Active Citizens: Addressing Discrimination against Children's Engagement in Political and Civil Society Processes.* Discussion Paper, 20th Anniversary of the Convention of the Rights of the Child, Geneva, October 2009.

United Nations. 2010. *Report of the Open-ended Working Group to Explore the Possibility of Elaborating an Optional Protocol to the Convention on the Rights of the Child to Provide a Communications Procedure.* Geneva: UN Human Rights Council Doc. A/HRC/13/43. Available at: http://www2.ohchr.org/english/bodies/hrcouncil/docs/13session/A.HRC.13.43_AEV.pdf [accessed 8 September 2010].

Van Bueren, G. 1995. *The International Law on the Rights of Children.* Dordrecht: Kluwer.

---

26   Found in the Preamble of the Declaration of the Rights of the Child 1924, which she drafted.

Van Bueren, G. 2008a. The separation of powers and the international legal status of the best interests of the child in assisting domestic courts to protect children's economic and social rights', in T. Collins, R. Grondin, V. Pinero, M. Pratte and M.C. Roberge (eds), *Rights of the Child: Proceedings of the International Conference, Ottawa 2007*. Montreal: Wilson and Lafleur, pp. 237–73.

Van Bueren, G. 2008b. *Child Rights in Europe: Convergence and Divergence in Judicial Protection*. Strasbourg: Council of Europe.

Chapter 6

Has Research Improved the Human Rights of Children? Or Have the Information Needs of the CRC Improved Data about Children?

Judith Ennew

The information about children generated and used by both governments and civil society determines the policies and programmes that directly affect children's experiences of childhood and the extent to which their rights are fulfilled. Thus the quality and reliability of data are of crucial importance. Rapid and near-universal ratification of the CRC provided a competitive edge to the reporting process, which has almost overwhelmed the CRC Committee with the number of reports received. However, more reports does not necessarily mean better reporting. Through focusing on three key areas – social research, information needs and data about children – this chapter examines the question of whether the demand for data to monitor the implementation of the CRC has resulted in better information to improve understanding of children's lives and to support the fulfilment of their rights. In conclusion, the chapter examines two possible (and not necessarily mutually-exclusive) propositions: that social research has improved the human rights of children independently of the CRC; and that CRC reporting has improved data about children.

What is Social Research?

The most succinct, and in many ways the most satisfactory, description of social research is Manfried Leibel's phrase 'systematic curiosity' (Liebel 2008). Throughout the nineteenth century, in Europe and North America, social data collection was carried out by philanthropists and journalists focused on 'new' social problems associated with the 'industrial revolution' and rapid urbanisation, collecting information through direct personal contact with individuals, combining ethnographic observation with case studies, interviews and statistics. Such data collection built increasingly on the new science of statistics (especially censuses and household surveys), developed by states for the purpose of governance

(Schweber 2001), and of increasing importance as the global nation-state system evolved (Anderson 1991).

It is no accident that the historical epoch that marked development of nation-states and statistics was also the period in which childhood began to be cognised as a separate ('quarantined') time in the life cycle, which requires control by states and state-accredited experts on children (Aries 1962, Donzelot 1979, Meyer 1984). Social research has a history of concern with children's welfare. Pioneers in the collection of information in the industrial heartlands of Europe and North America not only sought to improve housing and working conditions but also advocated legal reforms related to child work, schooling and the moral duty of women to remain at home to care for children.

Social Research with Children

Between 1900 and the first decade of the twenty-first century, three main periods of child research can be distinguished, all in various ways related to evolving discourses of childhood, and each exhibiting a continuous thread of social anxiety about children, which not infrequently builds into moral panics. Justice Elizabeth Butler-Sloss commented memorably on this tendency at the conclusion of a major inquiry into child abuse in the United Kingdom during the 1980s, that 'the child is a person and not an object of concern' (Butler-Sloss 1988: 245). In policy and research this might be glossed to mean that children should be regarded as subjects, including as subjects of rights.

From 1900 to 1979, the influence of nineteenth-century child savers and childhood reformers was noticeable in research on children and childhood (Platt 1969, Fyfe 1989, Zelizer 1994), in parallel with the development of experts and specialists on childcare, education and social work, all of which justified state intervention in the private realm of family life. The main areas of child research therefore became health, psychology and schooling. With the exception of psychometric tests devised by adults for investigation of children, information about children was gathered largely from adults (such as parents and teachers), by adults (such as psychologists, medical personnel and demographers).

What Happened in the 1980s?

The pivotal date for global child research and data on children is 1979, the United Nations International Year of the Child, which of course is also a key date for children's rights. In the 1980s, three overlapping developments within the social sciences ran parallel to the drafting process for the CRC. In anthropology, scattered studies had always recorded childhoods, although the focus was usually child-rearing practices and rites of passage (La Fontaine 1978). The few ethnographies of childhood itself tended to follow what might be called the 'gerund school', which analyses the process of *becoming* a social adult, the state of childhood being merely an unfinished process. This is reflected in the grammatical form of many published titles, such as *Coming of Age in Samoa* and *Growing Up in New Guinea* (Mead 1928, 1930), *Growing Up Agreeably* (Broch 1990) and *Growing Up in a Culture of Respect* (Bolin 2006). In contrast, from around 1979 onwards, both anthropologists and human geographers began to use ethnographic techniques, including participant observation, to research the lives of specific groups of children, such as street children, without considering them as 'objects of concern' who may result in unsocialised 'future adults' (for example, Aptekar 1988, Beazley 2003, Hecht 1998).

Within sociology, respect for children as human beings, rather than implicit disrespect for them as 'human becomings' (Qvortrup 1991), was more overt, linked to a methodological construction of children as research subjects with human agency, rather than inert objects of concern. This approach has been popularised as 'the new sociology of childhood' (or 'the new social studies of childhood') (James and Prout 1990). Superficially, it might appear that there is a link between this social conception of children and the rights-based emphasis on children's participation. Both recognise that children are important social actors, either because they are human subjects or because they are subjects of human rights. Yet, in practice, the two approaches seldom connect, even though both provide clear indication that there has been a major shift in perspectives on children. It was unprecedented that, when children, civil society organisations, state delegates, UN experts and advocates met in Geneva in October 2009 to celebrate 20 years of the CRC, the Chair of the CRC Committee, Professor Yanghee Lee, began the conference by saying that a crucial element of the Convention was to promote the view of children as 'beings rather than becomings' (albeit without reference to the new sociology of childhood).[1]

1990–2008 Childhood? Or Children? Or Children's Rights

The key change brought about within social research by the new sociology of childhood is that children are increasingly perceived as important in their own right. The new sociologists of childhood make the methodological point that children (like adults) are subjects of research, by emphasising their competencies in knowing, acting and constructing meanings (a position emphasised in Nordic social science; Brembeck et al. 2004). This contrasts with previous research on children, which used their supposed incompetence as an excuse for only collecting data from adults.

Beyond this methodological contribution, however, the new sociology of childhood has not enabled significant progress either in research techniques or in adding to data related to children's rights. Moreover, the funding and/or commissioning of academic social scientists by policy-making bodies, such as national research councils, often perpetuates the notion that children are objects

---

1   UN Press release, Geneva, 8 October 2009.

of concern, by focusing on 'problem' children rather than 'normal' childhoods (despite being essential for making causal inferences). Such is the underfunding of social science research that this is the case despite advances in methodological constructions of childhood and also in spite of the warning against researching only social pathology, made by Emile Durkheim in 1895.

The social sciences have not really connected with advances in the human rights of children, although both coexist within the late-twentieth-century discourse on children and childhood. Indeed, an almost wayward academic ignorance of children's rights persists among social scientists. For example, a recent account of childhood studies in anthropology, intended for student use, states that the CRC 'was opened for signature in 1979, came into force in 1989 … [with 54 articles] which aim to protect and promote children's rights in the fields of health, education, nationality and the family' (Montgomery 2009: 6). This far from unique example propagates misinformation, not only about the history of the CRC but also about the range of rights it involves. When academic social scientists do take note of the existence of the CRC, they tend to abuse it through a spurious assertion of cultural relativity, claiming that this Convention (if not the whole of the human rights agenda) is a 'white', 'Western', 'Christian' imposition, which fails to take into account local cultural norms (see for example, Boyden 1990, Burr 2006, Twum-Danso 2009). Arguments from within academic social science against the CRC, on the grounds of cultural imposition, seem to show little knowledge of the long debates within human rights circles about 'Asian Values' (Bauer and Bell 1999) or 'African Culture' (An'Naim 2002), which can so frequently be shown to be the result of political high-jacking of the issue. Debates about the way various cultures and national legal systems interpret the CRC characterised early discussions, published for example in the collections edited by Philip Alston (1994) and Welshman Ncube (1998), leaving little need for 'flat-earth' contributions in the twenty-first century. Social scientists should surely be the first to be aware that cultural traditions are not static and immutable. They are dynamic and progressive, adapting and developing in response to social and environmental changes. The conclusion might thus be that advances in the new sociology of childhood, the twentieth-century fascination with childhood (related to governance) and the development of legislation on the human rights of children, are no more than parallel processes within the same ongoing discourse on humanity.

Social Research with Children Two Decades after the CRC

A common thread through all periods is the paucity of accounts of 'normal' childhood and the assumption that childhood is fraught with difficulties, especially in the global South, where research is likely to focus on problem groups (child soldiers, child prostitutes or whatever is the current fashion for public concern or donor activity). In addition, researchers on these topics, particularly those commissioned by policy and programming agencies, show almost total ignorance of the new sociology of childhood and only a passing familiarity with children's rights. The picture gained from the available literature is of scattered, poorly-documented and non-comparable studies, which seldom involve children in systematic data collection, much less in planning research and designing research tools. Advocacy still largely relies on unsubstantiated information and/or ignores reliable research that does not agree with the ideological vision of campaigners. Thus, because it persists in using anecdotes and unreliable 'statistics', much advocacy cannot now be distinguished from the problems it addresses.

The Information Needs of the Committee on the Rights of the Child

The CRC Committee has made a particularly valuable contribution to the way the human rights of children are (or should be) perceived – through a lens of 'progressive achievement' rather than violation[2] – thus opening up possibilities for State Party reports to be transparent, rather than defensive. Yet the Concluding Observations of the Committee to all reports, from 1992 to the time of writing, include persistent requests to States Parties for better data for monitoring children's rights – data that are not beyond the wit of man (or woman) to devise, but that are a central absence in State Party reports. This continues to be the case despite a General Comment (2003), in which the Committee laid out the parameters for data collection and the development of indicators as 'an essential part of implementation':

- sufficient and reliable data;
- disaggregated data 'to enable identification of discrimination and/or disparities in the realisation of rights';
- data covering the whole period of childhood (up to 18 years);
- national coordination of data collection, evaluation and use in:
  - assessing progress in implementation
  - identifying problems
  - informing policy
- indicators and data covering all areas of the Convention;
- national distribution of comprehensive reports on the state of children's rights, including translations into minority languages and children-friendly versions.[3]

2   See Committee on the Rights of the Child, n/d. *Working Methods: Overview of the Working Methods of the Committee on the Rights of the Child.* IIB Constructive Dialogue: http://www2.ohchr.org/english/bodies/crc/workingmethods.htm [accessed 14 September 2010].

3   Committee on the Rights of the Child, 2003, *Convention on the Rights of the Child: General Comment No. 5 (2003) General Measures of Implementation of the Convention on the Rights of the Child (Arts. 4, 42 and 44, para. 6).* United Nations, Geneva, Committee

The final paragraph in this section of this General Comment is of vital importance:

> The Committee emphasizes that, in many cases, only children themselves are in a position to indicate whether their rights are being fully recognized and realized. Interviewing children and using children as researchers (with appropriate safeguards) is likely to be an important way of finding out, for example, to what extent their civil rights, including the crucial right set out in article 12, to have their views heard and given due consideration, are respected within the family, in schools and so on. (Committee on the Rights of the Child 2003, F paras 1–3)

Initial Government Reports to the CRC Committee (July 1992 – May 1993)

In the second half of 1992 and the first six months of 1993, the first 20 examples of an entirely new genre of text were published – the initial reports to the Committee of the Governments of Sweden, Bolivia, Sudan, Rwanda, Vietnam, Russian Federation, Egypt, Costa Rica, Peru, El Salvador, Indonesia, Mexico, Namibia, Pakistan, Belarus, Argentina, France, Colombia, Romania and Honduras. Despite the Guidelines provided by the Committee (1991)[4] the variety of information and style, as well as combination of insistence and absence in these first texts, were notable (Table 6.1). Structurally and stylistically, the reports fell into three groups:

- following the Committee Guidelines;
- following the Convention article-by-article;
- following a trajectory of their own (particularly Peru and Rwanda).

While it is tempting to comment on the paucity of information presented by the Governments of Rwanda and Peru, as well as on the fact that only two countries of the global North were represented in the first 20 reports, it is more interesting to examine and compare the texts on the basis of the issues that were emphasised (sometimes over-emphasised), and topics that were notable by their absence, in order to understand the state of global information on children at that early stage of CRC monitoring.

---

on the Rights of the Child, 34th session, 19 September–3 October 2003. CRC/GC/5, 27 November 2003.

4   Committee on the Rights of the Child, 1991. *General Guidelines Regarding the Form and Content of Initial Reports to be Submitted by States Parties under Article 44, Paragraph 1 (a), of the Convention.* Adopted by the Committee at its 22nd meeting (first session) on 15 October 1991. CRC/C/5, 30 October 1991. See http://www2.ohchr.org/english/bodies/crc/index.htm [accessed 9 December 2010].

Table 6.1   Comparison of the first 20 State Party reports received by the CRC Committee, July 1992 to May 1993

Government (in order of submission)	Submission date	Number of pages (+ indicates annexes)
Sweden	07.09.92	86
Bolivia	14.09.92	50
Sudan	29.09.92	15
Rwanda	30.09.92	7
Viet Nam	30.09.92	55
Russian Federation	16.10.92	70
Egypt	23.10.92	69
Costa Rica	28.10.92	64
Peru	28.10.92	17
El Salvador	03.11.92	57
Indonesia	17.11.92	20+
Mexico	15.12.92	50+
Namibia	21.12.92	94
Pakistan	25.01.93	43
Belarus	12.02.93	24
Argentina	17.03.93	46
France	08.04.93	76
Colombia	14.04.93	49
Romania	14.04.93	40
Honduras	11.05.93	60

Note: The texts considered here were printed and circulated by mail in hard copy in English by the (then) UN High Commission for Human Rights. Not all are available on the current United Nations Human Rights Council website. At the time they were circulated, not all were 'official versions'. Some, such as that of Sudan, were resubmitted (Sudan in 1993). However, for consistency, the analysis in Table 6.1 and associated text was made of the first versions to be made public. This analysis was first made public in the form of a conference presentation in 1994 (Ennew 1994).

Primarily, the states writing within this new genre represented themselves through constitutions, legislations or, not infrequently, the paternal concern for children manifested by the head of state (often stated in the text to be proven by attendance at the 1990 Summit for Children arranged by UNICEF in New York). The state itself was usually presented through information on geography and demography, or sometimes through history. Egypt wrote of the 'long history of child development starting in Pharonic days', although the form this took was unspecified, other than mentioning the fact that Pharaohs begot many children. Similarly, Indonesia found it necessary to begin with Java Man and to mention Marco Polo, although the role that either played in children's rights is unclear. Otherwise history was implicit in repetition of phrases such as 'before independence', encapsulating the moment when national history began. Many reports were either written against implied 'Western' standards that bear little relation to reality, or blamed current violations on colonial activities from around half a century earlier.

In general (and perhaps directed by the Guidance provided by the Committee) it appears that 'the state' wrote these reports, rather than any line ministry or person charged with the task, which means that the texts gave more information about the states than about their child denizens. It was not unusual for mention of children to be delayed until quite late in the text (page five of Argentina's 46 pages). Mexico was unusual in mentioning children in the first sentence, while Costa Rica was the only report in this first 20 to quote the actual words of a living child.

The logic of the nation-state system entailed (then as now) that data on stateless children formed a central absence in all reports. Some children simply do not exist in the global record and will thus be unable to access human rights throughout their lives. Even the population of children (less than 18 years of age) who did exist in civil registration systems could not be counted in the early 1990s, because census departments did not then disaggregate between adults and children other than in demographic quintiles. In addition, although children did (and do) appear in household-survey data, the unit of analysis tends to be the household/family.

Of course, it is impossible to ignore some individual authors, as in the case of the curiously detailed four-page record (around one third of the total text) from the National Commission of Culture and Arts in the Sudan report. This disproportionate contribution skewed the overall picture, beguiling the reader for a while with the notion that theatre, leisure and plastic arts opportunities provided by the government were the main occupations of Sudanese children – with the exception of delinquent children, data on whom also took up four pages.

Numerical information on juvenile delinquency was a common source of quantitative information presented in these initial reports, reflecting the lack of ability of states to penetrate and report on 'normal' childhoods taking place within the private or family sphere. The weaker a state's ability to investigate domestic activities, the more likely that a State Party report will contain numerical information *only* about children in state care – juvenile detention, orphanages and other institutions – or enrolled in formal education. Like health statistics, education was responsible for the majority of children-related data, although the vast array actually available was barely used to produce children-centred, age-related, gender-based or ethnic analysis (Ennew and Miljeteig 1996).

In some reports, national concerns that were current at the time affected the choice of data and topics. The government of France, for example, included long sections on reproductive technology, while Namibia concentrated a good deal of attention on refugees. In both cases, the data cited were not children-centred, nor did they have any direct bearing on the specific human rights of children. Likewise, even lists of legislation provided by States Parties in these reports referred largely to the human rights of adults, or of the whole population.

On the evidence of these 20 reports, in 1992/93, hard data on children appeared only to exist when the state, or a state apparatus, was *in loco parentis*. Even health data were surprisingly sparse, other than when children less than five years old died or were vaccinated. Despite much discussion of the ideal family, few data were presented about the families in which children actually lived; not even of the number of children – less than 18 years – in families or households. Almost no information was provided under Article 32 on the work children performed, particularly about children less than 10 years of age (much less the value they added to the Gross National Product), although an un-attributed number was frequently provided for street children.

The impossibly constructed category of 'street children' (Beazley 2003, Connolly and Ennew 1996, Glauser 1990) is not mentioned in any articles of the CRC, yet popped up repeatedly in odd locations, evidence of a global obsession that was at its height between 1979 and the mid 1990s. The fact that these children are generally conceptualised as 'outside childhood', because they are outside either family or institutional care (Ennew 1995), entails that they have no predetermined position in a State Party report, so that in 1992/93 they appeared variously under separation from parents, juvenile justice and economic exploitation, although more frequently under Article 36 (other forms of exploitation). 'Street children' were disproportionately focused on in some of these early reports from countries where their numbers were known to be relatively low, but strangely not mentioned at all in the Colombian report, despite worldwide association of that State Party with the existence of street children.

HIV and AIDS also took up a disproportionate amount of space (under Article 24) in several of the first 20 reports, although this did not then make epidemiological sense, even in Southern African countries. In such cases, the role of international civil society in the production of data on children was probably a major influence. To this day, State Party reports seem to include almost any data on children, simply because the data exist. Such data are frequently commissioned by international NGOs in response to donor fashions (in broad terms street children were overtaken as a donor obsession by child labour in the late 1990s, and by trafficking in the first decade of the twenty-first century). This tendency was also a feature of the civil society reports to the Committee, variously referred to over the years as 'NGO reports', 'alternative reports' or 'shadow reports'.

Country Reports Now

For a brief analysis of the state of the art in State Party reports now, the seven reports considered by the Committee on the Rights of the Child in its 54th session (May/June 2010) can be considered, along with the sections of the respective Concluding Observations related to data (Tables 6.2 and 6.3).

Table 6.2 Concluding observations and recommendations made about data in State Party reports considered by the CRC Committee in its 54th session (25 May to 11 June 2010)

State Party	Report	National data collection system		Concluding observations on data	
		Yes/No	Operational provisions, monitoring mechanisms, budget	Disaggregations	Other comments
Argentina	3rd and 4th	Yes	No	No	No systematic approach to data collection. Not all UNCRC areas covered
Belgium	3rd and 4th	No	No	Not mentioned	Fragmented data. Not all areas of UNCRC covered
Macedonia	2nd	No	No	Needed for gender, age, urban/rural	Statistics not related to 0–18 years. Not all areas of UNCRC covered
Grenada	2nd	No	No	No	Not all areas of UNCRC covered. Data not up-to-date
Japan	3rd	Not mentioned	Not mentioned	Not mentioned	Data do not relate to all areas of the UNCRC
Nigeria	3rd and 4th	Child Department of National Bureau of Statistics	National baseline survey	Not mentioned	Reminder about the 2003 General Comment on Implementation
Tunisia	3rd	Observatory; Annual National Reports	No	No	Not all areas of UNCRC covered. Reports descriptive rather than analytical

It is disappointing to note that these seven reports show little advance in the type and nature of data used in State Party reports. At the global level it seems that, 20 years after the adoption of the CRC, states have not moved on from the conventional 'object-of-concern' comfort zone of health, education and household statistics. Table 6.3 shows the glaring lack of information on 'vulnerable' children in the reports considered at the 54th session. The Committee recommends three States Parties (Argentina Grenada and Tunisia) to request technical help from UNICEF, with specific mention in the Recommendations to the Government of Tunisia of the UNICEF CHILD/INFO system. Yet the CHILD/INFO webpage refers to statistics that do not fall far outside the areas of health, education and household statistics.[5] Moreover, as Tables 6.2 and 6.3 demonstrate, the Committee does not seem to have a consistent and systematic approach to data. The lists of missing data on 'vulnerable children' (Table 6.3) do not always use the same terminology (for example referring in some observations to the 'juvenile justice system' and in others to 'children in conflict with the law'). These lists also underline the absence of data provided by States Parties on the rights of 'vulnerable' children (in itself a very imprecise term), which is often further emphasised by the list of research recommended throughout concluding observations and recommendations. Not one of the State Party reports examined in the 54th session contained information of children with disabilities. Meanwhile the Committee uses the defunct object-of-concern vocabulary of 'victims' when writing about abuse, exploitation and neglect but seems to have adopted one of the currently fashionable terms for street children ('children in street situations').

Thus it seems that between 1992 and 2010 there was little change in State Party reports, which continue to use data that sometimes have little bearing on children, let alone their human rights, as well as to include information on a limited range of the rights set out in the CRC. Above all, despite the General Comment of 2003, children have not been included in the data-collection, analysis and discussion processes. When children discover this, it can increase their sense that adults cannot be trusted. An example arose in a consultation with children on the CRC text and the Zimbabwe national report (1995) in Harare, organised by Save the Children Norway and Childwatch International, with children aged from 11 to 17 years. These children had not until then heard of the CRC but, including the youngest, proved themselves more than capable of passionate and rational discussion of the text, using neither 'games' nor a 'child-friendly' text. They expressed themselves astonished that there should have been a report from Zimbabwe that did not include the views of children, who had been neither consulted nor involved in data collection. 'It's a lie!' they declared; someone should tell the Committee members that the report they had received from Zimbabwe is unreliable.[6] It is worth remembering that human beings under 18 years of age were reported, in

---

5   http://www.childinfo.orgm [accessed 14 September 2010].

6   Personal notes from the Childwatch International Monitoring Children's Rights Project, 1993–98, data for the numbers of children less than 18 years of age were not

2008, to constitute 48 per cent of the total population of Zimbabwe in a paradox of democracy that affects many Sub-Saharan African nations.

Table 6.3   Information missing on child-protection issues, noted by the CRC Committee in concluding observations on the seven State Party reports considered in the 54th session (25 May to 11 June 2010)

State Party	Missing child-protection data
Argentina	Children with disabilities Children in the juvenile justice system Children in single-parent families Sexually-abused children Children in alternative care Children without parental care
Belgium	No systematic approach 'in particular to children in vulnerable situations' but no category mentioned by name
Macedonia	Child victims of abuse, neglect or ill-treatment Children with disabilities Refugee and asylum-seeking children Children in conflict with the law Working children Children in street situations
Grenada	Children with disabilities Children living in poverty Children in the juvenile justice system Children of single-parent families Victims of sexual abuse Institutionalised children
Japan	School-enrolment rates of children living in poverty Children with disabilities Non-Japanese children Violence and bullying in schools
Nigeria	Children deprived of family environment Refugees and internally-displaced children Children in conflict with the law Children with disabilities Single-parent families
Tunisia	Children living in rural areas Children with disabilities Children living in poverty Children in street situations Working children Child victims of sexual exploitation and abuse

available in 1997, which is why 2008 figures are quoted here: UNICEF, 2008: http://www. unicef.org/infobycountry/zimbabwe_statistics.html#68 [accessed 17 September 2010].

Since 1993, a few reports submitted to the Committee (especially the so-called 'shadow reports' from civil society) have included children's views. Children have also been members of national deputations to the CRC, particularly when associated with 'alternative' or 'shadow' reports. For example, on 11 June 2008, three members of *Draig Ffynci* (Funky Dragon, the permanent Children and Young People's Assembly for Wales) delivered a report, *Our Rights Our Story*,[7] to the Committee in Geneva as one of the submissions from the United Kingdom. This report had been researched and written by young people (including wide representation of children throughout Wales) with support from adult staff at *Draig Ffynci*, guided by social science professionals. Nevertheless, scientific data collected by children – or even collected from children – are generally notable by their absence. The inability of adults to provide realistic opportunities for children to express their opinions (rather than their 'voices') was summed up by 17-year-old Khairul Azri, a Malaysian delegate to the UN 'Special Session on Children', which took place in 2002:

> Adults miss the point. When is a child considered skilful enough to contribute and participate actively? If you do not give them the opportunity to participate, they will not acquire the skills. Give us the chance early and see how we fly. (UNICEF 2002: 1)

The UNICEF (2002) celebratory issue of the *State of the World's Children*, on participation and based largely on the Special Session experience, does not mention children collecting data (indeed does not mention data at all) but concentrates on their participation in meetings. In the Foreword, the then UN Secretary-General, Kofi Annan, praised children's 'passions, questions, fears, challenges, enthusiasm, optimism, ideas, hopes and dreams' during the meeting (Annan 2002), but paid scant attention to their knowledge and opinions.

The State of the World's Data on the State of the World's Children

With all their limitations, particularly with respect to child-protection issues, UNICEF country office five-year situation analyses provided continuous national records of children's lives in the last three decades of the twentieth century. Now that they have been largely (sub)merged into Common Country Reports, which use data provided by national offices of all United Nations agencies, information specific to children's rights is inadequately reported. The same is largely true of human rights in general. It also remains to be seen if CRC concerns will be relegated to concern with health and education within UN Human Rights Council Universal Periodic Reviews. This seems likely, because human rights experts tend to relegate children's rights to something akin to child welfare, partly because

---

7   http://www.funkydragon.org.uk/en/fe/page.asp?n1=1437&n2=2108&n3=2011) [accessed 17 September 2010].

child welfare organisations, which now tend to describe themselves as 'rights-based', do not engage in human rights issues beyond the CRC. A vivid example of this mutual misunderstanding occurred during a presentation on human rights violations in the conflict area South of Thailand, made in 2007 by the national office of one of the best-known international human rights organisations to a local children's rights organisation. The presenter failed to provide any information whatsoever about the violation of children's rights. When asked if such information could be provided, the speaker's response was that 'maybe some girls are raped by soldiers', although subsequent research did not reveal any such instances (personal notes 2007, UNICEF Thailand, 2008).

One reason why CHILD/INFO and other UNICEF data-gathering operations, such as the Multiple Indicator Cluster Survey (MICS), which is part of the CHILD/INFO system, have not moved much beyond health, education and demography since the CRC was adopted lies in the ambiguous relationship between UNICEF and children's rights. Although UNICEF is specifically mentioned, among UN specialised agencies, in Article 45a of the CRC as a source of expertise on national reporting – and referred to by name in the same respect within concluding observations – the data-collection and reporting mechanisms used by UNICEF do not cover the whole range of rights. The origin of this inattention rests in the lack of significant UNICEF involvement in the discussions around the drafting of the CRC (Detrick 1992). Throughout the 1980s, UNICEF focused on the Child Survival Revolution, urban poverty relief and Children in Especially Difficult Circumstances (CEDC) – especially street children in both the latter cases (Black 1996). UNICEF joined the children's rights debate somewhat reluctantly, starting with pressure from NGOs in 1985–86, and becoming involved (albeit with a child-survival-revolution perspective) in 1988, when submission to the United Nations General Assembly became inevitable (Black 1996). UNICEF then revealed its lack of understanding of human rights by locating children's rights within Public Affairs and seeking children's rights goals (goals being the key management tool of the then Executive Director, James Grant). Thus the first key goal was 'universal ratification' – using the UNICEF-organised World Summit for Children of 1990 to achieve this.

The World Summit, attended by 71 heads of state and government, together with 88 other senior officials mostly at ministerial level, adopted a Declaration on the Survival, Protection and Development of Children and a Plan of Action (UNICEF 1990) for implementing this. The Summit had consequences for data on children and their rights. Near-universal ratification within a rapid timeframe entailed that the CRC had monitoring 'teeth', producing a competitive reporting atmosphere, especially among States Parties in the global South. But the Summit goals limited the areas in which data were collected. As Table 6.4 shows, they missed out a wide range of rights, concentrating on survival and development (or 'provision') rights, but ignoring civil and political rights and paying lip service to protection. The first six goals only referred to Articles 6, 24 and 28 of the CRC, while two goals (b and f) reflected relevant aspects of adult human rights. It goes without saying that none of these goals have been met by 2010, even though they were largely repeated in the Millennium Development Goals of 2000.[8] The first Summit goals were related to existing indicators and information sets. In addition, the goal of a National Plan of Action (NPA) bamboozled States Parties into imagining that having an NPA fulfilled children's rights, obscuring (as the hasty ratifications at the Summit had already done) what the human rights of children actually entail. Thus the Summit goals acted as a drag on development of data on the full range of the human rights set out for children in the CRC text.

Table 6.4   Major goals of the 1990 World Summit for Children for Child Survival, Development and Protection in the 1990s

a. Between 1990 and the year 2000, reduction of infant and under-5 child mortality rate by one third or to 50 and 70 per 1,000 live births respectively, whichever is less
b. Between 1990 and the year 2000, reduction of maternal mortality rate by half
c. Between 1990 and the year 2000, reduction of severe and moderate malnutrition among under-5 children by half
d. Universal access to safe drinking water and to sanitary means of excreta disposal
e. By the year 2000, universal access to basic education and completion of primary education by at least 80 per cent of primary school-age children
f. Reduction of the adult illiteracy rate (the appropriate age group to be determined in each country) to at least half its 1990 level with emphasis on female literacy
g. Improved protection of children in especially difficult circumstances

Source: UNICEF (1990).

'Child Protection' Now Dominates the Field of Children's Rights

In 1990, a single vague goal (g) referred to 'CEDC' – a rag bag of issues, which can be linked roughly to CRC Articles 32–40 (now largely thought of as the 'protection articles'). On a visit to UNICEF HQ in 1993, I found 'children's rights' monitoring linked firmly and solely with CEDC, although the only CEDC indicator being contemplated was the number of children with (undefined) disabilities. This was suggested as a proxy indicator for all protection issues, on the assumption

---

8   http://www.un.org/millenniumgoals/ [accessed 17 September 2010].

that disabilities would reveal the rate of violation of child-protection rights. Unfortunately this ignored the fact that a large proportion of disabilities are due to congenital conditions or accidental injuries, rather than abuse, exploitation and even armed conflict (see for example, Phillippa 2005). Subsequently this particular indicator was never developed.

Nevertheless, by the twenty-first century, UNICEF had dedicated personnel for 'child protection', a classification that replaced the CEDC category on the suggestion of the CRC Committee.[9] Nevertheless, certain child-protection issues, such as child labour, commercial sexual exploitation of children, child soldiers, trafficking of (women and) children and, to a lesser extent than in the 1980s, street children, still dominate data collection on children's rights by organisations and academics working in the global South. Meanwhile, the understanding of the meaning of 'child protection' by UNICEF and most international non-governmental organisations – as protection from abuse, exploitation and violence – is not always shared by local civil society organisations. During analysis of data in rights-based research of Thai children's perceptions of child-protection issues after the 2004 Asian tsunami, it became clear that all Thai members of the research team classified children as 'protected' if they lived with two parents. This was subsequently corrected through awareness training on domestic violence and sexual abuse, which resulted in re-analysis of research data (UNICEF Thailand and Knowing Children 2007). Similarly, during a research evaluation of partner projects in Timor Leste, once again commissioned by UNICEF, it became clear that, far from thinking of child protection in terms of protection from abuse, exploitation and violence, local staff and grass-roots workers of partner organisations all conceptualised children's key protection needs as prevention of malnutrition and illiteracy. Given that health and education statistics corroborate the high prevalence of both malnutrition and illiteracy in this small nation, these could indeed be argued to be the main child-protection issues.[10]

Measurement and Children's Rights Data

One tendency within the data used for State Party reports is the dominance of the quantitative. Descriptive information is not especially useful within governance structures, where policies need to be justified and their impact measured using 'hard numbers'. Descriptive data are usually dismissed as 'merely qualitative', which is partly correct given that 'participatory research with children' so often lacks any kind of systematic data collection and analysis (see Chapter 7 in this

---

9   The revised policy on children in need of special protection measures (E/ICEF/1996/14) was endorsed by the Executive Board at its 1996 annual session (E/ICEF/1996/12/Rev.1, decision 1996/27).

10   Unpublished 2008 research evaluation for UNICEF Timor Leste. Child Protection Office, by Knowing Children.

volume). Yet the value of numerical data depends on conditions at the point of data collection. During a field trip in Vietnam in 1994, from capital city to commune level, taking in provincial and district statistical offices, for the Childwatch International Monitoring Children's Rights Project (Ennew and Miljeteig 1996) I found reason to doubt the widely-used low-birth-weight indicator of 250 grammes. From Hanoi to district level, I was assured that if better computers were provided, better statistics could be produced. At commune level, however, I found that the health workers who provided the data to the statistical offices lacked a set of scales to weigh the babies. Decisions about whether or not the newborns could be categorised as 'low birth weight' were made on the basis of a health-worker's judgement while holding the baby – a factor affecting national (and international) statistics that I suspect is not confined to Vietnam.

Definitions

Low birth weight, malnutrition and school enrolment rates, like most popular health and education indicators, have exact operational definitions, which makes it possible to monitor the incidence over time. But 'child-protection' topics, such as child labour, do not have agreed operational definitions. Despite the attempts of the International Labour Organisation to provide a definition of child labour in ILO Convention 182 on the 'worst forms' of child labour (Ennew, Myers and Plateau 2005), debates about the definition have not abated, partly because they are so frequently high-jacked by political agendas based on the spurious cultural-relativity argument that 'child work is necessary in our country because we are so poor'. Preventative measures are thus claimed to be an imposition from 'the West' where child labour is claimed to be 'eliminated' (Fyfe 1989). Similarly, child sexual exploitation is alleged in almost all published research to be unmeasurable because it is a hidden activity that cannot be researched (Ennew et al. 1996).

Anything can be measured – as long as it is adequately described (Ennew et al. 1996). It is not necessary to define child labour repeatedly to meet country cultural definitions (which effectively leaves exploitation unchecked). Nor is it necessary to limit the operational definition of child labour to trivial numbers, as in the ILO definition:

> To be counted as economically active ... a person must have worked for pay, profit, family gain, or for own final consumption, for at least one hour on any day during the preceding seven days (one week). (Ashagrie 1998)

Just to confuse the issue, this differs from the MICS definition: 'Children between the ages of five and 14 years, paid or unpaid, working at least four hours a day'.[11] Child labour is virtually the only child-protection issue included in CHILD/INFO,

---

11   http://www.childinfo.org/files/MICS4_List_of_Indicators_v2.1__20100407.doc [accessed 17 September 2010].

and not for all countries. Three indicators are supplied in the 2009–2011 MICS4 instructions, two of which relate to school attendance (Table 6.5).

Table 6.5   MICS 4 child labour indicators

Indicator	Description
Child labour	Number of children age 5–14 years who are involved in child labour
School attendance among child labourers	Number of children age 5–14 years who are involved in child labour and are currently attending school
Child labour among students	Number of children age 5–14 years who are involved in child labour and are currently attending school

Source: http://www.childinfo.org/files/MICS4_List_of_Indicators_v2.1__20100407.doc (accessed 17 September 2010).

Table 6.6   Six 'dimensions' for ranking 40 indicators of well-being in 'rich nations'

'Dimension'	Topics covered by indicators in this 'dimension'
Material well-being	Adult caretakers' jobs and income
Health and safety	Health care and injuries
Education	Schooling (not including quality indicators)
Family relationships	Family structure (not including indicators of emotional functioning)
Behaviours and risks	Adult measures of problem behaviours 'sex and drugs and rock and roll'
Young people's own subjective sense of well-being	According to adult measures of three (adult selected) criteria: Health rating Liking school Life satisfaction scale

Source: UNICEF (2007).

While debates about what is and what is not child labour rumble on, one of the most disturbing of current definitional tendencies in international work with children also reveals a potential trajectory away from the human rights of children. International civil society and intergovernmental organisations are currently exercising their collective intellect (although far from collectively or consensually) on defining 'well-being', a 'concept' that seems to be rapidly overtaking rights as the driving force of international programming for children. At times it seems as if strategists in international organisations working for children have sat around a table and agreed that 'Rights are "so last-century"'.

Organisational definitions of well-being differ, other than being uniformly vague. For example, UNICEF's (2007) definition of well-being in rich nations lists six 'dimensions', which are used to rank a total of 40 indicators (Table 6.6).

The implication of the final 'dimension' in Table 6.6 is that adults can only conceive of children's sense of well-being along a set of criteria dominated by the 'correct' spheres for children (such as school), and measured using adult assumptions and rating scales. The idea that children might know best about their own lives and especially about their 'subjective' feelings never arises in this report. Moreover, the choice of subjective well-being topics reveals that they have little to do with the full range of children's rights. Notable omissions are the right to have opinions taken seriously (Article 12), to be raised in an atmosphere of brotherly love and peace (Article 29) and review of placement (Article 25). Well-being is clearly a welfare notion, related to the construction of children as objects of concern, and not – on this evidence – considering children outside family care. This methodological stance can only result in data-collection methods that are adult-oriented, in research that produces data *on* or *about* children, without their participation (see Chapter 7 in this volume). The list of dimensions in Table 6.6 fails to note aspects of immense importance to children in all countries, whether 'rich' or 'poor', such as child work and other forms of exploitation, social justice and violence against children. Although bullying by other children appears in the report, domestic violence is not included within the dimension of 'family relationships' and there is no mention of violence by teachers in schools

The report claims that its 'concept of well-being' is guided by the CRC, which is surprising because the CRC text mentions well-being only in terms of factors that promote it (Preamble, Article 3(2) and Article 40 (3b)), or are injurious to it (Article 9(4) and Article 17 (e)). Indeed, mentioning a term does not amount to a definition of a concept. Furthermore, the report claims that 'The implied definition of child well-being that permeates this report is one that will also correspond to the views and experience of a wide public' (UNICEF 2007: 2–3). But an implication, also, does not amount to a definition, nor is an unspecified 'wide public' a valid citation or justification. Despite the extensive use of quantitative data and calculations, this report cannot be described as scientific because it does not even define its key term.

Monitoring Children's Rights is Not Rocket Science

A vast amount of data that could be collected about children's lives – time budgets, economic activities, domestic duties and so forth – tend not to exist, but could be collected using relatively simple research tools and analysis. Yet perhaps the greatest puzzle in the history of monitoring children's rights is that so little attention has been paid to rights-based recalculations of existing national statistical data: disaggregation and children-centred statistics. Once again, the scientific processes are already known and, indeed, have been demonstrated by non-governmental organisations and researchers on limited budgets (Ennew 1999, Saporiti 1994, Kibel et al. 2010).

Disaggregation

As already emphasised in this chapter, Concluding Observations on State Party reports almost routinely mention the need for accurate, disaggregated data. A dominant feature of both national and international statistics on children is that they almost always use aggregated national data, which rank countries with respect to 'performance' on overall goals, rather than examining disaggregated data that could indicate failures to fulfil the rights of specific groups of children within a nation. Children thus tend to be a statistically undifferentiated category, rarely disaggregated by gender and even less frequently by characteristics such as ethnicity, caste, religion, by 'evolving capacities' or sexual development. Un-disaggregated national data, such as the statistics reported in the annual UNICEF publication *The State of the World's Children*, are only useful for comparing achievements in children's rights between nations, and cannot be used to monitor children's rights in specific States Parties.

Rights-based data must, necessarily, be disaggregated in order to show which group, or groups, of people have their rights violated or not achieved. For example, the development of nations is commonly ranked according to the national infant mortality rate (IMR, or number of children, per 1,000 born alive, who survive to their fifth birthday),[12] which is a relatively accurate measure of the health and life chances of children under the age of 60 months. IMR can be used to track not only national development but also the impacts of various health-promoting interventions. But they are not usually disaggregated to show (for instance):

- if girls die more frequently than boys before they reach their fifth birthday;
- if children in rural areas die more frequently than children in towns;
- if proportionately more ethnic-group newborns fail to survive to the age of 60 months.

IMR is also not sensitive to the unknown number of children who do not appear on national records because their existence is not recorded in a civil registration system.

---

12   http://hdr.undp.org/en/reports/global/ [accessed 9 December 2010].

One disaggregation that almost never appears is age, in the sense of comparisons between age groups within childhood, even though various intra-state bodies do break down 0–18-years statistics into briefer divisions, such as the differentiation of early-childhood health statistics into under 12 months, under 24 months and under 60 months. Yet, age disaggregation can reveal crucial points for intervention, such as the rise in malnourishment among girls that occurs in some countries after the customary age for weaning. Likewise it could be useful to break down school attendance and drop-out rates by year of age between seven and 12 years, as well as by gender. Reports of school attendance tend to concentrate on a supposed universal violation of the right of girls to education. However, boys in more disadvantaged social groups often drop out earlier than girls, because there are labour-market opportunities for young boys, whereas girls may continue in school for some years more in spite of a heavy load of household chores, because there are few labour-market openings available or considered appropriate (Ennew and Young 1981, Ennew 1994). The relevant raw data for such disaggregations usually do exist, but are neither perceived as, nor calculated to develop, rights-based indicators.

Children-centred Statistics

The claim that children are discriminated against in statistics is a major innovation of academic child research, although effectively ignored by children's-rights monitoring (Qvortrup 1991, Saporiti 1994). According to this approach, because children are discriminated against in society they are discriminated against in statistics. National statistics discriminate against children – who appear as mere attributes of households, schools and other adult institutions (Qvortrup 1991). In most childhood data, the unit of analysis is the family, while the asymmetric relations that define children out of social life are taken for granted. Children are studied with respect to childhood institutions, such as the school or the family, but not with respect to the system of production or the labour market. Yet, as the annual 'Child Gauge' of the Children's Institute of the University of Cape Town clearly demonstrates, children-centred statistics can be calculated across many areas of children's rights, using existing statistics and disaggregated according to geographical region.[13]

The Consequences for Monitoring Children's Rights

Thus monitoring children's rights effectively carries the requirement to make significant qualitative changes at the level of surveys and also to carry out secondary analysis of existing material. If statistics are neither disaggregated nor

---

13   See for example, M. Kibel, L. Lake, P. Pendlebury and C. Smith (eds), 2010, *South African Child Gauge 2009/2010*, Children's Institute, University of Cape Town. Available at: http://www.ci.org.za/index.php?option=com_content&view=article&id=754&Itemid=2 09 [accessed 9 December 2010].

children-centred, it is not possible to measure the human rights of children. While the processes are not rocket science, it appears that most governments would prefer to allocate budgets to developing rockets and other weapons of war, in the name of national security, rather than to finding out about, and securing the fulfilment of, the rights of child citizens.

Conclusions: Consequences for Children of Being Improperly Researched

In my judgement, between the two propositions with which I began: 'Social research has improved the human rights of children independent of the CRC' and 'CRC reporting has improved data about children' I would suggested that 'the jury is out'. There has been very little progress in improving data over the two decades since the CRC came in to force. Some changes in research related to children can be observed, but the most notable feature is that these take place in disconnected discourses, and are not translated to the level of integrated practice. It cannot be argued either that academic research has affected CRC reporting, or vice versa.

The consequences of children being improperly researched are twofold, affecting both children's lives and the lives of adult researchers. From the child perspective the effects of poor research are that nothing happens to improve their lives, or that worse things happen when poor data are used as the basis of policy and programming. Disparities are enhanced and children, families and communities lose faith in both policy and research. On the other hand, the careers, jobs and status of adult researchers may be improved, while organisations are able to jockey for position in public acclaim and donor provision.

The greatest violation of children's rights is that we do not know enough about their lives or care enough to find out more. The poorest record in children's rights continues to be data on the children whose rights are most brutally violated through abuse, exploitation and violence. Money is spent on high salaries and expensive office space for men and women who play with numbers and formulae, staring at screens and arguing about definitions, rather than on scales for health workers, much less training for civil-registration officials whose culturally-blind eyes stare millions of stateless children out of existence – and out of entitlement to rights. Worst of all, children are not included as partners in the process of systematic curiosity, which might lead to policies and programmes that secure rights for all children, everywhere. Even more scandalous is that the technology and methods to collect and use relevant data exist, and are not used. The situation has not changed appreciably since UNICEF published the following statement in 1987:

> ... if the principle of protecting the most vulnerable is to be taken seriously, then it must be a process which can be monitored and measured. And the fact is that whereas most nations can and do produce up-to-date quarterly statistics on the health of their economies, few nations can produce even annual statistics on the health of their children. This failure to monitor the effects of economic and

social changes on the most vulnerable, and particularly on the growing minds and bodies of young children is both a cause and a symptom of the lack of political priority afforded to this task. Yet there could be no more important test for any government than the test of whether or not it is protecting the nation's vulnerable and whether or not it is protecting the nation's future – and its children are both. ...

Indeed, we know far more about changes in the weather or in viewing figures for television shows, or in consumer preferences and the monthly sales of video recorders, than we do about changes in the nutritional health of the under-fives. (UNICEF 1987: 30–31)

Thus it seems that the problem of inadequate data on children has been recognised for over two decades. And for over two decades we have had the tools for providing the solution. Why are scientific, rights-based data on children still as notably and universally elusive when the CRC is notably and universally ratified? There seems little point to the welter of State Party reports if they do not contain adequate information for monitoring and children, especially the most vulnerable, remain lost in statistics.

References

References to State Party reports to the Committee on the Rights of the Child can be retrieved from the Treaty Bodies Data Base of the UN Human Rights Council at http://tb.ohchr.org/default.aspx. References to some early reports are to the first (unofficial) versions distributed in hard copy by the (then) High Commission for Human Rights in 1992–93.

Alston, P. 1994. *The Best Interests of the Child: Reconciling Culture and Human Rights*. Florence, UNICEF and Oxford, Clarendon Press.

An'Naim, A.A. 2002. *Cultural Transformation and Human Rights in Africa*. London: Zed Books.

Anderson, B. 1991. *Imagined Communities: Reflections on the Origin and Spread of Nationalism*, 2nd edition. New York: New Left Books (Verso).

Annan, K.A. 2002. Foreword to UNICEF, *State of the World's Children 2003*. New York: UNICEF.

Aptekar, L. 1988. *Street Children of Cali*. Durham, NC: Duke University Press.

Aries, P. 1962. *Centuries of Childhood*. New York: Vintage Books.

Ashagrie, K. 1998. *Statistics on Working Children in Brief*. Geneva: ILO.

Bauer, J.R. and Bell, D.A. (eds). 1999. *The East Asian Challenge for Human Rights*. Cambridge, Cambridge University Press.

Beazley, H. 2003. Voices from the margins: street children's subcultures in Indonesia. *Children's Geographies*, 1(2) (August), 181–20.

Black, M. 1996. *Children First: The Story of UNICEF, Past and Present*. Oxford: Oxford University Press.

Bolin, I. 2006. *Growing Up in a Culture of Respect: Child Rearing in Highland Peru*. Austin, TX: University of Texas Press.

Boyden, J. 1990. Childhood and the policy makers: a comparative perspective on the globalisation of childhood, in A. Jones and A. Prout (eds), *Constructing and Reconstructing Childhood*. London: Falmer Press, pp. 184–215.

Brembeck, H., Johansson, B. and Kampmann, J. (eds). 2004. *Beyond the Competent Child: Exploring Contemporary Childhoods in the Nordic Welfare Societies*. Roskilde: Roskilde University Press.

Broch, H.B. 1990. *Growing Up Agreeably: Bonerate Childhood Observed*. Honolulu: University of Hawai'i Press.

Burr, R. 2006. *Vietnam's Children in a Changing World*. New Brunswick, NJ: Rutgers University Press.

Butler-Sloss, E. 1988. *Report of the Inquiry into Child Abuse in Cleveland 1987*. London: HM Stationery Office.

Connolly, M. and Ennew, J. 1996. Introduction: children out of place, *Childhood*, 3(2), 131–45.

Detrick, S. (ed.). 1992. *The United Nations Convention on the Rights of the Child: A Guide to the Traveaux Préparatoires*. Dordrecht, London and Boston, MA: Martinus Nijhoff.

Donzelot, J. 1979. *The Policing of Families*. New York: Random House.

Durkheim, E. 1895. *Les règles de la méthode sociologique*. Paris: F. Alcan.

Ennew, J. 1994. What is a country report? A symptomatic reading of the first 20 reports to the Committee on the Rights of the Child, Presentation to the European Conference on Monitoring Children's Rights, Children's Rights Centre, University of Ghent, Belgium, 11–14 December 1994.

——. 1995. Outside childhood: street children's rights, in B. Franklin (ed.), *The Handbook of Children's Rights: Comparative Policy and Practice*. London: Routledge, pp. 201–15.

——. 1999. *Monitoring Children's Rights*. Oslo: Childwatch International.

Ennew, J., Gopal, K., Heeran, J. and Montgomery, H. 1996. *Children and Prostitution: How Can We Measure and Monitor the Commercial and Sexual Exploitation of Children? Literature Review and Annotated Bibliography*, 2nd edition. Oslo: Childwatch International and Cambridge: Centre for Family Research.

Ennew, J. and Miljeteig, P. 1996. Indicators of children's rights: progress report on a project, *International Journal of Children's Rights*, 4, 213–36.

Ennew, J., Myers, W.M. and Plateau, D.P. 2005. Defining child labor as if human rights really matter, in B.H. Weston (ed.), *Child Labor and Human Rights: Making Children Matter*. London and Boulder, CO: Lynne Rienner, pp. 27–54.

Ennew, J. and Young, P. 1981. *Child Labour in Jamaica: A General Review*. London: Anti-Slavery Society.

Fyfe, A. 1989. *Child Labour*. Cambridge: Polity Press.

Glauser, B. 1990. Street children: deconstructing a construct. In A. James and A. Prout (eds), *Constructing and Reconstructing Childhood*. London: Falmer Press, pp. 136–56.

Hecht, T. 1998. *At Home in the Street: Street Children of North East Brazil*. Cambridge: Cambridge University Press.

James, A. and Prout, A. (eds). 1990. *Constructing and Reconstructing Childhood*. London: Falmer Press.

Kibel, M., Lake, L., Pendlebury, P. and Smith, C. (eds). 2010. *South African Child Gauge 2009/2010*.Cape Town: Children's Institute, University of Cape Town.

La Fontaine, J.S. (ed.). 1978. *Sex and Age as Principles of Social Differentiation*. ASA Monograph No. 17. London, New York and San Francisco, CA: Academic Press.

Liebel, M. 2008. Child-led research with working children. Paper presented to Child and Youth Research in the 21st Century: A Critical Appraisal, 28–29 May, 2008, European University Cyprus, Nicosia, Cyprus.

Mead, M. 1928. *Coming of Age in Samoa*. New York William Morrow.

——. 1930. *Growing up in New Guinea*. New York: William Morrow.

Meyer, P. 1984. *The Child and the State: The Intervention of the State in Family Life*. Cambridge: Cambridge University Press.

Montgomery, H. 2009. *An Introduction to Childhood: Anthropological Perspectives on Children's Lives*. Chichester: Wiley Blackwell.

Ncube, W.N. (ed.). 1998. *Law, Culture, Tradition and Children's Rights in Eastern and Southern Africa*. Farnham: Ashgate Dartmouth.

Phillippa, T. 2005. Poverty reduction and development in Cambodia: enabling disabled people to play a role. Available at: http://www.disabilitykar.net/pdfs/cambodia.pdf [accessed 22 January 2010].

Platt, A.M. 1969. *Child Savers: The Invention of Delinquency*. Chicago, IL: University of Chicago Press.

Qvortrup, J. 1991. *Childhood as a Social Phenomenon*, 2nd edition. Eurosocial Report 36/0. Vienna: European Centre for Social Welfare, Policy and Research.

Saporiti, A. 1994. A methodology for making children count, in J. Qvortrup, M. Bardy, G. Sgritta, and H. Wintersberger, *Childhood Matters: Social Theory, Practice and Politics*. Aldershot and Brookfield, VT, Hong Kong, Singapore and Sidney: Avebury.

Schweber, L. 2001. Manipulation and population statistics in nineteenth-century France and England, *Social Research*. Available at: http://findarticles.com/p/articles/mi_m2267/is_2_68/ai_77187774/ [accessed 9 December 2010].

Twum-Danso, A. 2009. The Convention on the Rights of the Child: turning international law into reality, in H. Montgomery and M. Kellet (eds), *Children and Young People's Worlds: Developing Frameworks for Integrated Practice*. Bristol: Policy Press.

UNICEF. 1987. *State of the World's Children, 1988*. Oxford: UNICEF.

——. 1990. *Plan of Action for Implementing the Declaration of the World Summit for Children*. Available at: http://www.unicef.org/wsc/goals.htm#Major [accessed 20 July 2010].

——. 2002. *State of the World's Children 2003*. New York: UNICEF.

——. 2007. *Child Poverty in Perspective: An Overview of Child Well-being in Rich Countries: A Comprehensive Assessment of the Lives and Well-being of Children and Adolescents in the Economically Advanced Nations*. Florence: UNICEF.

UNICEF Thailand. 2008. *Everyday Fears: A Study of Children's Perceptions of Living in the Southern Border Areas of Thailand*. Bangkok: UNICEF Thailand.

UNICEF Thailand and Knowing Children. 2007. Children's perceptions of post-tsunami child-protection issues in six provinces. Unpublished report. Bangkok: UNICEF Thailand.

Zelizer, V.A. 1994. *Pricing the Priceless Child: The Changing Social Value of Children*, 2nd edition. Princeton, NJ: Princeton University Press.

Chapter 7

How are the Human Rights of Children Related to Research Methodology?

Harriot Beazley, Sharon Bessell, Judith Ennew and Roxana Waterson

Introduction

Adopted unanimously by the United Nations General Assembly in 1989, the CRC has now entered its third decade. By any cultural or legal yardstick, it has 'come of age'. In this chapter, we ask what human rights mean for research with children. It is notable that even the preposition has changed – from *on* or *about*, to *with*. Research *on* and *about* children has a long, pre-rights history in education, psychology and history, being not only the impetus for scholarly debate, but also highly influential in shaping everything from public policies about children and families to recommended parenting styles and commercial marketing. Yet, both from a human rights perspective and within social sciences, the history of research on children is vexed. Children have usually been objects of research, with data collection aiming to advance a theoretical or policy perspective, rather than positioning children as research participants who are subjects of human rights.

In this chapter, we begin by documenting the emergence of the idea of rights-based research with children, outlining the methodology that underpins the approach. We argue that rights-based research ensures that both the process of research *and* the results are ethical, scientifically robust and respectful of children.

Rights-based Research with Children: The Emergence of an Idea

The research approach discussed in this chapter did not begin with the CRC, nor with earlier Declarations of the Rights of the Child adopted by the League of Nations and the United Nations. The origins were in the same year in which the drafting of the CRC was agreed by the international community (1979 being the UN International Year of the Child ['IYC']). In addition, the research that began the process was carried out for the IYC, having its roots in concern for the rights of child workers that was being expressed by UN specialist agencies (particularly the International Labour Organisation), the UN Human Rights Commission (through the Working Group on Slavery) and two of the many non-governmental human rights organisations that motivated and supported the IYC – Ford Foundation and

Anti-Slavery International (then the Anti-Slavery Society). The research on child labour that was commissioned by these two organisations had three characteristics that still typify rights-based research with children: children (in Jamaica) were asked to share their own opinions and experiences, questionnaires and interviews were not used with children, and 'qualitative' material from essays and drawings were analysed using the (pre-Windows version) Statistical Package for the Social Sciences, to produce statistical results from large samples (Ennew and Young 1982). This approach was later used successfully in other contexts, most notably in Peru (Ennew 1986) and the United Kingdom (Morrow 1999), inspired in part by similar innovations in South Africa (Swart 1990).

Parallel to this development, the drafting process for the CRC stimulated a more general discussion on what has, for three decades, been referred to as 'children's participation' (although better thought of as children's citizenship: Beers, Invernizzi and Milne 2006). Meanwhile, field-based practice in human geography, as well as in programming with street and working children, extended experience and skills in consulting with children (see for example Hart 1997, Cussianovich and Marquez 2002, Ratna and Reddy 2002, Liebel 2008). At the same time, academics, historians and social scientists were developing theories of 'childhood' as well as the methodological construction of 'child' as a social agent worthy of study in its own right (see for example James and Prout 1992). Nevertheless, these advances have not necessarily led to innovations in either methods or ethics for research with children (Ennew and Morrow 2002).

The impetus for the development of rights-based research with children was the submission of the first reports to the CRC Committee in 1992, and the Committee's realisation that available data, particularly information that fell outside the conventional health-education-psychology-demography nexus, were insufficient for monitoring the CRC. This kick-started regular meetings of an informal grouping of inter-governmental and non-governmental organisations, usually referred to by its members as 'The London Process'.[1] One outcome was a set of activities over a five-year period, which included analysing the methods that had been used to collect existing data (Ennew 1993, Ennew and Milne 1996), the development and testing of children-centred methods of testing data, as well as new ethical approaches, through experimental research that built the capacity both of the principal research designers and the researchers themselves, most of whom were grass-roots workers in local programmes (Boyden and Ennew 1997).

At that stage, this research could have been described as rights-motivated, rather than rights-based, and the data collected were principally 'qualitative' extensions of Participatory Action Research (PAR) techniques already developed for adults

---

1   The meetings were hosted by Save the Children UK in their London offices and principally attended by staff of Save the Children Sweden (Rädda Barnen), UNICEF (New York and Geneva), members of the Committee on the Rights of the Child, Defence for Children International, Childwatch International and two consultants (Jo Boyden and Judith Ennew).

(see Johnson, Hill and Ivan-Smith 1995). National studies, sponsored by UNICEF in Tanzania, Kenya, Bosnia and Herzegovina and Indonesia (Ahmed et al. 1999, Akunga et al. 2001, Robinson 2000, Čehajić et al. 2003, Hastadewi et al. 2004, and Setyowati et al. 2004) added and further developed the earlier qualitative-to-quantitative approach, through systematic use of PAR techniques, so that statistics could be developed for use by government and civil-society planners (Eversole 2009). In the first decade of the twenty-first century a number of manuals and research reports began to refer to this 'systematic curiosity' (Liebel 2010) as the 'rights-based approach to research with children' (Bangyai, Ennew and Noonsup 2009, Beazley et al. 2006, Beazley et al. 2009, Beazley and Alhadad 2008, Ennew and Plateau 2004, Ennew and Abebe 2010, RWG-CL 2003, UNICEF Thailand 2008).

Thus, two decades after the CRC came into force, the principle that children have the right to be properly researched has been well tested in a range of contexts. The resulting approach has five key characteristics. First, it is genuinely respectful of children as partners in research. Children's participation in research must be meaningful on their own terms, rather than on those dictated by researchers or by the strictures of funding arrangements. Second, this approach places ethics at the heart of research in practical and meaningful ways – children must engage in research voluntarily and must not be exploited through the research process. Third, research must be scientifically valid; data must be collected systematically using methods that can be justified and replicated. Fourth, analysis must be robust, where possible combining both statistical and descriptive techniques. Finally, like PAR and similar approaches, rights-based research prioritises local knowledge and expertise to produce insightful information on children's own experiences and opinions. Through the rights-based techniques of developing robust statistical results from qualitative materials, policy makers and programme planners can confidently use the information for planning and monitoring.

The CRC and Rights-based Research with Children

Although rights are indivisible, the rights-based approach to research with children is based on an interpretation of four articles of the CRC:

- Article 3.3: Children have the right to expect the highest possible standards of services from professionals who work with them – which implies high-quality, scientific research.
- Article 12: Children have the right to express their opinions in matters concerning them.
- Article 13: Children have the right to express themselves in any way they wish – not limited to the verbal expressions used by adults.
- Article 36: Children have the right to be protected from all forms of exploitation, including being exploited through research processes and through the dissemination of information (Ennew and Plateau 2004).

Children's Participation and Freedom of Expression in Research

Article 12, often presented (not entirely accurately) as entitling children to the right to 'participate', is perhaps the most controversial, most influential and most discussed article of the CRC (Beers, Invernizzi and Milne 2006). It is not, of course, an innovation because, as human beings, children have had the right to participate since the Universal Declaration of Human Rights in 1948. Yet the CRC drew attention to this right for human beings who are denied franchise on grounds of age (Franklin 2002), and emphasised the importance of the right of children to express opinions on matters concerning them. Much of the attention given to Article 12 results from the fact that children so rarely have the opportunity to do this. Nevertheless, there has, over the past two decades, been an ideational shift towards recognising the value of children's views (see Bessell 2009c), although there remains, as Badham points out, 'a gap between the high tide of the rhetoric of participation and the low tide of effective delivery of improved services' (Badham 2004: 153). The rhetoric of participation has frequently been put into practice as 'consulting with children' in adult-organised, policy-related events (Beers, Invernizzi and Milne, 2006). Within research, this often results in the collection of drawings, or children's 'voices', or unreferenced stories or 'mini case studies' about individual children – but not in the systematic analysis of children's perspectives, experiences or priorities (Beazley et al. 2006). Rights-based research with children insists that children should be able to express their opinions and contribute their knowledge and experiences alongside those of adults.

Freedom of expression (Article 13 CRC) is also a fundamental human right, the innovation in the CRC being that children are entitled to express their views in any way they wish, using whatever medium they prefer. Article 13 is thus an essential counterpart to Article 12, obliging researchers to consider carefully how they will implement their research questions in ways that ensure children understand, feel comfortable and are able to express themselves freely. The focus on 'listening to children's voices' in the past two decades, in academia, policy and programming, has often resulted in children being asked directly about topics they may not wish to discuss, or have not previously considered (or do not wish to consider), using words they may not understand, and in an environment that is unfamiliar. In such circumstances, children are 'consulted' but their rights are not respected. Moreover, the way in which they are consulted may render them re-traumatised, uncomfortable, fearful, threatened – or simply bored. Article 13 obliges researchers to adopt methods that are genuinely 'children-friendly'. It follows that such methods cannot be developed, used or evaluated independently of children. As partners in research, children should share in control of the methods used, the questions that are asked of them (and of adults), the way those questions are asked, as well as in the analysis and dissemination of results (Liebel 2010).

Methodology and Methods

At the heart of the right to be properly researched is Article 3 of the CRC: the right to the highest possible professional standards, which obliges those who work with children to ensure that professional standards are established and implemented – a principle that should be extended to include research activities. Rigorous, scientific method must be applied in research with children, especially if results are to be used in programmes designed in 'the best interests' of children (Article 3a, CRC). This is linked to the implication of Article 13 that appropriate, children-friendly methods are required to facilitate children's freedom of expression.

Yet, as Bessell (2009a) has pointed out, data collection techniques, while important, are 'alone incapable of facilitating children's positive involvement in research' (Bessell 2009a: 17). Appropriate, children-friendly methods are only one dimension of an overall methodology that posits children as bearers of human rights. Inappropriate methods undermine attempts to use a rights-based approach. The history of research with children over more than a century is awash with methods that silenced children or led to questionable results. For many decades, research on children, particularly that carried out within the discipline of developmental psychology, was (and often remains) dominated by the observation of children, often in environments unfamiliar to them, or by testing children without explanation of what researchers were seeking. Urie Bronfenbrenner, who was a pioneer within the 'ecological' approach to human development – which insists on the importance of real social contexts – wryly commented that his colleagues' laboratory work with children could best be described as 'the science of the strange behaviour of children in strange situations with strange adults for the briefest possible periods of time' (Bronfenbrenner 1979: 19). Such methods necessarily render children passive within the research process, and provide little scope for children to share and reflect on their own perspectives.

Children's Agency and Child Protection in Research

Article 36 entitles children to protection from all forms of exploitation, which should be interpreted as including exploitation through research. The spirit of Articles 3.3 and 36 obliges researchers to avoid 'extractive research', which has occurred most commonly in the past in countries of the global South, with researchers (usually from the global North) mining for data without considering how results can be communicated back to participants and their communities, let alone used for their benefit. Yet, historically, research with children has focused on the results, describing methodology and method only as means to an end. Articles 3.3 and 36 together oblige researchers to expand their focus, so that the emphasis on results is complemented by an equal emphasis on the manner in which research is conducted.

On its own (as well as in combination with other 'protection' articles in the CRC), Article 36 points to the necessity for revising the way key ethical principles

– 'do no harm', voluntary participation and confidentiality – have been, and are, largely ignored in research with children, because their agency in research has so often been handed over to parents, guardians and teachers, while children remain trapped as objects in the frameworks of bio- and psycho-ethics. Handing over agency to children, especially in societies where their agency is strongly limited by custom, is one of the challenges rights-based research has to meet. Cultural rules of seniority affect access to children worldwide. The idea of seeking informed consent from children – a fundamental concept within rights-based research – does not always sit easily with local practices embedded in age-based hierarchies whereby children (and many adults) are rarely asked for their individual perspectives (Abebe 2009). Negotiating seniority rules not only requires an understanding and appreciation of local norms, but may also consume considerable time. In addition, intergenerational hierarchies are complicated by gender and marital and reproductive status, as well as by politico-economic statuses such as class (Abebe 2009, Twum-Danso 2009, Jabeen 2009).

Research ethics are thus a common preoccupation for those who research with children and young people. By this we do not mean the commonplace concerns of university ethics committees but the ethical dilemmas of working with children, particularly those who are in some way vulnerable. We shall return to this topic in the final section of this chapter.

Constructing Children within Research

Rights-based methodology demands that researchers consciously confront the assumptions held about children. As Alderson and Morrow (2004: 22) have argued, we 'cannot avoid holding beliefs or theories about what children are and ought to be like'. These beliefs shape, and potentially undermine, the nature of our research with children (Bessell 2009a). Rights-based research requires us to examine the ways in which children and their worlds are represented, both in research and in both global and local cultures. We are not suggesting that researchers should engage in endless debate about the ways in which childhood is constructed in different societies, across time, culture and class. Rather than becoming preoccupied with myths of 'the discovery of childhood', we are sympathetic to the 'straightforward assertion that children live real childhoods rather than social constructs' (Ennew and Morrow 2002: 15). Yet, the representation of children's lives is often both adult-constructed and problematic, effectively reducing children's social agency by manipulating 'victim' categories. As Lucchini (1996) and Punch (2001) have both argued, children construct meanings that they use actively to negotiate and resist such adult imperialisms.

Three 'constructs' have shaped research with children in the global South, and each deserves scrutiny from a rights perspective: age, gender and 'problem' groups.

Ageless Children

Age-based categories underpinning childhood are problematic for research. The essentialist category 'the child' – ungendered and age-free (other than being less than 18 years old) – is often easier to conceptualise and research than more carefully differentiated age groups; for example, boys and/or girls of primary school age; young men and women aged between 15 and 17 years; infants and pre-school children. The issue of age is both important and neglected, and needs more work within a rights perspective. Childhoods are not divided universally into the same age categories, nor are such categories homogeneous, not only because of the evolving capacities and physical growth of human children, but also because the evolving capacities are largely culturally determined (Lansdown 2005). One factor is universal, however: childhood is the most heterogeneous stage in the human life cycle, comprising the fastest rates of change and development.

Within childhood, age differences possibly outweigh gender, ethnicity, religion and other discriminatory factors. An indication of the crucial, but often taken-for-granted, influence of age is that most 'participatory' research with children and young people tends to focus on older children, and even young adults. This does not have to be the case, but reflects the fact that working *with* (rather than *on* or *about*) the youngest children requires special skills and sensitivities, which do not have to be considered with children between 10 and 17 years (Dobbs 2002, Alderson, Hawthorne and Killen 2005, Kjørholt 2005, Dockett and Perry 2007).

Genderless Children and The 'Girl Child'

Gender analysis is rarely a feature of research with children, and the way in which gender shapes children's lives tends to be given scant consideration. Severe gender-based discrimination against girls in some countries has resulted in a handful of studies on some aspect of girls lives (for example Croll 2000). Such studies have been of enormous importance in highlighting the human-rights abuses suffered by girls in some parts of the world. Yet the often-used essentialist category of the 'Girl Child' suggests a necessary relationship between girlhood, discrimination and exploitation (Ennew 1994). Without dismissing the harm caused, particularly to girls, as a result of sex-based discrimination, we suggest that the category of 'Girl Child' is highly problematic as well as philosophically indefensible. In its many incarnations it has mutated into an empty mantra that serves only to homogenise girls' lives and the problems and opportunities they face, as well as largely ignoring the strategies they employ for coping, resisting or simply living. As Chakraborty has demonstrated in her study of young Muslim women in the *bustees* (slums) of Kolkata, girlhoods are not uniformly experienced as submissive, but may be both negotiated and subversive. With respect to the 'good Muslim girl' image, Chakraborty argues that:

> Rather than perform the 'good girl' all of the time, the reality is that young
> women perform multiple identities at different times and in different spaces as
> they consciously navigate through private and public domains. (Chakraborty
> 2009: 422)

In addition, 'girls' are all too often elided with 'women', and researched with
respect to their socialisation into gender roles – as 'not-yet women' or 'becoming
women'. This repeats the tendency identified by Durkheim a century ago (Durkheim
1956), and so ably reprised and used by Jens Qvortrup (1991): unless there is a
sociology that has childhood as its object, children are forever analysed as 'human
becomings' rather than human beings (see also Holloway and Valentine 2000).

If research with girls has often neglected the complexities of gender roles and
relations, the way in which gender shapes boyhoods is even more neglected. As is
the case with gender studies of adults, research with children – to the extent that
gender is considered at all – tends to assume that only girls have gender. From a
rights perspective, girlhoods and boyhoods are valid objects of research *in their
own right*, not simply the locus of accounts of becoming adult females or males.
Girls already *are* female-gendered human beings and boys already *are* male-
gendered human beings, yet we generally know too little about the experiences of
either girlhoods or boyhoods.

Children as Problem Groups

In the global South in particular, child research almost always focuses on
'problem groups' such as AIDS orphans, street children, child labourers, child
commercial sex workers and child soldiers. Research with children on these issues
is unarguably important, particularly in informing policy – indeed each of us has
been involved in research with children who can be labelled with one or more of
these descriptors. Yet our argument here is twofold. In the first place, children
who can be described as AIDS orphans or child labourers or child prostitutes are
not *only* members of one of these categories. These labels are not the sum total of
their lives, and research with children should understand, respect and reveal the
multiple dimensions of their realities, rather than reducing them to a category of
'at risk', 'disadvantaged' or 'vulnerable' children.

Secondly, there is a striking lack of research with children in the global South
who do not fit into 'problem groups'. As a result, childhood in the global South
is often presented as characterised by exploitation or abuse, because there is a
dearth of accounts of local 'normal' childhoods with which to compare these
pathological examples (a sociological error identified long ago by Durkheim).
The result is a tendency to make causal inferences based on an alien (usually
Northern) construction of normal childhood. This has serious consequences for
policy-making. For example, international policy focuses on ending 'child labour'
by placing working children in school classrooms, which, like 'the family', are
considered to be an appropriate location for childhood. While research on child

labour and children's work has increased dramatically over the past two decades, there is less research on the everyday experiences of children in formal schooling in the global South. The relatively few studies that have taken place indicate that school is often a hostile place for children, and not only for poor children in the poorest communities (see Bessell 2009b, Beazley et al. 2006). Yet international policy is remarkable uncritical of the nature of education on offer in much of the global South.

Rights-based Opportunities and Challenges for Researchers

Understanding children as subjects of human rights, worthy of respect and dignity, who lead complex and multi-faceted lives is essential to rights-based research. Nevertheless, our experiences as researchers have made us aware that there are challenges as well as opportunities in taking this approach.

Participation in Research is a Challenge for Adults and an Opportunity for Children

Participatory research by project workers with adults in communities has a comparatively long history, which has produced a battery of research techniques that are often now used with children (Boyden and Ennew 1997). While participatory techniques were not used comprehensively to target children until the mid-1990s (Johnson, Hill and Ivan-Smith 1995), they have grown in popularity over the past decade. As Twum-Danso (2009) has pointed out, participatory research with children in 'developing countries' has become attractive to donors, and is often a requirement of research funding. Yet there is little consensus about what participatory research with children means in practice (Beers, Invernizzi and Milne 2006). Such research is now often attempted, but it is not always (perhaps not often) done well (Twum-Danso 2009). Moreover, research carried out under the banner of 'participation' is not always genuinely participatory.

One key factor is that the development of agreed criteria for what counts as fulfilment of children's right to 'participate' is as yet an unmet challenge. Yet, we dispute the idea, so frequently voiced, that 'participation is not traditional in our culture' – it is not traditional in *any* culture (including for many adults). Participation can cause equal problems and challenges in countries of the global North as well as of the global South. Like participation by adults, research participation of children is a process that has to be developed, promoted and, above all, practised over time. Participation in research:

> ... is a process in which 'ownership of the problem' is increasingly shared between researchers and researched. In the first instance, researchers are likely to own the research problem and design the research, using methods that enable stakeholders to express themselves. Working directly with stakeholders

(including children), and gradually handing over responsibility to them for setting the research agenda, will change the role of researchers to 'facilitators', and turn the research process into a joint project. (Ennew and Plateau 2004: 15)

Moreover, children's participation challenges adults' preconceptions about children. Established researchers and university lecturers may find this difficult to accept. In past decades we have jointly and severally used the rights-based approach in many countries and on a wide range of topics – both in our own research and as capacity-building research advisors, working in close cooperation with local researchers. In the latter process we have found, on more than one occasion, senior participants, who feel their authority threatened and their prior research discounted, mounting initial resistance to trying out a participatory, multiple-method approach that also involves democratic relations of mutual respect and co-operation within the research team, whatever the age and status of members. However, our experience has been that, after experiencing fieldwork *with* children, the resisters turn into strong advocates for the rights-based approach.

Those whose activist work with children goes under the umbrella of 'participation' may be equally challenged. During one research capacity-building programme in which we were involved, girls who were former sex workers were among the 'trainees'. They had become involved in the research through their membership of a local non-governmental organisation, the staff of which were also taking part in the workshop. During group work to design a research protocol we noticed that adults in each group had delegated the girls to the task of entering the adults' ideas on a laptop. It took considerable discussion – and not a little practice – before the girls were reinstated as full group members, exchanging ideas, designing research tools and taking decisions.

The Opportunity to Collect Scientific, Children-focused Data

Choice of methods is important in ensuring the scientific rigour of research, with multiple methods allowing for triangulation of results. In this respect we would emphasise that a vital component of the approach is the refusal to accept the indefensible division between 'qualitative' and 'quantitative' research and data collection (Ennew and Plateau 2004). Rights-based research involves systematic research protocols that allow data, such as drawings and photographs (which are often thought of as 'merely qualitative') to be subjected to both statistical and ethnographic analysis, resulting in rich and verifiable information (RWG-CL 2003, Ennew and Plateau 2004, Ennew and Abebe 2010).

Policy makers and planners need hard numbers in order to design, implement and monitor policies and interventions. The bias toward quantitative data in government and organisations remains so powerful, in spite of the 'thinness' even of children-relative information – let alone children-centred statistics (Saporiti 1994) – that policy-makers can be unjustly dismissive of the value of richer, more close-textured, qualitative results. Unless the research methods allow for (indeed encourage) open-ended responses, there is no hope that children will have the opportunity to tell us what they themselves find significant. All too often, research with children relies merely on anecdotes about, or stories told by, individual children (so-called 'voices') that cannot be generalised across the population and are usually not collected using rigorous recording processes. The potential value and impact of qualitative results, with their richer insights into children's own perspectives, are thus lost.

Nevertheless, if numbers are essential to sound research, so too is discursive analysis, without which numbers are meaningless or misleading. Too often, researchers, seduced by the idea of participatory research with children, will collect dozens of drawings or photographs but, once back in the university or office, cannot think what to do with the images because these have not been collected systematically (Darbyshire, MacDougall and Schiller 2005). Adults may easily misinterpret children's drawings if they neglect to record what the children themselves had to say about them. The result is reports based on the staple methods of questionnaire, interview and focus group discussions, illustrated with children's drawings and boxed examples of their 'voices'. The opportunity to gain deeper insights into children's priorities, perspectives and experiences is lost. Children's words and pictures are worthy of more than just being used as illustrations; their right to give their opinions should not be reduced to anecdotes, presented as 'authentic voices'. We therefore argue for the need to acknowledge the inseparability of quantitative and qualitative methods, and to promote their integrated use in forms that are both children-friendly and rigorous.

The literature on research with children, like our own experience, indicates the importance of using a variety of methods. Developing and using methods that address the research questions, take account of children's age or life experience, and respond to the specific context in which children live can be challenging and time-consuming. There is, however, a growing literature documenting methods that have been used successfully. An early example of cultural sensitivity in choosing methods for research with children was the shift made by Johnson, Hill and Ivan-Smith (1995) in their research in rural Nepal. They found that children there were not accustomed to drama and role play, but were happy to express their ideas by composing songs, according to village custom. Chakraborty (2009) describes using a method based on yoga, which was particularly appropriate for her research with teenage girls in Kolkata, India. Novel and adapted methods may be necessary, not only across cultures but also according to individual children's ages, abilities and preferences (Morrow and Richards 1996). Using multiple methods can be an important means of ensuring that children are able to exert control over the techniques with which they feel most comfortable (see Darbyshire, MacDougall and Schiller 2005).

Research methods can be designed for more than one purpose and may need to be adapted for different social contexts. For example, in our research on children's views and experiences of physical and emotional punishment (see Beazley et al. 2005, 2006), we were concerned to ensure that we left children feeling positive about themselves, their lives and their participation in the research, despite the sensitive nature of the research topic. To achieve this, we drew on earlier work undertaken in Bosnia and Herzegovina (Čehajić et al. 2003) to develop a 'protection tool'. The original version of this method, based on the Bosnian tool, used a picture of a shield, divided into five sections, labelled:

1. The person I love most ...
2. If I was President/King/Prime Minister/etc. ...
3. I am best at ...
4. My happiest memory ...
5. I feel safe with ...

Children were to be invited to complete each sentence, and to take the completed shield home with them, thus ending the research with their own positive messages, rather than negative images of punishments they had witnessed or received.

In putting this method into practice elsewhere, however, we found it necessary to make adaptations. In Bosnia and Herzegovina the shield has strong cultural, social and historical meaning. In the eight countries of the Asia-Pacific region in which we conducted the study on punishment, however, a shield has little resonance. Indeed, in Indonesia, where the research was carried out in post-conflict areas such as Ambon, Maluku and Halmahera, traditional shields took a great variety of shapes quite unlike those of Europe, and local feedback suggested that their primary association with warfare and violence made this image inappropriate for use in the context of our research. After discussion with local partners, it was decided to change the image to an umbrella, which symbolises protection from the elements in most countries. Yet, in the Philippines, our research partners pointed out that only females carry umbrellas, so that boys might not readily identify with this image. Furthermore, children are often beaten with umbrellas. Thus, in the Philippines an umbrella is far from being a symbol of protection and was replaced with a drawing of a 'protection jacket', on which sentences for completion were written on the hood and pockets (Beazley et al. 2005). A different research project in Thailand used a drawing of a raised, open hand, which has strong resonances with one of the gestures often seen in statues of the Buddha, the five fingers providing convenient spaces for the children to write (Knowing Children and UNICEF Thailand 2007). Elsewhere, national flowers and a 'flower of peace' have also featured in protection tools in rights-based research protocols.

Whatever local form it takes, the protection tool achieves its purpose. In several countries, it has also yielded valuable data, if children give permission for copies of their drawings to be made and retained by researchers. For example in Fiji it revealed that the person most likely to punish children was also frequently the person with whom children felt safest (Save the Children Fiji 2006).

Ethical Opportunities and Challenges

Ethical considerations in research with children emphasise the duties of adult researchers and research managers to 'do no harm' at all stages of research – including dissemination of results. Moreover the lowly status of children in society, and their relative lack of information and understanding, provide additional complications for voluntary participation compared to research with adults. For the foreseeable future there will always be a role for adults in research with children, and we would refute the idea that research can actually be 'child-led' – even if children are involved in all aspects, including data collection and analysis (Robson et al. 2009, Liebel 2010). Children need adults to channel resources, lend legal status, negotiate permission and help with dissemination (Van Bueren 1995), as well as to protect them by maintaining ethical standards, as is adult responsibility under the provisions of the CRC.

As Morrow and Richards (1996) have suggested, the shifting sets of dilemmas and cultural considerations faced by researchers in the field sometimes make nonsense of university ethical checklists. What is needed is a deep commitment to a set of principles that can be implemented flexibly depending on circumstance, but are above compromise in terms of their fundamental integrity. Central to these principles is children's right to be protected from exploitation (Article 36 of the CRC).

We do not deny that formal ethical processes have their place – indeed some kind of peer-governed setting and monitoring of ethical standards is vital if children's rights to protection are to be met. Yet all too often, as Morrow and Richards (1996) have pointed out, the bio-medical model on which formal ethical processes tend to be based leads to rigid rules, based in clinical research, which either do not fit, or miss altogether, the ethical dilemmas thrown up by the real world. Two principles in particular present challenges for researchers working with children: voluntarism, expressed in the idea of 'informed consent', and confidentiality.

'Informed consent' means that research participants have been meaningfully informed about all aspects of the research: the purpose, what is expected of them, the methods, the person or organisation carrying out the research, and how the information will be used and by whom. Participants need to be assured that the information is confidential and that it will not be possible for people unconnected with the research to identify them. They should also be aware that they can refuse to take part, or stop their participation at any time, for any reason, without negative consequences. This is increasingly referred to as 'informed dissent' or 'informed refusal' (Ennew and Plateau 2004, Ennew and Abebe 2010). It is becoming common practice to treat informed consent as a legal requirement, with a document to be signed, as well as for the consent of adults – parents, teachers, caretakers, guardians – to be sought first, before children are involved.

The act of signing consent forms has several implications in different settings, particularly in the global South, where people may not be literate (Abebe 2009), or may be reluctant because giving a signature implies possible legal implications (Jabeen 2009), or afraid of repercussions, because of armed conflict for example

(UNICEF Thailand 2008). When research participants are children, there is often a requirement from ethics committees that parents or guardians provide informed consent, either in addition to or in place of children's informed consent. Yet, as Abebe (2009: 456) points out, 'it may not be clear which parental figures have the right to give or withhold permission'. Moreover, rights-based research insists that informed consent of children cannot be assumed from parental consent.

In rural Southern contexts local village heads are vital gatekeepers if access to community members of any age is to be possible. As Ahsan (2009: 393) writes:

> Even before I could seek their consent, I first of all had to negotiate for access with various hierarchies of adult gatekeepers … This made the young people vulnerable to power imbalances in the research settings, since they were unable to exercise their independent choice free from the influence of their adult guardians.

The process of negotiating with village leaders can be fraught, raising ethical as well as practical dilemmas. In some cases, a possible outcome of such negotiations is that individual children end up being identified or categorised in ways that cause embarrassment, stigmatisation or resentment. In one, rather extreme (but not altogether uncommon) example, researchers were faced with a village headman lining up 10 children outside his house in full view of other villagers and presenting them as 'the community AIDS orphans' (personal communication, Suleman Sumra, coordinator of the research described in Ahmed et al. 1999). In such a situation, researchers are faced with a sudden, acute ethical dilemma about what to say and do. The concept of informed consent is rendered meaningless and the potential for children to be exploited becomes very real. Moreover, the capacity of the researcher to reverse the situation is limited. Even in less challenging circumstances, the process of seeking informed consent can be a challenging one. As Ahsan has argued (2009), in practice, it is often difficult to determine if consent or dissent is 'real'.

Another specific problem is that children may be so eager to help a researcher (who has higher status or power), or unaware of the consequences of discussing private matters in a group discussion, that they disclose confidential information about other people, with negative consequences for themselves or others in their community. In such cases, researchers have a duty of protection, but may have to react quickly to a sudden ethical dilemma. As in modern moral philosophy, ethical decisions are situational. Each day in the field, each group of children, each moment may provide occasion for a troublesome decision in which the ethical priorities, as well as the methodological imperatives, may have to be ranked and weighed according to the priorities of the situation.

Finally, children may wish to have trusted adults present during research sessions. In prioritising confidentiality and privacy, researchers sometimes overlook the very real fact that they are relative strangers to children, while parents or other adults may provide them with security and reassurance during the research process.

Researchers' well-intentioned and often understandable efforts to undertake research outside the age-based hierarchies in which children in every society live may be tinged with an almost arrogant assumption that they know better than either children or the adults with whom they share their daily lives. We are not suggesting here that adult caregivers should always be present during research with children, since this can be equally problematic. Rather, we are calling into question any idea that researchers necessarily occupy a more ethical space than all other adults. If children are to be protected from exploitation during research, the position and role of all those involved must be the subject of critical reflection.

Concluding Remarks: Duties and Transformations

The discussion of informed consent and confidentiality demonstrates that research in the 'real world' does not fit neatly into the categories identified on the forms required by ethics committees, but requires negotiation between duty bearers and rights holders. Human rights are fulfilled when the responsibility to fulfil them for others is assumed by the groups, individuals or organisations who bear that duty. The academic research community bears an important responsibility for promoting and – to the extent that this is possible – monitoring ethical standards in research, including research carried out by non-academic bodies. Yet the ultimate duty bearers for the human rights of children are governments, which means that government research committees should play a greater role in ensuring that ethical standards are met in research with children – indeed in promoting such standards rather than merely licensing researchers and research projects. Moreover, all research ethics committees, within academia and beyond, should be highly cognisant of the on-the-ground reality of research with people, regardless of age. The aim should not be to make researchers jump through hoops or provide carefully crafted but unrealistic responses to potential ethical dilemmas, but to develop a culture in which the human rights and human dignity of research participants of all ages are respected and valued.

Thus the concept of duty-bearers is important for using a rights-based approach and avoiding the exploitation of children through research. Rights-based research with children acknowledges their agency as subjects of rights, rather than being the outcome of academic theory. The difference may be subtle, but it is crucial. The research that we (as rights-based researchers) carry out is less concerned with proving children's agency than with challenging the real-world notion that they are passive victims of abuse, exploitation or violence.

The conventional wisdom of doing research with children is changing rapidly, despite initial resistance from some established researchers. As Liebel (2010) has pointed out that scientific research is 'systematic curiosity' that should develop an equal partnership between researchers and researched – a partnership that, as we have found, is transformative for both. Abebe (2009: 460) notes that 'fieldwork is a personal experience rather than a mere academic pursuit', one in which it is effectively impossible not to become empathetically involved. The approach we have outlined here brings together both systematic curiosity and the deeply personal experience that is fieldwork, in a rigorous framework that places children at the core.

If this approach transforms researchers, what are (and/or might be) the effects on children's lives? We have experienced children's enthusiastic participation in research. Following recent rights-based research with children on their experiences and views of education in Fiji (Bessell 2009b, Bessell Low-McKenzie and Anise 2009) one girl commented 'This was the most amazing experience. For the first time in my life I felt like I really mattered.' As Jabeen (2009) observes, children can be personally empowered by being given the opportunity to share their opinions and experiences, particularly when no-one has ever before asked them. Children may be excited by their experiences as research designers, participants and researchers – but they are seldom irresponsible. A large body of research with children has already established beyond any question the value and eloquence of their contributions. Furthermore, a rights-based approach helps us to recognise diverse childhoods rather than constructing a single, universal (Northern) childhood, as well as promoting respect and value for children, as they are and in their diversity. Possibly most important of all for children and their futures, rights-based research provides a scientific basis for policy and action, which genuinely recognises children's experiences and priorities.

References

Abebe, T. 2009. Multiple methods, complex dilemmas: negotiating socio-ethical spaces in participatory research with disadvantaged children. *Children's Geographies: Advancing Interdisciplinary Understanding of Younger People's Lives*, 7(4) (November), 451–66.

Ahmed, S., Bwana, J., Guga, E., Kitunga, D., Mgulambwa, A., Mtambalike, P., Mtunguja, L. and Mwandayi, E. 1999. *Children in Need of Special Protection Measures: A Tanzanian Study*. Dar es Salaam: UNICEF.

Ahsan, M. 2009. The potential and challenges of rights-based research with children and young people: experiences from Bangladesh. *Children's Geographies: Advancing Interdisciplinary Understanding of Younger People's Lives*, 7(4): 391–403.

Akunga, A., Oriko, L., Muia, D., Mwangi, M., Mogere, J., Misi, L. and Muhati, D. 2001. *The Impact of HIV/AIDS on Education in Kenya, and the Potential for Using Education in the Widest Sense for the Prevention and Control of HIV/AIDS*. Nairobi: NICEF Kenya.

Alderson, P., Hawthorne, J. and Killen, M. 2005. The participation rights of premature babies. *The International Journal of Children's Rights*, 13, 31–50.

Alderson, P. and Morrow, V. 2004. *Ethics, Social Research and Consulting with Children and Young People*. Ilford: Barnardos.

Badham, B. 2004. Participation – for a change: disabled young people lead the way. *Children and Society*, 18, 143–54.

Bangyai, R., Ennew, J. and Noonsup, T. 2009. A necessary game of chance: knowledge of and attitudes towards migration to Thailand among children aged 7 to 13 years in two districts of Savannaket Province, Lao PDR. Paper presented at Perspectives on Children's Active Engagement with Migration in the Southeast Asian Context, a workshop in the ASEF Alliance Workshop Series, Bangkok, 19–20 February 2009.

Beazley, H. and Alhadad, M. 2008. *Participatory Child-led Research on the Feelings and Perceptions of Children Living in Three Children's Homes in the District of Lhokseumawe, North Aceh, Indonesia.* Jakarta: Save the Children US.

Beazley, H., Bessell, S., Ennew, J. and Waterson, R. 2005. *Comparative Research on Physical and Emotional Punishment of Children in Southeast Asia and the Pacific: Research Protocol.* Bangkok: Save the Children Sweden Southeast Asia and Pacific Regional Office.

——. 2006. *What Children Say: Results of Comparative Research on Physical and Emotional Punishment of Children in Southeast Asia and the Pacific, 2005.* Bangkok: Save the Children Sweden Southeast Asia and Pacific Regional Office.

——. 2009. The right to be properly researched: research with children in a messy, real world. *Children's Geographies: Advancing Interdisciplinary Understanding of Younger People's Lives,* 7(4), 365–78.

Beers, H. van, Invernizzi, A. and Milne, B. (eds). 2006. *Beyond Article 12: Essential Readings in Children's Participation.* Bangkok: Black on White Publications.

Bessell, S. 2009a. Research with children: thinking about method and methodology, in *Involving Children and Young People in Research.* Sydney: ARACY and the NSW Commission for Children and Young People.

——. 2009b. Strengthening Fiji's education system: a view from key stakeholders. *Pacific Economic Bulletin,* 24(3), 58–70. Available at: http://peb.anu.edu.au/pdf/PEB24_3_Bessell.pdf [accessed 28 June 2010].

——. 2009c. Children's participation in decision-making in the Philippines: understanding the attitudes of policy-makers and service providers. *Childhood,* 16(3), 299–316.

Bessell, S., Low-McKenzie, L. and Anise, S. 2009. *Having a Say on School in Fiji: Report of the Children and Young Person's Forum on Education in Fiji.* A Pacific Policy Project Paper. Save the Children Fiji and the Crawford School of Economics and Government.

Boyden, J. and Ennew, J. (eds). 1997. *Children in Focus: A Manual for Participatory Research with Children.* Stockholm: Save the Children Sweden.

Bronfenbrenner, U. 1979. *The Ecology of Human Development: Experiments by Nature and Design.* Cambridge, MA: Harvard University Press.

Čehajić, S., Cvijetić, V., Đarmati, I., Dupanović, A., Hadziosmanović, M. and Vuković, S.S. 2003. *Unaccompanied Children and Children at Risk of Being Institutionalized in Bosnia and Herzegovina.* Sarajevo: UNICEF Bosnia and Herzegovina.

Chakraborty, K. 2009. 'The good Muslim girl': conducting qualitative participatory research to understand the lives of young Muslim women in the *bustees* of Kolkata. *Children's Geographies: Advancing Interdisciplinary Understanding of Younger People's Lives*, 7(4), 421–33.

Croll, E. 2000. *Endangered Daughters: Discrimination and Development in Asia.* New York: Routledge.

Cussianovich, A. and Marquez, A.M. 2002. *Towards a Protagonist Participation of Boys, Girls and Teenagers.* Lima: Save the Children Sweden – Regional Office for South America.

Darbyshire, P., MacDougall, C. and Schiller, W. 2005. Multiple methods in qualitative research with children: more insight or just more? *Qualitative Research*, 5(4), 417–36.

Dobbs, T. 2002. The missing voice: what are children's views of physical discipline? Unpublished research study submitted in partial fulfilment of the requirement for the Post Graduate Diploma in Child Advocacy, Children's Issues Centre, University of Otago, Dunedin, New Zealand.

Dockett, S. and Perry, B. 2007. Trusting children's accounts in research. *Journal of Early Childhood Research*, 5(1), 47–63.

Durkheim, E. 1956. *Education and Sociology.* Glencoe, IL: Free Press of Glencoe. Translation of Durkheim, E., 1922. *Éducation et sociologie.* Paris: Alcan (published posthumously and reproducing essays from 1903, 1906, and 1911).

Ennew, J. 1986. Mujercita y mamacita: girls growing up in Lima. *Bulletin of Latin American Research*, 5(2), 49–66.

——. 1993. Homeless and working children, Part 1 of Boyden J. and Ennew J., Survey of surveys, social indicators for monitoring the convention on the rights of the child. Unpublished research paper for Rädda Barnen, Stockholm.

——. 1994. Defining the girl child: sexuality, control and development. *VENA: Special issue on The Girl Child*, 6(2), 51–6.

Ennew J. and Abebe, T. 2010. *The Right to Be Properly Researched: Ten Manuals for Scientific Research with Children.* Bangkok: Black on White Publications, Norwegian Centre for Child Research and World Vision International.

Ennew, J. and Milne, B. 1996. *Methods of Research with Street and Working Children: An Annotated Bibliography.* Stockholm: Rädda Barnen.

Ennew, J. and Morrow, V. 2002. Releasing the energy: celebrating the inspiration of Sharon Stephens. *Childhood*, 9(1), 5–18.

Ennew, J. and Plateau, D.P. 2004. *How to Research the Physical and Emotional Punishment of Children.* Bangkok: International Save the Children Southeast, East Asia and Pacific Region Alliance.

Ennew, J. and Young, P. 1982. *Child Labour in Jamaica.* London: Anti-Slavery Society.

Eversole, H. 2009. Asking children: the benefits from a programming perspective, *Children's Geographies: Advancing Interdisciplinary Understanding of Younger People's Lives*, 7(4), 484–6.

Franklin, B. 2002. Children's rights: an introduction, in B. Franklin (ed.), *The New handbook of Children's Rights: Comparative Policy and Practice*. London: Routledge, pp. 1–13.

Hart, R. 1997. *Children's Participation: The Theory and Practice of Involving Young Citizens in Community Development and Environmental Care*. New York: UNICEF and Earthscan.

Hastadewi, Y., Salam, A.Q., Nugroho, P.A., Cholilah, U., Isnaini, W. and Riyani, Y.A. 2004. *Situation and Condition of Child Labor at Several Sectors in District Tulungagung and Probolinggo*. Jakarta: UNICEF Indonesia.

Holloway, S. and Valentine, G. 2000. Children's geographies and the new social studies of childhood, in S. Holloway and G. Valentine (eds), *Children's Geographies: Playing, Living, Learning*. London: Routledge.

Jabeen, T. 2009. But I've never been asked!' Research with children in Pakistan. *Children's Geographies: Advancing Interdisciplinary Understanding of Younger People's Lives*, 7(4), 405–20.

James, A. and Prout, A. (eds). 1992. *Constructing and Reconstructing Childhood*. Brighton: Falmer Press.

Johnson, V., Hill, J. and Ivan-Smith, E. 1995. *Listening to Smaller Voices*. London: ActionAid.

Kjørholt, A.T. 2005. The competent child and 'the right to be oneself': reflections on children as fellow citizens, in A. Clark, A.T. Kjørholt and P. Moss (eds), *Beyond Listening: Children's Perceptions on Early Childhood Services*. Bristol: Policy Press, pp. 151–74.

Knowing Children and UNICEF Thailand. 2007. Situation analysis of child protection issues after the 2004 tsunami in Thailand. Unpublished report.

Lansdown, G. 2005. *The Evolving Capacities of the Child*. Florence: UNICEF, Innocenti Research Centre.

Liebel, M. 2008. Child-led research with working children. Paper presented to Conference on Child and Youth Research in the 21st Century: A Critical Appraisal, European University Cyprus Nicosia, 28–29 May 2008.

——. 2010. Foreword: systematic curiosity, in J. Ennew and T. Abebe (eds), *The Right to Be Properly Researched: Ten Manuals for Scientific Research with Children*. Bangkok: Black on White Publications, Norwegian Centre for Child Research and World Vision International. *Manual 1: Where do we start?*, 1.3–1.6.

Lucchini, R. 1996. The street and its image. *Childhood*, 3(2), 235–46.

Morrow, V. 1999. 'We are people too': children's perspectives on rights and decision-making in England. *International Journal of Children's Rights*, 7(3), 149–70.

Morrow, V. and Richards, M. 1996. The ethics of social research with children: an overview. *Children and Society*, 10, 90–105.

Punch, S. 2001. Negotiating autonomy: childhoods in rural Bolivia, in L. Alanen and B. Mayall (eds), *Conceptualising Child-Adult Relations*. London: Routledge, pp. 23–36.

Qvortrup, J. 1991. *Childhood as a Social Phenomenon: An Introduction to a Series of National Reports*. Vienna: European Centre for Social Welfare Policy and Research.

Ratna, K. and Reddy, N. (eds). 2002. *A Journey in Children's Participation*. Bangalore: The Concerned for Working Children. Available at: http://www.workingchild.org/Microsoft%20Word%20-%20A%20journey%20in%20children's%20participation-revised.pdf [accessed 10 September 2010].

Robinson, G.L. 2000. *Capacity Building on Child Research: A Documentation of the CNSPM Study*. Dar es Salaam: UNICEF Tanzania.

Robson, E., Porter, G., Hampshire, K. and Bourdillon, M. 2009. 'Doing it right?': working with young researchers in Malawi to investigate children, transport and mobility. *Children's Geographies: Advancing Interdisciplinary Understanding of Younger People's Lives*, 7(4), 467–80.

RWG-CL. 2003. *Handbook for Action-oriented Research on the Worst Forms of Child Labour, Including Trafficking in Children*. Bangkok: Regional Working Group on Child Labour. Available at: http://www.ilo.org/public/english/region/asro/bangkok/library/pub1.htm [accessed 10 September 2010].

Saporiti, A. 1994. A methodology for making children count, in J. Qvortrup, M. Bardy, G. Sgritta and H. Wintersberger (eds), *Childhood Matters: Social Theory, Practice and Politics*. Aldershot: Avebury, pp. 189–210.

Save the Children Fiji. 2006. *The Physical and Emotional Punishment of Children in Fiji: A Research Report*. Suva: Save the Children Fiji.

Setyowati, R., Wahyunadi, A., Suhanda, E., Susiladiharti, Kartika, I., Diryat, N. and Smith, E. 2004. *Anak yang Dilacurkan di Surakarta dan Indramayu*. Jakarta: UNICEF.

Swart, J. 1990. *Malunde: The Street Children of Hillbrow*. Johannesburg: Witwatersrand University Press.

Twum-Danso, A. 2009. Situating participatory methodologies in context: the impact of culture on adult-child interactions in research and other projects. *Children's Geographies: Advancing Interdisciplinary Understanding of Younger People's Lives*, 7(4), 379–90.

UNICEF Thailand. 2008. *Everyday Fears: A Study of Children's Perceptions of Living in the Southern Border Areas of Thailand*. Bangkok: UNICEF Thailand. Available at: http://www.unicef.org/thailand/Everyday_fears.pdf [accessed 10 September 2010].

Van Bueren, G. 1995. *The International Law on the Rights of the Child*. The Hague: Martinus Nijhoff.

Chapter 8

Using the Convention on the Rights of the Child in Law and Policy: Two Ways to Improve Compliance

Ursula Kilkelly

Introduction

The CRC was adopted by the General Assembly of the United Nations on 20 November 1989 and came into force a short time later, on 2 September 1990. The Convention has been praised for its wide range of comprehensive and detailed provisions (McGoldrick 1991: 133, Kilkelly and Lundy 2006). At the same time, the failure of States Parties to implement the duties imposed on them by the Convention has reinforced the need to address the absence from the Convention of an effective enforcement mechanism (for example Fottrell 2000: 1, Balton 1990: 125–9, Fortin 2009: 46). Although international dialogue on the addition of a protocol to provide children with a right of individual petition has finally begun,[1] it is important nonetheless to explore alternative ways in which the Convention's potential can be realised. The aim of this chapter is to consider two ways in which the Convention's provisions can be put to good effect. In particular, it focuses on the use of the Convention in litigation at national, regional and international levels, and the use of the Convention as an auditing tool with a view to promoting rights-based law and policy reform. In this regard, the chapter has three sections: the first will outline the Convention and related documentation that together define best practice and the scope of states' obligations in the area of children's rights; the second section will examine how auditing law, policy and practice for adherence to these standards can usefully be used to identify what states need to do to ensure greater compliance and to bring all three areas into line with children's rights; and the third and final section will consider the potential for using these standards to advance children's rights through litigation. The chapter will conclude with some

---

1   See Human Rights Council, *Report of the Open-ended Working Group to Explore the Possibility of Elaborating an Optional Protocol to the Convention on the Rights of the Child to Provide a Communications Procedure*, UN Doc. A/HRC/13/43, 21 January 2010, available at: www.ohchr.org [accessed 31st March 2010]. See also consideration of this development by Jaap Doek and Geraldine Van Bueren in this volume.

reflection on the lessons to be learned from both of these processes to ensure their potential is utilised.

The CRC

The CRC was the first comprehensive, internationally binding treaty to give full recognition to the individual rights of children. Its widespread ratification – by all UN members except the United States and Somalia – suggests its consistency with a strong level of international consensus on the way children should be treated in a wide variety of areas and circumstances. The Convention is widely regarded as the 'touchstone for children's rights throughout the world' (Fortin 2009: 49) and although it has been subject to some critical scrutiny (McGoldrick 1991, Lopatka 1992, Freeman 1992, Fortin 2009: 43–7), its merits include its breadth and the extent of its detailed provision for the autonomous rights of children (Kilkelly 2001: 308–26). Uniquely, the CRC encompasses civil and political rights and economic, social and cultural rights traditionally kept apart in international instruments, and it also includes humanitarian provisions (McGoldrick 1991: 133). Moreover, its comprehensive nature means that the CRC contains standards applicable to all areas of the child's life including school (Articles 28 and 29) and the family (Articles 3, 5, 12 and 18) as well as in specific settings of alternative care (Articles 20 and 21) and youth justice and detention (Articles 37 and 40) for example. It makes provision for children's wellbeing in a variety of contexts (Articles 6, 24 and 27) and makes specific provision for children with disabilities (Article 23), children whose parents have separated (Articles 3 and 9), children who have suffered abuse and exploitation (Articles 19, 30–34 and 37) and refugee children (Articles 7, 8 and 10). The Convention contains rights of general relevance (Article 7 on identity), rights of specific importance to children (Articles 18 on family support and 31 on the right to play, rest and leisure) and general human rights adapted to the specific needs of children (Articles 13 on freedom of expression, 14 on expression of religion and 17 on access to information). The navigation of the Convention's vast array of provisions is aided by the grouping together of the provisions under the headings of Participation, Protection, Provision and Prevention (Hammarberg 1990). At the same time, the CRC Committee has usefully reminded that these areas overlap in line with the understanding that children's rights are inter-linked and indivisible (CRC Committee 2003: 5).

According to the CRC Committee, the Convention has four general principles (CRC Committee 1991: 13). These are contained in Article 2, which provides for the right of every child to enjoy his/her Convention rights without discrimination of any kind; Article 3 which requires that the best interests of the child are a primary consideration in all actions taken concerning children; Article 6 which recognises the right of the child to life, survival and development; and Article 12 which provides that the state shall assure to every child capable of forming a view the right to express that view freely in all matters concerning him/her and to have it given due weight in accordance with the child's age and maturity. The legitimacy of singling out these provisions from the others in the CRC has never really been questioned, but it is clear nonetheless that these four principles are pivotal in nature, and they are also broad enough to allow them to be read together with all the other more detailed provisions. Taken together, the four provisions reflect the key obligations that states must fulfil to ensure the implementation of the Convention as a whole. The notions of treating children as equals, taking a child-centred approach and listening to children thus capture what the Convention as a whole is trying to achieve in bringing about a positive change in attitudes towards children.

Although the rights to life (Article 6) and to enjoy Convention rights without discrimination (Article 2) are clearly fundamental in nature, the terms of Article 3 (best interests) and Article 12 (right to be heard) arguably offer most support as tools of children's rights advocacy. Although Fortin (2009: 40) considers that Article 3 is the most important Convention provision insofar as it underpins all the others, the provision has also been criticised for watering down the requirement often applied in domestic law that the child's best interests are 'paramount'.[2] While this is explained by the fact that the scope of Article 3 is very broad and intended to apply in all areas including those in which there may be other legitimate considerations, like the public interest, a more serious but less cited criticism of Article 3(1) is that it is not in fact a right at all. It is one of few provisions in the Convention that does not use rights language and as a result it has an undeniably paternalistic feel that harkens back to when adults decided unilaterally 'what was best for children' without involving them in the decision-making process. The vague nature of the provision has been criticised for meaning 'all things to all people' (Kilkelly and Lundy 2006: 336), something which risks undermining its contribution to the rights approach to children's issues (Azer 1994, Kilkelly and Lundy 2006). At the same time, the non-threatening nature of Article 3 means that it is a useful tool in children's rights advocacy, and a familiarity with what it represents – that a child-centred approach to decision-making is important – means that it is a common touchstone for all those who work with and for children (Kilkelly 2006: 38–9). While the emphasis is nearly always placed on Article 3(1), the significance of Article 3(2), which imposes a duty on states to ensure that children receive 'such protection and care as is necessary for his or her well-being ... and to this end, shall take all appropriate legislative and administrative measures' tends to be underplayed. Yet, this overarching duty to take the necessary measures to ensure that children's needs are met is recognition of the important status of childhood and the particular vulnerability that children possess. Implicit in its terms is a duty to ensure that all legal and other measures are adopted to make this a reality. This undoubtedly serves to strengthen the impact of paragraph 1 of Article 3 (Kilkelly 2008a: 27–8).

---

2   See for example, s 3(1) of the Children Act 1989 of England and Wales and s 3 of the (Irish) Child Care Act 1991. See further Kilkelly (2008a: 7–8).

Article 12 of the UNCRC, which recognises the right of the child to express his/her views and have them given due weight in decisions made about them, is considered to be a defining principle of children's rights (Lundy 2007). Important both as a procedural and as a substantive right, the obligation to ensure that children are involved in decisions made about them serves to respect children's views and experiences, improve decision-making that affects them while also raising the profile of children and their views, ensuring their treatment as individuals in their own right (Parkes 2008). The provision is an enabler that can facilitate the exercise by children and young people of their rights in other areas and in this regard it is a powerful instrument of change and like Article 3, an important advocacy tool. The key to Article 12 is that it has two distinct but related parts: paragraph 1 places the general duty on the state to ensure that children have the right to express their views, and puts in place a dual test (in the form of age and maturity) with regard to giving effect to those views. Article 12(2) supplements the first paragraph by recognising that in order to ensure children are heard they must be provided the opportunity to be heard in any judicial and administrative proceedings affecting the child, either directly, or through a representative. Even though this particular requirement must bow to the procedures of domestic law, the provision is crucial nonetheless in laying down a benchmark on the child's right to participate in decision-making processes that concern him/her. This is manifest in literature across disciplines on the child's right to be heard (for example Sinclair 2004, Lundy 2007, Cashmore and Parkinson 2007, Franklin and Sloper 2005, Parkes 2011).

Remedying Shortcomings in the CRC's Text

At the same time it is clear that the Convention does not always deliver such clear messages and it suffers from many gaps and inadequacies. These are commonly revealed when the Convention is applied in a specific context or setting (for example, Kilkelly 2009: 243–68, Lundy 2006, Kilkelly 2006: 39). As noted above, Article 3 has been criticised for its vague meaning and as Parkinson (2001: 259) notes, Article 12 can be easier to state than to apply. Moreover, the CRC provisions on the rights of children with disabilities (Article 23) and children in armed conflict (Article 38) (Krill 1992: 353, Van Bueren 1994, Abraham 2003) represent two clear examples of where the CRC has set the bar too low. Research has also identified areas where the Convention is too vague and where its provisions fall short in the areas that really matter to children themselves. For example, Kilkelly and Lundy (2006: 337) have noted that the Convention is silent on the right of young people to access information on sexual health, and, similarly, that it does not reflect the importance to children of using public spaces without interference or of spending time with their friends. While Freeman (2000: 282) notes that this is a result of the failure to involve children themselves in the drafting process, these and other shortcomings can be addressed by the application of interpretive methods and tools that reinforce the indivisibility of Convention provisions and its object and purpose. One such approach is to read the Convention's provisions together to produce a meaningful standard (Kilkelly and Lundy 2006: 338, Kilkelly 2006: 39–41). In the example given above about the absence from the Convention of children's right to spend time together, this right can be drawn from the freedom of association in Article 15, the freedom of expression in Article 13 and the right to play and leisure in Article 31. Similarly, Article 31 and Article 19 (child protection) can produce children's right to a safe place to play and spend leisure time (Kilkelly and Lundy 2006: 339). Where such an approach does not remedy the inadequacy complained of, recourse may be had to the wealth of children's rights instruments that now make up international and regional human rights law under the United Nations, the Council of Europe and, increasingly, the European Union. These instruments are particularly detailed in areas like youth justice,[3] child protection[4] and aspects of family law including child abduction.[5] Moreover, the detailed jurisprudence of the European Court of Human Rights also explains States Parties' obligations under the ECHR in a wide variety of areas including alternative care, child abduction and adoption (Kilkelly 1999, Kilkelly 2004). Although there is much common ground between these instruments, together they have created an intricate web of standards that is mutually reinforcing. Similarly, reference to the General Comments of the CRC Committee serve to augment the Convention's potential by providing more detailed guidance on what States Parties must do to ensure compliance under various themes (Kilkelly 2006: 41). To date, particularly important General Comments have been published on

---

3   See the UN Standard Minimum Rules for the Administration of Juvenile Justice, 1985 (the Beijing Rules), adopted by General Assembly resolution 40/33 of 29 November 1985; The UN Rules for the Protection of Juveniles deprived of their Liberty, 1990 (the Havana Rules), adopted by General Assembly resolution 45/113 of 14 December 1990 and the Council of Europe Recommendation CM/Rec (2008)11 of the Committee of Ministers to member states on the European Rules for juvenile offenders subject to sanctions and measures.

4   See the CRC Committee's *General Comment No. 8, The Right of the Child to Protection from Corporal Punishment and Other Cruel or Degrading Forms of Punishment*, CRC/C/GC/8 (2006); the UN Study on Violence against Children, UN Doc. A/61/299, 29 August 2006. See also the supplementary report, The World Report on Violence against Children, United Nations, 2006; the Council of Europe Convention on the Protection of Children against Sexual Exploitation and Sexual Abuse, ETS No. 201 and Recommendation CM/Rec(2009)10 of the Committee of Ministers to member states on integrated national strategies for the protection of children from violence, 18 November 2009.

5   See the Council of Europe Convention on Recognition and Enforcement of Decisions concerning Custody of Children and on Restoration of Custody of Children, ETS No. 105; the Hague Convention on Child Abduction and Council Regulation No. 2201/2003 concerning Jurisdiction and the Recognition and Enforcement of Judgments in Matrimonial Matters and Matters relating to Parental Responsibility repealing Regulation (EC) NO 1347 (2000) [2003] OJL 338/1. See generally Lowe, Everall and Nicholls (2004).

children's rights in adolescent health,[6] in early childhood[7] and in youth justice.[8] A similarly valuable General Comment has been published by the Committee on general measures of implementation[9] – detailing the structures and systems states must establish to ensure children's rights are protected effectively – and a further General Comment deals with Article 12 of the Convention and sets out the range of measures implicit in securing the child's right to be heard.[10] The range and depth of guidance now available in these General Comments means that they provide a rich source from which to draw in the development of benchmarks under the Convention.[11]

While the General Comments provide an important statement of the Convention's application in specific contexts, the jurisdiction-specific guidance offered by the Concluding Observations that the Committee issues as part of the monitoring process is equally important (Kilkelly 1996). Following its consideration of each individual State Party report, submitted in accordance with the Convention's reporting requirements under Article 44, the Committee publishes its observations on what the state must do to ensure further implementation of the Convention's principles and provisions. While this document usually contains some general observations about the state's level of compliance, it may also incorporate very precise guidance to states whereby the Committee pinpoints to governments the need to take very specific measures. These can represent a very specific statement of the extent of national compliance with the Convention and can thus usefully inform any process designed to benchmark national law and policy against the Convention (Kilkelly and Lundy 2006: 340).

The Convention's Achilles Heel

The status of the CRC and the supplementary authority provided by the CRC means that there is now a substantial body of international law on children's rights. However, as international standards increase in number and in detail, the absence of effective means of securing the implementation of these rights becomes even

---

6   CRC Committee, *General Comment No. 4, Adolescent Health and Development in the Context of the Convention on the Rights of the Child*, CRC/GC/2003/4, 1 July 2003.

7   CRC Committee, *General Comment No. 7, Implementing Child Rights in Early Childhood*, CRC/C/GC/Rev. 7, 20 September 2006.

8   CRC Committee, *General Comment No. 10, Children's Rights in Juvenile Justice*, CRC/C/GC/10, 25 April 2007.

9   CRC Committee, *General Comment No. 5, General Measures of Implementation of the Convention on the Rights of the Child*, CRC/GC/2003/5, 3 October 2003.

10   CRC Committee, *General Comment No. 12, The Right of the Child to be Heard*, CRC/C/GC/12, 12 July 2009.

11   See also the documentation surrounding the General Day of Discussion, held annually by the Committee on the Rights of the Child. To date these have addressed topics like the girl child (1995), children and the media (1996), the private sector as a service provider (2002) and children without parental care (2005).

more glaring. At international level, the United Nations has no power to secure compliance with its treaty law and there is no police force to bring into line those States Parties that do not take their children's right's obligations seriously. Nor is there any formal means by which binding international obligations can be translated into justiciable claims at national level and those states that operate a dualist system have chosen to keep international and national law separate. Against this backdrop, the challenge of achieving the full implementation of the CRC can appear insurmountable. But, although the Convention's lack of teeth is indeed a negative feature, that is not to say that there are no other means by which CRC obligations can be observed, or the wider implementation of its principles and provisions promoted. The next two sections consider two such means: the first is the process of children's rights auditing or proofing, the second is the area of strategic litigation.

Children's Rights Auditing

Article 4 of the CRC requires States Parties to take all appropriate measures to implement the Convention. Various mechanisms must be put in place at national level to enable states to fulfil this duty and the CRC Committee has made it clear, in its General Comment No. 5 on General measures of implementation, that children's rights proofing of law, policy and practice is central to this process. According to the Committee, ensuring

> ... that all the provisions of the Convention are respected in legislation and policy development and delivery at all levels of government demands a continuous process of child impact assessment (predicting the impact of any proposed law, policy or budgetary allocation which affects children and the enjoyment of their rights) and child impact evaluation (evaluating the actual impact of implementation). (para. 45, General Comment No. 5)

Although this process of self-monitoring and evaluation is an obligation for governments, independent monitoring of progress towards implementation must also be undertaken by 'parliamentary committees, NGOs, academic institutions, professional associations, youth groups and independent human rights institutions' (para. 46, General Comment No. 5). The obligation requires states to keep under review the compatibility of law and policy with individual provisions of the CRC as well as holistically and states are encouraged to incorporate child impact assessments into their legislative and policy-making procedures (para. 47, General Comment No. 5). In this context, the Committee has noted the importance of collecting comprehensive and disaggregated data on every aspect of children's lives. It has highlighted that evaluation requires the development of indicators related to all Convention rights and emphasised that in many cases, only children themselves are in a position to indicate whether their rights are being fully recognised and realised. Accordingly, it notes that

> interviewing children and using children as researchers (with appropriate safeguards) is likely to be an important way of finding out, for example, to what extent their civil rights, including the crucial right set out in Article 12, to have their views heard and given due consideration, are respected within the family, in schools and so on. (para. 50, General Comment No. 5)

In addition, the measurement of the implementation of children's social, economic and cultural rights demands, according to the Committee, that children are visible in budgets and that the impact of economic and budgetary policy on their exercise of their rights is apparent. Finally, the Committee stresses the importance of adults working with and for children to receive on-going training and education on children's rights and highlights the need for periodic evaluation of the effectiveness of training, reviewing not only knowledge of the CRC, but also 'the extent to which it has contributed to developing attitudes and practice which actively promote enjoyment by children of their rights' (para. 51, General Comment No. 5).

As the General Comment makes clear, therefore, rights-proofing and auditing of law, policy and practice and of budgets is part of the state's legal duty to implement the CRC under Article 4. The fulfilment of this duty is to be undertaken both by government agencies and by independent researchers; it must be an evidence-based process and a continuous one, which is in itself compatible with the general principles of the CRC, notably the best interests of the child and the child's right to be heard.

Increasingly, research across a range of jurisdictions has sought to undertake such evidence-based assessments of the extent to which children's rights are being protected and promoted in specific areas of their lives. This has taken different forms and a variety of approaches and methodologies have been used. National NGOs and human rights institutions have undertaken rights-based analyses of law, policy and practice in order to produce shadow or alternative reports to the Committee on the state's progress in achieving full implementation.[12] These may be used to set national priorities for action either for government or for children's commissioners (Kilkelly et al. 2004, Kilkelly and Lundy 2006) and in many cases they are informed directly or indirectly by the views of young people. In many cases also, an initial or primary review is followed up with regular updates, or alternatively an annual audit takes place ensuring that progress can be kept under continuous review.[13] Governments too have been involved in the proofing of their

---

12   For guidance on this process see NGO Group for the Convention on the Rights of the Child, *A Guide for NGOs Reporting to the Committee on the Rights of the Child*, 3rd edition, Geneva, 2006, available at: www.crin.org [accessed 2 April 2010].

13   See for example, Children's Commissioner for Wales, *Annual Review 2008/2009*, available at: www.childcom.org.uk [accessed 1 April 2010].

national laws against the Convention's provisions. Although many governments limit their review of the Convention's implementation to when they must report to the CRC Committee, others have been persuaded about the merits of auditing law and policy independent of that process.[14] Numerous comparative and jurisdiction-specific academic and NGO-led research projects have sought to measure compliance with international children's rights standards in a multitude of areas and ways. The following are the author's reflections on the projects in which she has been involved as to the lessons to be learned from such auditing processes with a view to improving the understanding of and adherence to children's rights standards in practice (Kilkelly et al. 2004, Kilkelly and Donnelly 2007, Kilkelly 2007, Kilkelly 2008a, Kilkelly 2008, also Kilkelly 2006).

All of these approaches have important functions and many positive features. As efforts to engage in children's rights-proofing, they remind states of their international obligations under the CRC and promote an analysis of practice that takes place within a legal framework. Because these standards are based on international law, auditing research against them can produce clear statements about the rights of children and the treatment to which they are entitled. In this way, proofing produces not only conclusions about the extent to which these standards are being met, but facilitates the articulation of clearly worded and specific recommendations as to how this situation can be improved. The fact that children's rights auditing measures law, policy and practice against Convention-based standards means that the conclusions and recommendations emanating from the research are underpinned by the authority of international law, which the state is duty-bound to uphold.

The detailed and comprehensive nature of the international standards on children's rights adds further authority and credibility to the auditing process. The wide range of guidance available on specific aspects of children's rights means that the methodology can be usefully tailored to any particular group of children, or any area of the child's life. The wealth of standards means that auditing can be directed at specific groups of children or the general child population; it can be comprehensive, dealing with all areas of the child's life, or it can focus on a specific environment or issue. It is thus a very flexible model for monitoring the implementation of children's rights and an important way to examine the extent to which children's rights have been implemented in law, policy and practice. Children's rights auditing can be used at different levels. It can focus specifically on the rights-compliance of an individual piece of legislation examining the extent to which it expressly protects the child's right to be heard, or the principle of non-discrimination or best interests for example. Or it can consider the extent to which a specific statement of policy adheres to the Convention's principles and provisions. For example, a national strategy on youth justice could be scrutinised

---

14   See for example, Department for Children, Schools and Families, *Convention on the Rights of the Child: How Legislation Underpins Implementation in England* (March 2010), available at: www.dcsf.gov.uk [accessed 1 April 2010].

for its compliance with CRC Articles 37 and 40. For auditing purposes, the General Principles are an essential starting point and can be taken either in isolation or together with other provisions when developing benchmarks against which to measure law, policy and practice. Experience shows that some provisions are more useful than others. For example, while the concept of 'survival' in Article 6 can be used to measure mortality rates and levels of accidental death among children, concepts of 'development' are more difficult to measure. The vague nature of the best interests principle can mean that opinions as to whether and to what extent the principle has been implemented in areas such as child care, education and youth justice, can vary considerably. Thus, while research may usefully identify the extent to which the best interests principle is explicitly contained in law and policy, its application in practice will be far more difficult to measure effectively (Kilkelly and Lundy 2006). Although participation may be considered a nebulous concept, and the quality of participation difficult to measure, the extent to which children understand or are involved in decision-making processes is capable of precise evaluation as studies have shown (for example Kilkelly and Donnelly 2007, Kilkelly 2008). In relative terms, unequivocal language and strongly inferred equation with the right to participation make Article 12 an effective benchmark against which law, policy and practice can be measured. Its status as a provision with which all other provisions must be read supplements its value meaning that it can usefully be applied in all areas including family life, education, health and welfare, and youth justice and policing. The broad application and relevance of the Article 12 principle is clear from the more comprehensive benchmarking studies, while its use in a narrower or more targeted manner is apparent from its application to the more specific contexts like youth justice and healthcare.

Sometimes even the existence of legislation or policy will be the subject of investigation and, in this regard, researchers may choose to focus on whether national authorities have put in place the necessary systems to ensure effective protection of rights. The CRC Committee has recognised the importance of focusing on areas of added value where small changes, particularly in structural areas, can have a ripple or knock-on effect in the protection of children's rights. In this regard, the guidance set out in General Comment No. 5 (see above) provides several useful indicators of compliance with the duty under Article 4 to implement the Convention. Accordingly, research can usefully question the extent to which mechanisms exist to co-ordinate and monitor implementation at national level, it can interrogate the legal status of the Convention in domestic law, examine the justiciability of children's rights, the existence of advocacy and independent complaints mechanisms for children and the extent to which professionals working with and for children receive on-going training and education on children's rights and the CRC. Focus on these issues in an auditing process produces conclusions that are transparent and recommendations for structural and systemic change that are generally uncontentious. For example, studies in any sector can usefully conclude as to whether relevant professionals receive sufficient training on children's rights, and can similarly recommend that complaints mechanisms that address children's concerns are made available.

In terms of methodologies used for benchmarking exercises, it is clearly imperative that they are themselves rights-compliant. The involvement of children and young people, directly or indirectly, in research is a clear imperative under Article 12 of the CRC, although the best interests of the child requires that direct involvement is undertaken only within the defined parameters of ethical approval. Research shows that while the commitment to carry out research in line with children's rights values – particularly non-discrimination and the child's right to express themselves using age-appropriate media, to be heard and to have their views taken into account – is of central importance, it nonetheless represents a challenge, which necessitates the design, pilot and employment of appropriate methods which allow children to express their views in keeping with their age and ability (Kilkelly and Lundy 2006, Kilkelly and Donnelly 2007). Particularly vulnerable groups will require additional support and the investment of supplementary resources and these demands should not be underestimated especially in the planning phases.[15] Overall, while Article 12 requires children's views to be taken into account in research which affects them, therefore, ethical, practical and resource considerations together will determine whether and to what extent children are directly involved in any research. Avoiding tokenism, preventing research-fatigue and managing the expectations of young people involved in any research project are always important, especially in the long term. In light of these concerns, it is important to remember that indirect consultation with young people is also a valid way of attempting to measure the extent to which Article 12 is being implemented in practice. For example, while measuring the extent to which children are listened will require that they are directly involved, an alternative picture may be drawn from the collation of other viewpoints and perspectives. Witnessing the context in which the process under examination takes place, and observing its physical environment and any practical impediments to realising the child's rights under Article 12 are important and valid research methodologies. A youth justice study which uses observation of the court process as the principal tool, or a healthcare project that interviews adults on their interactions with children illustrate this point. In the former, for example, children's lack of involvement was apparent from the observation without talking to them directly and the study of the physical environment revealed at least one barrier to this direct involvement (Kilkelly 2008). On the other hand, a study into children and healthcare decision-making where children complained about the lack of their direct involvement in such decisions revealed through interviews with parents and health professionals that the reasons

---

15   This was the issue in one study ('Social integration of young people in contact with the youth justice system: a youth action research project') undertaken by the author, together with Dr Angela Veale of University College Cork supported by YAP Ireland, and funded by the Irish Research Council of the Humanities and Social Sciences. It is currently being prepared for publication. See also McAllister, Scraton and Haydon (2009).

for the poor communication were related *inter alia* to the tension between parents and health professionals regarding how much information children received about their treatment and what level of direct communication was appropriate (Kilkelly and Donnelly 2007). Health professionals also raised the practical problems of their lack of space and time for such consultation as well as the lack of adequate training. In this regard, the combination of the views of the three stakeholders in the healthcare process – children, parents and health professionals – ensured that the full picture regarding the implementation of Article 12 could be drawn. The curriculum audit, which reviewed the extent to which the training and education of a range of health professionals complied with children's rights standards, also clarified this situation further by identifying the lack of specific training for health professionals in children's rights, particularly on the child's right to be heard. Overall, therefore, it was the combination of these perspectives which helped to create a true understanding of the extent to which Article 12 is being implemented in the healthcare setting and to make recommendations regarding how the situation might be improved.

The Children's Court research also highlighted the importance of using varied methodologies in order to advance the understanding of the implementation of children's rights. The decision was taken at the outset of this research not to consult with young people for a variety of reasons including the available time and resources. The chaotic nature of the court system also suggested that identifying young people willing to participate would have been difficult. While it is recommended that any future research of this kind incorporate the views of young people directly, it is possible to argue that the approach taken to the research, namely one of observation of the court process, served to highlight young people's lack of understanding and participation in the process more effectively than speaking with them directly. In particular, it was patently clear from observing the court that young people's direct communication with the judge and the solicitor was extremely limited and that most young people spent the time in the courtroom staring at the floor or straight ahead, bored or without emotion (Kilkelly 2008). It was similarly clear from observation of the court that the physical layout of the courtroom posed a considerable obstacle to the child's involvement in the legal process and thus the implementation of Article 12 in this setting. These observations allowed practical recommendations to be made regarding the re-arrangement of the courtroom as well as the raising of awareness among judges and lawyers as to how they might bring about the child's participation and understanding of the process.

As these examples show, effective rights auditing requires that the methodology used be varied enough to ensure a variety of perspectives on the issue are achieved and flexible enough to ensure that the implementation of rights in practice are measured effectively. The objectives of the research will often dictate which approach or combination of approaches should be used. Involving young people directly in research which concerns them is both extremely important and valuable as children can provide a direct insight into the dissonance between law and policy and the way in which children's rights are being implemented in practice. A key lesson from research therefore is that those wishing to establish what is happening in children's lives must take the time and make the effort to talk to children and young people themselves. At the same time, not every project will have the resources necessary to do this in a meaningful or appropriate way. In this regard, it is important to recognise that involving children directly is not the only way in which the level of implementation of the CRC provisions like Article 12 can be measured. A combination of approaches appears to work best.

Overall, it is clear that auditing processes – attempting to measure the extent to which children's rights standards are implemented in law, policy and practice – have enormous benefits and very few drawbacks. They can be undertaken on a large scale or limited to a narrow, small basis. This is a flexible model whose precise methodology can be based on qualitative or quantitative methods, tailored to the special circumstances of the area under investigation. Informed by the authority of the CRC, its conclusions and recommendations carry added weight and, supplemented by the wider jurisprudence of the CRC, can represent a very specific application of more general principles and values. A rights-audit can throw up new perspectives on a well researched area of law or practice, demanding that a problem and its solution be viewed differently. The recommendations emerging can provide an authoritative impetus for reform, which, based on the Convention's standards, will enjoy the additional support of international law.

The Benefits of Strategic Litigation

It is clear, therefore, that research and auditing processes have significant merits and are valuable and important ways to monitor the enjoyment of children's rights in practice. At the same time, they offer a long-term and gradual strategy which, its authoritative basis notwithstanding, may not achieve progress quickly or at all depending on whether *inter alia* the political will exists to implement the recommendations made. Against this backdrop, the achievements of strategic litigation can prove attractive and although certainly not a panacea for the wide range of children's rights that are ignored, underplayed and indeed violated, they offer potential to achieve greater respect for children's rights that is worth exploring. Through the use of test cases, litigation can be used to challenge individual violations of children's rights and in doing so, take cases that have a broader positive effect on the lives of a greater number of children. The widely accepted practice of judicial review including under the Human Rights Act 1998 (and in Ireland the European Convention on Human Rights Act 2003) facilitate this process.

A further merit of a litigious approach to children's rights is, of course, that it can provide an effective remedy for an individual child whose complaint demands immediate resolution. Although litigation can also suffer from delays, it can in some instances deliver a more immediate response given the threat posed to children's rights by the passage of time. Similar to the auditing process described above, litigation based on international children's rights standards benefits from the authority that these instruments enjoy at international and in some cases regional and national level. Their value is supported further by the detailed and jurisdiction-specific standards that emanate from the CRC Committee (especially in the case of Concluding Observations) while this can also be supported by the conclusions of a children's rights audit as already outlined.

Accordingly, it is submitted, one strategic way of putting children's rights standards to effective use is to invoke them before judicial proceedings at national and international level. This approach has the potential to combine the enforcement potential of existing systems of individual petition such as the European Court of Human Rights, the Inter American Court of Human Rights and higher courts at national level, with the comprehensive and detailed standards of the CRC (Kilkelly 2001). As well as having the short-term result of providing individual children with an effective remedy based on CRC standards, this approach can also promote higher standards of children's rights protection in the long term by encouraging greater legal reliance on and reference to widely accepted children's rights values throughout the domestic and international legal system. Generating awareness among legal professionals and the judiciary can have a knock-on effect on the extent to which these standards are observed in other areas of legal practice. Thus, regardless of whether or not general principles like the best interests of the child could be said to have acquired the status of customary international law[16] it is possible to argue that the widespread support that the Convention enjoys gives its provisions standing beyond their strict legal quality. While, admittedly, national courts may be more constrained in this approach, particularly if the Convention has not been ratified by the state or where it is not part of domestic law, there can be little to stand in the way of any court seeking mere guidance or support from the widely accepted, minimum international standards which the Convention represents. Indeed, it is arguable that such an integrated approach to the protection of the rights of children promotes the cross-fertilisation of standards and mechanisms and aims to combine the benefits of both.

Litigation, strategic or otherwise, is a powerful tool. Lawyers in some national courts are accustomed to bringing constitutional or human rights challenges that seek to hold the state to account in respect of its treatment of individual or groups of children. However, the value of this approach can be further enhanced by an approach which uses all available legal instruments to secure greater protection for children's rights. Some examples from abroad make this point clearly (see also Parkes 2002). In Canada, for example, where the CRC is not part of domestic law, the Supreme Court nonetheless found the best interests principle set out in Article 3 to be more than persuasive in nature. In the case of *Baker v Canada (Minister of Citizenship and Immigration)*, the applicant challenged his deportation by relying on the CRC and, in particular, by arguing that the best interest of the (his child) child should be a primary consideration in the determination of the

---

16 See further below.

immigration matter.[17] When the case was heard by the Supreme Court, it held that the immigration officer did not adequately consider the best interests of the child, and the appeal was allowed. The Court considered the status of the Convention in Canadian law and before the courts in some detail. As the Convention had not been implemented by the Canadian parliament, its provisions had no direct application within Canadian law. That said, however, the Court went on to find that the values reflected in international human rights law might help inform the contextual approach to statutory interpretation and judicial review. More specifically, it was held that a reasonable exercise of the statutory power to allow a person to remain on humanitarian and compassionate grounds requires close consideration to the needs and interests of children as children's rights are important values in Canadian society. It was implicit in the judgment, therefore, that the provisions of the CRC would help inform whether the immigration officer had exercised his or her power reasonably. There was some disagreement in the Court regarding the status of international law within the domestic legal system and the approach of applying the underlying values of an unimplemented international treaty consistently. However, the overall conclusion was that the best interests of the child was required to be taken into account as a primary consideration in the immigration decision-making process. This has since been augmented by section 25(1) of the Immigration and Refugee Protection Act 2001.[18] The point being made here is that relying on the CRC can produce a requirement to undertake child impact analysis of immigration decisions, and this is something which the CRC Committee recommended in respect of Ireland in 2006.[19]

This conclusion – that immigration decisions must take into account the best interests of the child – has been reached by some US courts also, despite the United States not even having ratified the CRC. As well as its use in immigration cases similar to *Baker*,[20] the consensus represented by the Convention was an important factor in the case of *Roper v Simons* in 2005 when the US Supreme Court found the imposition of the death penalty on those under 18 to be contrary to the 8th and 14th Amendments to the US Constitution.[21] Here, the Court was persuaded by the international consensus – evidenced by widespread ratification of the CRC – against the imposition of the death penalty in juvenile cases. Even though the United States has not ratified the Convention, there was majority

---

17   *Baker v Canada*, 2 SCR 817 (1999).

18   See also *Martinez v Canada* (2003) FC 1341.

19   See Committee on the Rights of the Child, Concluding Observations: Ireland (2006) CRC/C/IRL/CO/2. This recommendation has its origins in research published in 2006 in Children's Rights Alliance, *All Our Children: Child Impact Assessment for Irish Children of Migrant Parents* (Dublin, 2006). See also the judgment of the High Court which advocated this approach although it was subsequently overturned on appeal by the Supreme Court. *Bode v Minister for Justice, Equality and Law Reform* [2006] IEHC 34 and [2007] IESC 62.

20   See *Beharry v Ashcroft*, 329 F.3d 51 (2003), US App. Lexis 8279.

21   *Roper v Simons*, 2005 US Lexis 2200.

support on the Supreme Court for relying on the CRC in this case. Returning to the role of academic research, however, it was the second element of the case that was even more critical. In particular, in reaching its conclusion that imposing the death penalty on juveniles was unconstitutional, the Court relied on what is now commonly known as the Brain Science Brief, a piece of neuroscience research which showed that that part of the brain associated with rational decision-making does not develop until early adulthood (see further Haider 2006). Although the case was ultimately decided on the basis of US constitutional law, the Court was clearly influenced by both the international consensus represented by the CRC's abolition of the death penalty, and the neuroscience evidence presented as an amicus brief before the Court in support of its conclusion. Beyond the significance of the individual case, therefore, Roper makes a highly persuasive case for a combined effort between researchers – whose job it is to audit or monitor compliance with the CRC and other instruments in as wide a range of disciplines as possible – and those well placed to take legal action to advance children's rights in areas of strategic importance. Overall, it makes the case for a much closer partnership between the legal profession and those in academia, and for continued engagement between all the partners working in children's rights to this end.

Of course there is potential for the use of this approach in Europe also. The fact that the CRC has been ratified by all States Parties to the Council of Europe means that it has arguably greater force in Europe than in the United States. On this basis, it is submitted that the European Court of Human Rights, set up to hear individual complaints concerning the ECHR, is entirely legitimate in referring to the CRC in cases involving children and it has done so in many cases with important effect, notably in cases concerning child protection and parental contact (Kilkelly 2001, Kilkelly 2002). Throughout the case law of the Court, evidence – sometimes inferred, sometimes overt – can be found of the Convention's influence.[22] Moreover, the former Commission on Human Rights referred directly to Concluding Observations of the CRC Committee on the United Kingdom when deciding that the defence of moderate and reasonable chastisement was too imprecise to ensure that children were effectively protected from abuse contrary to Article 3 of the ECHR.[23] This clearly provides another legal use to which the otherwise non-binding Concluding Observations can be put.

---

22   For example, see the cases of *T v UK* and *V v UK* (2000) 30 EHRR 121 (on effective participation in criminal proceedings); *C v Finland* [2006] 2 FLR 597 (on child's influence in domestic proceedings); *A v UK* (1993) 19 EHRR 112 and *Z v UK* [2000] 34 EHRR 97 (on the state's duty to protect children from harm).

23   No 25599/94 *A v UK*, Comm Rep, 18.9.97, Reports 1998-VI, no 90.

Conclusion

Overall, it is clear that there is considerable potential for utilising children's rights standards both in legal proceedings and in research in ways that are sufficiently flexible to be made fit for the range of challenges posed by the denial of children's rights. Such approaches are both distinct and separate – they have their own merits and stand in isolation – and they are inter-related in that an auditing process may usefully identify areas where a strategic legal challenge may succeed. They depend as much on the wealth and range of children's rights instruments that now govern and inform best practice in the treatment of children as they can compensate for the shortcomings of these instruments in the area of enforcement. In this respect, both approaches rely on international law that is widely supported and underpinned by a strong international consensus. The fact that reliance on these standards is now a tried and tested approach, domestically and internationally, encourages its continued use and development. Furthermore, in the era of globalisation, it is the cross-fertilisation of all of these standards – Article 24 of the EU Charter of Fundamental Rights with its CRC-based language of children's rights is an important case in point[24] – that will ensure enhanced protection of the rights of all children.

References

Abraham, S. 2003. Child soldiers and the capacity of the optional protocol to protect children in conflict. *Human Rights Brief*, 10(3), 15.

Azer, A. 1994. Modalities of the best interests principle in education. *International Journal of Law and the Family*, 8(2), 227–58.

Balton, D. 1990. The Convention on the Rights of the Child: prospects for international enforcement. *Human Rights Quarterly*, 12, 120–29.

Cashmore, J. and Parkinson, P. 2007. What responsibility do courts have to hear children's voices? *International Journal of Children's Rights*, 15(1), 43–60.

Committee on the Rights of the Child. 1991. *General Guidelines Regarding the Form and Content of Initial Reports to Be Submitted by States Parties under Article 44, Paragraph 1(a) of the Convention*. UN Doc. CRC/C/5.

———. 2003. *General Comment No 3. Adolescent Health and Development in the Context of the Convention on the Rights of the Child*. UN Doc. CRC/GC/2003/4.

Fortin, J. 2009. *Children's Rights and the Developing Law*, 3rd edition. Cambridge: Cambridge University Press.

Fottrell, D. 2000. One step forward or two steps sideways? Assessing the first decade of the Convention on the Rights of the Child, in D. Fottrell (ed.),

---

24   See further the discussion of the impact of the CRC on EU law and policy-making by Helen Stalford and Eleanor Drywood in the next chapter in this volume.

Revisiting Children's Rights 10 Years of the UN Convention on the Rights of the Child. The Hague and London: Kluwer Law International, pp. 1–14.

Franklin, A. and Sloper, P. 2005. Listening and responding: children's participation in healthcare within England. *International Journal of Children's Rights*, 13(1/2), 13–29.

Freeman, M. 1992. Taking children's rights more seriously. *International Journal of Law, Policy and Family*, 6(1), 52–71.

——. 2000. The future of children's rights. *Children and Society*, 14, 277–93.

Haider, A. 2006. Roper v Simons: the role of the brain science brief. *Ohio State Journal of Criminal Law*, 3, 369–77.

Hammarberg, T. 1990. The UN Convention on the Rights of the Child – and how to make it work. *Human Rights Quarterly*, 12, 97–105.

Kilkelly, U. 1996. The Committee on the Rights of the Child: an evaluation in the light of recent UK experience. *Child and Family Law Quarterly*, 8(2), 105–20.

——. 1999. *The Child and the ECHR*. Aldershot: Ashgate.

——. 2001. The best of both worlds for children's rights: interpreting the European Convention on Human Rights in the light of the UN Convention on the Rights of the Child. *Human Rights Quarterly*, 23(2), 308–26.

——. 2002. Effective protection of children's rights in family cases: an international approach. *Transnational Law and Contemporary Problems*, 12(2), 336–54.

——. 2004. Children's rights: a European perspective. *Judicial Studies Institute Journal*, 4(2), 68–95.

——. 2006. Operationalising children's rights: lessons from research. *Journal of Children's Services*, 4(1), 35–45.

——. 2007. *Barriers to the Implementation of Children's Rights*. Dublin: Ombudsman for Children.

——. 2008. Youth courts and children's rights: the Irish experience. *Youth Justice*, 8(2) 39–56.

——. 2008a. *Children's Rights in Ireland: Law, Policy and Practice*. Dublin: Bloomsbury Professional.

——. 2009. The child's right to religious freedom: time for reform?, in M. Fineman and K. Worthington (eds), *What is Right for Children? The Competing Paradigms of Religion and Human Rights*. Aldershot: Ashgate.

Kilkelly, U. and Donnelly, M. 2007. *The Child's Right to be Heard in the Healthcare Setting: Perspectives of Children, Parents and Health Professionals*. Dublin: Office of the Minister for Children and Youth Affairs.

Kilkelly, U., Kilpatrick, R., Lundy, L., Moore, L., Scraton, P., Davey, C., Dwyer, C. and McAlister, S. 2004. *Children's Rights in Northern Ireland*. Belfast: Northern Ireland Commissioner for Children and Young People.

Kilkelly, U. and Lundy, L. 2006. Children's rights in action: using the Convention on the Rights of the Child as an auditing tool. *Child and Family Law Quarterly*, 18(3), 331–50.

Krill, F. 1992. The protection of children in armed conflicts, in M. Freeman and P. Veerman (eds), *The Ideologies of Children's Rights*. Dordrecht: Martinus Nijhoff.

Lopatka, A. 1992. The rights of the child are universal: the perspective of the UN Convention on the Rights of the Child, in M. Freeman and P. Veerman (eds), *The Ideologies of Children's Rights*. Dordrecht: Martinus Nijhoff.

Lowe, N., Everall, M. and Nicholls, M. 2004. *The International Movement of Children*. London: Family Law.

Lundy, L. 2006. Mainstreaming children's rights in, to and through education in a society emerging from conflict. *International Journal of Children's Rights*, 14(2), 339–62.

——. 2007. 'Voice is not enough': Conceptualising Article 12 of the United Nations Convention on the Rights of the Child. *British Education Research Journal*, 33(6), 927–42.

McAllister, S., Scraton, P. and Haydon, D. 2009. *Childhood in Transition: Experiencing Marginalisation and Conflict in Northern Ireland*. Belfast: Queen's University Belfast.

McGoldrick, D. 1991. The United Nations Convention on the Rights of the Child. *International Journal of Law and the Family*, 5(2), 132–69.

Parkes, A. 2002. Children and the right to separate legal representation in legal proceedings in accordance with international law. *Irish Journal of Family Law*, 5(3), 18.

——. 2008. Children should be seen and not heard? A reflection on the proposed Constitutional Amendment. *Irish Journal of Family Law*, 11(3), 58.

——. 2011. *Children and International Human Rights Law: The Right of the Child to be Heard*. Routledge-Cavendish (forthcoming).

Parkinson, P. 2001. The child participation principle in child protection law in New South Wales. *International Journal of Children's Rights*, 9(3), 259–72.

Sinclair, R. 2004. Participation in practice: making it meaningful, effective and sustainable. *Children and Society*, 18, 106–18.

Van Bueren, G. 1994. The international legal protection of children in armed conflicts. *International and Comparative Law Quarterly*, 43, 809–26.

Chapter 9

Using the CRC to Inform EU Law and Policy-making

Helen Stalford and Eleanor Drywood

Introduction

Children's rights have, until relatively recently, seemed anathema to European Union (EU) law and policy; children were never regarded as particularly relevant to the EU's primarily economic and political pursuits. Rather, legal and policy provision targeting children has developed as something of an afterthought; a by-product of more adult-focused EU social law and policy. That said, the last five years have witnessed something of a sea change in children's rights at EU level, prompted largely by the publication in 2006 of the European Commission's Communication, *Towards an EU Strategy on the Rights of the Child* (EU COM 2006). This Communication set out a brave and ambitious new agenda for the future of EU activity in the field of children's rights, an agenda which would build upon the EU's existing achievements across a range of areas, and which would seek to integrate children's rights issues into all aspects of the EU regulatory architecture.

This public declaration of the EU's long-term commitment to children's rights is highly symbolic. However, the coherence with which the 2006 Communication applauds various EU achievements in the field of children's rights and sets out its programme of action for the future belies what has been, in reality, a highly fragmented and chaotic journey. There remains a degree of scepticism, therefore, as to whether the new-found children's rights agenda has sufficient substance and conviction to produce meaningful effects for children in the longer term. This scepticism is fuelled largely by the fact that EU children's rights measures to date have been devoid of any clear ideological reference point. More specifically, EU law and policy lacks persuasive and consistent allegiance to international children's rights principles. This, it is argued, has given rise to conflicting messages about the currency of children's rights at EU level and their vulnerability to being diluted or overlooked in the face of competing political and economic objectives.

The Commission itself has acknowledged that any future children's rights strategy, to be sustainable, has to be cast within a clearer and more persuasive normative framework, and explicitly identifies the CRC as its primary influence in this regard. Indeed, the Commission refers to the CRC on nearly every page of its 2006 Communication, and sets out an unequivocal ambition to use the instrument more strategically as a tool to audit future EU measures in the field of children's rights:

> It is important to ensure that all internal and external EU policies respect children's rights in accordance with the principles of EU law, and that they are fully compatible with the principles and provisions of the UNCRC and other international instruments. (EU COM 2006: 8)

There is no doubt then that the CRC has been singled out by the Commission as the definitive framework within which to formulate and implement its future children's rights strategy. But to some extent, this process had already gathered some momentum even before the Communication was issued: the Commission had already been engaging in regular consultation with international children's rights advocates from the academic and NGO sector well as representatives from international bodies such as UNICEF, with a view to drawing on their experience of applying the CRC; explicit references to CRC principles started to appear in legislative texts from 2004 onwards; and the instrument has been informing European Court of Justice (ECJ) interpretations of EU legislation during the course of the last decade.

The aim of this chapter is to critically evaluate the impact that more explicit integration of the CRC in these various EU contexts has had on children's rights. In doing so, it will explore how a more CRC-sensitive approach to EU law and policy-making might be achieved. The first part sets the scene for the discussion, with a brief summary of how children's rights have evolved under EU law over the past 50 years. The second part then examines the legal status of the CRC at EU constitutional level with a view to determining the extent of the EU's obligations to comply with the instrument. The third part will discuss how the CRC has been integrated into EU legislation and the effects of this. The fourth part will assess the extent to which the instrument has been used to inform judicial interpretations of EU law. The final part will suggest how the CRC might be incorporated more meaningfully into the EU decision-making process with a view to enhancing the EU's capacity to uphold and promote children's rights more effectively.

A Brief History of How Children's Rights Have Evolved at EU Level

The development of 'children's rights' at EU level over the past 50 years has been both gradual and random, characterised by isolated, largely social and economic, provisions with no explicit association with any fundamental rights agenda. Measures of relevance to children emerged initially in the 1960s in the context of free movement legislation when the rights available to EU workers to move to and reside within other member states and to access a range of social, welfare and tax-related benefits were extended to their families with a view to enhancing the allure of employment migration. Children within such families necessarily benefited from this entitlement, including the right to access education at all levels in the host state on the same basis as nationals.[1]

In the following decade, children became the indirect beneficiaries of another developing area of EU social law: employment equality legislation. This body of law was primarily aimed at re-integrating women within the labour market and enabling parents to balance work more effectively with their child-bearing and child-raising responsibilities. Children benefited at least indirectly from such measures insofar as it provided their parents (and particularly their mothers) with a modicum of financial security, a minimum level of protection whilst pregnant and immediately after giving birth, as well as more flexible working conditions that would better accommodate their domestic arrangements (for a full analysis of the various EU measures in this area see Caracciolo di Torella and Masselot 2009)

The 1980s was something of a fallow period for EU children's rights provision, but activities gathered pace again towards the end of that decade with the introduction of new protective measures within television advertising legislation (Council Directive 89/552/EEC of 3 October 1989 on the coordination of certain provisions laid down by law, regulation or administrative action in member states concerning the pursuit of television broadcasting activities[2]), followed by more targeted legislation aimed at protecting children and young people at work (Council Directive 94/33/EC of 22 June 1994 on the protection of young people at work[3]).

Priorities shifted again in the late 1990s when the EU gained competence to legislate on a range of external immigration and asylum issues, and to regulate procedural and jurisdictional matters in the field of cross-national family justice.[4] Responding to its new-found competence, the EU then engaged in a flurry of law-making activity in these two areas in particular, with children's rights measures afforded increasing prominence in many of the legislative texts.

Developments in the legislative arena reveal only part of the story of EU children's rights provision, however; the late 1990s also saw the emergence of a more prominent discourse on Europe's 'youth' in the context of civil dialogue, democratic participation, active citizenship and strategic investment in the skills and workforce of the future (see European Commission white paper – *A New Impetus*

---

1   See Article 12 of Regulation (EEC) No. 1612/68 of the Council of 15 October 1968 on freedom of movement for workers within the Community, OJ L 257/2, 19.10.1968.

2   OJ L 298/23, 17.10.1989. This instrument has since been amended, the latest version being Directive 2007/65/EC of the European Parliament and of the Council of 11 December 2007 amending Council Directive 89/552/EEC on the coordination of certain provisions laid down by law, regulation or administrative action in member states concerning the pursuit of television broadcasting activities, OJ L 332/27, 18.12.2007.

3   OJ L 216/12, 20.8.1994.

4   The former Title IV Part III EC Treaty. Amended provisions following the Treaty of Lisbon are now enshrined in Title V (entitled 'Area of Freedom, Security and Justice') of the Treaty on the Functioning of the European Union (TFEU), under a new Chapter 2 on 'Policies on Border Checks, Asylum and Immigration' (Articles 77–80).

for European Youth [EU COM 2001]). This, in turn, prompted the development of an 'EU Youth Strategy' which continues to invest in youth volunteering, educational and exchange projects, with a particular emphasis on activities that promote social inclusion.[5] Equally, there has been a surge of EU support for cross-national, cross-sectoral co-operation programmes aimed at protecting and empowering children and young people in the use of online technologies (operating primarily under the EU's Safer Internet Programme, established in 1999).

This brief and rather crude summary depicts the incremental evolution of children's rights within formal EU law and policy which has witnessed a progressively more explicit acknowledgement of the role of the EU in protecting and upholding children's interests with the turn of each decade. However, a closer analysis of these measures, and particularly of the legislation, reveals a rather less positive trend. In the context of free movement law as well as EU equality law, children's rights remain highly derivative and entirely dependent on their parents' decision to exercise those rights.[6] Similarly, EU immigration, asylum and family justice legislation, whilst conferring more direct and explicit entitlement on children, defers largely to member states' practice to determine the scope and application of those rights. The laws relating to child health and safety in the workplace and in relation to audio-visual media services arguably offer more direct protection but only within the limited contexts in which they operate. In that sense, children's rights across many of the EU areas summarised above remain restrictive and highly conditional. Moreover, they are still largely confined to a few *ad hoc* measures scattered sparingly across a dozen or so instruments with no ideological thread to link them together.

The extent to which the CRC could provide this ideological thread depends on a number of issues: whether the instrument has sufficient legal standing at EU level to legitimise using it as an authoritative source for the development and interpretation of EU measures; how the instrument can be integrated into EU law and policy in practice; and whether more explicit integration of CRC within official texts will necessarily lead to more child-sensitive interpretations of EU measures. It is to these questions that our discussion now turns.

The CRC and the EU's Fundamental Rights Framework

None of the treaties, which form the constitutional scaffolding of the EU, have ever made explicit reference to the CRC. However, since the late 1960s, the European Court of Justice (ECJ) has acknowledged that fundamental rights, as enshrined

---

5   The website of the 'Youth' directorate general of the European Commission provides a comprehensive summary of all these activities: http://ec.europa.eu/youth/ [accessed 13 September 2010].

6   For a recent illustration of this, see Case C149/10 *Chatzi v Ipourgos Ikonomikon*, judgment of 16/09/10.

in international treaties and in the constitutional traditions of the member states, are an integral part of EU law, guiding its interpretation (*Stauder v City of Ulm*,[7] *Internationale Handelsgesellschaft*[8]). In other words, they are integral to the 'General Principles' of EU law. These general principles refer to the unwritten sources of law that bind the EU institutions in the formulation, implementation and interpretation of EU law. The notion of fundamental rights as a source of EU law was formally recognised in 1992 with the introduction of the Treaty on European Union (TEU) (then Article F). Article 6(3) of the amended version of this Treaty now states:

> Fundamental rights, as guaranteed by the European Convention for the Protection of Human Rights and Fundamental Freedoms and as they result from the constitutional traditions common to the Member States, shall constitute general principles of the Union's law.[9]

Indeed, fundamental rights are now so firmly engrained in the constitutional fabric of the EU that they have even been used by the ECJ to confer directly effective rights on individuals even if, in doing so, the economic and political objectives of the EU itself are undermined (Arnull et al. 2006: 269–70). Some of the most striking examples of this are in the context of immigration whereby member states have been precluded from interpreting EU free movement law in a way that unduly prevents third country nationals from joining family members in the host state. This is on the grounds that such measures undermine individuals' right to family life as protected by Article 8 of the European Convention on Human Rights (ECHR). For example, in *Carpenter*, the ECJ considered the UK government's refusal to accept the application of Mrs Carpenter, a national of the Philippines and the spouse of a UK national, to remain in the UK.[10] Before making this application Mrs Carpenter had resided in the UK and, in fact, married her husband under an expired visa. Mr Carpenter's work had a particularly European dimension to it – he frequently dealt with clients in other member states and often travelled within the EU. The right to provide services across the EU member states is one of the fundamental freedoms recognised by the Treaty (Articles 26(2) and 56 Treaty on the Functioning of the European Union [TFEU]), the exercise of which is considered essential to the achievement of a common market. As such, legislation exists to ensure that, where possible, barriers to the provision of services across the EU are removed – which includes granting residence and any associated rights to the family members of those engaged in these activities (Council Directive 73/148/ EEC of 21 May 1973 on the abolition of restrictions on movement and residence

---

7   Case 26/69, (1969) ECR 419.

8   Case C11/70, (1970) ECR 1125.

9   Note that the Treaty on European Union was amended by the Treaty of Lisbon which came into force on 1 December 2009 (OJ 2007 C 306).

10   Case C-60/00 *Carpenter v Secretary of State for the Home Department*. [2002] ECR 1- 06279.

within the Community for nationals of member states with regard to establishment and the provision of services[11]). Mrs Carpenter claimed, therefore, that she had derived a right of residence from her husband under the free movement provisions insofar as he worked as a service provider in other member states. To support her claim, she argued that, as the primary carer of his children, she was instrumental to the success of her husband's business. The Court was reluctant to accept Mrs Carpenter's claim solely on the basis of her husband's role as a cross-border service provider, since her husband's business was primarily located within the member state in which they resided. However, the Court did concede that Mrs Carpenter's deportation would unduly interfere with her husband's right to respect to family life within the meaning of Article 8 of the ECHR. This decision both was inspired by and reaffirmed the status of the provisions of the ECHR as general principles of Union law. A consequence of decisions such as *Carpenter* is that member states and, indeed, the EU institutions can be held to account for alleged violations of fundamental freedoms that fall within the scope of EU activity (for further examples see *Baumbast and R v Secretary of State for the Home Department*,[12] *Metock and Others*[13]), including those relating to children's rights.[14]

By the same token, the ECJ has recognised the status of the CRC as another international human rights instrument of which it takes account in applying the 'general principles' of Union law (*Dynamic Medien Vertriebs GmbH*,[15] *Detiček*,[16] *Parliament v Council*[17]).

Of course, the CRC already provides a universal template for the development of international and domestic laws affecting children. However, it is a legal anomaly insofar as it is technically binding on States Parties but its legal enforceability varies from one member state to another. Therefore, its inclusion within the corpus of fundamental rights instruments, which inform the development and application of EU law, offers new possibilities for its enforcement, well beyond what it could achieve as a free-standing instrument. In other words, it can be directly relied upon before the ECJ to challenge EU measures that are deemed to be incompatible with the principles it enshrines.

---

11   OJ 1973 L 172/14, 28.6.1973.

12   Case C-413/99, ECR [2002] I-07091.

13   Case C-127/08, [2008] ECR I-6241.

14   This process is not dissimilar to that which already exists in England and Wales: following formal incorporation of the ECHR into domestic law by virtue of the Human Rights Act 1998, government departments are required to review any draft legislation that affects children to ensure its compatibility with the ECHR provisions and its accompanying case law (s. 19 Human Rights Act 1998). Moreover, national courts are empowered to set aside existing legislation that is deemed to be incompatible with the ECHR, giving the government and parliament the option to amend the legislation in line with the Convention (s. 4(2), s. 10 and Sch 2 para 4(4) Human Rights Act 1998). See further Fortin (1999).

15   Case C-244/06, judgment 14.2.2008.

16   Case C-403/09, judgment 23.12.2009.

17   Case C-540/03, (2006) ECR I-5769.

The Status of the CRC at EU Constitutional Level

In spite of the growing use of the CRC as an instrument that inspires general principles of EU law, until very recently there was virtually no reference to children in any of the EU's treaties or principal European declarations of rights.[18] On the one hand, this was understandable given the roots of these texts in the drive towards economic unity. However, it is a stance that became less defensible as the social and rights-based imperatives of the EU have increased in prominence and an increasingly explicit agenda in relation to young people emerged.

The landscape began to change at the turn of the millennium and, since then, references to elements of the CRC have begun to creep into specific constitutional texts. The first and most notable reference to the instrument is found in the Charter of Fundamental Rights in the European Union.[19] This was adopted in December 2000 and presents a detailed statement of the human rights principles to which the EU must adhere. One of the most significant innovations of the Charter is that it contains explicit reference to children's rights, granting them the right to, *inter alia*, such protection and care as is necessary for their well-being; the opportunity to express their views freely; and assurance that such views shall be taken into consideration on matters that concern them in accordance with their age and maturity (Article 24(1)). The Charter also provides that in all actions relating to children, whether taken by the public authorities or private institutions, the child's best interests must be a primary consideration (Article 24(2)). Such provisions resonate strongly with the general principles of the CRC, notably those expressed in Articles 3 and 12 of the CRC.

The most recent, and perhaps most significant, development at EU constitutional level is the introduction of the Treaty of Lisbon on 1 December 2009.[20] While this instrument does not refer directly to the CRC, it carries with it a number of legal and constitutional amendments that potentially impact upon the status of children's rights at EU level. Specifically, the Treaty specifies the 'protection of the rights of the child' as one of the stated objectives of the European Union (Article 3(3), TEU). This commitment is reinforced by a new Article which singles out protection of the rights of the child as an important aspect of the EU's external relations policy (Article 3(5), TEU), and by provisions which empower the European Parliament and the Council to adopt measures specifically aimed

---

18 Before the entry into force of the Treaty of Lisbon 2007, the sole exception to this was a reference in Article 29 TEU which related only to the specific area of cross-border criminal cooperation in relation to, *inter alia*, 'offences against children'. This reference has since been removed by the changes to the Treaties brought about by the Treaty of Lisbon 2007 (see the new Article 67 TFEU).

19 OJ C 83, 30.03.10.

20 OJ C 306, 9.10.08. Following the Treaty of Lisbon, the former EC Treaty has been amended and renamed the Treaty on the Functioning of the European Union (TFEU), although subject to updates and amendments the name of the Treaty on European Union remains the same (OJ C 83, 30.03.10).

at combating the sexual exploitation of and trafficking in children (Articles and 79(2)(d) and 83(1), TFEU). A range of more generic Treaty provisions relating to citizenship (Article 20, TFEU) and non-discrimination (Article 19, TFEU) also support the development of more inclusive, child-sensitive EU laws and policies (Stalford and Drywood 2009). Equally, the Lisbon Treaty enhances the status of fundamental rights at EU level within the amended Treaty on European Union. It affords 'Treaty-level' status to the provisions of the Charter of Fundamental Rights (Article 6(1), TEU) and states that the Union 'shall accede to the European Convention for the Protection of Human Rights and Fundamental Freedoms' (Article 6(2), TEU).

The enhanced visibility of fundamental rights at EU constitutional level following the Treaty of Lisbon bodes well for the future application of the CRC. It confirms, quite simply, that measures enacted within the scope of EU competence have to comply with human rights standards. While, in theory, this provides a more explicit basis for challenges to EU or member state actions that are deemed to be incompatible with international instruments such as the CRC (Craig 2008: 165), it may also encourage greater sensitivity to the compatibility of EU measures with the content of the CRC at the drafting stage.

Integrating the CRC into EU Legislation

The preceding analysis of the status of the CRC within the EU constitutional level prompts some discussion of the extent to which the instrument has filtered down to inform secondary legislation at EU level.

Direct references to the CRC have featured with increasing regularity in EU legislative and policy instruments over the course of the past decade. The most notable examples in this regard are the instruments relating to free movement, cross-national family justice, immigration and asylum. For example, the EU Citizenship Directive, which governs the entry, residence and social welfare rights of EU migrants and their family members, protects migrant children against expulsion from the host state, even if this would otherwise be justified on grounds of public policy or public security. The basis of this provision is that it upholds children's right to maintain links with their family in the host state, and expulsion is only permitted if it is compatible with the child's welfare, in accordance with the CRC (para. 24 Preamble and Article 28(3) Directive 2004/38/EC of the European Parliament and of the Council of 29 April 2004 on the right of citizens of the Union and their family members to move and reside freely within the territory of the member states[21]).

Other instruments, while they do not explicitly name the CRC as their source, allude directly to normative principles that are commonly associated with the CRC. Most notably, the primacy of the 'best interests' principle (as enshrined in Article

---

21   OJ L 158/77, 30.04.2004.

3 of the CRC) resonates throughout the immigration and asylum instruments, particularly in the context of provision for unaccompanied minors. For example, decisions to grant or withdraw residence rights from asylum seekers, or other illegal immigrants such as victims of trafficking, must be consistent with the best interests of any children involved (see for example para. 14 Preamble and Article 17(6) Council Directive 2005/85/EC of 1 December 2005 on minimum standards on procedures in member states for granting and withdrawing refugee status,[22] and Article 10 Council Directive 2004/81/EC of 29 April 2004 on the residence permit issued to third-country nationals who are victims of trafficking in human beings or who have been the subject of an action to facilitate illegal immigration who cooperate with the competent authorities[23]). Similarly, EU legislation governing the cross-national regulation of family law (where the parents live in different EU member states) demand that child welfare concerns must also inform decisions relating to jurisdiction, recognition and enforcement of matrimonial and parental responsibility decisions (para. 12 Preamble Regulation 2201/2003 of 27 November 2003 concerning jurisdiction and the recognition and enforcement of judgments in matrimonial matters and the matters of parental responsibility[24]). Thus, the Preamble of that instrument states:

> The grounds of jurisdiction in matters of parental responsibility established in the present Regulation are shaped in the light of the best interests of the child, in particular on the criterion of proximity. This means that jurisdiction should lie in the first place with the Member State of the child's habitual residence, except for certain cases of a change in the child's residence or pursuant to an agreement between the holders of parental responsibility. (para. 12, Regulation 2201/2003[25])

EU family law provision is also inspired by other normative principles enshrined in the CRC. For example, it requires that due account should be taken of the child's views before a decision regarding cross-national custody or residence will be enforceable (Articles 23(b) and 41(2)(c) Regulation 2201/2003); and in cases of parental child abduction, the objections of the 'competent' child can prevent the automatic return of the child to their country of habitual residence (Article 11(2)). Such measures clearly resonate with Article 12 of the CRC which provides that children should be given the opportunity to be heard in any judicial proceedings, and which requires that due account be taken of the views of the child in the light of his or her age and maturity.

The participatory ethic underpinning Article 12 of the CRC is also suggested in a number of EU immigration and asylum provisions which require member states

---

22   OJ L 326/13, 13.12.2005.
23   OJ L 261/19, 6.8.2004.
24   OJ L 338/1, 23.12.2003, repealing Regulation EC No. 1347/2000.
25   See also Articles 12(3)(b); 15(1) and (5); and 23(a) Regulation 2201/2003.

to provide children with appropriate assistance and legal representation during immigration proceedings (see e.g. Article 19(1) Council Directive 2003/9/EC of 27 January 2003 laying down minimum standards for the reception of asylum seekers,[26] and Article 30(1) Council Directive 2004/83/EC of 29 April 2004 on minimum standards for the qualification and status of third country nationals or stateless persons as refugees or as persons who otherwise need international protection and the content of the protection granted[27]).

The CRC's overarching commitment to non-discrimination, that is, to upholding the rights of *all* children on an equal basis (as enunciated in Article 2 of the CRC), is also reflected in EU immigration and asylum law, although to a much more subtle degree. For instance, the EU 'Procedures Directive', which sets out the procedures for granting and withdrawing refugee status (Directive 2005/85[28]), states that, *regardless of age*, reasoned, individual, objective and impartial decisions relating to their residence status must be communicated to the asylum applicant (Articles 8(2)(a) and 9(2) emphasis added). This instrument further provides that asylum procedures must be sensitive to the linguistic needs and limitations of the applicant (Articles 10(1)(a) and (b)). The same instrument requires member states to adapt immigration procedures to respond to the specific vulnerabilities of child asylum seekers, particularly unaccompanied minors: Article 17(4)(a), for example, requires member states to ensure that interviews with unaccompanied minors regarding their application are conducted '... by a person who has the necessary knowledge of the special needs of minors'. Such provisions reflect not only the general principles of Articles 2, 3 and 12 of the CRC, but also more substantive provisions such as Article 22 of the CRC which provides that young refuges are offered appropriate protection and humanitarian assistance in the enjoyment of their Convention rights.

It appears then that the EU has embraced the CRC, or at least the normative principles it endorses, across a range of key legislative areas in a manner that would have been inconceivable a decade ago. Questions abound, however, as to what mere reference to such principles achieves in practice; do they truly enhance children's rights in any tangible way or are they merely rhetorical? Closer examination of the children's rights provisions referred to above tempers any initial optimism: most fall into three categories corresponding to varying degrees of 'deficiency'.

The first category includes those instruments that simply fail to incorporate adequate provision for children or that discriminate against certain groups of children in their implementation. An obvious example of this is the notorious Family Reunification Directive (Council Directive 2003/86/EC of 22 September 2003 on the right to family reunification[29]). In contrast to some of the efforts summarised above to achieve comprehensive, non-discriminatory provision for

---

26   OJ L 31/18, 6.2.2003.
27   OJ L 304/12, 30.9.2004.
28   OJ L 326/13, 13.12.2005.
29   OJ L 251/12, 3.10.2003.

child immigrants, this Directive allows member states to impose 'integration conditions' on children over the age of 12 who apply to join their family in the host state. The provision offers no guidance on the nature and scope of this integration condition but, rather, vaguely posits that it will be determined by the legislation of the member state 'existing ... on the date of implementation of this Directive' (Article 4(1)).[30]

The second category includes those legislative instruments that, ostensibly, contain appropriate, binding provision for children but whose effectiveness depends entirely on how conscientious member states are in their implementation. Of course, the same could be said of much of the secondary legislation discussed above since any provisions included within EU Directives will only be as effective as the national implementing measures on which they hang and, indeed, on how rigorous the EU is in enforcing their implementation. The fact remains, however, that notwithstanding the range of enforcement mechanisms available to the EU, all too often even the most explicit, child-targeted EU legislation has largely been ignored. An example of this is seen in legislation, enacted in the 1970s, to address the educational (and particularly the linguistic) needs of migrant children (Council Directive 77/486 on the education of the children of migrant workers[31]). This instrument set out a comprehensive range of linguistic obligations aimed simultaneously at facilitating migrant children's integration in the host state and sustaining their linguistic and cultural heritage. Indeed, the Directive offered a strikingly intuitive vision of the CRC's educational rights realised over a decade later.[32] Subsequent analyses revealed, however, that only a minority of member states had taken any steps to implement the provisions, an indifference that was further fuelled by the Commission's failure to impose any sanctions.

A third, and more common obstacle hampering the impact of CRC-inspired measures, relates to the vague and conditional nature of many EU legislative provisions relating to children. In other words, they refer to the need to protect children's rights but only in accordance with existing national law or process. Such is the case for most of the immigration and family justice measures referred to above. These instruments may make numerous references to best interests and participatory rights but they do not endow the EU with any competence to dictate the content and scope of such measures at the national level; they rely instead on appropriate domestic procedures and guidance being in place at the national

---

30 An (unsuccessful) action for annulment initiated by the Parliament on the grounds that this provision failed to uphold the rights of the child, including that of non-discrimination, is discussed below. See further Drywood (2007).

31 OJ L 199/32, 6.08.2007.

32 See in particular Article 29(1)(c) of the CRC which provides that: 'States Parties agree that the education of the child shall be directed to ... The development of respect for the child's parents, his or her own cultural identity, language and values, for the national values of the country in which the child is living, the country from which he or she may originate, and for civilizations different from his or her own.'

(or, indeed, regional) level to give effect to such rights. For example, EU family justice legislation endorses the 'competent' child's right to be heard in cross-national family proceedings in accordance with national consultation processes. In practice, research has illustrated how easily domestic courts can dispense with the requirement to take account of the child's views (Smart et al. 2001, Douglas and Murch 2002, Butler et al. 2003). Similarly, although asylum legislation grants children a right to legal representation, the nature and extent of legal support, particularly for child asylum seekers, is notoriously inconsistent across the member states, not to mention across regions within each member state.

These deficiencies are further illustrated through the ECJ's interpretation of EU legislation relating to children, an issue to which our analysis now turns.

The Use of the CRC by the European Judiciary as an Interpretative Guide

Although historically the ECJ has been charged with providing guidance on the interpretation and application of the *economic* freedoms enshrined in EU law, it nevertheless has, as noted above, a long tradition of upholding and promoting fundamental rights.

Perhaps not surprisingly, however, there are only a handful of judgments by the ECJ that relate directly to children. While these judgments reveal a degree of judicial receptiveness to the CRC as an interpretative guide, they also suggest that the ECJ lacks the skill and knowledge required to deploy the CRC's central principles sensitively and appropriately. Needless to say, consideration of the CRC has been a relatively recent development in the EU's human rights jurisprudence, beginning rather sluggishly in 2002 when the Advocate-General attempted (unsuccessfully) to engage the ECJ in a discussion of the CRC implications of refusing a child's application to adopt his mother's surname (*Garcia-Avello*[33]).

Despite this initial reluctance, recent years have seen a growing number of references to the CRC by the ECJ. In its 2006 decision on the legality of the family reunification Directive, the ECJ, for the first time, explicitly acknowledged that the CRC should be taken into account in determining the compatibility of EU measures with fundamental rights (*Parliament v Council*[34]). The case concerned provisions that allowed member states to restrict the circumstances in which children who remained outside the Union territory could be reunited with their parents who were legally resident in Europe, on the basis of the child's age and

---

33   Case C-148/02, [2003] ECR I-11613. Advocate-General Jacobs' Opinion in this case referred to Articles 3(1), 7(1) and 8(1) of the CRC. In its full judgment, the ECJ declined to consider the implications of these provisions, basing its decision instead on the more familiar notions of EU citizenship (as enshrined in Article 20, TFEU, ex-Article 18 of the EC Treaty), and the right to respect for private and family life (as enshrined in Article 8 of the European Convention on Human Rights).

34   Case C-540/03, [2006] ECR I-5769.

likelihood of integration into the host society (Articles 4(1) and 4(6) Directive 2003/86[35]). The Court made reference, albeit fleeting, to the principle laid down in Article 10(1) of the CRC that children have the right to have their claims for family reunification dealt with in a positive, humane and expeditious manner, as well the child's right to maintain contact with both his/her parents, found in Article 9(1). On the one hand, symbolically, this was an important step in the legal recognition accorded to children at EU level: the Court acknowledged that CRC principles can, and should, serve as a point of reference in determining the legality of EU law. Ultimately, however, it rejected the European Parliament's arguments that the provisions breached the fundamental rights of the child and the principle of non-discrimination, choosing instead to uphold the legality of the provisions. In fact, aside from passing references to the relevant CRC principles, there was virtually no further discussion of whether they had actually been violated. The decision to uphold the offending provisions was determined instead on the basis of the legal framework surrounding immigration provisions at EU level. Furthermore, any rights-related discussion was confined to the scope and content of the right to a private and family life found in Article 8 of the European Convention on Human Rights, a text with which the Court of Justice is far more familiar, but that has, nonetheless, been noted for its traditionally 'adultist' focus (Drywood 2007).

The ECJ's ambivalence to the CRC in *Parliament v Council* has been superseded, in more recent years, with an increasing willingness to engage in a more meaningful discussion of the instrument. Recently, in *Detiĉec*,[36] the Court examined the relevance of CRC principles in the context of a cross-border abduction case pursued under the EU family justice legislation referred to above (Regulation 2201/2003[37]). The case concerned the daughter of an Italian father and Slovenian mother whose relationship had broken down. Custody of the child had been awarded to the father by the Italian family court but, for reasons that are not made clear in the ECJ's decision, that custody order requested that the daughter be temporarily placed in the care of an Italian children's home. Contravening this order, the mother travelled with her daughter to Slovenia and sought an order from the Slovenian court granting her custody there. At this point, the daughter informed the Slovenian court that she wished to remain in Slovenia with her mother. The question referred to the ECJ was whether the Italian court's original order must be upheld in Slovenia. In reaching its decision, the ECJ referred to the CRC-inspired provisions of the EU Charter of Fundamental Rights of the European Union (Article 24). In doing so, the Court emphasised the right of the child '... to maintain on a regular basis a personal relationship and direct contact with both parents' and added that '... respect for that right undeniably merges into the best interests of any child' (para. 54).

---

35   OJ L 251/12, 3.10.2003.
36   Case C-403/09, judgment 23.12.2009.
37   OJ L 338/1, 23.12.2003.

Notwithstanding the ECJ's acknowledgement that the child's best interests should be taken into account in determining how the Regulation should be interpreted, it conceded that such assessments fall to the discretion of the national courts. The ECJ thus upheld the Italian court's order on a point of procedure: the decision to place the child in the custody of the father had been legitimate and should not be undermined by the mother's actions in abducting her. Any further challenges to the decision, based on the best interests of the child, should be mooted before the Italian courts in accordance with the process of private international law.

Curiously, however, for all of its discussion of the best interests principle, the Court declines to consider the arguably more persuasive impact of Article 12 of the CRC (also enshrined in Article 24 of the Charter). This is particularly anomalous given that the child, who by the time of the ECJ's judgment was 13 years old, had told the Slovenian court that she wished to remain in Slovenia with her mother and that the objections of the 'competent' child can found an exception to return under EU law (Article 11 Regulation 2201/2003[38]).

As such, the court's preoccupation with upholding the rights of the child in *Detiĉec* appears somewhat disingenuous given its selective emphasis on those provisions that support the Court's judgment and its willing disregard for those that do not. Moreover, this anomaly raises questions as to the real purpose or value of the ECJ's allusion to the CRC principles if its main conclusion was that ultimately it had no real competence to rule on such issues. Indeed, this judgment is illustrative of a wider tension lying at the heart of the EU's unsteady relationship with children's rights; that is, the difficulty in upholding national sovereignty to determine the substantive application of children's rights, even when the question before the Court is primarily concerned with the interpretation of EU law.

Despite the 'hollowness' of the ECJ's consideration of the CRC in the *Detiĉec* judgment, there had been signs before then that protection of children's rights could act as a legitimate brake on the application of EU law. In *Dynamic Medien*[39] the legislation at issue was that governing the free movement of goods between the member states. The case concerned German laws prohibiting the sale of DVDs and videos via mail order that were not labelled as suitable for young persons. Proceedings were brought against a company that imported Japanese cartoons from the UK to Germany that bore no such label. This was in spite of the fact that they had been classified as 'suitable only for 15 years and over' by the British Board of Film Classification. The first question for the Court was whether these laws imposed unlawful limits on imported goods,[40] as prohibited

---

38   OJ L 338/1, 23.12.2003. This provision is itself informed by Article 13 of the 1980 Hague Abduction Convention.

39   Case C-244/06, judgment 14 February 2008.

40   The Court considers whether the laws fall into a category known as 'measures having equivalent effect', defined as above in Case 2/73 *Geddo v Ente Nazionale Risi* (1973) ECR 865.

by Article 34, TFEU (formerly Article 28 of the EC Treaty). Having answered this question in the affirmative, the Court then went on to consider whether this restriction on free movement of goods could be justified on grounds of public policy or public morality (as permitted by Article 36, TFEU, ex-Article 30 of the EC Treaty) and, in doing so, gave extensive consideration to the children's rights principles at play. In particular, Article 17 of the CRC was cited. This provision, whilst recognising the importance of the function performed by the mass media, also encourages signatory states to develop appropriate guidelines for the protection of the child from information and material injurious to his or her well-being. The ECJ again considered the broader general principles of the CRC found in Article 24 of the EU Charter of Fundamental Rights. On this basis the Court concluded that the German restrictions on the sale of the DVDs were justified by the overarching aim to protect young people. This judgment is therefore highly significant; it not only represents a rare derogation from the free movement of goods provisions, but marks an uncharacteristically confident deployment of children's rights principles to challenge the fundamental single-market ethos of the European Union.

These decisions demonstrate that, while there is a keen awareness by the ECJ of its obligations to comply with the provisions of the CRC, its application is unpredictable and rarely persuasive. It is important to note, however, that the CRC is not the only pathway to upholding children's rights. In fact, some of the most tangible benefits granted to children under EU law have come from decisions that hinge upon the notion of EU citizenship rather than the promotion of children's rights *per se*. For example, in *Baumbast*,[41] a family of migrants were entitled to remain in the UK, despite the fact that their parents no longer technically qualified for residence under EU free movement law, on the basis that any move to deport them would be prejudicial to the children's education. Furthermore, in *Chen*,[42] a child born to Chinese parents in Belfast who was granted Irish nationality (under the law applicable at the time) was subsequently entitled to exercise her free movement rights as an EU citizen and lawfully enter and reside in the UK. At the time she was an infant and, therefore, the Court ruled that her mother could also derive an associated right of residence in order to facilitate the exercise of her daughter's free movement rights as an EU citizen – to do otherwise would deprive these rights of any useful effect. Similar judgments were handed down in the subsequent cases of *London Borough of Harrow v Nimco Hassan Ibrahim, Secretary of State for the Home Department*[43] and *Texeira v London Borough of Lambeth, Secretary of State for the Home Department*,[44] although the ECJ went a step further and removed any condition that their ongoing residence rights be made conditional upon the family having sufficient independent financial resources and sickness insurance. Such

---

41   Case C-413/99 [2002] ECR I-7091.
42   Case C-200/02, *Zhu and Chen* [2004] ECR I-9925.
43   Case C-310/08, judgment of 23.2.10.
44   Case C-480/08, *Maria Teixeira*, Judgment of 23.2.10.

decisions serve to reinforce the children's status not only as independent rights holders under EU free movement law, but also as the 'anchors' of their parents' residence rights (see further Stalford 2008 and Currie 2009).

Developing a More CRC-based Approach to EU Law and Policy-making

The above analysis highlights the fickle and unpredictable nature of the EU's relationship with the CRC. Yes, the instrument now features more regularly in the parlance of the ECJ and the EU legislative process than it once did, but they remain uneasy bedfellows. These observations reinforce the point that genuine allegiance to the CRC implies more than passing reference to it in formal texts or judicial opinions; the entire process, investment and ideology surrounding the CRC also needs to be embraced. This obligation is captured in Article 4 of the CRC which obliges States Parties to the Convention to 'undertake all appropriate legislative, administrative, and other measures for the implementation of the rights recognised in the present Convention'. This obligation is further bolstered by Article 44 of the CRC which sets out the reporting obligations of States Parties on the measures they have adopted to give effect to its provisions. The UN Committee on the Rights of the Child has elaborated extensively on the meaning and scope of these commitments in its General Comment No. 5 on General measures of implementation.[45] The list of activities included within these guidelines is extensive and sheds new light on what genuine allegiance to the CRC demands of the EU: review of existing legislation; provision of effective remedies; a comprehensive child rights-based national strategy; coordination mechanisms; impact assessment, evaluation and other monitoring activities; making children visible in budgets; training, child rights education and awareness-raising; establishment of independent human rights/ombudsman institutions; cooperation with civil society; international cooperation; and working together with children directly (Ruxton 2010).

The Commission has already made a good start in identifying many of these issues in its 2006 Communication and, by the same token, there has been much talk at EU level of 'mainstreaming' children's rights into its law and policies. However, so far, this approach seems to consist primarily of sporadic references to CRC principles within legislative texts, with little evidence of the more comprehensive approach suggested by the General measures of implementation. To achieve this, we suggest that the following key issues demand urgent attention.

First of all, structural barriers within the EU, and particularly within the Commission, need to be addressed as an absolute priority. Currently, the Commission is ill-equipped to deal with the demands of developing the all-embracing children's rights strategy it envisages. Most notably, there is still insufficient co-ordination

---

45   CRC/GC/2003/5, 27.11.2003. See also the Committee's General Guidelines regarding the form and contents of States Parties' initial and periodic reports CRC/C/5, CRC/C/58 and CRC/C/58/Rev.1.

or collaboration between the different departments (Directorates-General – DGs) within the Commission; in fact the Children's Rights Strategy is largely associated with and driven by DG Justice, Freedom and Security despite the fact that other DGs have been leading highly innovative and far-reaching activities relating to children and young people for some years now.[46] Similarly, the Commission needs to be more directly responsive to the related activities of other EU agencies such as the Fundamental Rights Agency. There are prevailing concerns that this endemic divisiveness between the various Commission departments is hampering the joined up, comprehensive approach that the Children's Rights Strategy needs.

Secondly, in order to move forward with children's rights, the EU needs to reflect on past and existing achievements or failures in the area. This requires the development of much more effective, tailored monitoring mechanisms to test the impact of EU law and policy on children. While a number of methods might be used to achieve this, reference to high quality comparative statistical data is paramount. Currently, however, there is a distinct and worrying lack of data relating to children at EU level, making effective monitoring virtually impossible. Addressing this void is not just a question of resourcing the collation of new data, a process that would be both time-consuming and costly. Alongside this, further efforts could be made to disaggregate existing data to identify the distinct status of children and to expose the position of different groups of children. This could be achieved through detailed consultation with the European statistical body, EUROSTAT, and with national statistical bodies to develop a Europe-wide consensus on gathering more child-focused data. Additionally, greater effort should be made to collaborate with international statistical and monitoring activities to avoid unnecessary costs and duplication of effort.[47] Such efforts need to be complemented, however, by a more resolute commitment on the part of the Commission to transpose the findings of such monitoring activities into meaningful policy responses.

A third factor that would enhance the potential of the CRC at EU level is more routine engagement with those working on children's rights issues and service delivery at the grass roots level and, where possible, direct engagement with children and young people themselves. Further thought needs to be given as to how this will be achieved, but it must amount to more than simply broad brush surveys that have characterised the EU's consultation portfolio to date. Child participation must become integral to each legal and policy development at EU

---

46   See, in particular, the extensive work of DG Education and Culture which boasts 20 years of activities: (available at: http://ec.europa.eu/youth/index_en.htm [accessed 13 December 2010]); and DG SANCO has mainstreamed children and youth into a range of its public health initiatives in addition to establishing a number of campaigns on youth and safety health issues, see, for example, the Youth Health Initiative (available at: http://ec.europa.eu/health-eu/youth/index_en.htm [accessed 13 December 2010]).

47   Similar recommendations were proposed by the authors in 2009 following a study, conducted on behalf of the EU Fundamental Rights Agency, to develop a set of indicators to enable the EU to monitor the impact of EU law and policy on children. See Stalford, Sax, and Drywood et al. (2009).

level, and must be reinforced at national level in the implementation of EU law and policy measures. The lack of research and data reflecting the views of children is clearly an issue that the EU could address as a priority in itself through enhanced investment in programmes that support innovative and genuine participatory techniques with children from a diverse range of backgrounds.[48] Moreover, information on children and the EU could be made more accessible to young people, through more interactive and child-friendly media, consistent with Article 42 of the CRC.[49] Finally, further guidelines and training on how this research, where appropriate, can be translated into concrete policy recommendations could also be developed in collaboration with international stakeholders and NGOs with a view to avoiding tokenism.

Conclusion

The discussion in this chapter has demonstrated that the EU has accumulated an impressive catalogue of achievements in the field of children's rights. These activities have touched upon a diverse and, at points, somewhat disjointed range of areas. As progress has gathered pace, particularly in the past decade, attempts have been made to instil some semblance of coordination to ensure that these developments uphold and promote the rights of the child in a consistent and meaningful manner. However, in spite of these efforts, the absence of any ideological lynchpin underlying these activities is both striking and problematic.

There are signs, however, that the EU institutions are gradually embracing the CRC as an authoritative reference point in EU child law and policy processes. Isolated legislative provisions increasingly reflect the ethos of the CRC, particularly in the areas of migration and cross-border family disputes, where the Convention's central principles of best interests and child participation have clearly informed legal measures. However, the ideals espoused by the instrument have yet to permeate the policy, legal and judicial process in a more comprehensive and meaningful way.

Of course, it is important to remember that the CRC is just one of many tools at the EU's disposal in its journey towards achieving a more child-sensitive approach; children's rights can emerge and be enforced at the EU level even in the absence of formal and consistent allegiance to the Convention. The notion of EU citizenship and the provisions of the ECHR, for instance, have offered highly effective platforms for the development of children's rights at this level. Indeed,

---

48   There are some modest signs of EU support for large-scale, cross-national research involving children and young people, including the FRA's latest research on separated, asylum-seeking children in the European Union (EU Fundamental Rights Agency 2010).

49   Some progress has been made towards developing a dedicated website on children's rights issues but this is not readily accessible and there has been limited input of children and young people into this process.

the case law demonstrates that the judiciary is rather more at ease with advancing children's rights within these frameworks rather than through more direct reference to the less familiar framework of the CRC. The achievement of a more consistent and persuasive approach to children's rights, however, demands more emphatic allegiance to the unequivocally child-focused agenda of the latter. Indeed, with appropriate guidance on how to use the instrument as an auditing tool at various levels of EU activity, many of the current anomalies and, indeed, breaches of children's rights currently evident in EU law, could be ironed out. This, of course, demands that the EU's institutions move beyond simple rhetorical allegiance to the principles of the CRC itself, towards a more proactive engagement in the entire CRC ethos and process.

References

Arnull, A., Dashwood, A., Dougan, M., Ross, M., Spaventa, E. and Wyatt, D. 2006. *Wyatt and Dashwood's EU Law*. London: Sweet & Maxwell.

Butler, I., Scanlan, L., Robinson, M., Douglas, G.F. and Murch, M.A. 2003. *Divorcing Children: Children's Experience of Their Parents' Divorce*. London: Jessica Kingsley.

Caracciolo di Torella, E. and Masselot, A. 2009. *Reconciling Work and Family Life in EU Law and Policy*. Basingstoke: Palgrave Macmillan.

Craig, P. 2008. The Treaty of Lisbon: process, architecture and substance. *European Law Review*, 33(2), 137–66.

Currie, S. 2009. EU migrant children, their primary carers and the European Court of Justice: access to education as a precursor to residence under community law. *Journal of Social Security Law*, 16(2), 76–105.

Douglas, G.F. and Murch, M.A. 2002. Taking account of children's needs in divorce: a study of family solicitors' responses to new policy and practice initiatives. *Child and Family Law Quarterly*, 14(1), 57–75.

Drywood, E. 2007. Giving with one hand, taking with the other: fundamental rights, children and the family reunification decision. *European Law Review*, 32(3), 396–407.

European Union Commission. 2001. *A New Impetus for European Youth*. COM(2001) 681 final, Brussels, 681 final, 21.11.2001.

——. 2006. *Towards an EU Strategy on the Rights of the Child*. COM(2006) 367 final, Brussels, 4.7.2001.

EU Fundamental Rights Agency. 2010. *Separated, Asylum-Seeking Children in European Union Member States*. Summary Report, April 2010.

Fortin, J. 1999. The HRA's impact on litigation involving children and their families. *Child and Family Law Quarterly*, 11(3), 237–56.

Ruxton, S. 2010. Applying the UN CRC general measures of implementation in an EU context. Unpublished paper.

Smart, C., Neale, B. and Wade, A. 2001. *The Changing Experience of Childhood: Families and Divorce*. Cambridge: Polity Press.

Stalford, H. 2008. The relevance of EU Citizenship to children, in A. Invernizzi. and J. Williams (eds), *Children and Citizenship*. London: Sage.

Stalford, H. and Drywood, E. 2009. Coming of age? Children's rights in the European Union. *Common Market Law Review*, 46, 143–72.

Stalford, H., Sax, H. and Drywood, E. et al. 2009. *Developing Indicators for the Protection, Respect and Promotion of the Rights of the Child in the European Union*. Vienna: EU Fundamental Rights Agency.

Chapter 10

The Roles of Independent Children's Rights Institutions in Implementing the CRC

Brian Gran[1]

Introduction

What roles do independent children's rights institutions (ICRIs) play in implementing the CRC? After discussing what an ICRI is and the different types of ICRIs, this chapter will examine their objectives, their formal powers, their independence, and the resources they use to reach their objectives. Those resources include the circumstances in which ICRIs work to implement the CRC.

What is an ICRI?

Before proceeding to an analysis of the roles of ICRIs in implementing the CRC, a discussion of what exactly ICRIs and the CRC are will be useful. The CRC is the chief international treaty on children's and young people's rights. Adopted in 1989, and with nearly universal ratification, it is among the most widely ratified and most accepted of all human rights treaties.

An ICRI is a type of independent institution that concentrates on monitoring, promoting and protecting children's rights (Borgen 1996, Davidson, Cohen and Girdner 1993, Flekkoy 1991, Lansdown 2001a, 2001b, Melton 1991, UNICEF Innocenti Research Centre 1997). Although the first ICRI was set up over 30 years ago, since 2000 these institutions have been widely established, although in different shapes and sizes. However, with their increasing numbers, differences in their organisational features have become noticeable, resulting in debates over their efficacy. The CRC Committee, which is charged with monitoring governments' efforts at implementing the CRC, has strongly influenced what makes an ICRI.

1   The author thanks Jane Williams for her guidance and generous suggestions. He also thanks Robin Shura and Lynn Falletta for their assistance in gathering data for this project. The author is especially grateful to the ICRIs who have participated in his international study. Much of this chapter arises from an international project the author is directing on ICRIs. Data for this chapter are from interviews conducted with ICRIs during ENOC annual meetings, and from research on the four UK ICRIs, including interviews with those ICRIs, their staff, NGO representatives and government officials.

As part of its work, the CRC Committee publishes General Comments in an effort to encourage States Parties to advance young people's rights. These General Comments are designed to help States Parties and others interpret the provisions of the CRC. The CRC Committee has published a dozen General Comments from 2001 to 2009, with topics ranging from health to unaccompanied children.

The second General Comment (CRC/GC/2002/2, 15 November 2002) ('General Comment No. 2') published by the Committee focused on '[s]pecialist independent human rights institutions for children, ombudspersons or commissioners for children's rights ...' (para. 6). The Committee (para. 1) said it welcomed the 'establishment of NHRIs[2] and children's ombudspersons/children's commissioners and similar independent bodies ...'. The general idea of such an institution is that it is to be 'an independent institution for the promotion and monitoring of implementation of the Convention' (para. 1). The CRC Committee further states (para. 3) that the UN General Assembly and the Commission on Human Rights have 'repeatedly called for the establishment' of these institutions and that through periodic reporting, States Parties are expected to report on these institutions.

In its General Comment (at paras 3–4), the CRC Committee refers to the Vienna Declaration and Programme of Action (United Nations General Assembly 1993) generated in 1993 at the World Conference on Human Rights. According to the United Nations, the Vienna Conference was held to assess progress towards universal human rights. Held 25 years after the International Year of Human Rights, the Vienna conference was attended by over 7,000 participants, representatives of over 800 non-governmental organisations and representatives of 171 national governments (United Nations General Assembly 2010).

The Vienna Declaration emphasised that national human rights institutions (NHRIs) 'uphold the rule of law and democracy, electoral assistance, human rights awareness through training, teaching and education, popular participation and civil society' (para. 34). It further emphasises that the important roles of national human rights institutions are to promote and protect human rights (para. 36) and says that these institutions are to advise 'competent authorities', such as a government or parliament, remedy violations of human rights, and distribute information on and educate about human rights.

In its General Comment No. 2 (at para. 4), the CRC Committee refers to the Paris Principles. The Paris Principles were adopted in December 1993 by the UN General Assembly, the 'chief deliberative, policymaking and representative organ of the United Nations' (United Nations General Assembly 2010). The Paris Principles state that a national institution shall promote and protect human rights, and shall be independent of government. In doing its work, the Paris Principles state such a national institution should have as its objectives lobbying on and publicising human rights issues, including human rights violations, monitoring and lobbying for human rights legislation, and educating about human rights.

---

2   National human rights institutions.

The Council of Europe has taken a strong interest in ICRIs. In 2003, its Parliamentary Assembly made a recommendation on 'the institution of ombudsman', for which it seemed to have in mind human rights ombudspersons (Council of Europe 2003). It noted three purposes of national human rights ombudspersons: protecting human rights, promoting the rule of law and ensuring the proper behaviour of public officials. The Council of Europe said the central work of an ombudsperson is to be an intermediary between 'administration' and 'individuals'. Through this Recommendation, the Council of Europe notes that circumstances particular to each country will shape what its ombudsperson is expected to do. This Recommendation also notes how others are to work with the ombudsperson. It states that officials should turn to the ombudsperson when dealing with a particularly grave situation when normal procedures are ineffective.

However, the Council of Europe Assembly envisions an ombudsperson with limited powers. In their 2003 Recommendation, they hold that the ombudsperson's enforcement powers should be limited to moral persuasion through 'public criticism'. The Recommendation indicates this public criticism should be made through reports on 'maladministration', which the Assembly expects will result in the Council of Europe's 'political condemnation'. Given its vision of limited powers, the Assembly's Recommendation expects an ombudsperson would only access courts to ask for interpretive judgments of legal questions needed to fulfil its work, including an investigation, or for purposes of representing an individual who has 'no direct access' to court (even then, the Assembly states it is best for an individual to go directly to courts without help from an ombudsperson). The Council of Europe expects an ombudsperson would only ensure 'the procedural efficiency and administrative propriety of the judicial system'. Indeed, the Assembly recommends that the ombudsperson should not be able to initiate, intervene, or reopen judicial cases, with the exception of representing an individual who is without access to court.

Other definitions of ICRIs structure how ICRIs are established and how existing ICRIs implement the CRC. Membership requirements can shape the organisation and work of ICRIs. Probably the predominant network of ICRIs in the world is the European Network of Ombudspersons for Children (ENOC, formerly the European Network of Ombudsmen for Children). ENOC recently updated its membership guidelines. It designates two kinds of membership: full and associate. For an ICRI to be a full member, its government must be a member of the Council of Europe. Compared to the European Union, which has 27 members and is a governing structure, the Council of Europe has 47 members. Thus, this first membership criterion means ENOC membership is open to a broad group.

The second criterion to be a full ENOC member requires that the ICRI must have been established via parliamentary legislation. Third, this legislation must indicate the ICRI is independent (although in form and practice, even with a statement of independence, many ICRIs are encumbered with formal qualities that weaken their independence). Fourth, this legislation must indicate the ICRI has, at a minimum presumably, two functions: the first is to protect children's rights and the second is to promote children's rights. Fifth, conversely, the legislation establishing the office cannot limit the ICRI in pursuing the functions of protecting and promoting children's rights. Sixth, the legislation cannot limit the ICRI's ability to pursue 'core' functions outlined in the Paris Principles (it is not clear what those core functions are, but they are most likely the two functions noted above). Seventh, the legislation cannot limit the ICRI's ability to pursue these functions. This criterion downplays, if not ignores, limitations found in full members' legislation, which will be discussed below. Eighth, acknowledging that some ICRIs are part of human rights institutions, and sometimes are organised differently, ENOC requires that an official within the ICRI can be identified as exclusively devoted to protecting and promoting children's rights. Thus, a NHRI without an official wholly focused on children's rights will not meet this criterion. Finally, ENOC requires that processes for appointing new officials associated with an ICRI be set out in legislation. This legislation must identify the ICRI's length of term, and if another term may be served, how the renewal process works.

An associate ENOC member is an ICRI that does not fulfil a criterion. According to the ENOC website, numerous ENOC members are associate members. In fact, of the 36 ENOC members, eight are associate members: Andalusia of Spain, Georgia, England, Hungary, Portugal, Slovak Republic, Slovenia, and Styria of Austria. Associate status is sometimes given to encourage reform of the legislation governing an ICRI. In the case of the establishment of the Children's Commissioner for England, ENOC leadership hoped this ICRI would enjoy greater independence.

It should be noted that ENOC's membership guidelines raise questions of arbitrariness. An example is independence. Merely stating 'independence' in legislation ignores crucial features of ICRIs that undermine independence. Numerous ICRIs are accountable, directly or indirectly, to government officials. Similarly, the budget of many ICRIs is not automatically provided via legislation and instead, executive government officials control their budgets, determining increases and cuts. For example, the Prime Ministry of Iceland controls its ICRI's financial affairs.

Another example of arbitrariness concerns the ENOC membership criterion requiring that an ICRI's legislation cannot limit its ability to pursue the core functions of protecting and promoting children's rights, as this criterion ignores other ways ICRIs are impeded in their work. For instance, ENOC does not address what level of resources are needed for an ICRI to do its work. The staff of the English Commissioner numbers approximately 25, but this ICRI is expected to serve over 9 million children (Office for National Statistics 2010). In contrast, the staff of the Norwegian ICRI is about 15 (Barneombudet 2010), but it serves 854,000 children (CIA 2010).

From these comparisons, certain qualities begin to emerge regarding what is important in defining an ICRI. An ICRI is a specialist institution possessing extraordinary powers because children are outside normal politics. In contrast to some conceptions of an ombudsperson, an ICRI does not exist to point out extraordinarily awful situations, or maladministration, but because young people cannot enforce their rights like adults. For this reason, an ICRI maintains some degree of independence so that it can monitor what its government does and does not do in promoting young people's rights. It must be able to decry the failings of government and society to its young people.

Some definitions expect an ICRI will work towards CRC implementation, but not all. Indeed, while ENOC expects its members to pursue full implementation, this is not a condition of ENOC membership. Across these definitions are different visions of how an ICRI will pursue implementation of the CRC.

Why an ICRI, rather than an IHRI?

Why establish an independent *children's* rights institution? Why isn't an independent *human* rights institution good enough? This question seems especially relevant when national economies are under significant pressures and government's budgets are facing cuts. In France, for example, just such a situation may result in the closure of the French ICRI, despite the CRC Committee calling for its strengthening (CRIN 2009). Is, therefore, a separate independent institution for children's rights necessary?

A variety of answers have been given to this question. The CRC Committee, through its General Comment No. 2, calls for separate ICRIs because children are different from adults. According to the Committee, children need their own independent rights institution due to their development and different statuses in major social, economic and political structures. Because children are still developing (Lansdown 2001a, 2001b), the Committee (UN Committee on the Rights of the Child 2002: 2) states they are 'particularly vulnerable to human rights violations …'. Moreover, due to the way most societies are organised, in general young people are less likely to be heard. The CRC Committee's reasoning is that in very few places can young people effectively participate in political systems and legal systems. Likewise, only in rare circumstances can young people effectively work with organisations that might promote and protect their rights.

As a consequence, in para. 5 of General Comment No. 2, the CRC Committee points to several reasons why an ICRI is needed, as opposed to *only* a NHRI, but implicitly asks whether an ICRI based in a NHRI can serve as a voice in the political process and legal system for young people. In para. 6 of the General Comment, the CRC Committee seems to indicate a preference for an ICRI over an ICRI based in a NHRI when it says:

> Where resources are limited, consideration must be given to ensuring that the available resources are used most effectively for the promotion and protection of everyone's human rights, including children's, and in this context development of a broad-based NHRI that includes a specific focus on children is likely to constitute the best approach. A broad-based NHRI should include within

its structure either an identifiable commissioner specifically responsible for children's rights, or a specific section or division responsible for children's rights.

Yet it is important to note that the CRC Committee does approve here of governments that establish ICRIs based in NHRIs. The Committee states that if within the structure of an independent human rights institution there is an 'identifiable commissioner' who is responsible for children's rights, the CRC Committee is satisfied. The CRC Committee is implicitly saying that an ICRI based in a NHRI should be able to use resources for children's rights effectively, and that it should have a specific focus on children.

Kinds of ICRIs

As the various definitions suggest, there are different kinds of ICRIs, among whom appear the titles ombudsperson and commissioner. Historically, these ICRIs can trace their roots to the first ombudsperson, the Swedish Parliamentary Ombudsman, established in 1809. Gellhorn (1966: 195, 202) states that this ombudsman had the job of ensuring royal officers did not ignore the law, and refers to the Swedish Constitution's statement that the ombudsman must be an individual of 'known legal ability and outstanding integrity'. In his study Gellhorn refers to the work of Jägerskiöld (1961), who relates the history of a series of European national governments establishing ombudspersons after Sweden. This ombudsperson was also expected to hold Swedish governmental bureaucracy accountable.

Currently, the Parliamentary Ombudsman (Chapter 12, Article 6 of the Swedish Constitution) is elected by Parliament and numbers four: the Chief Parliamentary Ombudsman and three Parliamentary Ombudsmen. The Riksdag Act of 1974 (Article 11) states that terms are for four years, although an Ombudsman may be removed from office if Parliament carries out a vote of no confidence. The Parliamentary Ombudsman can institute criminal proceedings and can be present at court and administrative hearings. The Ombudsman has access to court records and other documents on request, and may also request assistance from a public prosecutor, which must be provided.

In general, some of these characteristics of the first Ombudsman are found in ICRIs, but many are not. The point is that what are now called ombudspersons, whether children's ombudspersons or other types of ombudspersons, only faintly resemble the Swedish Parliamentary Ombudsman. For instance, the Swedish Children's Ombudsperson, Barnombudsmannen, is appointed by government for six years. Governed by the Children's Ombudsman Act of 1993, the children's ombudsperson cannot institute criminal proceedings, but she or he can request reports from administrative authorities and officials of municipal and county governments on children's rights issues, to which they must respond. In addition, the children's ombudsperson can request meetings with these administrative authorities and government officials. Thus, while the Parliamentary and Children's Ombudspersons share similarities, they are distinct in important ways, particularly in terms of legal authority.

Some ICRIs are called children's commissioners. How does a children's commissioner differ from a children's ombudsperson? A commissioner is typified as having the primary responsibility of advocacy, which a children's ombudsperson does not. On the other hand, an ombudsperson is characterised as being able to hear and act on an individual's complaint. A children's commissioner cannot. Empirically, however, the labels 'ombudsperson' and 'commissioner' seem interchangeable at this point (SPICe 2001, UNICEF Innocenti Research Centre 2001). For instance, some commissioners, such as the Children's Commissioner for Wales, are empowered to investigate individual cases.

The form an ICRI takes is sometimes tied to its governmental system. For example, ICRIs based in federal governmental systems are often set up at subnational levels, such as the state. For instance, two ICRIs exist in Belgium, one in the Walloon region, and the other in the Flemish region. Similar arrangements are found in other countries whose national government systems are federal, including the United States, where almost half of the 50 states have ICRIs. In the United Kingdom, separate ICRIs exist for England, Northern Ireland, Scotland and Wales.

How do Independent Children's Rights Institutions Implement the CRC at the National Level?

Various factors are at play in the work of implementing the CRC at the national level, including ICRIs' legislative objectives. Indeed, an ICRI's legislative authority may not even indicate one of its objectives is to ensure national implementation of the CRC. A second critical factor is whether the ICRI possesses the necessary powers to ensure the CRC is implemented at the national level.

To identify differences among ICRIs in this regard, this chapter will contrast seven offices: three commissioners – Malta, Wales and the ICRI of the Australian state of Tasmania (Table 10.1); three ombudspersons – Norway, Belgium and the ombudsperson of the US state of Rhode Island (Table 10.1); and the Danish Council of Children's Rights, whose distinct arrangement sharply contrasts with the other six ICRIs.

Table 10.1   Examples of independent children's rights institutions (ICRIs)

	National	Devolved	State
Commissioner	Malta	Wales	Tasmania
Ombudsperson	Norway	Belgium	Rhode Island

Formal Objectives

Let us first examine the legislative objectives of each of these seven ICRIs. Objectives of the Malta ICRI, established in 2003, emphasise civil and social rights. Thus it has several objectives to fulfil, the first being advocacy of children's rights and interests. A separate but related objective is to promote compliance with the CRC, as well as with other international treaties. With regards to young people's civil rights, the Malta ICRI has the tasks of ensuring that young people can express their opinions, that government agencies and voluntary organisations take young people's rights and viewpoints into account, and of securing their protection from harm and exploitation. Furthermore, the Malta ICRI is expected to ensure institutions comply with the CRC. Its legislation also indicates that it will 'promote the highest standards' of social, education and health services, and it is further obligated to ensure that appropriate agencies prevent and mitigate poverty and the social exclusion of children. A focus on families sets the Malta Commissioner apart from many ICRIs. Indeed, it has the objective of advocating for the protection of the family, an objective reflected in the expectation that the Malta ICRI will advocate on behalf of parents in the raising of their children, as well as improving 'alternative care' for young people. This ICRI also has the objective of promoting high quality services to pregnant women. Moreover it is expected to promote 'special care and protection', including legal protection, to foetuses and infants.

The objectives of the Children's Commissioner for Wales, the first ICRI to be established in the United Kingdom, also emphasise social and civil rights, including safeguarding and advancing young people's rights and protecting and promoting the welfare of children in Wales. However, it does not have the objective of promoting compliance with the CRC, although it does have the statutory duty of considering the CRC in its work. In addition to its work for *all* children in Wales, this ICRI has goals that are focused on children in care, particularly monitoring arrangements, ensuring service providers respond to complaints and providing information about children who are in care. The Welsh ICRI also has the objective of providing assistance and representation to young people in legal proceedings involving care arrangements.

Objectives of the Tasmania ICRI emphasise social rights, chief among which is raising public awareness of children's well-being. Tasmania is a state in the federal structure of Australia and its ICRI is not tasked with promoting compliance with the CRC. Moreover, many objectives of the Tasmania ICRI, for example making an inquiry into a matter involving the welfare of children, may only be pursued at the request of the Minister for Health and Human Services, though the ICRI may advise the Minister on its own prerogative about an issue concerning young people's well-being. This latter objective explicitly applies to children in government custody or guardianship.

Established in 1981, the Norwegian ICRI has among its tasks that Norway complies with the CRC. As a result, its objectives incorporate civil, political, social and economic rights as their focus. Among its chief objectives is improving the conditions in which young people grow up. It is obligated to reduce conflict between young people and society, as well as to promote young people's safety through laws. A further objective is the protection of young people's interests as they pertain to planning by public and private authorities. In turn, the Norwegian ICRI is expected to provide information to public and private actors regarding young people's rights and interests.

Similar to Wales in relation to the United Kingdom, the Flemish region of Belgium possesses devolved powers, while some are reserved to the federal government of Belgium (Vandekerckhove 2001). The Flemish ICRI is an ombudsperson that is different from many ICRIs in that it is obligated to 'defend' young people's rights. Similar to the Norwegian ICRI, the Flemish ICRI is expected to ensure, within the Flemish community, that government legislation conforms to the CRC. Consequently, this ICRI's objectives emphasise civil, political, social and economic rights. Furthermore it is obligated to act as an advocate for young people's rights, interests and needs, and to do so, it is expected to analyse, even evaluate, and then make public the state of the living conditions of young people living in Flanders. In addition, the Flemish ICRI is obligated to distribute information about the CRC to people, including young people, living in Flanders.

In the United States, the first children's ombudsperson to be established was that in the state of Rhode Island. Called the Office of the Child Advocate, this ICRI was established in 1979, approximately two years before the Norwegian ICRI. Given the US government has not ratified the CRC, this ICRI is not obligated to take the CRC into account. The Rhode Island ICRI's objectives emphasise civil and social rights, but its focus is on children whose lives are directly affected by the Rhode Island Department of Children, Youth, and Families. Among these objectives, the Rhode Island ICRI aims to ensure that any young person in state care is aware of her rights and hence conducts investigations of children needing assistance who have been placed in institutions by a Rhode Island Family Court or the Department. This ICRI also has the objective of monitoring these facilities and their procedures. A further objective of this ICRI is to conduct reviews of procedures of the Department of Children, Youth, and Families, including reviewing any situation involving the death of a child who received Department services. The ICRI is also obligated to review Family Court orders pertaining to young people, and to train and offer technical assistance to guardians *ad litem* and other advocates in Family Court proceedings.

Denmark's Børnerådet (translated as the National Council for Children) (Børnerådet 2010), established in 1998, provides an interesting approach to an ICRI. Governed by six members, with another member serving as its chairperson, its overarching objective is to ensure young people's rights, as well as to promote attention to children's well-being. To this end it aims to assess the conditions in which young people live, particularly in comparison to the CRC, as a result of which, its objectives emphasise the civil, political, social and economic rights of Danish young people. Furthermore the Danish ICRI advises authorities on the conditions in which young people live and on what children's perspectives are of the work of those authorities. As one of its critical objectives is monitoring and publicising the circumstances of young people, it is expected to identify problems in laws and administrative practices that conflict with children's rights. The Danish ICRI is also obligated to distribute information about young people, including debates on issues involving them, and to strive to give young people opportunities to participate in and shape Danish society.

Table 10.2 summarises the objectives of these seven ICRIs.

Table 10.2   Objectives of ICRIs

	Civil rights	Political rights	Social rights	Economic rights
Malta	•	•	•	•
Wales	•	•	•	•
Tasmania			•	
Norway	•	•	•	•
Flanders (Belgium)	•	•	•	•
Rhode Island (United States)	•		•	
Denmark	•	•	•	•

Formal Powers

To reach their objectives, the ICRIs must possess legal powers. These can be separated into powers to change young people's circumstances, and powers to change how children are affected by others. The former consists of investigating, gathering evidence, providing legal assistance and removing children, while the latter consists of monitoring, researching, shaping opinion and lobbying.

The Malta ICRI has significant powers enumerated in its legislation. It can monitor, research, shape opinion and lobby. It can initiate measures promoting young people's rights and interests. It can gather evidence, as well as investigate violations of children's rights. It is also obligated to investigate deaths of children. Furthermore, it has the power to establish standards for government institutions in order for them to evaluate whether their processes respond to complaints involving young people; it then has the power to monitor whether those institutions are meeting those standards. This ICRI also has the power to monitor the work of social welfare services for young people. It has powers to collect information and conduct research. It can shape opinion through public education. And it can lobby, including by preparing and submitting legislation. However, this ICRI can neither provide legal assistance nor remove a child from a dangerous situation.

The Children's Commissioner for Wales also possesses significant powers. It has the power to monitor arrangements and to gather evidence about the well-being of young people in care. If information on these arrangements indicates illegal or dangerous behaviour, the Welsh ICRI has the power to ensure remedies are taken. In addition, the Welsh ICRI has the power to provide advice and information. These efforts extend to providing assistance and representation in a proceeding involving problems with in-care arrangements. It also has the power to make reports; it can acquire evidence, including the provision of information and examination of witnesses under oath. Moreover, it possesses the power to review extant or proposed legislation, policy, practice or service as it pertains to all children in Wales. Indeed, the Welsh ICRI can make representations to the Welsh Assembly on 'any matter affecting the rights or welfare of children in Wales'. This ICRI does not have the power to remove a child from a dangerous situation.

The ICRI of Tasmania, the Commissioner for Children, has the power to compel a person to answer questions or produce documents relevant to child abuse and protection. It also has the power to shape opinion and offer advice. If we broadly construe the powers of the Tasmania ICRI, it can also monitor, research and lobby. However, like others, its powers are in some respects limited. For example, its power to conduct an investigation may only be exercised when directed by the Minister of Health and Human Services (unless it involves a court). Similarly, the ICRI can only monitor impacts of legislation, policy or practice if requested by the Minister. Additionally, the Tasmania ICRI can gather evidence and it can compel a person to provide evidence for its work on child abuse and protection. However, it cannot provide legal assistance or remove children.

The Norwegian ICRI has the power to investigate and to gather evidence. Indeed, all institutions for children in Norway, whether public or private, are obliged to provide information to the ICRI to enable it to perform its tasks. As well as having the power also to monitor public and private institutions, it can conduct research, shape opinion and lobby public and private institutions. In some situations it can respond to individual complaints of a child, but it cannot provide legal assistance or remove children.

The Flemish ICRI of Belgium has powers similar to those of the Norwegian ICRI. The Flemish ICRI possesses powers to monitor and publicise the living conditions of young people. Furthermore, it can conduct or sponsor studies, and disseminate information about children's interests. This set of powers includes investigating complaints about violations of the CRC, but this power is constrained by the ICRI's inability to carry on the investigation when a judicial or administrative proceeding is underway. Nevertheless, the Flemish ICRI has the power to gather evidence, including documents from public officials, and can access government buildings. The ICRI can also evaluate national reports to the CRC Committee. It cannot provide legal assistance or remove children.

The powers of the Rhode Island ICRI, whose objectives are comparatively narrow, are at the same time weak. It has the power and responsibility to care for a child's estate while the child is in state custody, and it is able to receive a petition from a foster home that wants a child to stay with the home while its licensing process is completed. The ICRI also has the power to monitor foster care arrangements and to investigate when concerns arise. Moreover, it has the power to investigate the fatality of a child in the in-care system. In that role, the ICRI can collect evidence. However, this ICRI cannot remove a child from the system or from elsewhere. Nor can it offer legal assistance.

The Danish ICRI, the National Council of Children, can monitor, research and publicise circumstances in which young people live. It can also lobby government and others for changes to legislation and other practices. Furthermore, it can investigate and collective evidence. The Danish ICRI cannot, however, provide legal assistance or remove children.

The powers of each of these ICRIs are summarised in Tables 10.3 and 10.4.

Table 10.3   Powers of ICRIs to influence the circumstances of young people

	Investigate	Collect evidence	Provide legal assistance	Remove children
Malta	•	•		
Wales	•	Limited	•	
Tasmania	Limited	•		
Norway	•	•		
Flanders (Belgium)	Limited	•		
Rhode Island (United States)	•	Limited		
Denmark	•	•		

Table 10.4   Powers of ICRIs to affect others

	Monitor	Research	Shape opinion	Lobby
Malta	•	•	•	•
Wales	•	•	•	•
Tasmania	•	•	•	•
Norway	•	•	•	•
Flanders (Belgium)	•	•	•	
Rhode Island (United States)	•			
Denmark	•	•	•	•

A review of Tables 10.3 and 10.4 suggests that many ICRIs possess more powers to affect others than to influence the circumstances of young people. With the exception of Rhode Island, an ICRI endowed with limited powers, the ICRIs examined in this chapter tend to have fewer powers to shape the situations in which young people live.

Informal Powers

Another key aspect of an ICRI's make-up is its informal powers. Informal powers can be thought of as tools an ICRI possesses that are not set out in legislation or in another legal document. An international study of ICRIs I am directing indicates the informal power of communicating with the media is a powerful tool. Working with the media enables an ICRI to express opinions on children's rights, on how government and private institutions, including international ones, are treating children's rights and approaching children's interests. Results from this study indicate working with the media is strongly valued by many ICRIs. The legislation of none of the seven ICRIs compared in this chapter prohibits working with the media.

Independence

The ability to work with other institutions raises questions of the independence of ICRIs. All ICRIs have relationships with their governments, and many cooperate with private entities; some are located within national human rights institutions (NHRIs). What factors are important to an ICRI's independence? Does independence matter to an ICRI's work?

Studies of the independence of ICRIs have not been published and scholarly work on issues surrounding the independence of ICRIs is not available. Consequently, this chapter will turn to signals from the CRC Committee and other institutions for factors important to an ICRI's independence, then examine the qualities of independence of the seven ICRIs examined here. Paragraph 7 of the CRC Committee's General Comment No. 2 clearly articulates the Committee's viewpoint on the importance of independence to an ICRI: '... every State needs an independent human rights institution with responsibility for promoting and protecting children's rights. The Committee's principal concern is that the institution, whatever its form, should be able, independently and effectively, to monitor, promote and protect children's rights.' Thus, from the CRC Committee's standpoint, an ICRI's independence is crucial.

The CRC Committee refers to the Paris Principles and the Vienna Declaration as the sources of its ideas on ICRIs. The Paris Principles indicate factors to consider in evaluating the independence of an ICRI. Does the ICRI have adequate, stable funding it can use to advance children's rights? Does the ICRI have its own staff with premises that are identifiable as separate for children and young people? Questions can be drawn from the Vienna Declaration, such as whether relationships with other institutions hinder the ICRI from advising competent authorities, remedying children's rights violations, distributing information about children's rights, and assuming an educational role in regards to children's rights.

As mentioned above, one question regarding independence revolves around the idea of having an ICRI located in a NHRI. The CRC Committee points to several reasons why an ICRI is needed, as opposed to *only* a NHRI. These factors do not demand a separate ICRI, but point to concerns regarding the independence of an ICRI based in a NHRI. While paragraph 5 of General Comment No. 2 implicitly asks whether an ICRI based in a NHRI can serve as a voice in the political process and legal system for young people, paragraph 6, by emphasising that an ICRI based in a NHRI should not only have a specific focus on children but also be able to use resources for children's rights effectively, raises questions of whether an ICRI located in a NHRI can maintain independence in its work.

Many ICRIs are labelled 'independent', and of the seven ICRIs examined here, only the Rhode Island ICRI does not carry the 'independence' label. Labels of independence in charter or legislation, for instance, may seem like form over substance, but the ability to refer to this label may be an important resource for the institution. Yet the label of independence may be weakened by the formal qualities of an ICRI.

Given the paucity of studies and commentary, research on other independent institutions may suggest important qualities for an ICRI's independence. For example, research on central banks has tended to focus on four components of independence. The first component is the label of independence, which, as stated, six of the seven ICRIs studied in this chapter possess. The second component entails independence in doing work, which includes deciding on what work to undertake and how to conduct this work. Can another institution shape what work the ICRI undertakes? The third component relates to how the individual enters and exits the institution. Does another institution, such as government, influence how an individual takes and leaves the office of ICRI? Finally, control of the office's management and functioning once an individual holds an office is the fourth important component of independence. If a government official can control management of the ICRI office, this official may effectively stop or hinder the ICRI from reaching its goals.

Resources

ICRIs do not operate in a vacuum. Rather, ICRIs are located within a framework of other organisations, norms and resources, all of which may hinder or promote implementation of the CRC. Among the most crucial features of the children's rights landscape is the governmental system and leadership. If government responds to popular opinion on children's rights, the ICRI will, all things being equal, enjoy a significant advantage. Popular support of children's rights is also a critical factor. Another indicator of support is the number and strength of NGOs working to promote children's rights. Of course, strength of the civil society in which the ICRI functions shapes the efforts of the NGOs. And the legal system shapes civil society. Thus, the legal system, particularly its effectiveness, will affect the popular support of rights. If courts do not function, rights may be regarded as not worth pursuing. Overall, available resources are central to an ICRI's work of implementing the CRC. While a variety of resources shape the goals and functioning of individual ICRIs, both supporting and limiting their work, their budgets and staff sizes certainly are critical.

How Do ICRIs Set Their Agendas?

Given the vast differences in legislative objectives, legislated powers, independence, resources and other factors, including informal powers, how ICRIs go about setting their agendas is quite complicated. To a significant degree, the agendas of many ICRIs are set by their legislative schemes. However, the independence of an ICRI also shapes its agenda setting, and some ICRIs are bound to respond to requests from government officials. Not surprisingly, though, all ICRIs respond to issues, even crises, facing children and young people in their own countries. Finally, attitudes and beliefs about children, parents and other parts of society shape ICRIs' agendas.

We would expect that the objective of implementing the CRC to also be a critical component of any ICRI's agenda. For example, in Norway, despite the Norwegian ICRI having been established in 1981, eight years prior to the CRC, following CRC ratification the Norwegian government took steps to modify the legislation regulating the ICRI so that the office is tasked with ensuring Norwegian law and administration 'are in accordance with Norway's obligations according to the UN Convention on the Rights of the Child'. Given the United States has not ratified the CRC it is not surprising that a similar mandate does not affect the Rhode Island ICRI. What is surprising is that some ICRIs whose national governments have ratified the CRC are not obligated to help implement the CRC. While the United Kingdom ratified the CRC in 1991 and each of the four ICRIs in the United Kingdom – that is, England, Northern Ireland, Scotland and Wales – have a (differently expressed) obligation to pay 'due regard' to the CRC and all emphasise in their publications the importance of the Convention to their work, only the Northern Ireland and Scottish ICRIs have specific duties linked to CRC implementation. Even then, these duties do not encompass the general monitoring of implementation as such.

Independence of an ICRI also shapes its agendas, sometimes in restrictive ways. The Rhode Island ICRI, for example, filed a lawsuit against the Rhode Island state welfare system for purposes of reforming the Rhode Island in-care system. Through the lawsuit, the Rhode Island ICRI contends children who are in government care are being harmed by failures of the in-care system, including poor management. When the Rhode Island ICRI's term ended in January 2010, the Rhode Island governor indicated he would not consider the current ICRI among the new applicants, despite the express desire of the ICRI to serve a second term (*Rhode Island News* 2010).

As mentioned above, ICRIs do respond to crises involving young people. The Welsh ICRI in 2001 announced its intention to hold public inquiries into a sexual abuse case involving Ysgol Gyfun Rhydfelen school. During a period of almost 20 years, a number of children had been sexually abused, an injustice that had been covered up and ignored by some government officials. Whistleblowers, including current and past students, called attention to the crisis at the school. The ICRI's work consisted of public inquiries and other investigations over a period of three years, gaining international attention and demanding a great deal of time and resources of the Welsh ICRI (Children's Commissioner for Wales 2004).

Opinions, beliefs and attitudes can also shape the agendas of an ICRI. As noted, the Malta ICRI is obligated to provide legal protection to foetuses. In 2005, the Malta ICRI spoke out over IVF processes, raising concerns about how frozen embryos could be discarded and how research could not guarantee children conceived through IVF would live healthy lives (Sansone 2009). Given her legislated objectives, the Malta ICRI arguably was expected to raise such concerns, despite the fact that she faced criticism from medical doctors and media, among others.

Strategies to Implement the CRC

There are four broad strategies ICRIs take to implementing the CRC: using existing legislation, calling on government to institute new legislation, working with the media, and collaborating with other organisations. In relation to the first of these – insisting that government officials enforce national laws – ICRIs may use powers to monitor legislation, as well as to investigate and collect evidence of maladministration of laws that harm young people's rights. For example, the English ICRI publicly criticised the British government over its policies and practices of detaining immigrant children in asylum detention centres, contending young people held in these centres do not enjoy their rights according to British law (Aynsley-Green 2010).

In relation to the second strategy, ICRIs may lobby government officials to prepare and pass new laws that will implement rights identified in the CRC. For example, in early 2010, the first Russian federal ICRI, the former ICRI of the city of Moscow – who was fired after supporting the creation of a juvenile justice system (*The Moscow Times* 2010) – had loudly raised the alarm about the deterioration of children's rights in Russia over the last eight years.

In the third strategy approaching the media to discuss how national governments can further implement the CRC – an ICRI may find one of its most potent powers is not in the legislation governing the office but in working informally with other actors and institutions, including the media. This power may be used to set agendas beyond the legislated objectives of the ICRI. For instance, an ICRI may work with newspapers to set terms of public debate over issues affecting young people and their rights. With the availability of this informal power, an ICRI can take on significant issues of national importance, or issues affecting smaller groups of young people but in deeply serious ways. For example, in 2010, the Norwegian ICRI pressed employers to shorten working hours for parents, citing evidence of higher divorce rates among parents who work long hours and fail to spend time with their children (Sandelson 2010).

The fourth strategy, which is quite commonly employed, is to work with other organisations to implement the CRC. Nearly every ICRI who works in a country with a strong civil society cooperates with non-profit organisations. In some locations, these non-profit organisations are not local, but international. An important example is ENOC, which provides various forms of support to its members in their work towards CRC implementation. In many places, however, ICRIs work with domestic non-profit organisations to pursue CRC implementation. Iceland's ICRI, for example, works with universities to improve children's rights and wellbeing (Umboðsmaður barna 2007).

Barriers to and Successes in ICRIs' Implementation of the CRC

ICRIs may take on a variety of roles in their work to implement the CRC. This chapter has sought to demonstrate that a variety of factors shape how ICRIs go about this work. It is important, however, to emphasise that not all ICRIs are expected to work towards implementation of the CRC. In the United States, ICRIs do not focus on the CRC and only to a limited degree do they concentrate on children's rights. Even in countries whose national governments have ratified the CRC, not all ICRIs are obligated to consider the CRC in their work.

Two primary types of ICRI, ombudspersons and commissioners, are to be found, although notable exceptions, such as the Danish ICRI, do exist. Beyond these differences, which may only be superficial, varying objectives and powers often lead to ICRIs assuming different roles. Indeed, the objectives of an ICRI may emphasise certain aspects of the CRC, while the powers an ICRI possesses may enable it to pursue certain features of the CRC. Without the power to investigate, for instance, a young person's freedom from imprisonment with adults is difficult to evaluate. Additionally, an inability to collect evidence, particularly on a sensitive issue, may weaken the position an ICRI wants to take regarding young people's rights. Even with legal powers and adequate resources, compromised independence may hinder an ICRI from implementing the CRC.

In the bigger picture, ICRIs are unique institutions, positioned at public–private divides, between government and family and other institutions, appointed to safeguard and advance young people's rights. When government officials conclude young people's rights are not in their interest to pursue, or when such rights are overlooked by institutions in civil society, or are not pursued by parents and caretakers, advocacy and dogged pursuit by an ICRI may make critical differences to young people and their rights and well-being. Thus ICRIs may take leadership roles, guiding public and private institutions to implement the CRC and give credence to children's rights.

References

Aynsley-Green, A. 2010. Speedy end to child detention is needed. *The Guardian* [online, May 23]. Available at: http://www.guardian.co.uk/commentisfree/libertycentral/2010/may/23/child-detention-review [accessed 14 September 2010].

Barneombudet. 2010. Staffing and budget [online]. Available at: www.barneombudet.no/english/about_the_/staffing_a/ [accessed 10 June 2010].

Borgen, M. 1996. Developing the role of ombudsman, in E. Verhellen (ed.), *Monitoring Children's Rights*. The Hague: Kluwer Law International, pp. 541–4.

Børnerådet. 2010. Legal basis, Ministry of Social Affairs, Order no. 2 of 5 January 1998. Available at: www.boerneraadet.dk/english/legal+basis [accessed 9 June 2010].

Children's Commissioner for Wales. 2004. *Clywch: Report of the Examination of the Children's Commissioner for Wales into Allegations of Child Sexual Abuse in a School Setting*. Swansea: Children's Commissioner for Wales.

CIA. 2010. *CIA World Factbook*. Available at: www.cia.gov [accessed 11 June 2010].

Council of Europe. 2003. *The Institution of Ombudsman*. Recommendation 1615.

CRIN. 2009. France: children's ombudsperson at risk of being closed down [online]. Available at: crin.org/enoc/resources/infoDetail.asp?ID=20885&flag=news [accessed 11 June 2010].

Davidson, H.A., Cohen, C.P. and Girdner, I.K. (eds). 1993. *Establishing Ombudsman Programs for Children and Youth: How Government's Response to Its Young Citizens Can Be Improved.* Washington, DC: American Bar Association Center on Children and the Law.

Flekkoy, M.G. 1991. *A Voice for Children.* London: Jessica Kingsley.

Gellhorn, W. 1966. *Ombudsmen and Others: Citizens' Protectors in Nine Countries.* Cambridge, MA: Harvard University Press.

Jägerskiöld, S. 1961. Swedish ombudsman. *University of Pennsylvania Law Review*, 109(8), 1077–99.

Lansdown, G. 2001a. Children's Rights Commissioners for the UK, in B. Franklin (ed.), *The New Handbook of Children's Rights.* New York: Routledge, pp. 285–98.

——. 2001b. *Independent Institutions Protecting Children's Rights.* Florence: Innocenti.

Melton, G.B. 1991. Lessons from Norway: the children's ombudsman as a voice for children. *Case Western Reserve Journal of International Law*, 23, 197–254.

The Moscow Times. 11 January 2010. Children's ombudsman fired after 4 months.

Office for National Statistics. 2010. Table 4: mid-2008 population estimates: England. Available at: http://www.statistics.gov.uk/statbase/product. asp?vlnk=15106 [accessed 10 June 2010].

Rhode Island News. 8 January 2010. R.I. advertises child advocate's position.

Sandelson, M. 2010. Children's ombudsman puts working parents in their place. *The Foreigner*, 21 April 2010.

Sansone, K. 24 October 2009. Assisted procreation committee to focus on three issues. *Times of Malta.* Available at: URL [accessed 8 June 2010].

SPICe (Scottish Parliament Information Centre). 2001. *Report of the Children's Commissioner Seminar.* 25 June 2001.

Umboðsmaður barna. 2007. Report to the 2007 Annual ENOC Meeting. Available at: www.barn.is/barn/upload/files/english/enoc_annual_report_2007.pdf [accessed 9 June 2010].

UN Committee on the Rights of the Child. 2002. *General Comment No. 2 on the Role of Independent National Human Rights Institutions in the Promotion and Protection of the Rights of the Child.* CRC/GC/2002/2.

UNICEF Innocenti Research Centre. 1997. *Ombudswork for Children.* Florence: Innocenti.

United Nations General Assembly. 1993. Vienna Declaration and Programme of Action. 12 July 1993.

——. 2010. *Functions and Powers of the General Assembly.* Available at: www. un.org/ga/about/background.shtml [accessed 7 June 2010].

Vandekerckhove, A. 2001. A commissioner for children's rights in the Flemish community in Belgium, in B. Franklin (ed.), *The New Handbook of Children's Rights.* New York: Routledge, pp. 362–73.

Chapter 11

Multi-level Governance and CRC Implementation

Jane Williams[1]

Introduction

The obligations of the CRC are imposed on the States Parties. While others may be invited in to the CRC's processes it is only a State Party that is obliged to submit a report to and appear before the CRC Committee. The reporting and monitoring process under Article 44 generates a series of dialogues at and between the international and national levels. The central participants in these dialogues are the States Parties and the organs of the UN, principally the CRC Committee. The central texts are the State Party reports and the CRC Committee's Concluding Observations.

Of course, as reflected in Chapter 4 of this volume, other protagonists and other texts also feature in the process. Article 45 of the CRC explicitly encourages engagement of NGOs both in implementation of the substantive provisions and in the monitoring and reporting process. The potential for the reporting process to engage civil society and to advocate for changes in law and policy was noted from the initial reporting rounds (for example Woll 2000) and the CRC Committee has always 'systematically and strongly' (CRC 1990) encouraged NGOs as well as national human rights institutions to submit reports and information. Selected organisations are invited to participate in the CRC Committee's pre-sessional working group. There may also be a direct contribution by children and young people's organisations (Heesterman 2005). *Our Rights, Our Story*, featured in Chapter 15 in this volume, deserves to be regarded as a high point in this kind of involvement in the history of the CRC so far.

Thus in practice the CRC's process has never been limited to a dialogue between the CRC Committee and the State Party. The machinery of the CRC is designed to and does in practice take in the messages of other contributors and sends out messages intended to reach not only States Parties but also all organisations and persons wishing to involve themselves in some way. The role of non-governmental actors in gathering information and reporting on the State

---

1   The author is grateful to Professor Karen Morrow and Professor Volker Roeben for comments on drafts of this chapter and to Professor Roeben also for his guidance on the constitutional position of children's rights in Germany. The usual disclaimer applies.

Party's progress in implementing the CRC is well established and relatively well supported within the UN system (for example, NGOGroupCRC 2006). Yet little attention has yet been focused on the role of regional government *beneath* the level of the State Party.[2] Perhaps human rights protection in general might readily be assumed to be a matter for uniformity throughout the State Party, a matter of constitutional significance to be dealt with at the national level. Or perhaps no such assumptions apply, simply because the capacity of internal regional government in relation to implementation of international law is as yet only beginning to be recognised. There is some recognition of the need for the regions to be involved in the process of negotiation of international obligations: the Council of Europe's 1997 draft Charter of Regional Self-government went so far as to recognise minimum rights to consultation before obligations affecting the powers of local and regional government are undertaken (Council of Europe 1997: Article 10). But there has been no similar recognition of the role of the internal regional levels in implementation of obligations once undertaken.

Such lack of recognition is surprising given the extent to which implementation in practice can fall to the regions and localities within a State Party. By way of analogy, the European Union's Committee of the Regions estimates that some 70 per cent of all EU member state obligations fail to be administered at the local or regional level (Committee of the Regions 2009: 4). Furthermore, differential implementation between the regions has the potential to engage competing fundamental rights and principles, as the *Horvath* case, discussed later in this chapter, has shown. The full implications of this position remain largely to be explored.

It might well be thought appropriate that judicial enforcement of human rights standards deriving from international obligations should be uniformly available throughout the State Party, typically with a Constitutional or Supreme Court as ultimate arbiter of compatibility and/or precedence in relation to national law. However, judicial remedies for human rights violations are only one, albeit clearly a very important one, of the necessary tools for effective implementation. Arguably children's rights implementation has an accentuated need for non-judicial mechanisms since children face additional barriers to making legal claims simply because they are children, and those most in need of the protection of their rights are often least able to overcome those barriers. Consequently, whilst it is right that the UN system has turned its attention to the case for individual

---

2   Throughout this chapter the word 'level' is used to describe government institutions from international, including European, to (i.e. nation-state), regional and local government. Regional divisions within the nation-state may be called various names such as states, provinces, regions, territories or countries. It is arguable that 'level' is inappropriate to describe the units of some federal systems just as it is inaccurate to apply the term 'region' to an internal country or even constituent nation such as Wales or Scotland in the UK. Nonetheless in the interests of readability the term 'level' is adopted here, and 'regional' to denote a level internal to the State Party.

complaints and advisory mechanisms at the international level (see Doek, Van Bueren Chapters 4 and 5 respectively in this volume), it is also right for the CRC Committee to urge action on implementation across a range of administrative and political mechanisms and through various forms of what might be termed 'collaborative activism' (CRC 2003: I).

When it comes to these latter mechanisms, regional tiers of governance assume a particular significance. As illustrated later in this chapter, there is great diversity in provenance and form of regional government but it is common for responsibility to be allocated to the regional tier in fields such as health, education, social care, culture and recreation. These areas are of obvious importance in implementation of the State Party's obligations under the CRC.

This chapter discusses the various tools for implementation and how the power to make and to use them is in some cases distributed between levels of government within the State Party. It is argued that efforts towards more effective implementation need to take account of the range and parameters of legal and political power at internal levels and the nature of communication between the levels. For example, a more progressive approach to implementation at a regional level relative to the national level might utilise some of the developments in process and communication discussed by Doek (Chapter 4 in this volume). There may be scope for a dynamic relationship to emerge between a more CRC-friendly regional government and the CRC Committee. The effect might be both to further the regional policy and to exert pressure on the State Party to fulfil its obligations in areas where responsibility is retained at national level. It might also set an example for other regions to follow – always assuming the necessary tolerance on the part of the government at national level. On the other hand, experience in several countries suggests that internal distribution of governmental power can lead to fragmentation of scrutiny and lack of coordination. Multiple levels of governance therefore present both opportunities and potential problems in terms of CRC implementation. The UK since 1999 has experienced a form of regional government with devolution to Wales, Scotland and Northern Ireland and the impact of this on CRC implementation in the UK and its regions is offered here as illustrative of both the opportunities and the problems.

Judicial Enforcement, Administrative Mechanisms and Collaborative Activism

As Verhellen pointed out, the CRC has 'very few provisions that can be enforced directly' (1997: 86). That is not of course an argument against creating individual legal remedies for violations of those provisions that can be directly enforced. Verhellen suggests that the varying terminology of the text is the first indicator of which these might be. But even those formulations which are sometimes described as mere statements of intent ('encourage', 'strive', 'use their best efforts') rather than indicators of legal enforceability still create obligations to do something. It is perfectly possible to reach a judgment that a government has failed to encourage something if its actions positively discourage it, to conclude that it has not 'strived' to achieve something if there is no evidence of any serious consideration being given to the issue, and so on. At the other end of the textual spectrum of direct enforceability, words such as 'ensure', 'guarantee' and 'recognise' will not necessarily generate an individual legal remedy if the objective is perceived as being inappropriate for adjudication by the courts. This may often be the case where consideration of remedial action necessarily engages issues of social or economic policy.

In such a case, the limitations of judicial mechanisms are well-rehearsed. There is the principled objection rooted in the respective constitutional roles of judicial and political bodies and the pragmatic objection based on the lack of expertise and capacity of the courts to undertake review of resource-allocative decisions or provide effective supervision of systems for distribution. Despite these objections, in some jurisdictions there have been developments towards conferring a greater, more flexible and facilitative supervisory role for the courts. Fredman (2008) documents such developments, for example in South Africa and India, while also recognising that even where the courts are most active their intervention will never be enough alone. She argues for a 'synergistic approach' to implementation in which the traditional distinction between civil and political rights on the one hand and social and economic rights on the other is abandoned in favour of a focus on positive and negative duties and the relationship between them. This facilitates optimal use of judicial mechanisms by enabling less controversially justiciable issues such as discrimination and lack of due process to be identified when social and economic rights are engaged. It also paves the way for the development of deliberative approaches to the resolution of issues of the kind spearheaded by the courts in South Africa and India in litigation concerning such matters as evictions, homelessness, food distribution and access to treatment for HIV/AIDS. (See also, Van Bueren, this volume.) Where these approaches have been adopted, the courts have not crossed the boundary between judicial and political spheres by imposing a particular solution as to access to the desired material support. Instead they have used a variety of orders designed to ensure that political and administrative processes are followed in a way that will best secure the rights of the disadvantaged group concerned. Significantly, these developments also highlight the role of non-judicial actors. Fredman notes that a more pro-active judicial approach has been most effective where there are well-organised groups that can engage with government to negotiate solutions following upon the court's judgment. She cites as a recent high point in this regard the Treatment Action Campaign cases in South Africa where eventually 'the combined efforts of litigation, local activism, NGO involvement, and coordinated efforts by civil society achieved what could be called a genuinely deliberative approach' (2008: 172), leading to the adoption of a national strategic plan in 2007. Here, collaborative activism is one of a number of factors combining to produce an effect which could not be produced by the court's order alone.

For such an approach to be effective Fredman argues that 'all those who are genuinely able to make decisions or to influence decision-makers' need to be included in the process. In this regard she observes that multi-level government structures can present challenges in establishing a meaningful consultative forum (2008: 211). It is easy to imagine that when it comes to monitoring compliance, the existence of multiple internal mechanisms for regulation, audit, inspection and complaints may also produce difficulties at the very least of coordination.

If litigation can be seen as a hub around which activists can muster to produce a 'synergistic approach', it is not the only available hub, nor is it without its drawbacks. Apart from the cost and complexity of preparing a legal case, the judiciary are not, in most jurisdictions, either elected or representative of society at large and it can be argued that they are ill-equipped to generate the kind of change of approach to policy choices that the CRC demands. As Campbell (2006) remarks, there is a danger 'that human rights are diminished when we seek to cure democratic deficiencies by anti-democratic devices' – that is, when the primary focus of strategies for implementation is the judicial rather than political aspect of state power. In alternative models such as that propounded by Campbell in relation to human rights implementation in Australia, the courts may play no part or may acquire at most a role as backstop to bespoke political and administrative machinery. Campbell suggests that it is preferable to adopt a model based on a 'democratic bill of rights' with an enhanced role for parliamentary committees to scrutinise draft legislation, hold inquiries and bring forward proposed reforms. This would lead, he argues, to the development of 'a comprehensive set of human rights legislation with an enhanced legal status that would be respected and enforced' by the courts. An optimistic account of the recent developments in the UK, explained later in this chapter, might suggest that they represent incremental steps towards such a model.

Certainly, Campbell's parliamentary model goes some way to meet both the principled and the pragmatic objections to expansion of the judicial role. A parliamentary committee may instigate its own inquiries, either in response to communications from external advocates or of its own motion. Typically such a committee will have power to call witnesses and in particular to publicly examine and, where it deems necessary, publicly criticise ministers and their officials. These processes may be more accessible and amenable to participation by activist organisations than individual legal claims.

However, in practice the effectiveness of the parliamentary model just as much the court-centred model depends on the ability of activists to engage in deliberative processes as well as the willingness of governmental institutions to listen and act. Formal institutions such as national independent human rights institutions, children's commissioners and public service ombudspersons may play a crucial part. These institutions may undertake supportive roles including investigation of complaints, holding inquiries and promoting awareness and understanding of human rights. If empowered to institute proceedings alleging human rights violations and/ or to intervene in proceedings brought by other parties, such statutory bodies can support judicial enforcement. In the parliamentary model, they can refer matters to parliamentary scrutiny bodies and give evidence in their inquiries. All these activities can provide support for and a bridge between governmental and non-governmental actors thereby facilitating deliberative approaches.

It is not perhaps necessary (or practical) to take a doctrinal position about the relative merits of the judicial and the parliamentary models. There can be progress on both and this is indeed what is contemplated by the requirement in Article 4 for 'all legislative, administrative and other measures'. The CRC Committee asserts the necessity of judicial enforcement but at the same time has repeatedly drawn attention to the need for legislative reform, administrative changes and the application of resource in a wide sense from civic society, communities and family (CRC 2003). But broad-based deliberative engagement seems the common necessity and here localities are important because many of the organisations around which such engagement can be built are not State Party-wide or if they are, also have local groups which may or may not be coterminous with governmental sub-divisions within the State Party.

Institutions at Sub-Nation-State Levels

There are as many varieties of regional government and as many approaches to demarcation between regional and state levels as there are states which have a regional level. In many states the existence of a regional level is not of long standing. In Europe, for example, as Hopkins (2002: 330) points out, in 1939 within the area now spanned by the EU no state had democratic regional governments, yet by 2002 12 of the 15 EU member states had some form of it. Most of the member states admitted since then either have, or are working towards the establishment of, a level of democratic government between the national and the local. For the purposes of this section of this chapter, examples are drawn from Europe, whilst acknowledging that elsewhere in the world, further variations on the themes of federalism, regional autonomy and devolution may be found, in many cases with the same characteristic so far as allocation of CRC-relevant areas of government activity is concerned.

There was a flurry of constitution-building in Europe following the collapse of the Soviet Union in the late 1980s. Several of the new European constitutions made provision for a democratically-elected level of government between the national and local, with many including a directly elected regional assembly. A number of longer established European constitutions also feature such arrangements. Such democratically elected levels do not always possess significant law-making powers. Within the EU, whilst a number of states continue openly to consider or work towards delegation of legislative power to their regional assemblies, by 2008 there were only eight member states which consisted wholly or partly of regions with legislative powers.[3] On the other hand a relatively high proportion – 43.5 per cent – of the population of the EU is governed by the laws made by these regional legislative assemblies within their respective areas of competence.[4] And within the eight member states there are some 74 separate assemblies, the presidents of which have been meeting and networking formally for over a decade in a Conference of European Regional Legislative Assemblies.

The EU has a considerable interest in these regional bodies.[5] The EU Committee of the Regions is itself a reflection of recognition of the need to maintain and develop legitimacy of the expanding Union and to establish an interface with governance within member states down to local level, not just with national government. Regional assemblies are seen as channels through which the refreshing waters of subsidiarity can flow: laws can be debated and enacted at the closest possible level to the citizen, citizen participation in government can be facilitated and confidence in democracy can be strengthened. In giving institutional recognition and representation to internal regions and localities the Committee of the Regions is seen as a response to concerns about increasing remoteness of the EU institutions from its citizens. Indeed, some claims might be made for a 'bottom-up' impact: for example, pressure from the regional assemblies of Germany, Austria and Belgium is said to have resulted in recognition that the principle of subsidiarity first enshrined in the Treaty of Maastricht as governing EU/member state relations applies equally to the regional assemblies with legislative powers.[6]

The perceived need for democratic engagement, or re-engagement, is likewise often a driver for greater autonomy for the regions. Certainly in the UK, the 'democratic deficit' in law-making was at the heart of the case for devolution (Scottish Office 1997, Welsh Office 1997). Regional governments may spawn separate institutions such as the four children's commissioners within the UK, discussed further below, as well as separate arrangements for administrative complaints, inspection and audit. In some cases there are separate court systems. Non-governmental activists, children's organisations and alliances may be able to engage more closely with governments and assemblies at the regional level than the national level. In order to gauge the actual and potential impact of this in terms of implementation of the State Party's international obligations, including under the CRC, it is necessary to examine what powers are allocated to the regional level. This involves referring not only to the foundational texts of regional government but also to the practices that have emerged.

---

3   Regions with Legislative Powers (RLP) in the EU, 01.01.2008, Eurostat. Available at: http://www.regleg.eu/index.php?option=com_content&view=category&layout=blog&id=4&Itemid=5 [accessed 18 September 2010].

4   Ibid.

5   For a discussion of the trajectory of the EU's approach to regional variation, see Hunt (2010).

6   Declaration signed by Germany, Austria and Belgium, 1997. See: http://www.calrenet.eu/history.aspx [accessed 10 August 2010].

Obviously, the regional levels have a constitutional framework. All states seeking accession to the Council of Europe or European Union must adhere to common human rights standards, with the European Convention on Human Rights (ECHR) as a minimum. Human rights obligations can therefore be expected to be a core part of the constitutional framework of the regional governments just as they are for the national government. Indeed, express provision is commonly made in the regional foundational instruments, requiring the regional governmental bodies to comply with international obligations that have been accepted by the national level as State Party.

Such requirements of compliance with international obligations may be seen as facing two ways: inwardly, to ensure uniformity in application of international obligations within the State Party, and outwardly, to ensure that action taken at the regional level will not produce embarrassment in the context of international enforcement mechanisms. At the regional level, such provisions may also be seen as part of a set of binding principles for decision-making. In the UK, for example, each devolution statute contains a prohibition on action that is incompatible with Convention rights under the Human Rights Act 1998 (which covers most of the State Party obligations under the ECHR). If such a set of principles is not identical to those governing legislative and executive decision-making at the nation-state level, then a particular constitutional flavour is injected into law-making and governance at the regional level which is not present at the national level. This is the position in the UK and it seems it is not unique. In Germany, some of the Länder constitutions contain explicit protection for children's rights which is not derived from or replicated in the federal constitution.[7] In Italy, a number of the regions have adopted references to the rights of children in their governing statute, and even an express reference to the CRC.[8]

The powers, including legislative powers, of the regional institutions are legally defined, typically in founding statutes passed by the national legislature, sometimes supplemented by regional constitutions adopted by the regions

---

7   Of the 16 Länder, 11 Länder Constitutions grant special rights for children that enshrine one or several guarantees of the CRC. These children's rights can then be enforced by way of a constitutional complaint before the respective constitutional court of each Land. All Länder legislation has to comply with them. By contrast, the Federal Constitution does not contain an explicit guarantee of children's rights. The Federal Constitutional Court has, however, interpreted Art. 6(2) of the Basic Law, which contains the state-directed parents' right and obligation to raise and care for their children as constituting an obligation for the parents towards their children. This guarantee is then binding on the Länder via the general provision of Art. 1(3) Basic Law, according to which the Länder are directly bound by fundamental rights enshrined in the Federal constitution. It should be added that the Federal Government in 2010 withdrew a controversial reservation to the CRC that excluded its application in the field of federal asylum law, which is administered by the Länder.

8   See for example the list of objectives in the Statute of the Region of Tuscany: http://www.consiglio.regione.toscana.it/istituzione/Statuto-e-regole/Testo/Statuto-inglese.pdf [accessed August 2010].

themselves. Legislative competence may be conferred on the regional legislature exclusively, jointly or concurrently with the national legislature. The Italian Constitution, for example, confers legislative power on the Italian state and regions 'in accordance with the constitution and within the limits set by European Union law and international obligations' and then goes on to create three categories. Examination of these categories reveals that CRC-relevant areas are distributed between them. The first category comprises matters in which legislative power is exclusively reserved to the Italian state. For our purposes it is pertinent to note that this includes 'determination of the basic standards of welfare related to those civil and social rights that must be guaranteed in the entire national territory' as well as areas such as immigration, citizenship and registration – all matters touched by provisions of the CRC. The second comprises matters subject to concurrent legislation between the state and the region: this includes the CRC-relevant areas of education, health protection and regulation of media and communication. There is a residual category covering anything not mentioned in the first two. The region is granted exclusive legislative power on any matter falling into this third category. One such area of obvious significance for implementation of the CRC is children's social services.[9]

Of course, the delineation of powers and declarations of principles in founding statutes, whether at national or regional level, only ever tell part of the story: it is also necessary to look at how they are applied in practice. German federalism is a case in point. Article 30 of the German Basic Law enshrines the principle of subsidiarity by declaring that the exercise of governmental powers and the discharge of governmental functions are incumbent on the Länder. This general competence is qualified by the words 'except as otherwise provided or permitted by this Basic Law'. These words have provided a platform on which to build incrementally increased competence for the federal level, a tendency driven in part by Article 72 of the Basic Law which permits federal law-making where necessary to secure 'equivalent living conditions' throughout the country or 'the maintenance of legal and economic unity'. For some observers the effect of this has been to transfer power from the Länder to the federal level to the extent that Germany may be described as a 'disguised unitary state' (Reutter 2006). The picture is further complicated, however, when one factors in the influence the Land parliaments and the Land executives can have over political decisions at the federal level, together with the way in which federal 'framework legislation' has been developed, leaving considerable scope for detailed provision to be decided upon by the Länder. Unlike Italy, Germany does not regard the CRC or other international treaty obligations as self-executing. It is therefore especially intriguing to note that some of the

---

9   Article 117 of the Italian Constitution as amended by Constitutional Law No. 3 of 18 October 2001. See also the explanation of the position at Para 1.1 of the Italian State Party's 3rd and 4th periodic report submitted to the CRC Committee in December 2008 (CRC.C.ITA. 3–4). This report also describes both generalised and specific mechanisms for coordination and integration of information and other activities relevant to implementation.

constitutions adopted by the Länder contain provisions relating to children's rights. From this it may follow that the Land courts could find space to develop jurisprudence on children's rights distinct from that of the federal courts.[10]

Space does not here permit of an account of all of the different approaches to demarcation of legislative power. There are many variations, but the common point is that a significant amount of government action, including proposing and passing legislation, falls to be done not only at national level but also, and sometimes instead, at the level of a regional government or legislature enjoying a degree of autonomy.

If, as suggested above, it is easier for the non-governmental actors to engage with government at the regional level, NGOs' efforts to procure the changes necessary for effective CRC implementation might be more likely to succeed at the regional level. That would be in accord with the differently-grounded aspirations of both the EU Committee of the Regions and the CRC Committee. The EU Committee's three guiding principles are subsidiarity, proximity and partnership.[11] The CRC Committee urges collaborative activism contributing to and joined up with government action. The shared ideal would be constructive engagement of children's organisations and activists with government at regional level, producing better respect and protection for children's rights within the regions. Government decisions would be made at the level as close as possible to those affected by them (subsidiarity) and there would be public engagement through greater transparency and communication between government bodies and citizens (proximity). Some of the developments in the UK, explained below, can be seen as virtuous examples in this regard. But there are the potential negative effects already noted, in terms of co-ordination and accountability. Curiously, these negative effects are to some extent associated with the operation in practice of the third of the EU Committee's guiding principles: that of partnership.

By 'partnership' the EU Committee of the Regions means that the different levels of governance need to talk to each other, collaborate, co-operate and co-ordinate whilst also respecting the degree of autonomy accorded to each level. Such communication is no doubt essential for efficiency and conflict avoidance. However, in practice it may prove easier for the executive arm of government – in particular, government ministers and the civil service – with the relatively high level of administrative support that is available to them, to do this than it is for ordinary members of legislatures and other non-governmental actors. There is evidence to suggest that this can be experienced in practice as a barrier to effective accountability (for example, Hopkins 2002: 92, in relation to the co-operative arrangements between the German federal level and the Länder). Where other forms of institutional scrutiny such as children's commissioners, audit and inspection, are distributed between regional and national levels, co-ordination of

---

10   See fn. 6 above.

11   EU Committee of the Regions, PRESENTATION/Role. Available at: http://www. cor.europa.eu [accessed August 2010].

scrutiny of the performance of the State Party as a whole may be rendered difficult. The CRC Committee has drawn attention to this problem in State Party reports for the UK (CRC 2008: para. 13) emphasising the need for effective monitoring and evaluation of implementation across the whole of the State Party's territory. Counteracting this difficulty requires very good working partnerships between regional institutions.

It follows that when thinking about practical implementation of the CRC we need to think carefully about government structures at regional levels, how they link with the national level and how they communicate with one another. At this point it is apt to consider the particular example of the UK for a more detailed picture of one particular constellation of multi-level governance affecting a State Party.

Example of the UK

Several features about the UK make it an interesting case study. First, internal regional governance was established relatively recently as a result of three statutes passed by the UK Parliament in 1998 devolving powers to Scotland, Wales and Northern Ireland respectively. Accordingly, at the time of writing there has been just over a decade of operation of devolved governance (in the case of Northern Ireland this has been subject to interruption and revision following political events peculiar to that particular region). Secondly, the same period was one of significant wider constitutional change. This included the enactment of the Human Rights Act 1998 giving further effect in UK law to the ECHR and the creation of structures designed to promote equalities and human rights. These structures were created separately for Northern Ireland and then for the rest of the UK. Four separate children's commissioners have been established under laws passed separately for Wales, Scotland, Northern Ireland and England.

These developments might suggest a journey towards a better practice of democracy, better human rights protection and better children's rights implementation. However, a third feature of the UK in this period of constitutional change is ongoing ambivalence and sometimes hostility towards human rights in political and public discussion, together with increasing severance of children's rights from mainstream human rights discourse (this last exemplifying a wider trend – see Cantwell Chapter 2 in this volume). In March 2009 the UK Government published a discussion paper the title of which, *Rights and Responsibilities* (Ministry of Justice 2009), aptly reflected its central theme: a perceived need to introduce a notion of citizen responsibility in a contemporised re-statement of human rights designed for the UK. For children, the most the paper (at para. 3.71) postulated was the possibility of including in a future 'Bill of Rights and Responsibilities' a provision conferring a right to 'achieve well-being' – hardly an adequate concept to capture the breadth and specificity of the CRC (see further Ennew's comments on the ascendant concept of 'well-being', Chapter 6 in this volume). For our purposes it is interesting to note that one of the reasons put forward for not doing more at the UK level to give effect to the CRC is that many of the 'key policy levers' (para. 3.70) were now controlled by the devolved administrations and parliaments.

The devolved governments have in fact shown far less discomfort than the UK government about using the language of children's rights and about giving prominence to the CRC as a point of reference guiding policy (Williams 2007, Clutton 2008). It is therefore apt to consider the extent to which particular directions and dynamics have emerged at the sub-national level in terms of CRC implementation and what, if any, practical difference this has made.

Judicial Mechanisms

The UK has not seen developments towards judicial instigation of deliberative approaches comparable to those in South Africa and India. The Human Rights Act 1998, which gave 'further effect' in domestic law to the ECHR some 50 years after the UK accepted its international obligations under that Convention, has helped to stimulate a shift away from a blanket view of non-justiciability in relation to resource-sensitive areas of social and economic policy. There remains, however, firm resistance to substantive review by the courts of discretionary resource allocation decisions and of decisions with perceived resource-allocative impact (for example King 2007). On the whole the impact of the Human Rights Act has been to inject additional criteria (most obviously, proportionality) into the courts' retrospective assessment of the thought process of the governmental decision-maker, rather than to promote substantive review or to impose deliberative approaches to decision-making. Some members of the higher judiciary have been readier than others to embrace more expansive criteria, applying to the interpretation of the ECHR the human rights values of dignity and equality (for example Hale 2009) but the examples of successful challenges of that kind are few. The two examples given by Hale are *R (Bernard) v London Borough of Enfield*,[12] where the concept of dignity coloured the court's approach to the conditions necessary for the enjoyment by a disabled woman of her right to respect for private and family life under Article 8 ECHR, and *R(Limbuela) v Secretary of State for the Home Department*[13] where, Hale argues, dignity was effectively the conceptual tool which facilitated the court's conclusion that state-induced destitution of an asylum seeker violated his right not to suffer inhuman or degrading treatment under Article 3.

Parliamentary and Administrative Mechanisms

Such imaginative efforts in judicial interpretation notwithstanding, the Human Rights Act 1998 itself contains a crucial restraint on the judicial role. It prevents the courts from providing any remedy for incompatible action if the action in question

---

12   [2002] EWHC 2282 (Admin).
13   [2006] 1 AC 396.

is the necessary consequence of a provision in an Act of the UK Parliament. Instead, the courts are given the power to make a declaration of incompatibility which proclaims the incompatibility but leaves to the government the decision whether to introduce remedial legislation and to the UK Parliament the task of scrutinising any such proposal. In the post-Human Rights Act period the parliamentary role has been further enhanced by non-statutory developments, notably in a succession of inquiries and reports on human rights implementation by the UK parliamentary Joint Select Committee on Human Rights. These have included inquiries and reports specifically linked to the CRC process (for example, JCHR 2009, following publication of the CRC Committee's Concluding Observations on the UK's third and fourth periodic reports under the CRC). As long ago as 2002 this Joint Select Committee recommended incorporating 'at least some' of the CRC's provisions into UK law so as to be directly enforceable in the courts (JCHR 2002) and has reaffirmed that view on several occasions since (JCHR 2008, JCHR 2009).

These developments in parliamentary scrutiny at national level have been accompanied by the establishment of several human rights commissions with varying territorial scope. The Equalities and Human Rights Commission has responsibilities for England, Wales and Scotland, Northern Ireland has Commissions on human rights and on equality and Scotland has its own Commission on Human Rights. There are four separate children's commissioners, the 'English' commissioner having responsibilities also in relation to non-devolved matters throughout the UK. These are on the face of it important non-judicial mechanisms supporting human rights implementation in the UK. Taken together these developments can be seen as steps towards a parliamentary and administrative model of human rights implementation. However, the introduction of the devolved parliamentary bodies introduces a special twist in this narrative. While many CRC-relevant governmental functions are now devolved, and while the devolved governments and legislatures operate under additional constraints as to human rights obligations compared to the UK level, none of the devolved parliamentary bodies had by 2010 established either a human rights or a children's rights scrutiny committee.

Devolution

Devolution in the UK is often described as being asymmetrical. This refers to the fact that the demarcation of powers between the devolved and national level is different for Northern Ireland, Wales and Scotland. Prior to devolution Scotland and Northern Ireland each had their own legal system whereas Wales was part of the legal system of England and Wales. Each country has a unique historical relationship with England. In the cases of Northern Ireland and Scotland this historical relationship is rooted in conflict, diplomatic negotiation and agreement; in the case of Wales, conquest and assimilation. The common legal system of England and Wales, dating back to the sixteenth-century assimilation of Wales by England, was a factor leading in 1998 to a more tentative arrangement for conferring governmental functions to Wales compared to Scotland and Northern Ireland. Revision of the Welsh settlement in 2006 still left the National Assembly for Wales with less legislative competence than the Scottish Parliament and the Northern Ireland Assembly. The details are complex, but essentially the Welsh legislature can make laws only in relation to matters that are explicitly transferred whereas the Northern Ireland and Scottish legislatures enjoy general legislative competence subject only to (differently) specified exceptions or reservations. These differences notwithstanding, all the devolved institutions enjoy wide powers in relation to the areas of social welfare, child protection and well-being, education, health, language, culture, transport, sport, environment and planning.

Constitutional Human Rights

Common to all three devolution arrangements is that the Human Rights Act's protection of the traditional English constitutional lawyer's notion of parliamentary sovereignty is not replicated for the devolved parliamentary bodies. The UK Acts that established the devolved legislatures and executives for Scotland, Wales and Northern Ireland all contained provision putting beyond their competence any act that is incompatible with Convention rights under the Human Rights Act 1998 (and indeed anything contrary to EU law). There has not as yet been a successful challenge calling in aid this constraint in relation to a law passed by a devolved legislature, although the Northern Ireland Commissioner for Children and Young People has twice used the argument in litigation. In a sense the Northern Ireland Commissioner's cases simply serve further to illustrate the limitations of judicial mechanisms. In the first, which concerned the adoption of anti-social behaviour legislation,[14] the Commissioner argued that the government's decision to promote legislation on anti-social behaviour was irrational, that the minister concerned was tainted by bias and that there was a failure of due process because of inadequate consultation especially with children and young people. The Commissioner also argued that the proposed legislation was incompatible with the CRC and ECHR and in breach of the general duty on public authorities to promote equality of opportunity under section 75 of the Northern Ireland Act 1998. The court dismissed all the arguments, noting that those directly based on ECHR Convention rights were difficult for the Commissioner to deploy because of lack of 'victim' status. This point also proved a barrier in the second case which concerned the continuation in law of the defence of reasonable chastisement to the criminal charge of common assault.[15] The reason given by the Northern Ireland Commissioner for not pursuing the latter case to appeal was lack of resource.

---

14   *In the Matter of an Application for Judicial Review by the Northern Ireland Commissioner for Children and Young People of the Decisions Announced by the Minister of State for Criminal Justice, John Spellar* [2004] NIQB 40.

15   *Northern Ireland Commissioner for Children and Young People's Application* [2009] NICA 10.

Even though no legal challenge has yet succeeded, the human rights constraints on devolved governments within the UK can properly be regarded as reflecting a constitutional protection of a different nature from that which exists at the UK level. In areas where governmental decisions about implementation are now made separately, there may be potential to challenge government at either the devolved or national level. This could arise if it were to be argued that a facility was enjoyed differently by a child in England compared to a child in Wales, Scotland or Northern Ireland, in such a way as to amount to a violation of an obligation of non-discrimination (Article 2, CRC; Article 14, ECHR). There is no example in relation to a children's rights issue as yet, but a brief diversion to note the position in relation to differential implementation in the UK of EU obligations shows that this type of argument has at least entered in to the litigator's lexicon in England and Wales.

The case of *R (Horvath) v Secretary of State for Environment, Food and Rural Affairs*[16] concerned the implementation by separate regulations for England and Wales of an EU requirement to impose conditions for receipt of direct support for farmers under the common agricultural policy. Mr Horvath argued that as a farmer in England he was subject to more onerous conditions than a farmer in Wales and that this constituted a violation of the principle of non-discrimination under EU law. The European Court of Justice, to which the case was referred by the High Court of England and Wales, found that differential implementation did not in itself constitute discrimination contrary to EU law and that member states were allowed to allocate responsibility for implementation to regional levels of government where national law permitted this, subject to the overriding need to implement 'correctly'.

Perhaps Mr Horvath's experience augurs badly for any attempt to use judicial mechanisms to highlight inequalities of access to CRC rights in the different regions of a State Party. Yet it seems reasonable to anticipate concerns arising if differences in organisation and provision of services lead to stark instances of less favourable treatment of children from one region compared to another. This might arise for example where young people from England and Wales are put together in a young offender institution (as is often the case, there being limited availability of secure accommodation for young offenders in Wales, and criminal justice remaining a non-devolved matter). Responsibility for assessment and provision of support rests with the local authority in which the young people normally reside and to which they will return on release. Local government funding, structures and the general governance of support services would fall in Wales to the Welsh Ministers and the National Assembly for Wales and in England to the UK government and Parliament. Deficiencies experienced by one young person and not the other, flowing from different policy choices or structural arrangements in Wales and England, could be characterised as unequal access to CRC rights within the State Party. There may be many barriers in the way of successful pursuit of

---

16   Case C 428/07, European Court of Justice, 16 July 2009.

this issue as a legal claim (including of course the lack of direct enforceability of the CRC in the UK, a matter which did not need to trouble Mr Horvath as he was asserting a directly enforceable right under EU law), but that does not stop it from being an issue about differential enjoyment of access to human rights, demanding to be addressed.

Tentative Innovations in Implementation: The Welsh Ministers' 'Duty to Have Due Regard' to the CRC

Post-devolution, each of the devolved administrations has been able to develop its own position in relation to the CRC, in addition to the national position taken by the UK government. Divergence can be discerned, for example by reference to the separate statutory remits for the children's commissioners and associated government statements (Williams 2005). In Wales, the political commitment of the devolved administration to the CRC was striking (Clutton 2008, Williams 2007). The executive as early as 1999, and then the National Assembly for Wales as a whole in 2004, proclaimed that the CRC was their overarching set of principles for all devolved policies on children and young people. Welsh Ministers sought to implement this position by ensuring that key strategy documents, for example on child poverty and on young offenders, made express reference to relevant articles of the CRC. The legislative competence of the National Assembly for Wales was extended under the Government of Wales Act 2006 and in the summer of 2009, the then First Minister, Rhodri Morgan, made the bold announcement that it was his government's intention to 'explore further the possibility of introducing a Measure to embed the principles of the United Nations Convention on the Rights of the Child into law on behalf of Welsh children' (NAW 2009).

The National Assembly for Wales had already generated the first legislative reference to the CRC in the UK when, in 2001, it enacted a regulation requiring the Children's Commissioner for Wales to 'have regard to' the CRC in exercising functions.[17] (This was followed by references to the CRC, though not in identical form, in the respective enactments establishing children's commissioners in Northern Ireland, Scotland and England.) Now, it seemed that Welsh Ministers were committed to achieving, so far as possible within devolved competence, a general legislative measure of implementation. No general legislative measure was proposed by the Northern Ireland, Scottish or UK governments, although at UK level a broadly-based children's rights coalition was collaborating over a Private Members' Bill (that is, a Bill introduced to Parliament without government support) on children's rights (CRAE 2010). That Bill, modelled on the Human Rights Act 1998, would if enacted have UK-wide application, but would stand no chance of being enacted without government support, which was not forthcoming.

The legislative model eventually published by Welsh Ministers in 2010 was, in the event, a cautious one. Broadly, the Rights of Children and Young Persons

---

17   Regulation 22, Children's Commissioner for Wales Regulations 2001.

(Wales) Measure as introduced to the Assembly's legislative process in June 2010 would have applied only to 'decisions of a strategic nature' by Welsh Ministers, attaching to such decisions a duty 'to have due regard to the requirements' of the CRC. The intended effect would be to

> ... require the Welsh Ministers to put in place arrangements so that when they ... make strategic decisions about how to exercise their functions, they will comply with a duty to have due regard to [the CRC] ... (WAG 2010, at para. 2.5)

However following legislative scrutiny the scope of this duty was extended so as to require Welsh Ministers to have due regard to the CRC when exercising any of their functions (whether or not at a 'strategic' level). This Welsh initiative is significant as an attempt to use a legal duty to enhance the profile of the CRC within government decision-making processes. It also seeks to tie a degree of local parliamentary scrutiny in to the monitoring and reviewing process of the CRC by means of a bespoke scrutiny role for the National Assembly for Wales and a requirement of consultation with children and young persons, the Children's Commissioner for Wales and other persons or bodies as the Welsh Ministers consider appropriate as to how to carry out the duty to have due regard. In this way the Welsh Measure might even be presented as an effort towards addressing within governmental thought processes what Stalford and Drywood in this volume describe as the need to embrace 'the entire process, investment and ideology surrounding the CRC'. Certainly it is the first attempt in the UK to make a general legislative provision about CRC implementation, and as such it is interesting not only that it comes from regional rather than national government but also that the region concerned is the one enjoying the weakest legislative competence.

It should be acknowledged that the central mechanism of the Welsh Measure, the 'due regard' duty, is calculated to contain the possibilities of legal challenge (compared for example to the much stronger provision in the Human Rights Act 1998 which makes ECHR compatibility a criterion of legality of governmental action). The Welsh mechanism thus reflects the traditional caution about judicial review discussed earlier in this chapter. In view of the joint England and Wales legal system and the relative weakness of Welsh devolved competence, it would perhaps be unrealistic to expect any different approach to this issue to emerge from Wales, especially in the still early years of Welsh devolution. To the extent that the Welsh Measure increases the visibility and accountability of government's performance in CRC implementation, the mechanisms for doing so are clearly intended to be primarily parliamentary and administrative rather than judicial.

Devolution and Engagement of Non-governmental Actors

The story of the CRC in the UK post-devolution has been heavily influenced by non-governmental actors. The Wales NGO Monitoring Group for the CRC engaged intensely in lobbying for and responding to the Welsh legislative measure as well as attending to its main business of co-ordinating the Wales NGOs' report to the CRC Committee (Save the Children 2006, Save the Children 2008 and, on the role of the Group generally, see Croke and Williams 2008). Proximity of governmental and non-governmental actors is reflected in the observer status on the Wales NGO Group of Welsh Assembly Government officials as well as the office of the Children's Commissioner for Wales (Croke and Williams 2008). Indeed each of the UK's four commissioners reports constructive engagement within their respective territories with government and with a wide range of statutory and voluntary agencies, children's organisations and with children themselves, through a variety of mechanisms (Marshall and Williams 2011).

In so far as devolution in the UK can be presented as a success story for non-governmental actors, the experience also suggests that, echoing Gran in this volume, progress is dependent on a coincidence of good NGO organisation and a number of other factors. NGO collaboration, however vibrant, will not suffice alone to bring about change. The UK coalition which produced the unsuccessful Children's Rights Bill 2009 attracted an impressive array of support from NGOs, statutory bodies including children's commissioners and equality and human rights commissions, individual Members of Parliament and even local authorities (CRAE 2010). But without at least the acquiescence, if not support, of the UK government, that Bill stood little chance of becoming law, whereas at the level of devolved government in Wales, there was a coincidence of Ministers' political aspiration and NGO activity.

State Party Co-ordination and the CRC's Process

As noted above, the CRC Committee has emphasised the importance of co-ordination across the State Party. Distribution of governmental responsibility amongst regional and national levels presents challenges in this regard. The experience of the UK post-devolution suggests that these challenges can be met if effective collaboration can be achieved between the respective institutions, but that this may be harder in practice for the NGO community to achieve than it is for governmental and statutory bodies. In the third and fourth periodic reporting period (culminating in hearings at the CRC Committee session in September 2008) the four children's commissioners were able to collaborate on and submit a joint report to the CRC Committee (11 Million et al. 2008) and the UK government consulted and collaborated with the devolved administrations on the writing of the UK State Party report (CRC 2008a.). The UK government also played a role in bringing together non-governmental actors in the early stages of its own process (CRC 2008a). In the event, however, the UK NGOs' report was only one of several submitted, with separate reports submitted in addition by children's rights alliances in England, Scotland and Wales as well as the Wales children and young people's report (see further Funky Dragon Chapter 15 in this volume). CRC Committee rapporteurs visited both the UK level and the separate regions.

The issues about coordination as to monitoring and reporting are essentially of a practical rather than a principled nature. The same cannot be said about coordination in implementation, since there is an inherent tension between the need for national coordination and the devolution of decision-making powers in CRC-relevant areas. Devolution is intended to allow for difference, for the exercise of local discretion as to policy priorities and for variations in service delivery driven by decisions made in exercise of such discretion. Separate responses were developed in the UK to the CRC Committee's Concluding Observations on the UK's third and fourth periodic report. In addition to the Welsh legislative measure described above, a Welsh Assembly Government Action Plan was produced as a specific and ongoing response to the Concluding Observations (WAG 2010a). In Scotland, a consultation paper was issued proposing a raft of actions within existing Scottish policy and legislative frameworks but no legislative steps towards further implementation (Scottish Government 2009). In Northern Ireland indications are that consideration of any legislative measures will be viewed in the context of ongoing consideration of a Bill of Rights for Northern Ireland (NICCY 2008) and its existing 10-year strategy on children and young people (Northern Ireland Government 2006). At the UK level, the government coordinated a joint statement of commitment to CRC implementation to coincide with events to mark the twentieth anniversary of the CRC on 20 November 2009 (DCSF 2009) but its more detailed responses to specific calls for action demonstrate the complexities of partial and asymmetrical devolution. They span the minimalist notion of a potential 'right to achieve well-being' as part of a re-statement of 'rights and responsibilities' (Ministry of Justice 2009, and see above), measures concerning the operation of law and policy in England (such as local provision of children's services), matters concerning England and Wales (such as youth justice), matters concerning England, Wales and Scotland (such as equalities legislation) and UK-wide matters (such as immigration and children in armed conflict) (JCHR 2010). Whatever the virtues of devolution, it cannot be said to ease the task of national coordination of CRC implementation.

Conclusion

Smaller territorial units of governance ought to facilitate closer engagement between the governed and the governing: this is indeed a major part of the justification for the delegation of powers from the national to the regional and local levels. Participative and deliberative approaches, and the type of collaborative activism that is necessary for CRC implementation, may be easier to achieve at these levels. The proximity of institutions and greater accessibility of decision-makers in these smaller spaces may be particularly conducive to constructive engagement with children and young people themselves, always assuming the necessary will on the part of the institutions and decision-makers concerned. Certainly, aspects of the story of children's rights in the UK post-devolution support these propositions.

Yet multi-level governance also introduces complexities and sometimes surprises of a less positive kind.

First, at least in principle, differences in approach to implementation might in the extreme manifest as issues about violation of the requirement of non-discrimination in Article 2 of the CRC. Second, and of more immediate practical import, internal distribution of functions within the State Party renders the task of reporting and monitoring more complex. Third, the goal of national coordination of implementation becomes particularly difficult, perhaps impossible, to achieve. Fourth, this difficulty tends to arise mainly in the social, economic and cultural field, that is those most likely to be allocated to the regions, and these happen also to be the areas that are most problematic in terms of judicial enforcement. This in turn engages the problem articulated by Campbell (2006: 326) that 'the language of rights is a language of entitlements, and this is a notion that makes little sense when there is no way of securing that to which one is entitled when it is under threat'. Parliamentary and administrative mechanisms of accountability are therefore especially important for securing accountability of governments for CRC implementation in these fields. The fifth and perhaps most important challenge presented by multi-level governance is precisely that – of accountability. The story of the CRC in the UK post-devolution illustrates all of these problems and demonstrates that at least in transitional stages parliamentary and administrative mechanisms for scrutiny may take time to catch up with the internal distribution of governmental powers amongst executives.

Counter-balancing the positive effects in terms of easier NGO engagement with regional government are the additional difficulties of coordination which NGOs face without the benefit of the resource available to governmental organisations. This may have an impact on the CRC Committee which, already facing serious challenges in coping with its volume of work (Doek, Van Bueren in this volume), must grapple not only to understand the implications of formal distribution of responsibility within the State Party but also to deal with multiple NGO submissions stemming from the internal regions.

On the other hand, the way in which devolved administrations in the UK have been ready to promote the CRC offers an opportunity for the CRC Committee to engage constructively with NGOs at those levels, injecting its messages into local practices and into lobbying for law reform in a way which would not be possible if communication were limited to the national level. The development of the Welsh legislative measure illustrates the potential for this, engaging as it did not only the NGO community but also through them, UNICEF and the CRC rapporteurs in an informal, advisory capacity.

Multi-level governance is a factor in transformations of several kinds, to which there is no predictable or perhaps any end point. The matters touched upon here each form part of larger transformations in politics, policy, law and government. The pertinent point in the context of this collection of reflections and experiences of the vision of the CRC and its implementation is simply that since the CRC was adopted there have been changes and developments in distribution of governmental powers within a number of States Parties and that this carries implications for the undertaking and evaluation of all 'appropriate legislative, administrative and other measures of implementation'.[18]

References

11 Million et al. 2008. *UK Children's Commissioners' Report to the UN Committee on the Rights of the Child*. London: 11 Million.

Campbell, T. 2006. Human rights strategies: an Australian alternative, in T. Campbell, J. Goldsworthy and A. Stone (eds), *Protecting Rights Without a Bill of Rights: Institutional Performance and Reform in Australia*. Aldershot: Ashgate.

Clutton, S. 2008. Devolution and the language of children's rights in the UK, in A. Invernizzi and J. Williams (ed.), *Children and Citizenship*. London: Sage.

Committee of the Regions. 2009. *White Paper on Multilevel Governance*. CdR/89/2009/fin. Brussels: EU Committee of the Regions.

Council of Europe. 1997. *Draft European Charter of Regional Self-Government* (Recommendation 34 (1997) of the Congress of Local and Regional Authorities in Europe 5 June 1997).

CRAE. 2010. *Children's Rights Part of UK Law: Summary of Action to Promote a UK Children's Rights Act* [online, Children's Rights Alliance for England]. Available at: http://www.crae.org.uk/protecting/uk-law.html [accessed June 2010].

CRC. 1990. *Guidelines for the Participation of Partners in the Pre-Sessional Working Group of the Committee on the Rights of the Child*. CRC/C/90 Annex VIII.

——. 2003. *General Comment No. 5 on General Measures of Implementation*. CRC/GC/2003/5.

——. 2008. *Concluding Observations on the Third and Fourth Periodic Reports Submitted by the United Kingdom*. CRC/C/GBR/CO/4.

——. 2008a. *Third and Fourth Periodic Report of the United Kingdom under Article 44 CRC*. CRC/C/GBR/4.

Croke, R. and Williams, J. 2008. Institutional support for the UNCRC's 'Citizen Child', in A. Invernizzi and J. Williams (eds), *Children and Citizenship*. London: Sage.

DCSF. 2009. *Working Together, Achieving More, A Joint Commitment to Take Action in Response to the UN Committee on the Rights of the Child's Concluding Observations*. London: Department for Children, Families and Schools.

Fredman, S. 2008. *Human Rights Transformed*. Oxford: Oxford University Press.

Hale, B. 2009. Dignity. *Journal of Social Welfare and Family Law*, 31(2), 101–8.

---

18   Article 4 of the CRC.

Heesterman, W. 2005. An assessment of the impact of youth submissions to the United Nations Committee on the Rights of the Child. *International Journal of Children's Rights*, 13(3), 351–78.

Hopkins, J. 2002. *Devolution in Context: Regional, Federal and Devolved Government in the European Union*. London: Cavendish.

Hunt, J. 2010. Devolution and differentiation: regional variation in EU law. *Legal Studies*, 30(3), 421–41.

JCHR. 2002. *The UN Convention on the Rights of the Child*. 10th Report of the UK Parliament's Joint Committee on Human Rights, Session 2002–03, HL Paper 117, HC 81, London.

——. 2008. *A Bill of Rights for the UK?* 29th Report of the UK Parliament's Joint Committee on Human Rights, Session 2007–08, HL Paper 165, HC 150, London.

——. 2009. *Children's Rights*, 25th Report of the UK Parliament's Joint Committee on Human Rights, Session 2008–09, HL Paper 157, HC 318, London.

——. 2010. *Government Response to the UK Parliament's Joint Committee on Human Rights*. 25th report of 2008–09 on children's rights, 23 February 2010.

King, J. 2007. The justiciability of resource allocation. *Modern Law Review*, 70(2), 197–224.

Marshall, K. and Williams, J. 2011. Children's commissioners: representing children's interests and views, in *Professionals, Children and the Community: Working Together*. Pearson [forthcoming].

Ministry of Justice. 2009. *Rights and Responsibilities: Developing Our Constitutional Framework*, Cm 7577 March 2009. London: Ministry of Justice.

NAW. 2009. Record of proceedings of the National Assembly for Wales, 17 July 2009.

NGO Group CRC. 2006. *Third Edition of the Guide for Non- Governmental Organisations Reporting to the Committee on the Rights of the Child*. Geneva: NGO Group for the CRC.

NICCY. 2008. *Review of Children's Rights in Northern Ireland, Northern Ireland Commissioner for Children and Young People*. Belfast: Northern Ireland Commissioner for Children and Young People.

Northern Ireland Government. 2006. *Our Children and Young People – Our Pledge: A Ten Year Strategy for Children and Young People in Northern Ireland 2006–2016*. Belfast: Office of the First Minister and Deputy First Minister.

Reutter, W. 2006. The transfer of power hypothesis and the German Lander. *Publius: The Journal of Federalism*, 36(2), 277–301.

Save the Children. 2006. *Righting the Wrongs: The Reality of Children's Rights in Wales*. Cardiff: Save the Children.

——. 2008. *Stop, Look, Listen: The Road to Realising Children's Rights in Wales: A Summary of the NGOs' Report to the United Nations on Children's Rights in Wales*. Cardiff: Save the Children.

Scottish Government. 2009. *Do the Right Thing: For People Who Work with Children or Work on Their Behalf, A Scottish Government Response to the Concluding Observations of the UN Committee Concluding Observations.* 1 September 2009 [online]. Available at: http://www.scotland.gov.uk/Publications/2009/08/27111754/0 [accessed June 2010].

Scottish Office. 1997. *Scotland's Parliament.* Cm. 3658. Edinburgh: HMSO.

WAG. 2010. Explanatory Memorandum accompanying the proposed Rights of Children and Young Persons (Wales) Measure, Welsh Assembly Government, Cardiff, 14 June 2010.

——. 2010a. *Getting It Right: The Welsh Assembly Government's 5-Year Action Plan in Response to the CRC Committee's 2008 Concluding Observations.* Cardiff: Welsh Assembly Government.

Welsh Office. 1997. *A Voice for Wales: The Government's Proposals for a Welsh Assembly*, Cm. 3718. London: HMSO.

Williams, J. 2005. Effective government structures for children? The UK's four children's commissioners. *Child and Family Law Quarterly*, 17, 37–53.

——. 2007. Incorporating children's rights: the divergence in law and policy. *Legal Studies*, 27, 261–87.

Woll, L. 2000. Reporting to the UN Committee on the Rights of the Child: a catalyst for domestic debate and policy change? *International Journal of Children's Rights*, 8(1), 71–81.

Verhellen, E. 1997. *Convention on the Rights of the Child: Background, Motivation, Structure, Main Themes*. Leuven: Garant.

Chapter 12

Human Rights and Child Poverty in the UK: Time for Change

Rhian Croke and Anne Crowley

Introduction

Child poverty scars the lives of too many children and young people living in the UK. It limits their future life chances for employment, for training, for enduring, positive family and social relationships, for good physical and mental health and longevity and it affects their childhood experiences profoundly (Bradshaw and Mayhew 2005).

In research conducted on behalf of Save the Children with 1,500 families living on a low income across the UK, eight of 10 parents said their children missed out on activities such as after-school clubs, school trips and inviting friends for tea (Save the Children 2006). Difficulties in making ends meet meant that children in at least a quarter of these households went without warm coats in winter, proper meals and heat in the home. Poverty is the single biggest threat to the well-being of children in the UK. Poor children often have little or no space to play and live in areas with few shops or amenities; children from the bottom social class are four times more likely to die in an accident and have nearly twice the rate of long-standing illness than those living in households with high incomes. Children who grow up in poverty are far less likely to do well in school and are much more likely to leave the education system with no qualifications at all (Bradshaw and Mayhew 2005).

Despite being one of the richest countries in the world, the UK experiences some of the highest levels of poverty in the developed world with nearly one in three children living in households with below the commonly agreed poverty threshold of 60 per cent median income. Among the 25 European Union countries only Italy, Portugal and the Slovak Republic have higher levels of child poverty (UNICEF 2007).

Following Tony Blair's historic pledge to end child poverty in the UK in a generation (Blair 1999) and the introduction of welfare to work and tax credit policies, child poverty started steadily falling in the early 2000s. However, progress on reducing the numbers of children living in child poverty in the UK stalled in 2005 and even before the recession hit, began to increase. The UK government has failed to reach its target of halving child poverty by 2010 and on current performance they will fall way short of their target of eradicating child poverty by 2020 (Hirsch 2008).

This chapter outlines the essential elements of a human rights based approach to tackling child poverty in the UK including the inter-relationship between child poverty and the relevant international human rights treaties. Current approaches to child poverty in the UK and Wales are reviewed, with a particular focus on how the dynamic of the CRC reporting process has influenced policy development in Wales. The case for a human rights approach to tackling child poverty in the UK is set out before the chapter concludes with a summary of current opportunities to further the implementation of a rights based approach to addressing child poverty at both the UK and Wales levels of governance.

Before exploring these substantive issues it is necessary to set out a brief explanation of the multi-levels of governance operating in the UK as it affects Wales (see further, Williams in this volume). Following a referendum on establishing a devolved parliament or assembly in Wales, the National Assembly for Wales was established in 1999. The new National Assembly for Wales was given the power to pass secondary legislation in a number of fields including health, education, transport and rural development. Power to determine policy relating to tax and benefits, foreign affairs, immigration and criminal justice was retained by the UK Parliament sitting in London. In May 2007, the new Government of Wales Act 2006 came into force. The Act increased the powers available to the National Assembly and granted further legislative powers in relation to the devolved policy areas but retained power for the hitherto non-devolved areas with the UK government.

Early on in its history, the National Assembly for Wales demonstrated a strong commitment to children. A number of ministers had a background in working in the voluntary sector on child, youth, family and women's issues and were very receptive to prioritising children's rights. An early task of the first Welsh Assembly Government was to respond to the recommendations of an inquiry into the abuse of children in public care in Wales (Waterhouse 2000). Their response included the establishment of the UK's first children's commissioner or ombudsperson. In 2004, the Welsh Assembly Government formally adopted the CRC as the basis of all its policy making for children and young people.[1] This represented a divergence from the New Labour UK Government's approach for children's policy in England which preferred to focus on the outcomes of public services for children and young people.[2] This presented an opportunity in Wales if not in the UK as a whole to re-assert the value of a human rights framework for tackling child poverty and reclaim the values and principles that should underpin the shared lives of people.

---

1   The Assembly formally adopted the UNCRC in Plenary Session on 14 January 2004. Record of Proceedings, National Assembly for Wales, 14 January 2004.

2   See HM Government (2004).

Current Approaches to Tackling Child Poverty at the UK and Wales Levels of Governance

Efforts to eradicate child poverty have of course to be understood in the wider context of overcoming poverty and social exclusion. At this point in time there seems to be a broad political consensus that poverty and disadvantage in the UK are avoidable and need to be tackled with persistence and co-ordination and that the starting point should be about helping everyone play full economic and social roles. The variation in approach comes when we try to define just how much help, of what sort and for whom; the relative value of economic and social roles; and what should be done to support those who are unable to flourish in the market economy (Darton, Hirsh and Strelitz 2003).

The UK government of 1997–2010 summed up its anti-poverty strategy as 'work for those who can, security for those who cannot' and introduced a range of policies to get people into paid work and to make work pay (Lister 2008: 11). Such policies contributed significantly to the reduction in child poverty in the early 2000s with the risk of poverty being much lower in working families, but the rise in child poverty rates in England and Wales since 2005 has been among children in working households and it is this that has undermined progress towards the target to end child poverty by 2020 (MacInnes, Kenway and Parekh 2009).

Undoubtedly, reforms to tax and benefits (a non-devolved area) and support to get parents into decent, well paid work (largely non-devolved) make the largest contributions to eradicating child poverty in Wales. However, the Welsh Assembly Government has a role to play in supporting parents into work by, for example, ensuring adequate provision of childcare and the efficient administration of certain benefits. It has a significant role in reducing inequalities and addressing discrimination in the medium to longer terms through education, health, transport and other key social policies which are all devolved.

Tackling child poverty in Wales has more recently become a real political issue. For a nation setting its sights on renewed prosperity, children and young people assume particular importance for their future economic value. A focus on children and the development of skills in the next generation are essential to the vision of a vibrant and prosperous Wales as set out in the Welsh Assembly Government's strategic plan *Better Wales* (Thomas and Crowley 2007). Child poverty is seen as especially wasteful, carrying huge costs both for the children and families involved and also for society (Hirsch 2009).

It was not immediately clear how Tony Blair's ambitious and welcome target of eradicating child poverty by 2020 was to be played out in Wales. However, in 2003 the Welsh Assembly Government formally adopted the UK government's child poverty targets and set about developing its first child poverty strategy focused on policy within its control including education, health, social care and transport. From the outset, the Welsh Assembly Government adopted a children's rights approach, consulting with significant numbers of children and young people affected by child poverty in Wales. These consultations provided powerful evidence of the isolation and stigma experienced by poor children in Wales; action to tackle these aspects of child poverty and the forging of a rights based approach were prominent in the Welsh Assembly Government Strategy, *A Fair Future for Our Children* (WAG 2005).

The 'One Wales' programme of the new Labour/Plaid Cymru coalition Welsh Assembly Government of 2007 made eradicating child poverty a high priority and introduced a number of additional commitments. These included the establishment of an 'Expert Group' to advise the Assembly Government on policy and progress. It also included the regular publication of data on the extent of child poverty in Wales and regular government reporting on progress against its own set of child poverty targets and milestones, as well as a commitment to legislate to place statutory duties on public agencies in respect of tackling child poverty (Winckler 2009).

The Children and Families Measure[3] enacted in February 2010 imposed new duties on a range of public bodies in Wales including the Welsh Assembly Government and local government. The key duty is for these public bodies to demonstrate their commitment to reducing child poverty. The duties in the Measure reflect similar duties imposed on the UK government in the UK Child Poverty Act 2010 to work toward a new target of reducing the proportion of children in poverty to between 5 to 10 per cent by 2020. The Welsh Assembly Government produced in 2010 a comprehensive strategy for reducing child poverty with a much clearer focus on what could be achieved in Wales. Central to this new strategy is improving outcomes for children and young people living in disadvantaged families in Wales and reducing inequalities. The strategy is built around the Welsh Assembly Government's seven core aims for children which themselves derive from the CRC and aims to tackle both the causes and effects of child poverty through a range of cross-cutting policies and programmes (WAG 2010).

Towards a Human Rights Based Approach to Tackling Child Poverty

What is a Human Rights Based Approach to Tackling Child Poverty?

A human rights based approach to poverty is based on the concept that the 'poor have rights or entitlements that give rise to legal obligations on the part of others. Poverty reduction then becomes more than charity, more than a moral obligation – it becomes a legal obligation' (OHCHR 2004: 33). The emphasis on universal human needs challenges the 'otherness' of those experiencing poverty (Lister 2008). It shifts the debate from the personal failures of the 'poor' to the failure of macro-economic structures and policies. The recognition of the existence of legal entitlements of the poor and legal obligations of others towards them is the first step towards empowerment. The empowerment of those living in poverty is an essential precondition for the elimination of poverty and for the upholding of

---

3   A Measure is a law passed by the National Assembly for Wales.

human rights. The human rights based approach 'acknowledges the agency of people living in poverty – that they are not just passive victims but also agents in their own lives, capable of making choices and of contributing the expertise borne of experience to policy-making' (Lister 2008: 13). Human rights can help to equalise the distribution and exercise of power both within and between societies (OHCHR 2004).

Human rights violations are both a cause and consequence of poverty, in other words human rights violations are 'part of what it means to be poor' (British Institute of Human Rights 2008: 6). Despite the clear link between poverty and human rights, the international human rights instruments do not contain an explicit human right to freedom from poverty. Poverty cannot be subdivided into separate rights. Poverty is instead defined and understood by examining the interrelationship and indivisibility of civil, political, and social and economic and cultural rights. Poverty by nature is complex and a human rights based approach to poverty eradication goes beyond the focus of increasing income and toward the recognition that poverty is multi-dimensional, affecting many areas of life and infringing numerous human rights.

Traditionally across the UK child poverty has been seen as a consequence of family poverty resulting from a lack of economic resources. The key measure of child poverty used in the UK and across the European Union is a relative income measure; child poverty is defined as the percentage of children aged 0–17 years living in households with an income below 60 per cent of the national median income. It is this relative income measure that is used as the prime measure of progress against the UK's child poverty targets. A human rights perspective on the other hand sees children as units of observation in their own right and focuses the analysis on a broader concept of resources to explain the well-being of children (Eurochild 2007: 1).

Conceptualising child poverty from a human rights perspective privileges this broader perspective incorporating economic, social and cultural rights, such as a right to health care as well as civil and political rights such as the right to be heard. Understanding child poverty as a denial of children's fundamental human rights resulting from a lack of resources emphasises the interrelated and interdependent dimensions of deprivation. For example, access to decent housing, health care, a balanced and adequate diet will contribute to children's success in school. By contrast, overcrowded accommodation, located in a deprived neighbourhood may contribute to poor health, low educational attainment and disaffection from school (Eurochild 2007).

In 2007, UNICEF published an assessment of the well-being of children in the 21 nations of the industrialised world (UNICEF 2007). The report compared different dimensions of a child's well-being using 40 indicators spanning health, education, peer and family relationships and was a significant and important departure from previous analyses which just used income poverty as a proxy measure for overall child well-being (Eurochild 2007: 2). The UK fared badly in the assessment, coming bottom in the resultant UNICEF league tables. This caused some shock waves in the UK with the report lauded as a 'wake up call' to the fact that despite being a rich country, the UK was failing its children and young people (BBC 2007). The comparisons with the performance of countries such as the Netherlands, Sweden, Denmark and Finland at the top of the league tables demonstrated that in prosperous, industrialised countries, inequalities in childhood were not inevitable and it was possible to support every child to fulfil his or her potential (UNICEF 2007).

Exploration of poverty 'through the eyes of a child' reinforces the importance of the human rights perspective. To understand the lived experience of child poverty we need to bring a child's perspective to the analysis of child poverty and social exclusion (Ridge 2009). A review of qualitative research in the UK with low income children and families commissioned by the Department of Work and Pensions presents a powerful picture of the 'lived experience' of poverty (Ridge 2009). The evidence from children reveals the experience of poverty in childhood can be highly damaging and the effects of poverty both pervasive and disruptive. As Ridge summarises:

> Poverty permeates every aspect of children's lives from economic and material disadvantages, through social and relational constraints and exclusions, to the personal and more hidden aspects of poverty associated with shame, sadness and the fear of difference and stigma. (2009: 2)

Consultations with over 300 children and young people in Wales identified a common set of themes and messages about the effects of poverty on the lives and experiences of children and young people. Children and young people of all ages raised issues relating to education, health, crime, drugs, participation, leisure, transport, the unique pressures on families living on a low income and the profound effects of the stigma and shame that poverty brings (Crowley and Vulliamy 2002).

In this research as in similar research in other parts of the UK (Ridge 2009) children and young people talked about going without clothing and heating because of the lack of money in their household. Some children and young people were concerned to point out that most parents in low income households often went without themselves so that their children could have what they needed and prevent their children being singled out by their friends as poor.

A strong cross cutting theme in this research across the UK relates to the exclusion children and young people living in poverty experience. Children and young people living in low-income households repeatedly described how they are made to feel different to other children and young people. The fact that children begin to experience the reality of their 'different-ness' at an early age has been highlighted by a number of studies in the UK (Middleton, Ashworth and Walker 1994, Horgan 2007).

Children and young people across the UK clearly understand the stigma and shame that living in poverty brings and acutely feel the lack of respect their 'different-ness' evokes in some of their peers and some of the adults around them. The impact of this on children and young people's sense of worth and self-esteem cannot be underestimated.

The research illustrates how living in low-income households affects all aspects of children's lives. Children and young people in Wales highlighted the inaccessibility of leisure and social activities (Crowley and Vulliamy 2002). Children and young people complained about how crime and drugs affected their use of public space by, for example, the proliferation of discarded syringes and the vandalism of play facilities for younger children.

The key messages from children and young people in the UK studies reviewed by Tess Ridge (2009) provide a glimpse of the social and human costs of child poverty in the 'here and now' of childhood and in the longer term and reinforce the need for a rights based approach which challenges 'povertyism' and the discrimination children experience on the grounds of poverty (Killeen 2008). The next section examines the direction given by the most relevant international human rights treaties as to the key elements of a rights based approach.

Poverty and International Human Rights Treaties

The international treaty of most relevance to poverty alleviation is the International Covenant on Economic, Social and Cultural Rights (ICESCR). It enshrines the economic, social and cultural rights contained in the UN Declaration on Human Rights (UDHR). Under Article 11 of the ICESCR States Parties must 'recognize the right of everyone to an adequate standard of living for himself and his family, including adequate food, clothing and housing, and to the continuous improvement of living conditions'. States Parties are required to take appropriate steps to ensure the realisation of this right. In its most recent Concluding Observations on the UK, the UN Committee on Economic, Social and Cultural Rights expressed its concern that child poverty remains widespread in the UK, and called on the government to develop human rights based poverty reduction programmes. The Committee has also criticised the UK government for failing to fully incorporate human rights standards into UK law (Committee on Economic, Social and Cultural Rights 2009).

The CRC is the most comprehensive of the international human rights treaties and places high importance on children's basic socio-economic rights. It recognises that poverty, and especially persistent poverty early in the child's life has a significant impact on the healthy development of the child and can result in breaches of numerous of the civil, political, social and economic rights contained within the Convention.

The first articles of the CRC that come into focus when considering child poverty are Articles 27 and 4, however, due consideration must always be given to the guiding principles of the CRC (Articles 2, 3, 6, 12) that are instrumental to all the other articles and depending on the given context other articles of the CRC. Additionally the CRC Committee has issued 12 General Comments to date in relation to specific rights or aspects of specific rights. These General Comments provide information on what are traditionally known as socio-economic rights and they complement what is included in the Committee on Economic, Social and Cultural Rights General Comments.

Article 27 calls on States Parties to implement 'the right of every child to a standard of living adequate for the child's physical, mental, spiritual, moral, and social development'. The CRC acknowledges that parents and guardians have primary economic responsibility for the child but that states should provide material assistance to children either indirectly through their parents or directly to children themselves in cases of identified need. Thus under Article 27 of the CRC States Parties have to fulfil their obligations 'in accordance with national conditions and within their means'.

Turning to Article 4 the State Party has a duty to take measures 'to the maximum extent of available resources'. It distinguishes between socio-economic rights and civil and political rights by requiring that, 'with regard to economic, social and cultural rights, States Parties shall undertake such measures to the maximum extent of their available resources and, where needed, within the framework of international cooperation'. There is an acceptance within this article that the full realisation of socio-economic rights may not be achieved immediately as resources may not be available. However each State Party is required to show that it has used all the resources that it has available to the maximum extent as a matter of priority and this requires an adequate and transparent budget analysis. The CRC guidelines for periodic reports further state that children should be made visible in budgets (CRC Committee 1996).

Article 2 of the CRC sets out the basic duty to 'respect and ensure' all rights in the Convention to all children in the State Party's jurisdiction, without discrimination of any kind. Vulnerable groups of children are deserving of special measures of protection and additionally there must also be protection against discrimination between different groups of children. Arguably those groups of children that are most disadvantaged in enjoying their rights (e.g. living in poverty) require the highest standard of protection. The principle of non-discrimination applies to all state policies and practices, including those concerning healthcare, education etc. and access to services.

Article 3 makes it clear that in all actions concerning children, whether undertaken by public or private or social welfare institutions, courts of law, administrative authorities or legislative bodies, the best interests of the child shall be a primary consideration. This also includes any decisions regarding a child's economic welfare. Article 6 of the CRC directs states to 'ensure to the maximum extent possible the survival and development of the child'. Article 12 of the CRC requires states to 'assure to the child who is capable of forming his or her own views the right to express those views freely in all matters affecting the child, the views of the child being given due weight in accordance with the age and maturity of the child'. The international monitoring bodies have often stressed the importance of participation as an essential element of anti-poverty strategies (Economic and Social Council 2001: paras 9 and 12), particularly for children for whom poverty is a major obstacle to participation in a number of contexts (CRC Committee 2009).

At a minimum, the cumulative effect of the guiding principles of the CRC reflected in the articles described above alongside what the CRC Committee describes as the 'general measures of implementation' make sure that due priority must be given to children, particularly vulnerable groups of children, that the best interests of children are protected, that the survival and development of the child is fulfilled and, finally, that the child's views have been respected when making decisions about any situation that affects them. All states should use a children's rights perspective, giving active consideration to the guiding principles when making any decision that has a direct or an indirect effect or impact on children (CRC Committee 2003). (See further Kilkelly for discussion on children's rights auditing, Chapter 8 in this volume.)

The United Nations has identified key principles of a human rights based approach that can be applied by governments and public institutions. The first of these is to explicitly apply human rights values, legal standards and norms across policy, planning and practice – that is examining how decisions and actions impact on human rights. The other principles relate to how this is achieved – ensuring accountability mechanisms to claim rights, the identification of immediate, intermediate and long-term targets; effective monitoring methods, the empowerment and participation of people in identifying and addressing rights issues, and non-discrimination, prioritising those most vulnerable to human rights abuses (OHCHR 2004). The adoption of a human rights conceptualisation of poverty should be about recognising dignity, respect and participation as well as about the indivisibility of civil, political, economic, social and cultural rights.

The international human rights instruments, UN Guidelines, General Comments and the General Principles and General Measures of Implementation of the CRC provide an intricate web of standards presenting an invaluable framework for developing programmes and policies for addressing child poverty.

By ratifying the CRC and ICESCR, the UK State Party has taken on the obligation to provide material assistance and to support policies and programmes for the poor. The CRC Committee also emphasises that economic, social and cultural rights, as well as civil and political rights, must be regarded as justiciable (CRC Committee: para. 25).

To What Extent Do Current Approaches to Tackling Child Poverty in the UK Reflect a Human Rights Based Approach?

So far the rights based approach to poverty has not been taken on board by the UK government in relation to domestic poverty even though ironically it underpins the Department for International Development's understanding of poverty in the global South (Lister 2008). Traditionally, the approach to tackling child poverty in the UK has not been focused on the accountability of the state, rather as we noted above, the approach to date has been premised on getting parents into work.

Neither does the human rights legislation in the UK (Human Rights Act 1998) confer social, economic and cultural rights, as it focuses almost exclusively on civil and political rights. Contrary to a recommendation by the Joint Committee on Human Rights of the House of Lords and the House of Commons (JCHR) (JCHR 2004), the government has consistently resisted UN pressure to incorporate the International Covenant on Economic, Social and Cultural Rights into UK law.

In the UK, precedence is given to the immediate protection of civil and political rights while it is argued economic and social rights must depend on affordability. The UK government view is to see 'economic and social rights not as enforceable rights, but as aspirational policy goals' (JCHR 2004: para. 52). There is also the belief that many aspects of these rights are already incorporated into other legislation, such as that on social security, and that there is no need to make UK law on these matters subject to any external authority. The UK Government rejected EU proposals which would have incorporated the European Charter of Fundamental Rights into UK law. This Charter builds on the rights protected by the European Convention on Human Rights to create more comprehensive protection for economic, social and cultural rights (see further Stalford and Drywood Chapter 9 in this volume).

In 2006 the Equality Act established a single body with responsibility for equalities legislation and for promoting and protecting human rights in Great Britain and dissolved the Commission on Racial Equality, the Equal Opportunities Commission and the Disability Rights Commission. The Equality and Human Rights Commission set up in 2007 is a statutory body covering Great Britain (England, Scotland and Wales). The Equality and Human Rights Commission is required to prioritise rights protected by the UK's Human Rights Act, which, as referred to earlier, generally excludes economic, social and cultural rights (Killeen 2008).

The 2010 Equality Act is intended to streamline the law giving individuals greater protection from unfair discrimination and to make it easier for employers and companies to understand their responsibilities. It also sets a new standard for those who provide public services to treat everyone with dignity and respect. Section 1 of the Act places a duty on certain public bodies to consider socio-economic disadvantage when making strategic decisions about how to exercise their functions. This is essentially about public bodies making strategic decisions such as deciding priorities and setting objectives (in relation to, for example, health, housing, crime rates etc.) to consider how their decisions might help to reduce the inequalities associated with socio-economic disadvantage. If implemented this would be a step forwards, in that it places a legal obligation on certain public bodies to consider inequalities associated with disadvantage when they are carrying out their planning (almost akin to an equality impact assessment that includes socio-economic disadvantage as an indicator) but this is as far as it goes. Its purpose is to support the achievement of broad economic policy objectives and accountability is limited to show to one another, auditors, inspection bodies that they have processes in place and are taking these aspirations seriously. It does not entrench a human rights accountability framework that holds public bodies to account to implement people's socio-economic rights and it is hard to envision that legal challenges will arise from this duty.

Therefore, there is currently limited recourse to justice for people to claim their individual social and economic rights in the UK. Additionally and disappointingly, there was no noticeable public outcry that the UK government failed to meet its first target of reducing child poverty by a quarter in 2005 or when in March 2010, the Treasury conceded that it will miss the target of halving child poverty by 2010 by a long way (approximately 600,000 children).

The need for the adoption of a rights based approach to child poverty was set out by the CRC Committee in its 2008 Concluding Observations on the UK's State Party report (CRC/C/GBR/CO/4 [20 October 2008]). The Committee welcomed the State Party's commitment to end child poverty by 2020 and the proposed introduction of legislative measures to enhance and clarify the state's accountability, however, it expressed concerns that child poverty remained a serious problem affecting all parts of the United Kingdom and questioned whether the government's strategy was sufficiently targeted at those groups of children in most severe poverty. The Committee highlighted the necessity of 'an adequate standard of living ... for a child's physical, mental, spiritual, moral and social development and that child poverty also affects infant mortality rates, access to health and education as well as everyday quality of life of children'. In accordance with Article 27 of the Convention, the Committee recommended that the State Party: adopt and implement legislation aimed at achieving the 2020 target; prioritise those in greatest need; do more to provide material assistance and support programmes to children particularly with regard to nutrition, clothing and housing.

The Child Poverty Act 2010 of the last Labour UK government is in some ways (as the Joint Committee on Human Rights has described it) a 'human rights enhancing measure' (JCHR 2004 para. 122) in that it introduces some accountability for the State to meet its child poverty reduction targets. As the JCHR stated:

> providing an unqualified duty to meet the four income targets by the end of the financial year 2020–21, and establishing a detailed framework both for driving and monitoring progress towards the achievement of those targets, the Bill does on its face appear to provide a mechanism for the progressive realisation of children's rights to an adequate standard of living in Article 27 CRC and Article 11 ICESCR. It goes some way towards implementing the recent recommendation of the UN Committee on the Rights of the Child that the Government adopt legislation aimed at achieving the target of ending child poverty by 2020, including by establishing measurable indicators for its achievement. We therefore welcome the Bill as a human rights enhancing measure. (JCHR 2009: para. 1.22)

The Act places specific duties on the UK government, the government of Scotland and local authorities in England to work towards the target of eradicating child poverty by the year 2020. A similar duty is imposed on the Welsh Assembly Government and Welsh public bodies, including but not restricted to, local authorities in Wales with the Welsh Assembly's Children and Families Measure, 2010. The 'eradication of child poverty' target is defined in the UK Child Poverty Act 2010 as a reduction in the proportions of children living in households with less than 60 per cent of the median income (currently standing at 30 per cent after housing costs) to between 5 to 10 per cent.

Interestingly, as there is a divergence in the UK government domestic policy on poverty and UK government international development aid policy, there is also a divergence in the language underpinning poverty policy within the confines of the UK. The UK Child Poverty Act is based on income targets and economic policy objectives whereas the Welsh Assembly's Children and Families Measure encompasses a broader approach to child poverty encapsulating 13 Broad Aims that include aims that can be clearly connected to human rights principles, such as non-discrimination, participation and survival and development. Furthermore, for Wales, the strategy that flows from the Children and Families Measure is set within the framework of CRC via the Welsh Assembly Government's seven core aims. Having said that, neither the UK nor the Welsh poverty legislation allows children to claim their individual socio-economic rights: instead they aim to hold Government to account to meet targets of eradicating child poverty and therefore aim to progressively fulfil children's socio-economic rights in the longer term.

The issue of the justiciability of socio-economic rights is contested. The Joint Committee on Human Rights (JCHR) agrees with the UK government that social and economic rights should only be given limited legal effect. The JCHR argue that the government instead should be under a duty to make progress towards the realisation of economic and social rights as in accordance with the targets laid out in the Child Poverty Act 2010 and that this should go alongside a requirement to report regularly to Parliament. The courts they argue should only have a circumscribed role to review how successful the government has been in reaching the targets that have been set (JCHR 2009). The JCHR argue that fully justiciable and legally enforceable economic and social rights carry too great a risk that the courts will interfere with legislative judgments about priority setting. They are of the opinion that the government and Parliament must retain the responsibility for economic and social policy, in which the courts they consider lack expertise and have limited institutional competence or authority (JCHR 2009: para 1.26) (see further Williams, Van Bueren Chapters 11 and 5 respectively in this volume).[4]

---

4   This position stands in contrast with the one adopted in South Africa, where there were similar concerns. In South Africa they have proved able to deliver judgements on economic and social rights made enforceable under the South African constitution. South Africa has entrenched justiciable socio-economic rights in its Constitution, and the judiciary has made it clear that 'civil and political and socio-economic rights are inter-related and mutually supporting', and that '[t]here can be no doubt that human dignity, freedom and equality … are

Legislative target-setting (i.e. that included in the Child Poverty Act 2010) is relatively new[5] and it remains to be seen how the UK and the Welsh Assembly Governments will be held to account to meet their 2020 target to eradicate child poverty. It is not completely clear how a case of judicial review could be brought if governments fail to meet their targets. The approach to legislative target setting can be compared to the international treaty reporting process which encourages State Parties to incrementally and progressively improve their records to realise the rights of children without recourse to an individual complaints mechanism (see further discussion Doek and Van Bueren Chapters 4 and 5 respectively in this volume). These are certainly important aspects of an overall human rights based approach to the realisation of children's socio-economic rights but does this approach go far enough, and in reality will government be effectively held to account to redistribute resources to remove children from a life of poverty?

This new legal framework for child poverty reduction is not enough in itself. Governments of the UK are also obliged under the CRC (Article 4) and the International Covenant on Economic, Social and Cultural Rights (Article 2) to invest the maximum available resources into eliminating child poverty. The Institute of Fiscal Studies and the Joseph Rowntree Foundation estimated in 2008 that an additional investment of £4 billion per year was needed to meet the government's poverty target of 2010 (Hirsch 2008). This investment was not forthcoming with government saying it could only afford to invest 1 billion. This even though in 2007, London city bonuses totalled £14 billion and BP made £3.44 billion in three months. It is clearly not just about affordability – governments make choices with regard to tackling priorities as the UNICEF report of 2007 indicated even though the Trade Union Congress estimates that £40 billion a year is wasted on tackling the consequences of child poverty (Crowley 2009). As the UN has consistently recommended, the CRC and the ICESCR need to be fully incorporated into UK domestic law if children's rights are to be respected, protected and fulfilled.

A Children's Rights Based Approach in Wales?

This penultimate section briefly reviews the progress made by Welsh Assembly Governments over the last 10 years in adopting a children's rights approach to tackling child poverty and discusses how the reporting process of the CRC has been an important catalyst for fostering the commitment to the children's rights based

---

denied to those who have no food, clothing or shelter' (Constitutional Court in *Government of the Republic of South Africa v Grootboom* 2000 (11) BCLR 1169 (CC), para. 23).

5   See Court of Appeal decision in *R (Friends of the Earth) v Secretary of State for Energy and Climate Change* [2009] EWCA Civ 810 (30 July 2009), a challenge to the Secretary of State's failure to implement his Fuel Poverty Strategy under the Warm Homes and Energy Conservation Act 2000, in which the Court noted, at para. 19, 'the relatively sudden upsurge of this type of target-setting, duty-creating legislation' and describing it as 'a rapidly developing area of public law'.

approach in Wales. There is a clear divergence in the attitudes and commitment to children's human rights between the Welsh Assembly and UK government (see further Williams 2007, Clutton 2008).

The rights and well-being of children and young people have been significant on the Welsh political landscape for many years not least because of the strong links between governmental and non-governmental organisations in Wales (Croke and Crowley 2006). Devolution accelerated and supported this commitment to children. In 2002, the Assembly Government was commended by the CRC Committee for using the Convention as the framework in its strategy for children and young people. In 2004 the commitment to the CRC was consolidated when the Welsh Assembly Government adopted the CRC as the overarching set of principles for all its policy on children and young people, at the same time issuing *Rights to Action* a policy document adopting seven core aims for children, presented as a direct translation of the CRC's articles into broad policy aims. Further to the Assembly's resolution of adopting the CRC in 2004, the Children Act 2004 guidance for Wales requires local authorities and their partners to have regard to the CRC:

> The Assembly Government has adopted the UN Convention as the foundation for all its dealings with children and young people, and local authorities and their relevant partners should have regard to its principles in providing services. (Welsh Assembly Government 2004: 7)

Rights to Action heralded an approach to children that aimed to see them as rights-holders and make them more visible in policy making. Welsh Assembly Government policy makers recognised that children should be understood as 'beings' as well as 'becomings' (see further Freeman Chapter 1 in this volume). The Minister for Children, Jane Hutt, stated:

> Children and young people should be seen as citizens, with rights and opinions to be taken account now. They are not a species apart, to be alternately demonized and sentimentalised, nor trainee adults who do not yet have a full place in society. (Welsh Assembly Government 2004: 7)

Interestingly in Wales, policy for children based on the language of rights and entitlement was developed not solely up to age of 18 years but up to 25 years. The *Ten Entitlements* became the Welsh Assembly Government's legal direction on youth services for young people aged 11–25 years. The government discourse shifted to talk of children *and* young people (see further Cantwell in this volume).[6]

---

6   It is beneficial that the language of government refers to children *and* young people. As Cantwell illustrates in Chapter 2 of this volume there has been a tendency to 'infantalise older CRC rights holders' (Cantwell: 43) and 'over-zealous use of the word "child" when

Children and young people's access to political participation and governmental decision making was increasingly supported and funded by the Welsh Assembly Government via Funky Dragon, the children and young people's assembly for Wales (see further Chapter 15 in this volume), local authority youth forums, the Children's Commissioner for Wales, and the funding of the Participation Unit which has a lead strategic role in developing children and young people's participation across the public and non-governmental sectors in Wales (Thomas and Crowley 2007).

During this time constructive dialogue increased between the Welsh Assembly Government and the non-governmental community, centred on the establishment of the Wales UNCRC Monitoring Group, a national alliance of agencies tasked with monitoring and promoting the implementation of the CRC in Wales. The Group took the Concluding Observations 2002 and reported how far the Welsh Assembly Government and UK government had progressed in reaching compliance with these recommendations. *Righting the Wrongs: The Reality of Children's Rights in Wales* was the first extensive report on the state of children's rights in Wales and was launched and debated at an oversubscribed conference in 2006. Key speakers inspired the delegation on the importance of children's rights, including the first Children's Commissioner for Wales, Peter Clarke, and the then Chair of the Committee on the Rights of the Child, Jaap Doek (see Williams and Croke 2008 for further discussion).

The report and conference effectively launched the next round of periodic reporting to the CRC Committee and succeeded in securing a commitment from the Minister for Children to oversee the Welsh Assembly Government submission

---

referring to CRC rights-holders has in turn created invisibility for adolescents as a whole' (Cantwell: 46). In Wales, particularly via the channel of Funky Dragon, young people made it clear to government that they wanted to be identified as young people and not children. It is also beneficial that the discourse on rights and entitlements includes young people up to the age of 25 years. The Welsh Assembly Government acknowledges that there should be a continuum of support from childhood, to adolescence and into early adulthood. For example, young people from the age of 18, making the transition from foster care to self-supported living, children leaving the care system and the many young people facing unemployment are some of the most vulnerable young people living in Wales. Support and realisation of rights should not end at 18. However it becomes confusing when the framework of the CRC is said to cover those young people up to the age of 25. The CRC is a legal instrument that covers the human rights of anyone under the age of 18 years. The other international human rights instruments can be turned to support the rights of young people included in the 18–25 years age group and the human rights principles drawn from all of the international human rights treaties (as well as the UK Human Rights Act 1998) can be used as the rights based framework when considering the policy underpinning their support. As Cantwell outlines, and this is pertinent to the Wales case study, discourse dominates on 'children's rights' as opposed to 'human rights' or the 'human rights of children', so it is often forgotten that the fulfilment of human rights does not stop when a person reaches adulthood, they continue along the life course and are accessible via the other international human rights treaties.

to the State Party report as well as regular and focused dialogue between government and NGOs, more inclusive 'NGO Alternative' reporting (resulting in greater credibility and authority) and perhaps most importantly raised the profile and importance of children's rights with a wider constituency of policy makers and practitioners from across Wales. The dialogue had certainly begun and in early 2007 (released well in advance of the UK State Party report to encourage debate within Wales) the Welsh Assembly Government responded with a cross-governmental report (WAG 2007) demonstrating the Government's commitment to monitoring the progress of children's rights in Wales.

More and more partners were mobilised around the importance of monitoring and reporting on children's rights. As well as both the Welsh Assembly Government (WAG 2007) and the Wales UNCRC Monitoring Group (Croke and Crowley 2006) reports to the CRC Committee, the first UK-wide Children's Commissioner's report was submitted which gave significant weight to the importance of children's rights. Funky Dragon (Chapter 15 in this Volume) also became a global pioneer in children and young people's reporting, carrying out a large-scale, peer-led piece of research on the CRC and communicating children's own voices directly to the CRC Committee. All of these reports were the result of significant collaborative activity between members and their various professional networks and of engagement with relevant bodies elsewhere in the UK and at international level. The movement for children's rights had gained in authority and momentum as a direct result of the dynamics of monitoring and reporting on the CRC (see further Doek in this volume).

Policy advocacy and the collective voice of the NGOs continued unabated – the UK Concluding Observations 2002 anchored in the authority of the international human rights framework had become an unparalleled tool for stimulating discussion at Welsh Assembly Government level, in exerting pressure on government to address these recommendations and make changes to legislation and policy. Throughout this time period Welsh Assembly Government strategic policy making became increasingly underpinned by the CRC.[7]

Child poverty policy in particular has been heavily influenced by the children's rights movement in Wales. Child poverty has been a key focus of non-governmental organisations throughout the reporting process and non-governmental organisations have engaged regularly with Government, working collaboratively to influence the direction of policy. Two key members of the Wales UNCRC Monitoring Group are also members of the Welsh Assembly Government's Child Poverty Expert Group, both of whom are outspoken advocates for children's rights. The framework of the 2010 Child Poverty Strategy is set within the seven core aims (directly derived from the CRC) acknowledging the interrelated and interdependent dimensions of

---

7   Examples of Welsh Assembly Government policies underpinned by the UNCRC: *National Service Framework for Children, Young People and Maternity Services (NSF),National Youth Offending Strategy, Sexual Health and Well-Being Strategy, Rights to Action, Extending Entitlement* and *A Fairer Future for Our Children*.

deprivation that children face. It follows clear human rights principles such as a focus on the most disadvantaged children and reducing inequalities.

The Welsh Assembly Government has carried out consultations on the development of the child poverty strategy with a wide range of constituents, for example health, education, social care, community safety professionals; children and young people's partnerships; local politicians, non-governmental organisations and children and young people. This again reinforces the commitment to a response to child poverty that is multi-sectoral and multi-dimensional.

The Welsh Assembly Government took much notice of the UNICEF Well-being report (UNICEF 2007) referred to earlier in this chapter. The Welsh Assembly Government was concerned that progress in Wales as a result of the divergent rights based approach would be lost within overall UK rankings. It commissioned its own report on the well-being of children in Wales (WAG 2008) and plans to publish updates every three years to inform service planning cycles at both an all-Wales level of governance and at the local, municipal level. The well-being monitor's collation of statistics is based around the seven core aims, however, the set of indicators could be more rights based and the data collection needs to be further disaggregated to better capture the true reality of all children's lives in Wales.

Government officials in Wales are aware that the causes and impact of child poverty are complex and need to be understood in a holistic way if child poverty is to be reduced. In other words it is increasingly understood that civil and political as well as social, economic and cultural rights are breached when a child lives in poverty and these all need to be met if the child's full potential is to be realised. The Children and Young People Partnerships[8] at local authority level compliment this understanding of child poverty as they are multi-disciplinary and multi-sectoral, which helps to foster a more holistic rights based approach. The Welsh Assembly Government fund a flag ship project hosted by Save the Children that is supporting public bodies throughout Wales, including local authorities and the Children and Young People's Partnerships to address child poverty using a multi-sectoral and multi-dimensional approach.[9]

The recommendations contained in the Concluding Observations of the CRC Committee in 2002 gave strength to NGOs holding government to account to monitor transparently the proportion of their expenditure on children. Reporting to the UN Committee in 2007, the Welsh Assembly Government included an analysis of the proportion of its budget spent on children (the only nation in the UK to do so) (WAG 2007). In 2009, they released a further report analysing public

---

8   Strategic partnerships (known as children and young people partnerships) have been in place since 2002 and have been on a statutory footing since 2004. Local authorities and key partner agencies are required in law to cooperate to improve the well-being of children and young people in the local area.

9   For further information on this project go to www.childpovertysolutions.org.uk [accessed 20 September 2010].

expenditure on children (Dolman 2009). More needs to be done to monitor and plan expenditure that takes into consideration the needs of the poorest children and non-governmental organisations still need to consistently hold government to account to meet their Article 4 CRC obligation to spend to the maximum extent of resources available.

As a direct outcome of the 2008 reporting process, in 2009, the Welsh Assembly Government published its first National Action Plan on Children's Rights (Welsh Assembly Government 2009) which sets children's rights targets for all government departments to be achieved by the time the UK State Party next reports to the CRC Committee in 2014. Children's rights standards cut across Welsh Assembly Government policy making, but still more needs to be done to ensure that these standards are a part of planning and practice at the level of implementation.

There is an increasing recognition that both Welsh Assembly and local governments are duty bearers with responsibilities and obligations to respect the rights enshrined by the CRC and to be accountable to the children and young people of Wales. This level of accountability has been furthered by the development of the Children and Families Measure (referred to above) but also a Children's Rights Measure (see further Williams Chapter 11 in this volume) which was proposed by the First Minister in July 2009 and really symbolises the culmination of a decade of commitment to embedding the UNCRC into policy making. At the time of writing, the proposed Children's Rights Measure of the Welsh Assembly Government is currently passing through the legislative process. If passed, this will serve to in effect give children access to more human rights in Wales than adults, due to the comprehensive nature of the CRC encompassing social, economic and cultural rights. In Williams' words earlier in this volume this measure will certainly 'increase the accountability of government's performance in CRC implementation' but as she explains this will be a parliamentary and administrative not a judicial approach to CRC implementation, so it will not be possible to judicially enforce individual social and economic rights. However, due to the earlier discussed executive and National Assembly's appetite for supporting children's rights implementation and the strength of civil society, Children's Commissioner, and children and young people assembly for Wales, this approach if harnessed appropriately has the opportunity to further embed a children's rights framework of accountability in Wales.

In conclusion, Wales has witnessed a clear movement towards attempting to adopt a children's rights based approach to policy making including policy making concerning child poverty. Also within the limits of its legislative powers the Assembly is working towards the incorporation of the CRC into legislation in Wales. This divergence has been mostly as a result of a devolved government that has been responsive to a vibrant non-governmental community which has taken advantage of the power and dynamism of the CRC reporting process and a government that has opened the corridors of power to children and young people. Government, NGOs and children and young people, however, are clear sighted enough to acknowledge that much more needs to be done to entrench and translate the children's rights based approach from policy into practice and to make children's rights a reality in Wales.

Time for Change

There is now acknowledgement amongst governments as well as non-governmental organisations that the current approach to tackling child poverty in the UK is not working as fast or as effectively as is required by a rich country with one of the worst child poverty rates of the industrialised world. Inequality in the UK is getting worse as noted above. Writing about the socially damaging effects of unequal societies, Wilkinson and Pickett (2010) estimate that on average the richest 20 per cent in the UK are seven times richer than the poorest 20 per cent; in Japan and Sweden, which represent more equal societies, the gap is less than four times. Levels of child poverty in the UK have been rising since 2005 with the proportion of children living in poverty doubled in the past generation. The UK still has proportionately more children living in poverty than most other rich countries. It is definitely time for change.

Arguably, in the UK we have squandered the real opportunities that valuable economic growth over the last 15 years afforded to the fight against child poverty, but there remain many opportunities (as well as considerable challenges) for enhancing a human rights approach to tackling child poverty in Wales and the UK in the second decade of the twenty-first century. The UK is a wealthy but highly unequal society, there is an unfair distribution of resources exacerbated by the current economic situation, but this is no justification for any child living a life of poverty.

The new child poverty legislation at the UK and Wales levels of governance are a welcome move. Both governments have an opportunity now to work together to make progress in the fight against child poverty and some important new mechanisms to persuade some of the most relevant public bodies to do more in this regard.

Lessons can also be learned in the longer term from the holistic rights based approach to policy and planning being adopted by the Welsh Assembly Government including their clear recognition that children are rights holders and their efforts to encourage children's participation in governmental decision making as well as reporting transparently on the proportion of government expenditure on children. In Wales there is a broader understanding of child poverty that places the child at the centre, privileges children's experiences of poverty and the complex and interrelated nature of the deprivation they face. Additionally the Children's Rights Measure will provide the opportunity to increase the accountability of the Assembly to children and therefore improve the overall well-being of children in line with a human rights based approach.

But much will depend on continuing political will and the effectiveness of the new monitoring and scrutiny procedures which represent a key influencing opportunity for child poverty organisations. Both the UK and the Welsh Assembly Governments need also to work with voluntary and community partners to improve the public's understanding of child poverty, its causes and the impact on children and society at large. They need to show leadership in treating those living in poverty with respect and recognition. Lister (2008) identifies two important strands of poverty 'politics' in the UK, one being more traditionally focused on redistribution and particularly meeting the child poverty targets, the second, the more recent politics of recognition and respect concerned with how people in poverty are treated. She concludes by reminding us that these two strands are not in conflict with each other and to be effective need to be 'mutually reinforcing' (Lister 2008: 14).

Public support is necessary to encourage governments to do what is required to tackle child poverty and a number of recent research projects (for example Delvaux and Rinne 2009) have highlighted both negative attitudes and a lack of understanding in respect of both poverty and human rights. It is important to find new ways of communicating and talking about these issues and the values underpinning the society we want to live in. Developing grassroots activism and building the capacity of children, families and communities to speak out and claim their rights could help to challenge the notion of poverty as a personal failure and support children and young people affected by poverty to claim their rights. Popular attitudes reflected and amplified by much of the media have arguably made it difficult for governments in the UK to promote fully re-distributive approaches to combating poverty (Killeen 2008).

The reporting systems for international human rights agreements also represent key influencing opportunities. The UK Government has to produce a 'periodic' report every 4–5 years for the core international human rights treaties they have signed up to including the ICESCR and the CRC. The government is under obligation to consult on NGOs over these reports, and NGOs can also produce shadow reports and provide evidence to the UN Committees that consider these reports. The devolved administrations including the Welsh Assembly Government are enabled to contribute to these State Party reports. The next reporting rounds later in the decade present valuable opportunities for once again holding the State Party to account for its progress on reducing child poverty. As has been evidenced in Wales, the dynamics of the reporting process can have a considerable influence over policy development and the movement for children's rights.

Activists and child poverty organisations in the UK have been frustrated by the limitations of the Human Rights Act 1998 in terms of the lack of enforceable economic, social and cultural rights and the UK government's refusal to incorporate these rights in its new equality framework set out in the Equality Act 2010. However, the debate on the introduction of a new Bill of Rights for the UK is a key opportunity to raise the importance of the incorporation of economic, social and cultural rights into UK law. Additionally the Equality and Human Rights Commission has an important role to play as an independent advocate for human rights giving full consideration to addressing poverty and working towards realising a UK society that is fully based on the principles of equality and the full range of human rights.

The context of devolution has demonstrated that there are different levers in action that are influencing the development of policy and legislation. Unlike the UK government, the Welsh Assembly Government has been influenced by the machinery of the CRC, its jurisprudence, standards and the dynamics of the reporting process this has resulted in policy and legislation that is clearly underpinned by human rights principles. The test of time will now bring clarity to whether this approach will serve children best.

Finally each state, including the UK must acknowledge that, with a serious commitment to child poverty eradication, it is possible to make rapid progress towards the fulfilment of many children's rights even within existing resource constraints. Political willingness is the most powerful barrier but with a concerted effort to improve the efficiency of resource use, the reduction of expenditure on activities that are not for the public good and by reducing spending on activities that disproportionately benefit the rich there is no excuse for failing to achieve the elimination of child poverty in the UK by 2020.

References

BBC News On-line. 14 February 2007. UK is accused of failing children [online, BBC News On-line]. Available at: http://news.bbc.co.uk/1/hi/uk/6359363.stm [accessed 31 March 2010].

Blair, A. 1999. Beveridge Lecture, Toynbee Hall. Reproduced in R. Walker (ed.), *Ending Child Poverty*. Bristol: The Policy Press.

Bradshaw, J. and Mayhew, E. 2005. *The Well-being of Children in the UK*. London: Save the Children.

British Institute of Human Rights. 2008. *Human Rights and Tackling UK Poverty: Report of Roundtable Meeting, 17 January 2008*. London: British Institute of Human Rights.

Clutton, S. 2008. Devolution and the language of children's rights in the UK, in A. Invernizzi and J. Williams (eds), *Children and Citizenship*. London: Sage, pp. 171–81.

Committee on Economic, Social and Cultural Rights. 2009. *Concluding Observations of the Committee on Economic, Social and Cultural Rights on the United Kingdom of Great Britain and Northern Ireland*. E/C.12/GBR/CO/5 (22 May 2009).

Committee on the Rights of the Child. 1996. *General Guidelines Regarding the Form and Contents of Periodic Reports to be Submitted under Article 44, Paragraph 1(b), of the CRC*. CRC/C/58, 20 November 1996, para. 20.

———. 2003. *General Comment No 5. on General Measures of Implementation of the CRC*. CRC/GC/2003/5.

——. 2009. *General Comment No. 12 on the Right of the Child to be Heard.* CRC/C/GC/12.

Croke, R. and Crowley, A. (eds). 2006. *Righting the Wrongs: The Reality of Children's Rights in Wales.* Cardiff: Save the Children.

Crowley, A. 2009. Failing to end child poverty will cost us dearly. *Western Mail,* 2 October 2009.

Crowley, A. and Vulliamy, C. 2002. *Listen Up! Children and Young People Talk: About Poverty.* Cardiff: Save the Children.

Darton, D., Hirsch, D. and Strelitz, J. 2003. *Tackling Disadvantage: A 20-Year Enterprise.* York: Joseph Rowntree Foundation.

Delvaux, J. and Rinne, S. 2009. *Building Public Support for Eradicating Child Poverty in the UK.* York: Joseph Rowntree Foundation.

Dolman, R. 2009. *Financial Provision for Children within the Welsh Assembly Government Budget.* Cardiff: Statistics Wales and Welsh Assembly Government.

Economic and Social Council. 2001. *Poverty and the International Covenant on Economic, Social and Cultural Rights: Statement of the Committee to the Third UN Conference on the Least Developed Countries* (25th session). E/2002/22- E/C.12/2001/17, annex VII.

Eurochild. 2007. *A Child Rights Approach to Child Poverty: Discussion Paper* [online, Eurochild]. Available at: http://www.eurochild.org/index.php?id=343 [accessed 31 March 2010].

Hirsch, D. 2008. *What is Needed to End Child Poverty in the UK?* York: Joseph Rowntree Foundation. Available at: http://www.jrf.org.uk/publications/what-needed-end-child-poverty-2020 [accessed 3 March 2010].

——. 2009. *Estimating the Costs of Child Poverty.* York: Joseph Rowntree Foundation. Available at: http://www.jrf.org.uk/publications/estimating-costs-child-poverty [accessed 3 March 2010].

HM Government. 2004. *Every Child Matters: Change for Children.* London: Department for Education and Skills.

Horgan, G. 2007. *The Impact of Poverty on Young Children's Experience of School.* York: Joseph Rowntree Foundation. Available at: http://www.jrf.org. uk/publications/impact-poverty-young-childrens-experience-school[Accessed 31 March 2010].

JCHR. 2004. *The Implementation of the International Convention on Economic, Social and Cultural Rights.* 2 November 2004.

——. 2009. *Legislative Scrutiny: Child Poverty Bill.* 26 November 2009. HL 183/ HC 1114.

Killeen, D. 2008. *Is Poverty in the UK a Denial of People's Human Rights?* York: Joseph Rowntree Foundation. Available at: http://www.jrf.org.uk/publications/ poverty-uk-denial-peoples-human-rights. [accessed 3 March 2010].

Lister, R. 2008. Poverty eradication in the UK: overview of key issues, challenges and current responses in, *Human Rights and Tackling UK Poverty: Report of Roundtable Meeting, 17 January 2008.* London: British Institute of Human Rights.

MacInnes, T., Kenway, P. and Parekh, A. 2009. *Monitoring Poverty and Social Exclusion*. York: Joseph Rowntree Foundation. Available at: http://www.jrf. org.uk/publications/monitoring-poverty-2009 [accessed 3 March 2010].

Middleton, S., Ashworth, K. and Walker, R. 1994. *Family Fortunes: Pressures on Parents and Children in the 1990s*. London: Child Poverty Action Group.

Office of the High Commission on Human Rights (OHCHR). 2004. *Human Rights and Poverty Reduction: A Conceptual Framework*. New York and Geneva: United Nations.

Ridge, T. 2009. *Living with Poverty: A Review of the Literature on Children's and Families' Experiences of Poverty, Research Number 594*. London: Department of Work and Pensions.

Save the Children. 2006. *Hard Times*. London: Save the Children.

Thomas, N. and Crowley, A. 2007. The state of children's welfare and rights in Wales in 2006, in *Contemporary Wales: An Annual Review of Economic and Social Research*, 19, 161–79.

UNICEF. 2007. *Child Poverty in Perspective: An Overview of Child Well-being in Rich Countries*, Report Card 7. Florence: UNICEF Innocenti Research Centre.

Waterhouse, R. 2000. *Lost in Care: Report of the Tribunal on Inquiry into Abuse of Children in Care in the Former County Council Areas of Gwynedd and Clwyd*. London: HMSO.

Welsh Assembly Government. 2004. *Children and Young People: Rights to Action. Guidance on Local Cooperation under the Children Act 2004*. Available at: http://www.assemblywales.org/N00000000000000000000000016990.pdf [accessed 20 September 2010].

——. 2005. *A Fair Future for Our Children: The Strategy of the Welsh Assembly Government for Tackling Child Poverty*. Available at: http://wales.gov.uk/ topics/childrenyoungpeople/publications/fairfuture/?lang=en [accessed 20 September 2010].

——. 2007. *Rights in Action: Implementing Children and Young People's Rights in Wales*. Available at: http://wales.gov.uk/docs/caecd/publications/ 090415rightsinactionen.pdf [accessed 20 September 2010[.

——. 2008. *Children and Young People's Well-being Monitor for Wales*. Available at: http://wales.gov.uk/about/aboutresearch/social/ocsropage/2008monitor?lang=en [accessed 20 September 2010].

——. 2009. *Getting it Right: A 5 Year Rolling Action Plan for Wales Setting Out Key Priorities and Actions to be Undertaken by the Welsh Assembly Government in Response to the Concluding Observations of the UN Committee on the Rights of the Child 2008*. Available at: http://wales.gov.uk/docs/dcells/publications/0 91117gettingitrighten.pdf [accessed 20 September 2010].

——. 2010. *Child Poverty Strategy for Wales*. Available at: http://wales.gov. uk/consultations/childrenandyoungpeople/cpstrategy/?lang=en [accessed 20 September 2010].

Wilkinson, R. and Pickett, K. 2010. *The Spirit Level: Why More Equal Societies Almost Always Do Better*. London: Allen Lane.

Williams, J. 2007. Incorporating children's rights: the divergence in law and policy, *Legal Studies*, 27(2), 261–87.

Williams, J. and Croke, R. 2008. Institutional support for the UNCRC's 'Citizen Child', in A. Invernizzi and J. Williams (eds), *Children and Citizenship*. Sage: London.

Winckler, V. 2009. *What is Needed to End Child Poverty in Wales?* York: Joseph Rowntree Foundation. Available at: http://www.jrf.org.uk/publications/poverty-wales-2009 [accessed 3 March 2010].

Chapter 13

An Exploration of the Discrimination-Rights Dynamic in Relation to Children

Elspeth Webb

Introduction

This chapter will explore the relationship between discrimination and rights, and how this relationship is used in developing a conceptual framework that can be of practical use in the promotion of the rights of children.

The twentieth century saw the growth of a global commitment to the promotion of children's rights leading to the CRC in 1989, and the establishment of Children's Rights Commissioners in many jurisdictions. In the UK, as in many countries around the world who have ratified the CRC, the Convention has been used to inform central policy and strategy (for example, Kilkelly, Stalford and Drywood, Croke and Crowley Chapters 8, 9 and 12 respectively in this volume). In tandem with this we have seen local councils, hospitals, public health authorities and schools making use of it in the development of local services. But, despite this, there is a growing gap between rhetoric and policy; indeed it could be argued that since 1989 the situation in the UK *vis-à-vis* the rights of children has worsened. Table 13.1 lists UK Acts of Parliament in this period that have disadvantaged children, and reduced their rights and civil liberties.

It is proposed that the explanation for this apparent paradox is a failure to understand the relationship between child rights and discrimination against children. This chapter explores, in a mainly UK context, what forms discrimination against children can take, the mechanisms via which it operates, and what its effects are on the lives and welfare of children. The objective is to outline many different aspects of discrimination as broadly as possible: rather than provide an up-to-the-minute review of child rights abuses it will instead draw on a range of examples that best represent the complexity of the phenomenon. As the author has a health background, the examples provided draw mainly, although not exclusively, from a health, or health services, perspective. A conceptual framework is developed, which is represented schematically in Figure 13.1. 'Child' is taken here to refer to those persons covered by the CRC, that is, those aged less than 18 years.

Table 13.1   Acts of the UK Parliament disadvantaging children since 1989

Act	Impact on children and young people
1994 Criminal Justice and Public Order Act	Incarceration for 12 to 14 year-olds Repeal of 1968 Caravan Sites Act local authority duty to provide sites, with serious consequences for the health and welfare of traveller children
1996 Asylum and Immigration Act	Detention of children, denial of benefits, and poor service access for children of parents seeking asylum
1998 Crime and Disorder Act	Anti Social Behaviour Orders, curfews, truancy sweeps
2003 Anti-social Behaviour Act	Penalty notices for disorderly behaviour (16-17 year-olds with provision for 10 year-olds and over)
2003 Sexual Offences Act	Criminalises sexual behaviour in under 16 year-olds
2004 Children Act	Law confirms the 'right' to hit for parents
2010 Equality Act (Phillips 2009)	Explicitly excludes under 18s from equality legislation

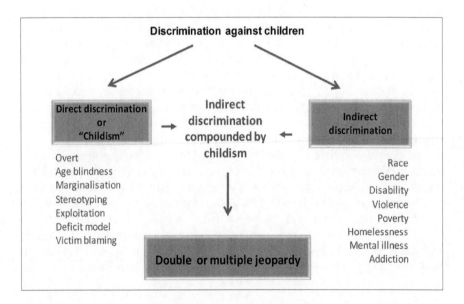

Figure 13.1   Conceptual framework of discrimination against children

Discrimination and Rights

Although the seeds of the American civil rights movement were sown much earlier than 1 December 1955, for most people the movement truly began that day when Rosa Parks refused to give up her seat on her bus returning home from work. The movement gained momentum in the next decade, a decade which saw similar developments in many other parts of the world, e.g. the Aboriginal rights movement in Australia, the radicalisation of the African National Congress in South Africa and British race riots in Nottingham and London's Notting Hill district. That these movements were challenging the pervasive racism experienced by Black people at the time is unquestionable – these were civil and political protests which sought to combat racism and make those societies, in which Black people experienced so much injustice, fairer and equitable. The last forty years have seen huge changes, social, political and legislative, which have resulted in, to some extent, greater justice for Black and Aboriginal peoples in many countries.

In another corner of the UK a second civil rights movement was gaining pace at much the same time, one that grew out of the systematic discrimination experienced by Roman Catholics in Northern Ireland, and which led to a 30-year civil war. Addressing this problem has required that this discrimination was openly admitted and acknowledged.

These examples provide a clear link between human rights and discrimination, that is, upholding the human rights of vulnerable groups, be they ethnic or religious minorities, women, or people with disability, requires the identification and eradication of discrimination. In fact the same relationship between rights and discrimination exists for children too, but the history of the child rights movement, and the very unique position of children in society, makes this link less intuitively obvious.

The Origin of Child Rights Paradigms

> I saw a child brought in ... at the sight of which men wept aloud, and I heard the story of little Mary Ellen told ... that stirred the soul of a city and roused the conscience of a world that had forgotten, and as I looked, I knew I was where the first chapter of children's rights was being written. 9 April, 1874, New York Evening Sun. (Riis 1874 cited in Stevens and Eide 1990)

This famous case, in which philanthropists attempted to apply animal cruelty legislation to protect an abused child, is sometimes seen as the beginnings of child rights, although the notion appeared earlier: Thomas Spence, the English revolutionary, in a pamphlet published in 1796 entitled 'The Rights of Infants' argued that all children, including those born to the very poor, had a right to the basic necessities of life. Thus the beginnings and development of child rights is one largely dominated by a desire to protect children from abuse and neglect (but see further, Cantwell Chapter 2 in this volume). But if the disadvantage and harm that children experience are analysed, as they are here, through a discrimination lens it becomes clear that their rights are closely linked to discrimination. In the Western world it has taken over 40 years to fully understand the mechanisms by which people are affected by racism, and the forms racism can take. Even as late as 1995, unrecognised institutional racism in the UK police led to the inappropriate and ineffective investigation of the murder of a Black teenager, Stephen Lawrence (Macpherson 1999). We have hardly begun to understand how discrimination against children affects their lives and welfare.

Discrimination against Children

Discrimination can be direct or indirect. Indirect discrimination is the inequitable treatment of one group disadvantaging another, as opposed to direct discrimination in which the focus of discriminatory attitudes, actions and policies is the group itself. I will refer to direct discrimination against children, i.e. discrimination against them as children *per se*, as childism.

Discrimination can act at the level of the individual, but can also be institutional, occurring when the structures or operating policies of organisations result in certain groups being disadvantaged. This concept is most familiar as institutional or structural racism but can apply to any group disadvantaged by stigma and discrimination, including children.

Direct Discrimination

This can be manifest in the following ways:

Overt discrimination   In Britain the late nineteenth and early twentieth centuries saw the beginnings of the 'exclusion of children from adult spaces', not for their safety or well-being but for the convenience of adults (James 1993). This separateness of the child's world is now seen as a natural state of being. The resulting discrimination is so much a cultural given that it is both ubiquitous and unrecognised, with hotels in the UK routinely refusing access to children, and occasionally to dogs too. At the time of writing the Good Hotel Guide includes the following text:

> Once again, everything was found 'first class' at this 'handsome' conversion of a non-working 19th-century farmhouse and its outbuildings overlooking the foothills of ... a remote peninsula. For 11 years it has been run by the 'warmly welcoming' (except to children) owners ... Children: not under 16. Dogs: allowed in annexe bedroom only ...[1]

---

1   http://www.goodhotelguide.com/index.html [accessed March 2010].

Marginalisation Through their constructed otherness, children's status in British society is as non-persons relegated to a social, economic and political marginalisation (James 1993: 72). Marginalisation describes when a group experiencing discrimination is not seen as part of the core business or service. In the context of health care it is not only a modern phenomenon:

> ... when sick children are admitted promiscuously with adults, the former never have so much attention paid them as the latter ... (Armstrong 1783, cited in Dunn 2002: F228–31)

In 1994 the confidential local audits performed by the Audit Commission (S. Farnsworth and B. Fitzsimon, personal communication, 1994) and other research (Webb, Naish and MacFarlane 1996) revealed that the needs of children were not prioritised in health commissioning. Little has changed since (Viner and Keane 1998, NCB 2000). When the UK government first announced the creation of National Service Frameworks (NSF) for health, they did not include children. The children's NSF was agreed only after pressure was brought to bear on the government by NGOs, the media and academics (Aynsley-Green et al. 2000); even so, unlike the disease-centred NSFs which focus almost exclusively on adult services, the children's NSF is not accompanied by resources or investment.

Children are similarly under-represented in funding for research and development resulting in an inadequate evidence-base for much paediatric practice (Smyth 2001, AHCPR 1997), particularly evident in the development of new therapeutic drugs. In 2000 over two thirds (67 per cent) of 624 children admitted to wards in five European hospitals received drugs prescribed in an unlicensed or off-label manner (Conroy et al. 2000). Although the problem was and is complicated by the ethical problems encountered around consent for child participation in trials (Stephenson 2002, Sutcliffe 2003), it is largely profit driven. Drugs were not tested in children and thus not licensed for paediatric use. Even licensed drugs are prescribed off label 'resulting in children becoming therapeutic orphans sometimes with tragic consequences' (Sutcliffe 2003). In response to this unsatisfactory situation the European Union passed the European Paediatric Medicines Regulation in 2007, which it is hoped will improve the safety of sick children (Vassal 2009).

Age blindness This is equivalent to colour blindness in racial parlance – treating everyone in the same manner, so ignoring or denying different needs. Such an approach can exclude children: for example, marina developments with inadequate barriers between toddlers and deep water.

Although huge strides have been made within the health sector to respond to the accommodation needs of children – providing facilities for play, and ensuring parents can accompany their children – there are still examples of poor practice, with shared waiting rooms in primary and secondary care in which carers have to spend considerable time with very young children in surroundings that are unsuitable and stressful.

The deficit model of childhood   Children are seen as immature, i.e. incapable or unfinished; simply on the road to adulthood rather than people in their own right. This is very evident in the field of child participation. The notion of incorporating the views of children has become ubiquitous, with many departments of sociology studying the phenomenon, and no shortage of guidance.[2] But again we find a gap between what is said and what is done: out of 509 Trusts and health authorities in the UK just 27 consulted children on services for chronically ill or disabled children (Sloper and Lightfoot 2003). At an individual level young people with serious illness have reported feeling marginalised in decision making (Young et al. 2003). Although there are problems in achieving full and meaningful participation, not least the competing rights of children and parents (DFES 2001, Walker and Doyon 2001), children can be effective partners in the management of their own treatment (Emilio and Sanz 2003), and there is plenty of convincing evidence from the Child-to-Child programme showing how children can contribute effectively to health alliances and transform their lives and health (Pridmore and Stephens 2000). This approach, initially developed in a developing world context, is one in which children are involved in identifying health priorities for their community and then becoming active or leading partners in the development and implementation of health promotion to combat these problems.

Even older adolescents are denied the right to express their views in ways open to adults. At the start of the latest war in Iraq, many sixth form students aged 16–18, who technically could have been serving in the armed forces at that time, missed school to join anti-war marches; some of them were suspended or even excluded. David Hart of the National Association of Head Teachers expressed the following view:

> Heads should ban all protests during school. They should take disciplinary action against any members of staff who encourage the demonstrations and against any pupils who are absent when they should be in school ... The right way to go about it is to give pupils the opportunity in school to debate the issues ... They might benefit more from learning about the causes of war than by demonstrating against it. (BBC News 2003, cited in Miller 2005)

Moffit and Caspi (2001) calls this 'a contemporary maturity gap' in which, in modern post-industrial societies, essentially mature individuals are infantilised by extended education and delayed work opportunities. For some young people this results in antisocial behaviours 'that are normative and adjustive'. This is an important issue. Around 25 per cent of British men under 25 will have accrued criminal records to accompany them through their adult life, of which over half will have been adolescent-onset delinquents.

---

2   For guidance within health services alone see BMA (2000), Brook (1997 and 2000), DFES (2001) and NSPCC (2001).

Victim blaming This term describes the phenomenon in which a vulnerable group are blamed when they experience disadvantage or harm. Pedestrian injuries, a leading cause of childhood mortality, provide a good example. Children are blamed, with prevention strategies continuing to stress child behaviours, rather than addressing necessary and more effective changes in the structure of transport systems.

> The strength and pervasiveness of the ideology of victim blaming in child pedestrian injuries is explained by the special position that the road transport system holds in relation to dominant economic interests. Victim blaming ideology is a strategy that serves to maintain these interests at the expense and suffering of children. (Roberts and Coggan 1994)

Another example is the 'Lolita' syndrome, in which children are blamed for their own sexual abuse. In 1993 a man found guilty of the rape of a girl, aged nine, was given two years probation. The presiding judge said 'I have been provided with information which leads me to believe that she was not entirely an angel herself ...'.[3] Although Lord Taylor stated on appeal that this comment should not have been made, it is a view met elsewhere. On Alice Liddell, the girl with whom both John Ruskin and Lewis Carroll were infatuated, Prose writes 'what seems clear is that Alice was by no means a frail flower attracting these predatory bees; she pursued and actively encouraged their attentions' (Prose 2003, cited in Hughes 2003).

Poverty provides the most pernicious example of victim blaming. During the 1980s much of the West moved towards more laissez-faire free market economies; some countries took steps to protect children from these developments whilst others did not (Watt 1998). The UK and the United States saw significant increases in the numbers of their child populations growing up in poverty, unlike many continental European countries (UNICEF 2005) – see Table 13.2.

Child poverty is a policy choice (Wilkinson and Pickett 2009) that some governments make, despite the overwhelming body of evidence documenting the detrimental impact of poverty on the development and health of children (Spencer 2000). For example, evidence shows clear links between life-course-persistent delinquency and abuse, poor parenting, relative poverty and socially disorganised communities (Moffit and Harrington 1996, Farrington 1995), which ought to, but does not, inform both preventive and responsive strategies to this problem. Instead governments of all persuasions in the UK have tended to focus largely on a punitive approach. Other well documented consequences of relative poverty in rich countries include teenage pregnancy, drug and alcohol abuse, truancy, poor school performance and subsequent unemployment, for which these young people are also held responsible. We both condemn and blame children for these outcomes.

---

3   *Attorney-General's Reference No. 13 of 1993 (Karl Justin Gambrill)* (1994) 15: Cr. App. R. (S.) 292 CA (Crim Div).

Table 13.2   Percentage of children living below national poverty lines

Mexico	27.7	Austria	10.2
USA	21.9	Germany	10.2
Italy	16.6	Netherlands	9.8
New Zealand	16.3	Luxembourg	9.1
Ireland	15.7	Hungary	8.8
Portugal	15.6	Belgium	7.7
UK	**15.4**	France	7.5
Canada	14.9	Czech Republic	6.8
Australia	14.7	Switzerland	6.8
Japan	14.3	Sweden	4.2
Spain	13.3	Norway	3.4
Poland	12.7	Finland	2.8
Greece	12.4	Denmark	2.4

Source: UNICEF, 'Child Poverty in Rich Countries, 2005', *Innocenti Report Card*, No. 6. UNICEF Innocenti Research Centre, Florence.

Stereotyping   Children can be viewed as poor witnesses, more likely to lie than adults. This has had serious consequences for vulnerable children in care, whose reporting of abuse was dismissed: 'the negative response (to complaints) ... especially in relation to reports of physical abuse, justified the pervading cynicism of most residents in care about the likely outcome of any complaints that they might make' (Waterhouse 2000).

There is also a pervasive stereotype of distressed and disadvantaged children as inherently bad, a stereotype that has been both encouraged and exploited by politicians:

> During the election campaign I heard too often people talk about a loss of respect in the classroom, on the street corner, in the way our hard-working public servants are treated as they perform their tasks ... People are rightly fed up with street corner and shopping centre thugs, yobbish behaviour sometimes from children as young as 10 or 11 whose parents should be looking after them ..., of the low-level graffiti, vandalism and disorder that is the work of a very small minority that makes the law-abiding majority afraid and angry. (Tony Blair quoted in the *Times* newspaper, 13 May 2005)

The media is also guilty with significant consequences for policy – contrast its response in the early 1990s to the murder of James Bulger to that of people killed by mentally ill adults, the most high profile of which was the stabbing of Jonathan Zeto by Christopher Clunis on a London tube station. James Bulger's death was just as much a health issue as was Jonathan Zeto's. But while the media argued that inadequate community mental health services, not Christopher

Clunis, were responsible for Jonathan Zeto's death, it demonised James Bulger's killers, both of whom had experienced deprivation, neglect and abuse (Morrison 1998). The link between James Bulger's death and a lack of child protection and child mental health services was not made, although professionals working in the area of child protection recognise that the interventions available for neglected and abused children, both in terms of post abuse work and in mental health promotion, reached only a fraction of those who could benefit. Nearly 20 years on, the media response to a severe attack on two children, in the town of Darlington in the north of England, by two other children, two brothers in the care of the local authority with extremely adverse childhood experiences, showed how little had changed.[4]

Internalised discrimination Discrimination can be internalised. A member of a group experiencing discrimination adopts and shares the views of a hostile society, thus seeing him/herself as inferior. A powerful example of internalised racism is provided by Nelson Mandela (1995) in his autobiography. He describes an incident during a period of exile in which he panics on noticing that the pilot of the aeroplane in which he is travelling is Black – even Mandela had internalised the view that a Black person could not be capable of such a task.

Children also take on society's view of themselves – as someone adults can pass in a queue unchallenged, as people having nothing to say worth hearing, as lawful victims of physical assault.

Exploitation As with any powerless group children are vulnerable to exploitation by the powerful, in this case, adults. This may be private and secret, for example the sexual exploitation of children within families. It may be commercially driven, for example, child labour (including sexual exploitation), advertising aimed at, or using, children; or politically driven – consider the exploitation of athletic prodigies in former Eastern Europe, given anabolic steroids in adolescence with serious consequences for their health.

Child labour is traditionally seen as a problem of low- and middle-income countries, but Field (2003) argues that we see emerging another equally exploitive form of labour – a tests and outcomes dominated education system, an 'insatiable schooling industry' of considerable economic value, and from which many people are making a great deal of money, with education as 'endless labour'. Although Field is writing about Japan, her work has many resonances for children in the UK.

Ironically valuing and requiring the participation of children has encouraged their exploitation. Consider the example provided earlier regarding participation of children in service development in which just 27 of 509 health providers consulted children on services for chronically ill or disabled children (Sloper and Lightfoot

---

4   http://www.mirror.co.uk/news/top-stories/2009/04/07/edlington-boys-tortured-by-thugs-while-on-a-fishing-trip-played-dead-to-scare-attackers-115875-21259408/ [accessed March 2010].

2003). Only 11 of these 27 went beyond consultation to meaningful participation in policy, with the other 16 cynically making use of children, somewhere between rungs one and three of Hart's (1992) Ladder.

Indirect Discrimination

As children are dependent and powerless they are particularly vulnerable to indirect discrimination, in which their carers are disadvantaged as a result of gender discrimination, racial discrimination, or the disadvantage many marginalised groups experience because they are poor, ill, disabled or stigmatised for other reasons. Table 13.3 provides examples of how indirect discrimination affects children.

Racial discrimination as an example of indirect discrimination against children

Poverty   As a result of societal racism many Black Ethnic Minority (BEM) communities in the UK are at risk of poverty, with 50 per cent of the Pakistani and 60 per cent of the Bangladeshi communities in poverty (Kenwaywe and Palmer 2007). Many adults in BEM communities are either unemployed or in low-paid work and their children may be more likely to attend poorly resourced inner-city schools. African, African Caribbean, traveller and children of mixed heritage are more likely to be in the public care, excluded from school – see Table 13.4 – and living in lone parent households. All these factors are linked with adverse health outcomes. The types of adversity may vary between BEM groups.

Table 13.3   Indirect discrimination against children in the UK

Primary focus of discrimination	Mechanisms via which children are disadvantaged
Girls/women	Low pay; single mother households trapped in poverty Poor maternity provision: working mothers returning to work when babies are very young Reduced educational opportunities/expectations (in some communities)
Parents	No or little paternity leave (MacDonald 2003) No parental leave for child illness Little acknowledgment of dual role of working parents in occupational law (Leach 1995) Inadequate childcare services for young children Inadequate provision for prams in public transport – difficulty in accessing appointments
Black and ethnic minority communities	Increased risk of growing up in poverty (Kenwaywe and Palmer 2007) Increased risk of being in care (27% of looked-after population in England are of Black Ethnic Minority origin)* Poor access to health care (Webb 2000) Inadequately protected from harm (Webb, Maddocks and Bongilli 2002)
Asylum seekers	Poor health care In detention In poverty
Homeless families	Stigmatised; poor access to services; low uptake of surveillance and immunisation (Webb et al. 2001, Tischler et al. 2002)
Disabled	Access difficulties; marginalised in policy
Mentally ill carers	Stigmatised; unsupported – children acting as carers (Wilson 2000)
Families and communities in poverty	Stigma, shame and difference (see Croke and Crowley Chapter 12 in this volume), with a range of negative outcomes for children

Note: *Children looked after in England (including adoption and care leavers) year ending 31 March 2009. Available at: http://www.dcsf.gov.uk/rsgateway/DB/SFR/s000878/SFR25-2009Version2.pdf [accessed 23 December 2010].

Table 13.4   Permanent school exclusions and lone parent families by ethnic group: England

Ethnic group	Permanent school exclusions (% of school population) (DCSF 2007)	% lone parent families with dependent children (ONS 2004)
White	0.13	22
Indian	0.3	10
Pakistani	0.8	13
Bangladeshi	0.8	12
Black Caribbean	0.41	48
Black African	0.16	36
Mixed or other Black	0.36	52
Chinese	–	15
Irish traveller	0.36	–
All	0.14	23

Access to information   Many parents in BEM populations, particularly mothers, do not have a working knowledge of English, and may not read. Without adequate provision of interpreters these parents are unable to access information crucial to their ability to make informed choices, to liaise with health, welfare and education, and to advocate for their children when they are in need. Their situation is somewhat analogous to that of an illiterate mother in the developing world, a factor long known to be linked to high infant mortality (Cleland and Van Ginneken 1998). It would seem reasonable to hypothesise that the language status of unsupported migrant parents is likely to impact on the health of their children.

Access to health services   BEM communities do not have equality of access to services (Webb 2000). There are examples of institutional racism: for example, services are dependent on postal addresses, which disadvantage asylum seekers and travellers; services are often planned using whole population data. For BEM populations there is a mean age shift to the left. Nineteen per cent of white British people are aged under 16, but 38 per cent of British Bangladeshis are under 16 (see Table 13.5). Using whole population data to plan services ensures that areas with high BEM populations are undermanned and under-resourced for children's services, despite the increased needs of these communities as a result of poverty.

Table 13.5   UK percentage of ethnic groups aged under 16

White	19
Mixed*	55
Indian	22
Pakistani	35
Bangladeshi	38
Other Asian	22
Black Caribbean	25
Black African	33
Other Black	35
Chinese	18
Other	20

Note: *A UK census category designating someone with antecedents from two or more ethnic or racial groups.
Source: Office of National Statistics 2002

Services are also discriminatory in that they are culturally inappropriate, inaccessible, with BEM clients stereotyped in ways that interfere with their care (Webb 2005).

Attitudes to children   Within Wales, the first part of the UK to appoint a Children's Commissioner, and despite a very public commitment to children's rights, the policy choices made by the Welsh Assembly Government (WAG) still indicate that children's needs are not prioritised. Consider, for example, the state of Child and Adolescent Mental Health Services (CAMHS). Following recognition, in 2000, of the serious under funding of children's mental health services over many years in England there was a massive investment – £440m, for a total population of around 50 million. An equivalent spend per capita in Wales, total population 3 million, would be £26.4m. What has been spent, at the time of writing, is about £7m, although it is difficult to access this information. Although the Welsh CRC highlighted the parlous state of CAMHS in several reports (Office of the Children's Commissioner for Wales 2007), there remained a huge shortfall of investment in these services. During this period WAG spent £30m on free prescriptions for adults aged 18–65. It is timely to ask what are the mechanisms by which children's issues are lost in prioritisation and allocation of health service spending in the face of obvious and demonstrated need.

Why are we witnessing this apparent paradox, i.e. that as politicians and journalists increasingly integrate 'children's rights speak' into their rhetoric, policy seems either blind or hostile to children and young people? The answer may lie in ambivalence in adult representations of, and attitudes towards, children. Many examples of discrimination against children in Western societies, particularly in the Anglo-American axis, contrast with the general view that people have positive attitudes toward children. In a web-based pilot, part of an ongoing research project investigating the measurement of attitudes towards children, researchers tested whether implicit measures of attitudes reveal less favourability toward children than conventional self-report measures. Results indicated an *explicit* preference for children, and an *implicit* preference for adults (Leygue et al. 2008). Implicit attitudes, those cultural givens that are usually unconsciously held, are generally good predictors of behaviour: this may provide an explanation for the practice–rhetoric gap. More work is needed to explore this hypothesis.

Conflicts of rights and values   Value conflicts occur when an accepted set of values or beliefs are at variance with other value sets, which may be valid within their own context. Conflicting values occur as groups may have differing attitudes or ideologies for cultural, economic, social or historical reasons. They occur not just across ethnic or religious divides, but as a result of differences of class, education, gender, age and profession. Conflicting values can also be held by an individual: personal values, for example, those held in consequence of a religious belief, may be at odds with what is expected of them professionally; an individual may be unaware of these value conflicts if explicit, i.e. conscious, attitudes are at odds with implicit, i.e. unconscious, attitudes.

In the field of child health there are four ways in which value conflicts may be manifest:

1. When for cultural, historical or religious reasons groups have widely differing moral frameworks and thus conflicting values. Examples include:

    *   The conflict between parents who are Jehovah's Witnesses refusing to allow their child a blood transfusion, and the right of a child to appropriate treatment.
    *   Sex education in schools – the right of children to information may be in conflict with the withdrawal of children belonging to particular religious groups from this curriculum.
    *   Child abuse: a difficulty facing professionals in this area is the unresolved debate around whether child abuse is a relative or an absolute concept (Webb and Moynihan 2010). Chand (2000) states: 'Overall cultural differences in the way families rear their children should be … respected, but where child abuse does occur it should be understood that this particular family has gone beyond what is acceptable not only in the British culture, but in their own.' But this relativistic approach, which leads directly to cultural deficit, is dangerous. It would mean that female genital mutilation (FGM) is not abuse since, in the context of the cultures in which it is traditional, it is perceived as a responsible act by parents ensuring their daughter a place in society, whereas it is recognised to be seriously harmful to children and outlawed by the CRC (Webb and Hartley 1994, Wynne 1994).

2. When, within a culture, accepted values in one area of activity are in contradiction to accepted values in another. For example:

- Within the CRC itself, the right to family life may be at odds with a child's right to protection from harm, and a child's right to freedom from exploitation may conflict with a child's right to work.
- At a macroeconomic level there is a tension between free market economics and the protection of children from poverty (Watt 1998).

3. When the needs or rights of one group are in conflict with those of another. For example:

- Priority setting in healthcare in which resources are inadequate to meet the needs of the population. How does one balance the needs of disabled children for rehabilitation services against the needs of osteoarthritis sufferers for joint replacement surgery?
- Where a parent's views on the medical care of a child may be in conflict with the views of the child, or perceived to be in conflict to a child's best interests, such as whether to continue or terminate a pregnancy in a 14-year-old girl, or when to terminate treatment in a dying or profoundly disabled child.
- Conflicts between the needs of different groups of children. For example a child with severe learning difficulties and profoundly challenging behaviour has a right to family life and to educational inclusion. However there are circumstances where this may be harmful to a sibling's health and welfare, or severely compromise the education of other children. Resolving conflicts of interest between groups of children is particularly challenging. Indeed the examples given here are not only unresolved, but unmentioned, unacknowledged and taboo. We need honest open debate.

For children, indirect discrimination always compounds direct discrimination, with some children experiencing multiple jeopardy. An example of such multiple jeopardy is provided by the predicament of children in the education system who are both male and black. These factors appear to act together, affecting how these children are perceived and how they fare (Strand 2007). Child welfare professionals can be faced with individual cases of great complexity: a child may be disabled, belong to an ethnic minority community, be living in poverty, and have a parent with mental health problems. Not only will such a child be victim to layers of discrimination, all of which will increase the risk of his or her rights being contravened, but protecting children who experience such complex adversity presents professionals with many competing rights and values. There are many examples from the child protection arena in which layers of complexity are associated with failures of the protection systems with devastating consequences for the children involved; for example child abuse complicated by:

- being in care (Waterhouse 2000)
- domestic violence (Owers, Brandon and Black 1999)
- Black or Ethnic Minority (BEM) status (Bridge Child Care Consultancy Services 1991)
- BEM status and disability (Kenwaywe and Palmer 2007)
- BEM status and trafficking (The Victoria Climbié Inquiry 2003)

The value conflicts that arise may be such as to paralyse services and leave children in danger. Resolving them requires sophisticated responses and may require recourse to the courts; but welfare systems for children must be able to respond effectively to complexity.

Conclusions

Marrying traditional responses to disadvantage and disparities with a rights-based approach – in effect complementing the robust evidence provided by social scientists and public health with a tool, the CRC, that incorporates both moral and legal imperatives – should strengthen the effectiveness of any strategy that aims to promote the health and welfare of children. How this can be done has been explored elsewhere: for example in the context of obesity (Goldhagen and Mercer Chapter 14 in this volume) and in the context of child maltreatment (Reading et al. 2009).

But if one accepts that discrimination and rights are part of the same dimension, rights-based approaches must be informed with an understanding of what comprises discrimination against children, and how it exerts its effects. Without this how is it possible to identify the appropriate focus for action? Is a child disadvantaged because she is a member of a minority ethnic group, because she is disabled, or because children's services in general are marginalised and under-resourced?

The conceptual framework developed here provides a structure that can help recognition of discrimination towards children and improve understanding of the mechanisms and pathways by which it exerts its often malign effects. It complements the 'root cause analysis' approach described by Goldhagen and Mercer (Chapter 14 in this volume) by broadening the scope of the analysis to incorporate discrimination as a risk factor, and providing a tool to help identify not just the fact of disadvantage but why and how children are disadvantaged. Exploring the causes and roots of discrimination must include recognising conflicts of rights and values. Resolving these in the best interests of children allows the development of child-centred responses and interventions that promote social justice and equity.

References

AHCPR. 1997. Policy on the Inclusion of Children in Health Services Research, in *NIH Guide*, 26(15), Agency for Health Care Policy and Research. Available at: http://www.ahcpr.gov/fund/nih5997.htm [accessed March 2010].

Aynsley-Green, A., Barker, M., Burr, S., Macfarlane, A., Morgan, J., Sibert, J., Turner, T., Viner, R., Waterston, T. and Hall, D. 2000. Who is speaking for children and adolescents and for their health at the policy level? *BMJ*, 321, 229–32.

BMA. 2000. *Consents, Rights and Choices in Healthcare for Children and Young People*. London: BMA.

Bridge Child Care Consultancy Services. 1991. *Sukina: An Evaluation Report of the Circumstances Leading to Her Death*. London: The Bridge.

Brook, G. 1997. Help me make choices too! Developing and using a framework to help children, with their families, to contribute to decisions about treatment. *Cascade*, 26, Action for Sick Children.

——. 2000. Children's competence to consent: a framework for practice. *Paediatric Nursing*, 12(5), 31–5.

Chand, A. 2000. The over-representation of Black children in the child protection system: possible causes, consequences and solutions. *Child and Family Social Work*, 5: 67–77.

Cleland, J.G. and Van Ginneken, J.K. 1998. Maternal education and child survival in developing countries: the search for pathways of influence. *Soc. Sci. Med.*, 27, 1357–68.

Conroy, S., Choonara, I., Impicciatore P., Mohn, A., Arnell, H., Rane, A., Knoeppel, C., Seyberth, H., Pandolfini, C., Pia Raffaelli, M., Rocchi, F., Bonati, M., Jong, G., de Hoog, M. and van den Anker, J. 2000. Survey of unlicensed and off label drug use in paediatric wards in European countries. *BMJ*, 320, 79–82.

DCFS. 2007. *Permanent and Fixed Period Exclusions from Schools and Exclusion Appeals in England 2005/06*. Available at: http://www.dcsf.gov.uk/rsgateway/DB/SFR/s000733/index.shtml [accessed August 2010].

DFES. 2001. *Core Principles for Involvement of Children and Young People*. Children and Young People's Unit. London: Department for Education and Schools.

Dunn, P.M. 2002. George Armstrong MD (1719–1789) and his dispensary for the infant poor. *Arch Dis Child*, 87(3), F228–31.

Emilio, J. and Sanz, E.J. 2003. Concordance and children's use of medicines. *BMJ*, 327, 858–60.

Farrington, D.P. 1995. The development of offending and anti-social behaviour from childhood: key findings from the Cambridge study in delinquent development. *J Child Psychol Psychiatry*, 36, 929–64.

Field, N. 2003. Education as endless labour, in H. Montgomery, R. Burr and M. Woodhead (eds), *Changing Childhoods: Local and Global*. Haddington: Open University/Wiley, pp. 35–7.

Hart, R. 1992. *Children's Participation from Tokenism to Citizenship*. Florence: UNICEF / Innocenti Research Centre.

James, A. 1993. *Childhood Identities: Self and Social Relationships in the Experience of the Child*. Edinburgh: Edinburgh University Press.

Kenwaywe, P. and Palmer, G. 2007. *Poverty among Ethnic Groups: How and Why Does It Differ?* New Policy Institute research brief: DCSF-RB002, July. Available at: http://www.poverty.org.uk/reports/ethnicity.pdf [accessed February 2010].

Leach, P. 1995. *Children First*. London: Random House.

Leygue, C., Maio, G.R., Karremans, J., Gebauer, J.E. and Webb, E. 2008. *Implicit Mental Representations of Children and Adults*. Paper presented at the 15th General Meeting of the European Association of Experimental Social Psychology, Opatija, Croatia, June 2006.

MacDonald, R. 2003. Childcare for working parents (Website of the week). *BMJ*, 326, 170.

Macpherson, W. 1999. *The Stephen Lawrence Inquiry*, Volume 1:46.25. Available at: www.archive.official-documents.co.uk/document/cm42/4262/sli-46.htm [accessed March 2010].

Mandela, N. 1995. *Long Walk to Freedom*. London: Abacus.

Miller, T. 2005. Across the great divide: creating partnerships in education, in *The Encyclopedia of Informal Education*. Available at: www.infed.org/biblio/partnerships_in_education.htm [accessed 20 September 2010]. First published in R. Carnwell and J. Buchanan (eds) (2005), *Effective Practice in Health and Social Care: A Partnership Approach*. Buckingham: Open University Press.

Moffit, T.E. and Caspi, A. 2001. Childhood predictors differentiate life-course persistent and adolescence-limited antisocial pathways among males and females. *Development and Psychopathology*, 13(2), 355–75.

Moffit, T.E. and Harrington, H.L. 1996. Delinquency: the natural history of antisocial behaviour, in P.A. Silva and W.R. Stanton (eds), *From Child to Adult: The Dunedin Multidisciplinary Health and Development Study*. Auckland: Oxford University Press, pp. 163–85.

Morrison, B. 1998. *As If*. Granta: London.

NCB. 2000. *Improving Children's Health: A Survey of 1999–2000 Health Improvement Programmes*. London: NSPCC, Children's Society, National Children's Bureau.

NSPCC. 2001. *Two-Way Street Training Video and Handbook about Communicating with Disabled Children and Young People*. London: NSPCC.

Office for National Statistics. 2002. Age distribution, in A. White (ed.), *Social Focus in Brief: Ethnicity*. London. Available at: http://www.statistics.gov.uk/downloads/theme_social/social_focus_in_brief/ethnicity/ethnicity.pdf [accessed August 2010].

——. 2004. Households and families. *Social Trends*, 34. London: TSO. Table 2.5; page 28. Available at: http://www.statistics.gov.uk/downloads/theme_social/Social_trends34/Social_Trends34.pdf [accessed August 2010].

Office of the Children's Commissioner for Wales. 2007. *Somebody Else's Business? Report of a Scoping Exercise of Child and Adolescent Mental Health Services in Wales in 2007.* Available at: http://www.childcomwales.org.uk/uploads/publications/5.pdf [accessed March 2010].

Owers, M., Brandon, M. and Black, J. 1999. *A Study of Part 8 Reviews Reports for the Welsh Office.* Norwich: Centre for Research on the Child and Family, University of East Anglia.

Phillips, T. 2009. What will the Equality Bill mean in practice? Speech given at the NHS London Equality Conference, Wednesday 8 July 2009. Available at: http://www.equalityhumanrights.com/legislative-framework/equality-bill/commission-speeches-on-the-equality-bill/speech-what-will-the-equality-bill-mean-in-practice/ [accessed March 2010].

Pridmore, P. and Stephens, D. 2000. *Children as Partners for Health: A Critical Review of the Child-to-Child Approach.* London: Zed Books.

Prose, F. 2003. *The Lives of the Muses: Nine Women and the Artists They Inspired.* London: Aurum. Cited in Hughes, K. Pas de deux. *Guardian*, Review, 8 November 2003. p 15. Available at: http://www.guardian.co.uk/books/2003/nov/08/highereducation.biography [accessed August 2010].

Reading, R., Bissell, S., Goldhagen, J., Harwin, J., Masson, J., Moynihan, S., Parton, N., Santos Pias, M., Thoburn, J. and Webb E. 2009. Promotion of children's rights and prevention of child maltreatment. *Lancet*, 373, 332–43.

Roberts, I. and Coggan, C. 1994. Blaming children for child pedestrian injuries. *Soc. Sci. Med.*, 38(5), 749–53.

Sloper, P. and Lightfoot, J. 2003. Involving disabled and chronically ill children and young people in health service development. *Child: Care, Health and Development*, 29, 15–20.

Smyth, R.L. 2001. Research with children. *BMJ*, 322, 1377–8.

Spencer, N. 2000. *Poverty and Child Health*, 2nd edition. Oxford: Radford Medical Press.

Stephenson, T. 2002. New medicines for children: who is protecting the rights of the child? *Curr Paediatr*, 12, 331–5.

Stevens, P. and Eide, M. 1990. The first chapter of children's rights. *American Heritage Magazine*, 41. Available at: http://www.americanheritage.com/articles/magazine/ah/1990/5/1990_5_84.shtml [accessed March 2010].

Strand, S. 2007. *Minority Ethnic Pupils in the Longitudinal Study of Young People in England (LSYPE).* Centre for Educational Development Appraisal and Research, University of Warwick. Available at: http://www.dcsf.gov.uk/research/data/uploadfiles/DCSF-RB002.pdf [accessed February 2010].

Sutcliffe, A. 2003. Testing new pharmaceutical products in children. *BMJ*, 326 (7380), 64–5.

The Victoria Climbie Inquiry: Report of an Inquiry by Lord Laming London. 2003. London: HMSO. Available at: http://www.victoria-climbie-inquiry.org.uk/finreport/finreport.htm [accessed March 2010].

Tischler, V., Vostanis, P., Bellerby, T. and Cumella, S. 2002. Evaluation of a mental health outreach service for homeless families. *Archives of Diseases of Childhood*, 86, 158–63.

UNICEF. 2005. *Child Poverty in Rich Countries, 2005*. Innocenti Report Card No.6. Florence: UNICEF Innocenti Research Centre.

Vassal, G. 2009. Will children with cancer benefit from the new European Paediatric Medicines Regulation? *European Journal of Cancer*, 45, 1535–46.

Viner, R.M. and Keane, M. 1998. *Youth Matters: Evidence-Based Best Practice for the Care of Young People in Hospital*. London: Caring for Children in the Health Services.

Walker, N.E. and Doyon, T. 2001. Fairness and reasonableness of the child's decision: a proposed standard for children's participation in medical decision making. *Behav Sci Law*, 19(5–6), 611–36.

Waterhouse, R. 2000. *Lost in Care: Report of the Tribunal of Inquiry into the Abuse of Children in Care in the Former County Council Areas of Gwynedd and Clwyd since 1974*. Part VI: 29.30. London: The Stationery Office.

Watt, G.C.M. 1998. Not only scientists, but also responsible citizens. *J R Coll Phys Lond*, 32, 460–65.

Webb, E. 2000. Health care for ethnic minorities. *Current Pediatrics*, 10, 184–90.

——. 2005. Problem solving in clinical practice: stereotypes and semaphore, keep them coming back for more, pieces missing, nothing fitting, complications galore. *Archive of the Diseases of Childhood, Educ Pract Ed*, 90, 11–14.

Webb, E. and Hartley, B. 1994. Female genital mutilation: a dilemma in child protection. *Archives of Diseases in Childhood*, 70, 441–4.

Webb, E., Maddocks, A. and Bongilli, J. 2002. Effectively protecting Black and minority ethnic children from harm: overcoming barriers to the child protection process. *Child Abuse Review*, 11, 394–410.

Webb, E. and Moynihan, S. 2010. An ethical approach to resolving value conflicts in child protection. *Arch Dis Child*, 95, 55–8.

Webb, E., Naish, J. and MacFarlane, A. 1996. Planning and commissioning of health services for children and young people. *Journal of Public Health Medicine*, 18(2), 217–20.

Webb, E., Shankleman, J., Evans, M.R. and Brooks, R. 2001. The health of children in refuges for women victims of domestic violence: cross sectional descriptive survey. *BMJ*, 323, 210–13.

Wilkinson, R. and Pickett, K. 2009. *The Spirit Level: Why More Equal Societies Almost Always Do Better*. London: Penguin.

Wilson, J. 2000. *The Illustrated Mum*. London: Corgi.

Wynne, J. 1994. Female genital mutilation: a dilemma in child protection (commentary). *Archives of Diseases in Childhood*, 70, 444–5.

Young, B., Dixon-Woods, M., Windridge, K.C. and Heney, D. 2003. Managing communication with young people who have a potentially life threatening chronic illness: qualitative study of patients and parents. *BMJ*, 326, 305–7.

Chapter 14

Child Health Equity:
From Theory to Reality

Jeffrey Goldhagen and Raúl Mercer

Introduction

The well-being of children is firmly rooted in the social, political, economic, cultural and environmental determinants of health. Medicine, to the contrary, remains mired in a biomedical 'diagnose and treat' dialectic that is mostly irrelevant to the health and well-being of children and adults. Using the Alma Ata[1] conference as a point of reference, attempts to change this classical practice paradigm over the past several decades have mostly failed. As a result, health disparities within and among countries have increased (UNICEF 2007a, Goldhagen et al. 2005); public health and medicine have continued to diverge (Goldhagen 2005, Beitsch et al. 2005); 'health for all' remains a hollow echo; the emerging 'millennial' morbidities – health outcomes resulting from adverse social and environmental determinants – remain unaddressed (Palfrey et al. 2005); and national and global health systems are unprepared to respond to the rapidly emerging threats of globalisation and climate change (Wamala and Karachi 2006, UNICEF 2007b).

This *status quo* has contributed to the unnecessary suffering and deaths of billions of children and adults (Black, Morris and Bryce 2003, UNICEF 2009). The more we have come to understand social epidemiology and the biology of health, the wider the chasm between knowledge and medical practice has become (Wilkinson 1996). We know that it is not only genetics that defines the trajectory of an individual's health status, but also the environment (epi-genetics) in which genes are expressed (Shelley et al. 2009). We know that racial, class and gender disparities in health are not the result of race, poverty or gender, but rather racism, classism and sexism (Webb 2004, Williams 1999, Case, Lubotsky and Paxson 2000). Elspeth Webb (Chapter 13 in this volume) describes the emerging concept of 'childism' as the next contribution to the culture of 'ism' that so profoundly affects the health and well-being of children.

---

1   The International Conference on Primary Health Care, meeting in Alma Ata, USSR, in September 1978, expressed the need for urgent action by all governments, all health and development workers, and the world community to protect and promote the health of all the people of the world. The Declaration of Alma Ata is available at: www.who.int/hpr/NPH/docs/declaration_almaata.pdf [accessed 22 March 2010].

With respect to health care, we know that it contributes relatively little to health outcomes (McGinnis and Foege 1993, Klerman et al. 2001). Yet despite the evidence-base of social epidemiology accrued over the past several decades, and the rapidly expanding knowledge-base of the life-course sciences – genetics, developmental neurology and endocrinology, embryology, child development, etc. (Bartley, Blane and Montgomery 1997, Hertzman et al. 2001, Lu and Halfon 2003, DiPietro 2000) – medicine has yet to fully integrate these advances into its discipline. As a profession, medicine maintains a cloak of conservatism that precludes the transformational changes that will be required for it to respond to the millennial determinants of children's health.

The intent of this chapter is to present an equity-based approach to child health that responds to the millennial determinants of children's well-being (Spencer 2003, Nazroo 2003, Keating and Hertzman 1999, Marmot 2006). This new paradigm translates the principles of child rights, social justice and health equity into child health practice. The CRC is used as the framework to ensure the full inventory of social, economic, civil-political, cultural and environmental determinants of children's well-being are addressed. Elements of this equity-based practice have been accrued over many years through the global experience of multiple disciplines and stakeholders in children's health and well-being. This model for global health is positioned at the intersection of social epidemiology and the biological, medical, public health and social sciences. The figures and tables that follow provide the blueprints and tools for building this new discipline of Child Health Equity.

Child Health Equity – Structure

The emerging discipline of Child Health Equity is structured to respond to the complex and dynamic interaction of the global political, social, economic, cultural and physical environments that impact every aspect of children's lives. It uses an interdisciplinary set of strategies and tools to translate the knowledge and evidence base of social epidemiology and the life course sciences into the practice of Child Health Equity. The foundational blueprint for this architecture is presented in Figure 14.1.

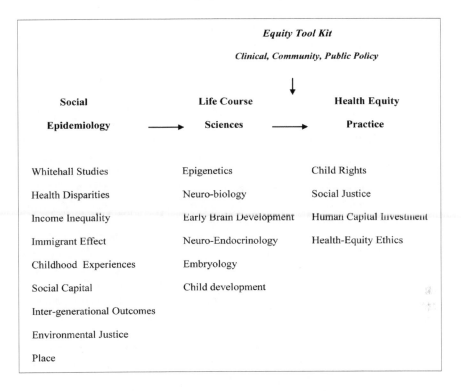

Figure 14.1   Blueprint for the new practice of Child Health Equity

This model reflects the process of innovation in medicine. Accumulated observations become established as an epidemiology. Epidemiological findings catalyse advances in science. The knowledge and evidence-bases of epidemiology and science are then translated into practice. In the scenario of Child Health Equity, observations related to the root causes of health, accumulated over the past several decades, have become the substrate of the evolving discipline of social epidemiology. An in-depth presentation of this epidemiology is beyond the scope of this chapter. The following examples represent only a sample of the sentinel observations of social epidemiology that have catalysed recent advances in the life course sciences:

- The Whitehall studies conducted by Sir Michael Marmot identified the social gradient for health (Bosma et al. 1997, Marmot 2009).
- Studies related to health disparities, and in particular those demonstrating the ineffectiveness of quality health care to address disparities in infant mortality, exposed the disconnect between health care and health outcomes (Lu et al. 2003).

- The relationship between income inequality and health outcomes has provided insight into the complex relationship between wealth distribution, poverty and health (Kawachi, Kennedy and Prothrow-Stith 1997, Corak et al. 2005).
- Observations related to the negative impact of living in the United States on the health of immigrants, and in particular the better birth outcomes of newly arrived African immigrant women compared to wealthy educated African American women, has provided insight into the relationship between racism, discrimination and health (David and Collins 2007).
- Accumulated knowledge related to 'Adverse Childhood Outcomes' has contributed to advances in our understanding of the life course impact of infant and child well-being on the trajectory of adult health.[2]
- Application of the sociological construct of social capital to health has demonstrated the importance of positive relationships and social cohesion to child and adult well-being (Zolotor and Runyan 2006, Runyan et al. 1998).
- Consistent findings of inter-generational poverty, educational failure, risk-behaviours, poor health, etc. reflect the impact of social and environmental determinants on health (Kahn, Wilson and Wise 2005, Marmot and Wilkinson 1999).
- Knowledge related to the effects of the physical and social environment on health, and in particular the health of minorities, has redefined the importance of 'place' in the health trajectory of individuals and communities (Frumkin 2005[3]).

The accumulated findings of social epidemiology demanded an explanation rooted in human biology and physiology. Over the past decade, seminal work in early brain development, the neurobiology and endocrinology of foetal development, the effects of the environment on the expression of the genome, and other life course sciences have begun to explain the observations of social epidemiology (Halfon, Shulman and Hochstein 2001, Shonkoff and Philips 2000, Halfon and Hochstein 2002).

What now remains is the challenge to translate the knowledge and evidence-bases of social epidemiology and the life course sciences into practice (Figure 14.1). This will require a change from current medical and health paradigms. Child Health Equity, as recently presented in a policy statement of the American Academy of Pediatrics, is composed of four elements – child rights, social justice, human capital investment and health-equity ethics (Goldhagen, Etzel and Melinkovich 2010). The statement provides the foundation and framework to support this paradigm change. It is critically important to understand that 'health

---

2 Adverse childhood experience study. Available at: http://www.acestudy.org [accessed 22 March 2010].

3 Policy Link. Available at: http://www.policylink.com [accessed 25 March 2009].

equity' is not only an outcome to be achieved, but also provides the strategies and tools with which to achieve these outcomes. With respect to the four core elements of Child Health Equity:

- The principles of *child rights*, as defined by the CRC, establish the prerequisites for the health and well-being of all children; and redefine the status and role of children in society as participants and contributors to their own health and that of the communities in which they live (Article 12). As a result, the relationship between professionals and children will assume a new balance through which the predominant determinants of children's well-being can be more effectively addressed.
- The principles of *social justice* provide insight and instruct how to allocate and distribute finite resources to ensure no children are discriminated against (Article 2, CRC), that the best interests of children are considered when resource allocation and distribution decisions are made (Article 3, CRC), and that their rights to survival and development are fulfilled (Article 6, CRC) (Foege 1993).
- *Human capital investment* defines a value for investment in venues and relationships critical to children's health and development, and reconstructs the world of children and adults as the sum total of these investments. It includes education, environment, social, financial and personal capital. The concept of personal capital attempts to identify and quantify what is required to provide children hope and confidence in the future for themselves and their families (Heckman 2006, Lucas et al. 2007, American Academy of Pediatrics 2003).
- *Health-equity ethics* uses the articles of the CRC to establish an expanded set of ethical principles as a lens through which to view and analyse the world of children and the decisions that impact them. The four core elements of bioethics can be translated into the four themes identified by UNICEF as of particular and pervasive importance,[4] the core components of child rights (Table 14.1).

Table 14.1   Relating the principles of medical ethics and child rights

Children's rights principles	Ethics principles
Non-discrimination	Justice
Promote best interest	Beneficence
Survival and development	Non-maleficence
Listened to and taken seriously	Autonomy

4   http://www.unicef.org/crc/files/Guiding_Principles.pdf [accessed 20 September 2010].

Once this translation has been established, the articles of the CRC can now be used to analyse the ethics of decisions impacting children's health and well-being (Table 14.2) (Nixon and Forman 2008).

Table 14.2 Translating the elements of bioethics into 'four themes' of the CRC

Taxonomy of rights	Inventory of rights	Ethics principles	Assessment criteria
Economic	Adequate standard of living Social security Protection from economic exploitation	Justice – distributive and allocative	Is there a morally defensible system for allocating resources?
Cultural	Respect for language, culture and religion Abolition of traditional practices likely to be prejudicial to health	Autonomy	Do children feel they are respected?
Social	Life, survival and development Access to best possible health care Education Play Family life or alternative care Family reunification Fullest inclusion for disabled children Support for parents to ensure protection of children's rights	Beneficence	Do participants in policy making processes consider the best interests of the child when decisions are made?
Protective	Promotion of a child's best interests Protection from abuse/exploitation Protection from armed conflict Protection from harmful drugs Protection from trafficking Rehabilitative care post abuse	Non-maleficence	Is the dictate of '*primum no nocere*' (first do no harm) adhered to in decisions made related to the child?
Civil and political	Heard and taken seriously Freedom from discrimination in the Exercise of rights Freedom of religion, association and expression Privacy and information Respect for individual's integrity Freedom from all forms of violence, torture or other cruel, inhuman or degrading treatment Due process in the law Respect within the justice system Not to be detained arbitrarily	Autonomy	Do children consider themselves participants in their environment?

Child Health Equity – Function

With this perspective of the history and structure of Child Health Equity, its principles can now be translated into the practice of paediatrics and child health. In order to accomplish this, child health professionals must move beyond the traditional perimeters of their disciplines to reframe their identity as child advocates functioning at three levels of practice – clinical/programme services, community and systems development and policy formulation (Figure 14.2). This will facilitate a holistic approach to the definition and mitigation of the social and environmental determinants impacting children's health and well-being.

Figure 14.2   Child Health Equity and the three levels of child advocacy

In order to translate the principles of Child Health Equity into practice in these three advocacy domains, a new and expanded set of tools and strategies is required (Figure 14.1). These tools will differ from those currently used in medicine. They are divided into foundational, diagnostic and intervention tools (Figure 14.3, Table 14.3), though most can be used for multiple purposes.

- The foundational tools provide perspective, context and principles to enable professionals to employ the diagnostic and intervention tools. These foundational tools include human rights and related documents relevant to the practice of Child Health Equity (Table 14.3).
- The diagnostic tools provide the capacity to dissect and understand the complexity and dynamics of the root causes of a particular health issue.
- The intervention tools allow for a holistic and integrated approach to children's health and well-being in the domains of clinical service, community development and policy formulation.

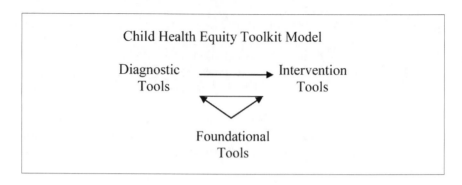

Figure 14.3   Child Health Equity toolkit model

Table 14.3   Child Health Equity toolkit

Foundational tools	Diagnostic-planning tools	Intervention tools
Human rights documents UN Convention the Rights of the Child Covenant on Civil and Political Rights Covenant on Social, Economic and Cultural Rights Convention on the Elimination of all forms of Racial Discrimination Convention on the Elimination of Discrimination against Women Convention against Torture and other Cruel, Inhuman and Degrading Treatment UN Convention on the Rights of Persons with Disabilities ***Other sources*** Social justice Equity-based ethics Life-course science Alma Ata Declaration Ottawa Charter for Health Promotion Millennial Development Goals	Health system framework Root cause analysis Budget Analysis Intergenerational justice analysis Periods of risk analysis Health and environmental impact assessment Ethnography Media/arts/photovoice Environmental justice GIS (Geographic Information System) Health-related quality of life Equity indicators Early childhood development indicators Children's participation indicators Logic models for planning Social capital scales	Child-friendly hospitals Gender tool Cultural competence Children's participation Pain and palliative care Evidence-based practice Ombudsperson Child-friendly cities Medical home Children's participation Medical-legal collaboration Human capital investment Built environment/urban planning Intergenerational justice Wealth transfer Early childhood education Community-based participatory and translational research Children's allowances Evidence-informed policy

A basic principle of health equity is that operating in only a single domain will preclude successful mitigation of any health issue. A systems approach that addresses issues in the context of service, community and systems development and policy formulation is required to respond to the complex contemporary health challenges facing children and families.

Implementing the Child Health EquityToolkit

The complexity of the health issues impacting children requires an analytical approach to determine their root causes in order to implement appropriate interventions. Childhood obesity will be used as a case scenario to demonstrate the utility of the Child Health Equity toolkit to address this complex health issue. Although many tools will be required to address the health issues affecting children, most assessments will begin by using root cause analysis (Wu, Lipshutz and Pronovost 2008) to define issue components, and a health system model (Goldhagen and Lansdown 2008) to provide a structural framework to support and understand how the components interrelate.

Health System Model

Figure 14.4a. presents a health system model that can be used to structure an equity-based approach to complex child health issues. The model provides a linear representation as to how health systems are structured and function.

In general, our current biomedical approach to health issues begins with the identification of morbidities, e.g. obesity, asthma, abuse, infant mortality, etc. (Figure 14.4b). Our system then immediately moves along the continuum to establish incidence, prevalence, distribution mortality, disparity, etc. indicators to characterise the morbidity and monitor interventions. Interventions are most often fragmented and focus primarily in the domain of clinical care. Few systems of care integrate interventions across the domains of clinical care, community and systems development and public policy. As a result, little progress has been made in dealing with the critical health issues impacting children in economically developed and less developed countries.

In an equity-based health system, the array of determinants of children's morbidities is defined prior to moving along the continuum (Figure 14.4c). These determinants are established through the use of root cause analysis (see following section) – a process that engages interdisciplinary professionals, consumers and other stakeholders in a holistic assessment of the complex aetiologies and determinants of a particular health condition (Wu, Lipshutz and Pronovost 2008). This differs from the traditional biomedical practice paradigm in which the root causes of health conditions are rarely defined, and 'subspecialists' work independently to diagnose and treat. Once these root causes are defined, equity-based indicators are generated to both drive and evaluate the clinical, community and public policy interventions. These interventions are framed using the core elements of Child Health Equity – children's rights, social justice, human capital investment and health-equity ethics. The Child Health Equity toolkit (Table 14.3) provides the capacity to translate these principles into practice.

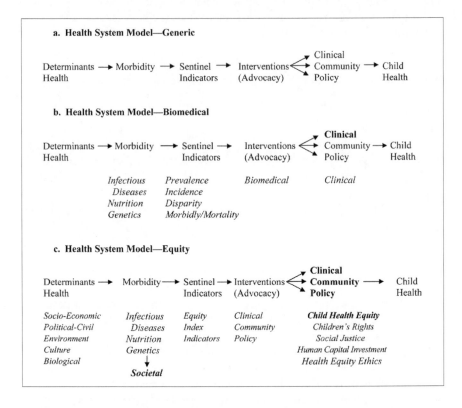

Figure 14.4   Child Health Equity: Health system model

Root Cause Analysis (Wu, Lipshutz and Pronovost 2008)

Root cause analysis (RCA) is a method to identify the proximal (root) aetiologies of problems, conditions and/or events. The practice of RCA is predicated on experience that problems are best solved by correcting and/or eliminating root causes, as opposed to merely addressing symptoms (morbidities). RCA principles applied to health systems recognise that identifying and responding to root causes are more effective than merely treating the symptoms of a condition. To be effective, RCA must be performed systematically, with conclusions and causes substantiated by knowledge and evidence bases. There is usually more than one potential root cause for any given condition. Therefore, a single intervention will seldom succeed. To be effective, the analysis must establish all known causal relationships between the root cause(s) and the defined condition. The process must be iterative as a tool for structuring ongoing interventions and quality improvement.

There are several steps involved in defining the causes of a health issue and that drive the intervention.

- *Identification:* the problem is defined, data/evidence gathered, causal relationships associated with the defined condition are identified and causes are identified which, if removed or changed, will mitigate or prevent the condition
- *Intervention:* effective solutions are identified to prevent recurrence: these must be possible to implement, meet desired goals and objectives and not cause other problems. These recommendations are implemented, results are observed and resultant knowledge and experience is used to continuously improve interventions.

Root cause analysis has the capacity to catalyse the transformation of an aging, conservative medical culture into an equity-based discipline that solves problems by establishing systems of care that operate across the advocacy domains of clinical care, community and systems development and policy formulation. Using obesity as an example, a root cause analysis might reveal, as outlined in Table 14.4, the root determinants, indicators and equity-based interventions for the global epidemic of obesity. The determinants and interventions of root cause analyses will differ depending on a number of factors, e.g. the disciplines and perspectives of the participants; the socioeconomic, political and cultural context; geographical environment, etc.

Table 14.4 Root cause analysis: Childhood obesity

Domains	Determinants	Indicators	Equity approaches and tools
Social Economic Political Civil Cultural	Working families Access to parks and recreation Neighborhood safety School funding Increase agricultural production Business deregulation TV deregulation Media consolidation Corporate growth expectations	Outside meals Supervised meals Outside play School meals Physical education Marketing 'junk' food Calories consumed Marketing to children Commercials: time, focus, number Expansion of fast food chains	Human rights Social justice Human capital investment Ombudspersons Root cause analysis Child-friendly cities Health impact assessment Media Budget analysis Best interests Baby-friendly hospitals Cultural competence Social indicators Medical-legal programme Equity-based ethics GIS/mapping Gender tools

Once the root cause determinants of a condition (obesity) have been identified, interventions can then be developed in the advocacy domains of clinical service, community development and public policy formulation (Table 14.5). Using the articles of the CRC as a health-equity tool, a response to the root causes of childhood obesity can be structured using the health system model framework. This is presented in Figure 14.5.

Table 14.5   Intervening at the three levels of advocacy

Advocacy domains	Determinants	Intervention
Clinical	Working families	Outside meals Supervised meals Outside play Calories consumed
Community	Access to parks and recreation Neighbourhood safety School funding	School meals Physical education
Public policy	Increased agricultural production Business deregulation TV deregulation Media consolidation Corporate growth Expectations	Marketing 'junk' food Marketing to children Commercials Expansion of food chains

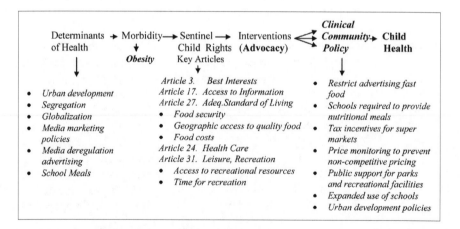

Figure 14.5   Health system model framework

As presented in Figure 14.5, the articles of the CRC can be used as a health-equity tool to establish a holistic framework to support and legitimise a comprehensive assessment and broad array of political, social, economic, environmental and cultural interventions to address the issues impacting health. For example, with respect to childhood obesity:

- *Article 3. Best interests*: are the best interests of the child served by the extensive advertising of fast foods focused specifically on children? Are the menus for school meals developed in the best interests of children?
- *Article 17. Access to information*: is there access to appropriate information to allow children and families to make rational choices about nutrition?
- *Article 27. Adequate standard of living*: is an adequate standard of living ensured by a system that provides insufficient food security for a significant number of children? Is there equity in geographic access to quality food sources between poor and minority communities? Are the price differentials for food between poor and more affluent communities equitable? Does the system ensure financial support equivalent to the purchase requirements of families for food?
- *Article 24. Health care*: is there access to the health services required to prevent or treat obesity?
- *Article 31. Leisure, recreation and cultural activities*: do children have access to the recreational resources they need to provide the physical activities required to remain healthy? Does the need for poor children to work (Article 32), at the expense of time spent in developmentally appropriate recreation and educational pursuits, contribute to poor health outcomes?

Consideration of these potential root cause determinants for obesity leads to a set of equity-based interventions in the three advocacy domains. For example, using the CRC as a tool in the domain of services/programmes, professionals can implement its core principles to ensure overweight children: a) are not discriminated against in the health care setting (Article 2), b) have their best interests considered whenever clinical and institutional decisions are made that could have an impact on them (Article 3), c) have a voice and are listened to (Articles 12, 13, 14 and 15), and d) are provided age and developmentally appropriate nutritional information to enable them to make informed decisions that will affect their lives (Article 17). In addition, respecting the privacy and confidentiality of overweight children will do much to facilitate their involvement in prevention and treatment endeavours and to improve their self-esteem (Article 16).

In the domains of community development and public policy formulation, multiple responses can be implemented that respond to root cause determinants of obesity:

- The density of parks and recreational facilities and the amount of tax dollars used to support sports and recreational programmes in communities could be assessed and potentially increased to ensure access to developmentally appropriate and necessary physical activity for all children.
- Percentage and demography of adolescents employed, and weekly hours of employment, could be monitored and analysed in relation to graduation rates and health status.
- Restrictions on advertising for 'fast food' and other high fat foods could be implemented similar to the restrictions on tobacco advertising.
- Schools could be required to provide nutritional meals. In many urban communities in the United States more than 50 per cent of school age children are enrolled in school lunch programmes.
- The density of food stores and average cost of food items could be monitored to ensure equitable access to food among communities.
- Tax and other economic incentives could be provided to food store chains by local governments to encourage strategic location of food stores and ensure equitable geographic access to food.
- Local governments could also prohibit non-competitive 'price gouging' in poor and minority communities that often have access to only small convenience stores and/or single food chain stores.

In this example, the CRC serves as an effective tool to guide and support the expanded involvement of child-serving professionals in clinical care, child advocacy, community development and public policy formulation. There is an important role for professionals and organisations to play in advocating for the rights of children in their communities and globally.

Other Health Equity Tools

In addition to the use of human (child) rights as a health equity tool, multiple other resources in the Child Health Equity toolkit (Table 14.3) are relevant and can be applied in response to the epidemic of childhood obesity (Table 14.4).

- *Social justice.* The principles of social justice provide an approach to assess the allocation and distribution of resources required for the prevention and treatment of obesity in children (Foege 1993).
- *Human capital investment.* An analysis of how we invest in at-risk children in the multiple currencies of human capital, in particular in schools (educational capital), urban development (environmental capital), social relationships (social capital), provides an expanded context for interventions for at-risk children (Heckman 2006, Lucas et al. 2007, American Academy of Pediatrics 2003).
- *Ombudspersons.* The ombudsperson's role in fulfilling the rights of all

children without discrimination is vital to ensuring the prerequisites for optimal nutrition are available to all children, and access to care is accessible for overweight children.[5]

- *Child-friendly cities.* UNICEF's Child Friendly Cities initiative is a powerful tool for engaging children and youth in building environments that respond to their needs for optimal growth and development.[6]
- *Health impact assessment.* Health impact assessment is an evidence-based analytic tool which can be used to assess the health impact of political decisions affecting overweight children and youth.[7]
- *Budget analysis-best interests.* Budget analysis tools facilitate the evaluation of resource allocations made by elected officials as they relate to considering the best interests of overweight children.[8]
- *Baby-friendly hospitals.* UNICEF's Baby Friendly Hospital movement is a structured evidence-based strategy for increasing the prevalence and duration of breastfeeding (Southall et al. 2000).
- *Cultural competence.* Training and skills in cultural competence ensure that culture is used in a supportive way to effect positive health outcomes for overweight children (Joseph et al. 2005).
- *Health-equity indicators.* Quality of life indicators for communities that address the root cause social and environmental determinants of childhood obesity are critical to understand, monitor and mitigate the complex and interrelated causes of obesity.[9]
- *Medical-legal partnerships.* Medical-legal partnerships provide clinicians with a mechanism to ensure overweight children are receiving the services and resources for which they are eligible.[10]
- *Equity-based ethics.* Equity-based ethical analyses provide an expanded lens through which to view the ethical basis of decisions made by professionals and those in power that impact at-risk and/or overweight children and youth (Nixon and Forman 2008).
- *GIS/mapping.* This technology provides the capacity to map and analyse

---

5   European Network of Ombudspersons for Children. Available at: http://www.crin. org/enoc/resources/InfoDetail.asp?ID=15044 [accessed 4 February 2009].

6   Child Friendly Cities. Available at: www.childfriendlycities.org [accessed 4 February 2009].

7   Centers for Disease Control and Prevention. Health impact assessment. Available at: http://www.cdc.gov/healthyplaces/hia.htm [accessed 4 February 2009]. CDC Healthy Places. Health Impact Assessment. Available at: www.cdc.gov/healthyplaces/hia.htm *[accessed 22 March 2010].*

8   International budget partnership. Available at: www.internationalbudget.org/ themes/ESC/index.htm *[accessed 22 March 2010].*

9   Global Equity Gauge Alliance. Available at: www.gega.org.za/ [accessed 4 February 2009].

10   National Center for Medical Legal Partnership. Available at: http://www. mlpforchildren.org [accessed 4 February 2009].

the distribution of resources, e.g. food stores, parks, recreation facilities, required to prevent and mitigate childhood obesity.[11]

- *Gender tools*. These tools facilitate the analysis and definition of how systems consider and respond to the needs and best interests of overweight girls and boys (Joseph et al. 2005).

In summary, restructuring our approach to childhood obesity using an equity-based framework will require a systemic response to the threats and challenges facing children and families. These threats and challenges manifest as the social, economic, political, cultural and environmental determinants of children's well-being. Child health professionals will need to move beyond their limited roles as clinicians to conceptualise themselves as child advocates functioning in the advocacy domains of practice, community and systems development and public policy formulation. The Child Health Equity toolkit will provide the capacity to translate these principles into practice.

Beyond Obesity

On a global scale, the complex interplay and impact of social and environmental determinants on the lives of children throughout the world dictate the need for professionals and organisations to translate the principles of Child Health Equity into practice. Among the many available resources, the CRC in particular provides professionals in economically developed and less economically developed countries with a template for community advocacy and policy formulation. Examples of the relevance of the CRC to several global health challenges that professionals will increasingly confront include (Waterston and Goldhagen 2007):

- The movement of children across borders through immigration, trafficking, adoption, etc. is a global issue. Articles 7, 8, 9, 10, 11, 20, 21, 22, 30 and 35 deal specifically with these concerns.
- In a global economy, the exploitation of children for and by adults within and outside a child's community is both a local and international matter. Articles 32, 34 and 36 relate specifically to the protection of children from child labour and sexual and other forms of exploitation.
- International standards of conduct required to develop civil societies and peace benefit all countries. Societies cannot reach these standards unless children are extended the rights required to ensure they are protected from abuse and marginalisation. Articles 19, 37, 38 and 40 extend the rights of children to be protected from abuse and neglect, torture and deprivation of liberty, armed conflicts and aberrant juvenile justice systems.

---

11   GIS mapping. Available at: www.who.int/health_mapping/en/ [accessed 22 March 2010].

- Investment in the health and development of children (Articles 23, 24 and 31), standards of living (Articles 26 and 27) and education (Articles 28 and 29) will pay significant dividends across the life course.

Conclusion

Most social movements of consequence throughout modern history have been built on a foundation of human rights and social justice. The emerging discipline of Child Health Equity inherits this pedigree – the relevance and importance of an equity- and rights-based approach to the global health and well-being of children cannot be overstated. At a minimum, this approach requires the incorporation of the principles and practices of children's rights and social justice into all professional pursuits and aspects of children's lives. The CRC provides a foundation and framework to support this work in relation to the delivery of children's services, community and systems development and the generation of public policy.

Restructuring our approach to children's health and well-being, using the strategies and tools of Child Health Equity, will allow us to recognise, understand and respond to the challenges facing children and families in the context of the social and environmental determinants of their well-being. It will reframe our understanding of children and childhood and allow us to relate to children as people in their own right, with their own voices. Integrating the principles of Child Health Equity – children's rights, social justice, human capital investment and health-equity ethics – into practice will require a fundamental shift in the education of child-serving professionals, the work of public and private sector institutions and research agendas and methods.

The global health of children remains an indictment of the world community. If we are to succeed in ensuring the optimal health and well-being of all children, and if child-serving professionals and organisations are to remain relevant to the needs of children, we must expand our roles and capacity to integrate an equity- and rights-based approach to all domains of child health practice. The practice of Child Health Equity will build on the practice paradigms of the past to ensure the relevance of paediatrics and child health into the future.

References

American Academy of Pediatrics, Committee on Environmental Health. 2003. *Pediatric Environmental Health*, 2nd edition, edited by R. Etzel and S. Balk. Elk Grove Village, IL: American Academy of Pediatrics.

Bartley, M., Blane, D. and Montgomery, S. 1997. Health and the life course: why safety nets matter. *BMJ*, 314(7088), 1194–6.

Beitsch, L., Brooks, R., Glasser, J. and Coble, Y. 2005. The medicine and public health initiative: ten years later. *American Journal of Public Health*, 29(2), 149–53.

Black, R., Morris, S. and Bryce, J. 2003. Where and why are 10 million children dying every year? *Lancet*, 361, 2226–34.

Bosma, H., Marmot, M., Hemingway, H., Nicholson, A., Brunner, E. and Stansfeld, S. 1997. Low job control and risk of coronary heart disease in Whitehall II (prospective cohort) study. *BMJ*, 314, 558–62.

Case, A., Lubotsky, D. and Paxson, C. 2000. Economic status and health in childhood: the origins of the gradient. *American Economic Review*, 92, 1308–34.

Corak, M., Lietz, C. and Sutherland, H. 2005. *The Impact of Tax and Transfer Systems on Children in the European Union*. Innocenti Working Paper No. 2005-04. Florence: UNICEF Innocenti Research Center.

David, R. and Collins, J. 2007. Disparities in infant mortality: what's genetics got to do with it? *American Journal of Public Health*, 97(7), 1191–7.

DiPietro, J. 2000. Baby and the brain: advances in child development. *Annual Review of Public Health*, 21, 455–71.

Foege, W. 1993. Preventive medicine and public health. *JAMA*, 270(2), 251–2.

Frumkin, H. 2005. Health, equity, and the built environment. *Environmental Health Perspectives*, 113(5), 290–91.

Goldhagen, J. 2005. Integrating pediatrics and public health. *Pediatrics*, 115(4 Suppl), 1202–8.

Goldhagen, J. and Lansdown, G. 2008. Child Rights, in K. Heggenhougen and S. Quah (eds), *International Encyclopedia of Public Health, Vol. 1*. San Diego, CA: Academic Press, pp. 605–12.

Goldhagen, J., Remo, R., Bryant, T. III, Wludyka, P., Dailey, A., Wood, D., Watts, G. and Livingood, W. 2005. The health status of southern children: a neglected regional disparity. *Pediatrics*, 116(6), 746–53. Available at: http://pediatrics.aappublications.org/cgi/content/full/116/6/e746 [accessed 20 September 2010].

Goldhagen J., Etzel, R., Melinkovich, P. 2010. Policy Statement with the Council on Community Pediatrics and Committee on Native American Child Health. Health equity and children's rights. *Pediatrics*, 125(4), 838–849.

Halfon, N. and Hochstein, M. 2002. Life course health development: an integrated framework for developing health, policy, and research. *Milbank Q*, 80(3), 433–79.

Halfon, N., Shulman, E. and Hochstein, M. 2001. *Brain Development in Early Childhood: Building Community Systems for Young Children*. Los Angeles, CA: UCLA Center for Healthier Children, Families and Children. Available at: http://www.healthychild.ucla.edu/Publications/Documents/halfon.health.dev.pdf [accessed 4 February 2009].

Heckman, J. 2006. Skill formation and the economics of investing in disadvantaged children. *Science*, 312, 1900–902.

Hertzman, C., Power, C., Matthews, S. and Manor, O. 2001. Using an interactive framework of society and lifecourse to explain self-rated health in early adulthood. *Soc Sci Med*, 53(12), 1575–85.

Joseph, R., Betancourt, J.R., Green, A.R., Carrillo, J.E. and Park, E.R. 2005. Cultural competence and health care disparities: key perspectives and trends. *Health Affairs*, 24(2), 499–505.

Kahn, R., Wilson, K. and Wise, P. 2005. Intergenerational health disparities: socioeconomic status, women's health conditions, and child behavior problems. *Public Health Report*, 120, 399–407.

Kawachi, I., Kennedy, B. and Prothrow-Stith, D. 1997. Social capital, income inequality and mortality. *American Journal of Public Health*, 87(9), 1491–8.

Keating, D.P. and Hertzman, C. 1999. *Developmental Health and the Wealth of Nations: Social, Biological, and Educational Dynamics*. New York: Guilford Press.

Klerman, V., Klerman, L.V, Ramey, S.L, Goldenberg, R.L, Marbury, S., Hou, J. and Cliver, S.P. 2001. A randomized trial of augmented prenatal care for multiple-risk, Medicaid-eligible African American women. *American Journal of Public Health*, 91(1), 105–11.

Lu, M. and Halfon, N. 2003. Racial and ethnic disparities in birth outcomes: a life-course perspective. *Maternal Child Health Journal*, 7(1), 13–30.

Lu, M.C., Tache, V., Alexander, G.R., Kotelchuck, M. and Halfon, N. 2003. Preventing low birth weight: is prenatal care the answer? *Journal of Maternal, Fetal and Neonatal Medicine*, 13(6), 362–80.

Lucas, P., Dowling, S., Joughin, C., et al. 2007. Financial benefits for child health and well-being in low income or socially disadvantaged families in developed world countries. *Cochrane Database Syst Review*, 1, CD006358.

Marmot, M. 2006. Health in an unequal world. *Lancet*, 368, 2081–94.

——. 2009. Health inequalities among British civil servants: the Whitehall II study. *The Lancet*, 337, 1387–93.

Marmot, M. and Wilkinson, R. 1999. *Social Determinants of Health*. Oxford: Oxford University Press.

McGinnis, J.M. and Foege, W.H. 1993. Actual causes of death in the United States. *JAMA*, 270(18), 2207–12.

Nazroo, J. 2003. The structuring of ethnic inequalities in health: economic position, racial discrimination and racism. *American Journal of Public Health*, 93(2), 277–84.

Nixon, S. and Forman, L. 2008. Exploring synergies between human rights and public health ethics: a whole greater than the sum of its parts. *BMC International Health and Human Rights*, 8(2).

Palfrey, J., Tonniges, T., Green, M. and Richmond, K. 2005. Introduction: addressing the millennial morbidity – the context of community pediatrics. *Pediatrics*, 115, 1121–3.

Runyan, D., Hunter, W., Socolar, R., Amaya-Jackson, L., English, D., Landsverk, J., Dubowitz, H., Browne, D., Bangdiwala, S. and Mathew, R. 1998. Children

who prosper in unfavorable environments: the relationship to social capital. *Pediatrics*, 101(1 Pt 1), 12–18.

Shelley, L., Berger, S.L., Kouzarides, T., Shiekhattar, R. and Shilatifard, A. 2009. An operational definition of epigenetics. *Genes and Dev*, 23, 781–3.

Shonkoff, J. and Philips, D. (eds). 2000. *From Neurons to Neighborhoods: The Science of Early Childhood Development*. Washington, DC: National Academies Press.

Southall, D., Burr, S., Smith, R., Bull, D., Radford, A., Williams, A. and Nicholson, S. 2000. The Child-Friendly Healthcare Initiative (CFHI): healthcare provision in accordance with the UN Convention on the Rights of the Child. *Pediatrics*, 106(5), 1054–64.

Spencer, N. 2003. Social, economic, and political determinants of child health. *Pediatrics*, 112, 704–6.

UNICEF. 2007a. *An Overview of Child Well-being in Rich Countries*. UNICEF Innocenti Report Card, Issue No. 7. Florence: UNICEF Innocenti Research Centre.

——. 2007b. *Climate Change and Children*. New York: UNICEF. Available at: http://www.unicef.org/publications/index_42166.html [accessed 9 August 2009].

——. 2009. The state of the world's children 2009. Available at: www.unicef.org/sowc09/report/report.php [accessed 22 March 2010].

Wamala, S. and Karachi, I. 2006. *Globalization and Health*. Oxford: Oxford University Press.

Waterston, T. and Goldhagen, J. 2007. Why children's rights are central to international child health. *Archive of Diseases of Childhood*, 92, 176–80.

Webb, E. 2004. Discrimination against children. *Archive of Diseases of Childhood*, 89(9), 804–8.

Wilkinson, R.G. 1996. *Unhealthy Societies: The Afflictions of Inequality*. London: Routledge.

Williams, D. 1999. Race, socioeconomic status, and health: the added effects of racism and discrimination. *Ann N Y Acad Sci*, 896, 173–88.

Wu, A., Lipshutz, A. and Pronovost, P. 2008. Effectiveness and efficiency of root cause analysis in medicine. *JAMA*, 299(6), 685–7.

Zolotor, A. and Runyan, D. 2006. Social capital, family violence, and neglect. *Pediatrics*, 117(6), 1124–31. Available at: http://pediatrics.aappublications.org/cgi/content/full/117/6/e1124 [accessed 20 September 2010].

Chapter 15

Our Rights, Our Story:
Funky Dragon's Report to the United
Nations Committee on the Rights
of the Child

Funky Dragon

Introduction

Funky Dragon Mission Statement

Funky Dragon – the Children and Young People's Assembly for Wales – is a peer-led organisation. Our aim is to give 0–25 year olds the opportunity to get their voices heard on issues that affect them. The opportunity to participate and be listened to is a fundamental right under the United Nations Convention on the Rights of the Child. Funky Dragon will try to represent as wide a range as possible and work with decision-makers to achieve change.

Funky Dragon's main tasks are to make sure that the views of children and young people are heard, particularly by the Welsh Assembly Government, and to support participation in decision-making at national level.

Funky Dragon is the Children and Young People's Assembly for Wales. It was set up in 2002 and achieved charitable status in 2004. It became the first charity in the UK to have under 18s recognised as trustee members and currently works with children aged 6 to 25 years old, through a variety of methods. It was established to enable the participation of Children and Young People and as an instrument for the Welsh Assembly to listen to the views of young people on issues that affect them.

One way this is achieved is through the Grand Council which consists of 100 young people from all over Wales aged 11 to 25. They meet directly with Ministers at the Funky Dragon Annual General Meeting to discuss the issues and concerns of the young people they represent. The Grand Council meets up another three times a year and drives the work of the organisation which ensures it is young people-led. Through this mechanism the Our Rights, Our Story project developed.

On 11 June 2008, three young people from Wales travelled to Geneva to debate issues from their two reports with the CRC Committee. Their reports – *Our Rights,*

Our Story and *Why Do Peoples Ages Go Up Not Down?* contained the views and opinions of over 14,000 children and young people from Wales. The themes of the reports covered education, information, health, participation, environment and play.

This chapter outlines the process undertaken by a steering group made up of members from the Funky Dragon Grand Council. It starts with the development of an organisation run by young people and goes on to describe the formation of a project which concludes with Welsh representation at the CRC Committee in Geneva.

Funky Dragon

The organisation we now call Funky Dragon – the Children and Young People's Assembly for Wales – had its origin in two different places. The first was a group of young people who, having attended a conference run by Children in Wales in 1998, had been inspired by the Member of Parliament Julie Morgan to build an organisation that was run by young people and represented the views and opinions of young people to the newly formed Welsh Assembly Government (WAG). The second was an initiative started by the then First Minister of the National Assembly for Wales, Alun Michael. The group called 'Young Voice' was a steering group of professionals from a range of different backgrounds including education, children's rights and government officials from supporting departments. The group was facilitated by Wayne David, later to become a Member of Parliament, and worked out of the Wales Youth Agency, in Caerphilly (a quasi non-governmental organisation representing youth workers in Wales).

In the summer of 1999, the two groups became aware of each other and began to work in partnership initially to facilitate a conference entitled 'Breaking Barriers'. The event was held at the National Assembly for Wales and the one hundred young people that attended spent the day debating the question: 'If Wales had an organisation run by young people, what would it look like and what would it do?'

Alun Michael's preference at the time was a single annual event to consult with young people. However, the unanimous feeling of the young people at the event was that once a year would not be enough, mainly for reasons of continuity. The event itself was facilitated entirely by young people, with Wayne and his team arranging logistics and providing support.

The event was a great success and provided a clear mandate from the young people, to establish a permanent structure for young people across Wales. Both groups formed what was to become Funky Dragon's management committee and with funding from the National Assembly for Wales set about building an organisation. The mission of the organisation was to incorporate both the CRC and Article 12 in particular, setting out the young people's aspirations and intentions for being a national platform to engage with government and other policy makers. Article 12 states:

1. Parties shall assure to the child who is capable of forming his or her own views the right to express those views freely in all matters affecting the child, the views of the child being given due weight in accordance with the age and maturity of the child.

2. For this purpose, the child shall in particular be provided the opportunity to be heard in any judicial and administrative proceedings affecting the child, either directly, or through a representative or an appropriate body, in a manner consistent with the procedural rules of national law.

The National Assembly for Wales funding was provided with a number of caveats. The first being that professionals from the Young Voice steering group and a National Assembly for Wales observer were members of the Funky Dragon Management Committee, the second was that the organisation kept the name 'Young Voice'. The young people debated these conditions and whilst they were not happy about the name, they were prepared to compromise for £280,000 funding per year (especially as they had never agreed on a name for their organisation and had been using the name 'Bite Back' which had been the title of a conference they had run).

With the funding in the bank the group set about building an organisation. The first steps of this included constituting as both a charity and a company limited by guarantee. When trying to register 'Young Voice' as a company it turned out that there was already a company called Young Voice in existence and British law prohibits two companies having the same name.

This gave the young people an opportunity to name the organisation themselves. After much deliberation, they came up with 'The Children and Young People's Assembly for Wales'. However, it transpired that the law would not allow the organisation to be called that as it had legal connotations and could not be used by a registered company. On advice from Companies House, the young people decided to register under the name of the website they had created called 'Funky Dragon, Draig Ffynci' but to operate as the 'Children and Young People's Assembly for Wales'. However, the name Funky Dragon, Draig Ffynci stuck and is still being used to this day.

Funky Dragon Grand Council

The membership of the organisation, known as the Grand Council, was to be made up of representatives from all of Wales' 22 local authorities, as well as specific interest places and co-options. Each Local Authority Youth Forum elects two young people, one representing the statutory sector and the other representing the voluntary sector. The special interest places included representation from minority groups such as disabled, gay, homeless, looked-after and ethnic minority young people. The co-options spaces were left open. The latter two categories of spaces were specifically designed to ensure as wide a representation of young people as possible. This allowed for 60 spaces for young people in total.

However, this changed in 2005. When school councils became statutory in Wales the Grand Council wanted to ensure that representation was enabled for these groups so the Grand Council increased to three spaces per local authority with the eight specific interest and 12 co-option spaces remaining. This took the total number of available spaces to 86.

There was another change to the structure in 2007 when the young people representing the specific interest spaces wanted to instigate a change. The specific interest representatives decided that they did not like the title 'specific interest' or the way they were represented. From the young people's point of view they felt it was stigmatising and would discourage others to join. They also felt that the categories were too strict and may act to exclude other young people. In view of this the representatives took the idea of renaming the position as 'equality representative' to the rest of the Grand Council. It was discussed, voted and was passed that the name would change along with the structure of Funky Dragon.

The young people agreed that eight specific interest representatives would change to 22 equality representatives (an equality representative elected from each local authority). The new equality representative is no longer limited to the previous eight categories and now includes young farmers, teenage parents and any other group that are under represented through the youth forum elections. In addition to this the new structure has 12 spaces for co-options where young people from anywhere in Wales can be co-opted onto the Grand Council if they feel the group they represent is not represented. This has therefore taken the number of representatives of young people up to 100.

Funky Dragon Management Committee

In constituting the organisation the Grand Council decided that the board of trustees (known as the Management Committee) would be made up of 12 people. Four professionals (from the former Young Voice group) and eight young people from Funky Dragon's Grand Council (four aged 11 to 17 and four aged 18 to 25). This balance was deliberate in ensuring that the organisation was truly young people led.

In attempting to constitute the organisation as a charity, the Charity Commission at first turned down the application, on the grounds that British Law stated that trustees of a charity had to be at least 18 years old. The rejection was debated by the Management Committee and it was decided that rather than compromise and not have under 18s on the board, the young people felt that it would be better to continue as a registered company (Company Law at that time had no such age requirements) but also to continue to try to achieve charitable status with under 18s on the board.

With the assistance of lawyers and years of letters back and forth to the Charity Commission, Funky Dragon finally secured its charitable status in May 2004.

With no compromise from the Management Committee, Funky Dragon became the first charity in British history to have under-18 year-olds as trustees, an honour which is still taken very seriously by Funky Dragon's members today. The Charity Commission has since published information on their website on how other charities can involve under 18s on their board.[1]

The CRC Reporting Process

During the early development of Funky Dragon, two young people from the original steering group were offered the opportunity to accompany Save the Children (Wales) staff to Geneva as part of the NGO reporting process in 2002. If you look at the CRC Committee's records you will see the group at this stage was called Young Voice. Development of Funky Dragon had not got as far as naming the organisation.

In the evaluation of the process the young people admitted they had taken very opposite approaches to the event. One had read all papers sent to them whilst the other had simply turned up. However, in their evaluations of the event they both concluded the same thing; they had both gone along as individuals and whilst the experience had been a mostly positive one for both of them, they each felt that they could only respond to the committee's questions as individuals and not as representatives. This in turn meant that all of their answers to the Committee members' questions were of their own personal experience and not in any way representing others. On their return, their joint recommendation was that should Funky Dragon ever form as an organisation and return to the CRC Committee, then whoever went should do so as representatives of young people in Wales and not as individuals.

Due to Funky Dragon's two year membership rule, when it came to starting the reporting process the two young people that had originally attended the meeting of the CRC Committee in Geneva were no longer around for the next reporting round in 2008. However, the next group of young people used their evaluation and its subsequent recommendations as both an inspiration and a guide to the next report produced by Funky Dragon.

The Our Rights, Our Story Steering Group

In February 2006 Funky Dragon held one of its Grand Council residential weekends in Bala, North Wales. As part of the weekend Funky Dragon staff ran a workshop on both the CRC and the reporting process. As part of this workshop the young people decided that a steering group should be set up to explore the idea of Funky Dragon reporting to the CRC Committee. Membership of the steering group was

---

1   Further information can be found on the Charity Commission website: http://www. charity-commission.gov.uk/ [accessed 20 September 2010].

open to all Funky Dragon's Grand Council members, and a total of eight young people signed up there and then.

Membership of the group would remain open to other Grand Council members throughout the period of the project and other young people could join later. This random self-selection process produced a cross-section of young people aged 12 to 22. The individual members of the group represented male, female, Welsh speakers, ethnic minorities, disabled, gay, lesbian, looked after and homeless. Throughout the project 18 different young people took part; some stayed for the duration of the project whilst others stayed for a few months. In terms of the young people's geographical spread they came from 14 different Local Authorities from across Wales.

Learning from Others

Starting with a blank canvas and a self-confessed lack of knowledge the staff and steering group set about finding out what others had done before and who could help the project on its journey.

Funky Dragon staff conducted a literature search looking for previous children's reports to the UN; in total 12 others were found. Of these only one was similar to what was trying to be achieved. This was the Belgian 'What do you think?' project. Whilst the Belgian project had been initiated by UNICEF and had a steering group of professionals it had also had a steering group of 50 young people aged mainly between 13 and 18. Charlotte Van Den Abeele, the project co-ordinator was contacted and she kindly invited the steering group over to Brussels to meet her and some of the young people involved in the project. With support from the WAG's Brussels office in terms of logistics (Brussels is not in any way wheelchair friendly) the steering group spent three days there.

The group spent a day with Charlotte and three young people from the original 'What do you think?' project and were given the opportunity to learn about what they did, how it was done and anything that should be avoided! The group spent the second day thinking about how they would start their research, what themes they would like to cover and, more importantly, a name for the project. The name took up much discussion! A short list of choices was put together which went back to the rest of the young people on the Grand Council for a vote, where Our Rights, Our Story (OROS) won.

Funky Dragon approached Dr Kevin Haines at Swansea University for guidance. Dr Antonella Invernizzi also volunteered her support. Kevin met with the steering group during its first residential. He also provided training on what is research, data collection and stratification. It is important to note that whilst providing knowledge and advice at the outset neither Kevin nor Antonella took part in any of the decisions around the project.

To enhance the staff's capacity to support young people each of the Senior Staff (six) embarked on Social Research Masters Courses at Swansea University to gain an understanding of research techniques. Their knowledge was then used to advise the young people on their chosen methods.

Staff Recruitment

Having established a name for the project and some general aims and objectives, the steering group set about recruiting staff to carry out their research. Job descriptions and person specifications were written and jobs advertised. Members of the steering group then shortlisted and interviewed candidates; in total six project workers were appointed.

The role of the project workers was to identify groups, schools etc. Once identified in terms of the project's agreed stratification, the project workers were tasked with data collection. They were supported and monitored in their work by both their Funky Dragon line managers and the steering group.

Themes and Issues

As part of their planning process the steering group had considered the CRC's framework for NGOs compiling alternative reports. Whilst the framework may have suited the CRC Committee and NGOs' purposes it did not fit with what the young people had envisaged. Whilst Jaap Doek, then chair of the CRC Committee, was in Wales speaking at a conference, members of Funky Dragon met with him and discussed the reporting frameworks response. Jaap informed the young people that children's reports could be in any format they wish.

With this in mind the steering group started its process by examining the CRC in detail. Understanding the Convention and the articles contained within it was a time-consuming but important process which would enable the steering group to make informed decisions on which issues should be taken forward by their research. It felt that many articles of the CRC whilst very worthy and agreeable didn't really offer them any scope for further exploration within a Welsh context. For example with Article 35 – to protect children from abduction – whilst the steering group would not challenge this right as part of the Convention they did not feel that their ability to claim this right was in any way challenged.

In deciding which articles the steering group felt would be relevant to children and young people in Wales they developed five themes to focus on – education, health, information, participation and specific interest; which the relevant articles came under. After the themes had been decided the steering group decided its main research question would be: *To what extent are young people in Wales able to access their rights (as defined by the CRC)?*

Under the five themes, the steering group devised questions in a brainstorming activity which was repeated in a consultation with over 100 young people at Funky Dragon's AGM in July 2007. The steering group then revisited the questions and handed them to staff, along with the decision to carry out both quantitative and qualitative research for development into research tools.

At this point, the staff team matched the questions, by theme, to articles in the CRC. They were then divided into those that would provide interesting national statistics for the quantitative survey and those that were of lesser statistical significance, yet interesting and insightful. These were explored by smaller groups through qualitative workshop activity. The maximum number of survey questions was agreed, formed into closed questions, technically improved, piloted using the survey's electronic voting system and reduced in number to fit the time period for a school assembly.

Qualitative workshop activities were devised to cover the five themes and piloted. Feedback from the pilot sessions was used to refine them. A pre-requisite to data collection was a desk-based research exercise, in order to identify young people's services, organisations and groups, by local authority, across Wales.

Welsh Language

Wales is a bi-lingual country with approximately 22 per cent of its population using Welsh as its first language. Funky Dragon has written and implemented a Welsh Language Scheme ensuring its activities are carried out in both languages. All OROS publicity, research tools, websites, information and reports were available in Welsh as well as English. Many data collection sessions with young people, particularly those in Welsh-speaking schools were run entirely through the medium of Welsh.

In producing publicity materials for the OROS project Funky Dragon was unable to find an officially recognised Welsh translation of the CRC. Funky Dragon sought permission from the United Nations and had the entire convention translated into Welsh then published the Convention along with a guide explaining both the history and the mechanisms of the CRC. This guide, *The Complete Explanation of the CRC*, was freely available in hard copy and downloadable from Funky Dragon's website.

The Research

Having established the themes which the project was going to cover and asked over 100 young people 'what would you ask young people if you were doing the research?' the steering group began to think about how they would conduct their research. It was decided to carry out three very different types of research in order to reach as wide a range of young people as possible and explore young people's issues in depth.

Even though Funky Dragon ran two websites – www.funkydragonjunior. co.uk aimed at 7 to 10 year olds and www.funkydragon.org, the latter receiving over 10,000 individual users per month – it was decided not to use either for the purposes of data collection. The reason for this was reliability, there was no way of ensuring that those completing the on-line survey were who they said they were and therefore it was considered to be an unreliable source of information.

A research protocol was written to ensure consistency and validity of the research when it came to analysis; it made sure that the research was carried out correctly by everyone irrespective of who was running each workshop.

The National Survey

Fifty questions and statements were generated from what young people had told us they would ask. All of the questions were closed by means of multiple-choice answers. Answers to questions ranged from 'yes/no'/ 'don't know' to 'always/ 'sometimes'/ 'occasionally'/ 'never'. Statements asked young people to 'agree' or 'disagree' to varying degrees. The steering group wanted to conduct the research in a fun and interactive way, doing something very different from the normal, paper-based survey.

Further to this they felt it was vitally important that all the young people who took part in the survey had to have a clear understanding of both the questions and answers the survey contained. This meant ensuring sure that the survey was accessible to all young people, even if their reading skills were not great. It was felt the only way to do this was to make sure that every question and its answers were read out aloud and explained. This would give all young people the opportunity to ask questions to clarify any points.

In order to carry out the survey in this way Funky Dragon purchased an electronic 'voting system'. The system had 180 individual keypads which worked in conjunction with a PowerPoint presentation. A public address system was also purchased to ensure that large venues with a high number of young people could also be accommodated.

The surveys were mainly carried out in school assembly settings. Each of the questions and their corresponding answers were projected onto a large screen and then read aloud by Funky Dragon staff. Once satisfied that everybody understood the question, young people were then asked to 'vote'. Each young person had their own remote control and then pressed their chosen answer. As no record was kept of which young person had which remote, the survey was completely anonymous.

All data was then stored on a central computer in the office, which was later analysed using a statistical analyses software tool 'SPSS'.

The Workshops

A series of fun and interactive methods were developed for each of the themes, each theme having a number of different activities. As well as activities to gain data from children and young people, there were also icebreaker games, scene-setting activities and evaluation exercises. The full session with all activities included took around two and a half hours to run. Project staff adapted the sessions to take into account time available, the size of the group and the needs of individuals. The games and activities were not changed, ensuring consistency.

The workshops were designed to work with young people in a participatory manner using a rights based approach. Funky Dragon uses different methods to ensure that all young people can access workshops whilst taking into consideration differing literacy and physical skills. Activities differed according to the theme being discussed but each workshop started with an introduction to the CRC and what are the differences between a 'right' (according to the CRC) and a 'privilege'. In the Living in Wales workshop young people were asked what was good about living in Wales and what they would change; this was carried out using a method called a 'post it storm'; and 'value continuums' were carried out for questions in the Education workshops which allowed the young people to move around and find further information to back up their choices on the value continuum. These could be written down or recorded by a Dictaphone.[2]

Adaptations were provided in the research protocol to ensure inclusivity for all young people but the objectives of the workshop were not lost.

The Interviews

In total 37 one-to-one interviews were carried out with young people from specific interest groups. Each young person was given a disposable camera and asked to take photographs of their community, people and places that were important to them. This was to help them put their rights into the context of their own lives. The photographs were then used as discussion throughout the interview. Due to the nature of specific interest groups this method allowed differing levels of confidence and competence to be taken into account. It also provided an opportunity to express opinions in a variety of ways.

Analysis

It was important that the steering group was involved in decision-making throughout all stages of the research process to ensure it was young people led from start to finish. Once the data collection research period had been completed the next step was to analyse the findings.

The national survey was carried out in 45 secondary schools (two schools per local authority plus one extra school) with 10,035 young people. The quantitative data generated was analysed using SPSS. The young people were given a brief training session on what the package could do, and they then ran frequencies and explored significant findings that could be reported on.

For the qualitative data, 140 workshops were run with 2,170 young people. This research was coded using the Atlas software package, and again, once the young people received a brief training session, they were left to run queries and explore significant findings.

---

2   Further information on these methods can be seen in the Dynamix (2002) publication, *Spice It Up.*

Members of staff that had been trained to use both software packages were on hand to support the young people so that they could make best use of the information gathered. The steering group split into groups and two or three members worked together to focus on one theme.

Due to their confidential and complex content, the analysis of the 37 interviews with young people with specific interests were undertaken by two members of Funky Dragon staff.

Writing the Report

Following the analysis, the steering group was left with a wealth of statistical findings which they wanted to discuss further with other young people. As they had been involved in the process from the start, they took the opportunity of discussing their most significant findings with the rest of the Grand Council at the residential in Aberystwyth in July 2007. The aim of this was not only to show the findings but also to gather views and opinions of the young people on what had been found. It provided additional insight and further questions to be considered in producing the final report.

The Grand Council split into four workshops: health, information, participation and education. Two or three members of the steering group presented their findings in each workshop and asked for the thoughts of the young people. They also whittled down the findings to the most significant ones. The enthusiasm for the work was incredible especially as the young people voluntarily worked up until 11pm. The staff had to put a stop to the work that was going on otherwise they might never have gone to bed!

The staff then took the findings and comments to draft the first version of the report. Once this had been done, it was taken back to the steering group for further comments and to ensure the report reflected what the young people wanted to say.

The Children's Report

Although the main aim of the steering group was to lead the report for 11 to 18 year olds, Funky Dragon were able to include children aged 7 to 10 in the research through additional funding from the WAG in early 2007. The initial funding did not allow for this age group to be included in the research and the additional funding received made it possible to expand the research age group. As a result of the funding two Children's Project Workers and a part-time Web Designer were recruited.

The role of the new staff members was to adapt the questions and methods designed by the young people's steering group for use with 7 to 10 year olds, and to create a new website specifically for children of that age group to tell them of their rights under the Convention. Ideally a children's steering group would have been established. However, the funding and time available did not allow this.

Young people from the Grand Council were involved in the process of the recruitment of the staff from devising job descriptions to short-listing to interviews. The Children's Project Workers were based in Funky Dragon's Swansea and Wrexham offices. The North Wales Project Worker was a fluent Welsh speaker. Their first task was to adapt the methods used with the 11 to 18 year olds into workshops that were more fun with an emphasis on play and creativity, while helping the children to learn about rights. However, as well as the four themes being used by the 11 to 18 age group (information, participation, education, health) the children's team also developed workshops for play, environment and living in Wales.

The first session the project workers ran with each group and class was designed to help them distinguish between a right and a privilege. This proved challenging at times as some children had a concept of rights that was different from a human rights, or CRC-generated, perspective, and seemed to think that owning an iPod was a right and not a privilege!

In total the project workers gathered data from 2,525 children from all over Wales. Children were consulted in schools, play schemes, after school clubs, through children's events and various other groups.

The methods used to gather the information were all qualitative. It was felt that repeating the survey method used for the 11 to 18 year olds would have been inappropriate. Pilots showed that when using multiple choice questions with 7 to 10 year olds, children would go for what they thought an adult would expect them to say, rather than what they genuinely thought. Instead open ended questions such as 'if I were head teacher I would …' were used.

The workshops were adapted slightly for play schemes as activities were sometimes held outside which meant that they could generally be messier! There was also more of an unstructured feel to them as staff did not want to interfere with any other activities that were going on. This also allowed the children to opt in voluntarily rather than be forced to take part. It was felt there would be a certain hypocrisy in stopping children playing to ask them about their rights.

During analysis, Funky Dragon staff were able to use the data collected through qualitative methods to produce quantitative data. In order to distinguish between the research collated from the young people and the research collated from the children, the children's workers wrote a separate report called *Why Do People's Ages Go Up Not Down?* a name which originated from a question a child asked in one of the 'information' themed workshops.

The writing of the children's report, *Why Do People's Ages Go Up Not Down?* had to be undertaken solely by staff as no steering group for children existed within Funky Dragon. However, to gain an input from children all findings were taken to a primary school that had been involved in the initial research where they indicated which of the findings were most important to them, and they wanted the CRC Committee to know about.

Ethical Considerations

All work that involves children and young people should attempt to address ethical dilemmas that may arise. All Funky Dragon's work follows its statement of ethical practice which defines the framework of all research practices and has been approved by Funky Dragon's Management Committee. In addition to this all of Funky Dragon's work adheres to its child protection procedure which outlines the steps for staff to take if they are concerned about the possible abuse of a child. All Funky Dragon staff have been CRB checked, and any staff that the young people came into contact with outside of Funky Dragon would not be left alone with any of them.

Discussions have always taken place regarding the balance between conducting ethical research and gaining valuable research data. The declaration of Helsinki developed by the World Medical Association has become deemed the basis of human research ethics (Tyebkhan 2003). In addition to this, since the ratification of the CRC in 1991, children's rights have become a major influence in research with children (Alderson and Morrow 2004, Kellett 2005).

Combining the ideas of Helsinki with a rights based approach, which ensures children and young people the same privacy and information rights as adults (MacNaughton and Smith 2005), guarantees their safety. This approach meant that if a situation arose that meant addressing the balance between gaining research and conducting ethical research, the child or young person's safety would have been paramount and the project would have been suspended if required.

Informed Consent

The gatekeepers are the adult initial point of contact regarding any work with children. They judge the scheme of work and weigh up the risks and benefits involved for the children and young people they work with (Walsh 2005). They judge the project based on their own ethical, and moral, guidelines. When working with children and young people, obtaining consent from the gatekeepers to access schools, youth forums and so on to involve children and young people in the research is the first step.

It was only once access was gained from the gatekeepers that the children could be asked if they wanted to participate. Funky Dragon's approach to this was the informed consent process. The standpoint for this project was simply to provide all the information we had to allow the children and young people to make an informed decision.

Consent forms were obtained for all young people taking part in the research. It was an integral part of the process and all participants were made aware of what was being asked and why; and given the opportunity not to take part if they didn't want to.

Findings from the Reports

In total, 66 recommendations came out of both reports. However it wasn't possible to take all 66 to the CRC Committee as the young people only had 15 minutes to present their reports at the pre-session in Geneva. The three findings the young people took to the Committee were from both reports; the finding and recommendation for extra play came from the *Why Do People's Ages Go Up Not Down?* children's report; whilst the other two came from the *Our Rights, Our Story* young people's report:

Play

Finding – children were asked an open question 'where do you like to play?' They drew their favourite place or activity. Over 1,700 responses were received and the findings were:

- 25 per cent of children said their local park was their favourite place to play;
- 21 per cent of children said they enjoyed playing in their local area, e.g. local field or street'
- 35 per cent of children said sport was their favourite activity with football receiving the most responses followed by swimming and the trampoline;
- Of all the responses given, 93 per cent named an outdoor space or outdoor activity, only 7 per cent of children drew their favourite place to play indoors, e.g. their bedroom.

Recommendation – Funky Dragon recommends that all children have access to a park that is safe to get to, is clean and has working apparatus. Attention needs to be given to providing more outdoor facilities for this age group such as an increase in outdoor sport and play centres. Where local facilities are available such as leisure centres, adventure playgrounds and playschemes, attention is needed on encouraging this age group to utilise them and processes should be made as child friendly as possible.

Bullying

Finding – when young people were asked if they had been a victim of bullying in school, 46 per cent answered yes, 52 per cent answered no, whilst the remaining 2 per cent abstained. When asked if there were systems in place in school to stop bullying 58 per cent answered yes, 38 per cent answered no and 4 per cent abstained.

Recommendation – Funky Dragon recommends that anti-bullying policies within schools need to be promoted more, so that all members of the school (staff and pupils) are aware of the systems which are in place.

The design of these policies should be worked on with pupils, so that they are as effective as they can be in meeting young people's needs. Funky Dragon also recommends that more is done to monitor and evaluate the implementation of these policies, to ensure their constant improvement and effectiveness.

Funky Dragon recommends that anti-bullying policies are extended to cover both after-school activities and school transport – ensuring young people's safety and well-being in all aspects of their education.

Personal and Social Education in Schools (PSE Lessons)

Finding – young people were asked to grade the question 'I find PSE lessons useful and informative' from 'Agree Strongly' to 'Disagree Strongly'. The results were:

- 15 per cent agree strongly
- 30 per cent agree
- 19 per cent don't know
- 13 per cent disagree
- 23 per cent disagree strongly

Recommendation – Funky Dragon feels the government needs to give clearer directives as to how PSE is taught. Currently schools have the freedom to deliver PSE as they see fit (whether this be as an individual subject or across the curriculum). Funky Dragon feels this is leading to inequalities in the experiences that young people are having in this area, despite the existence of a national curriculum for this subject.

Funky Dragon also recommends that more 'value' be given to PSE in schools. We suggest the government looks towards offering a qualification in this subject, and that specialised teachers should deliver lessons. Funky Dragon recommends that the government (possibly through its inspecting body ESTYN) look at the various ways in which PSE is taught across Wales, and highlight examples of good practice.

Once the *Why Do People's Ages Go Up Not Down?* report and the *Our Rights, Our Story* report were finalised, the CRC Committee received copies for reading, plus an executive summary of both reports which concentrated on the most significant findings as determined by the steering group.

Reporting Back

The main aim of the OROS project was to produce a report to submit to the CRC Committee informing them how young people in Wales were accessing their rights. No-one envisaged how big the process would become and its impact on a Welsh level.

Geneva

The reports were sent to the CRC Committee along with other reports from the UK. Funky Dragon was invited to present its findings to the CRC Committee along with other young people's organisations from the UK; *Get Ready for Geneva* from England and *Article 12* from Scotland. Non-governmental organisations and the Children Commissioners from across the UK also presented evidence at the same session.

In June 2008, three members of the steering group, Rebecca, Chris and Ben, travelled to Geneva to verbally present the findings of the reports gathered from more than 14,000 children and young people from Wales. The steering group decided that they should focus on three main findings; play, bullying and personal and social education lessons in schools.

A DVD was produced showing the journey to Geneva, and included interviews with the three presenters giving their feedback on the process.

Before:

> ... um I think it's important because not many young people go and give evidence to the UN and I think it's important because we've been involved in the project and we know all about it, like more than like another outsider person would or could read about. We know what we've done and what we haven't done and then ... the research (Rebecca).

After:

> we started with each of the nations giving a presentation on what their main results were. We were limited to five minutes, so we quickly went through our main findings and then we went round the committee and they each asked a big load of questions of what they wanted answered and how we went about the report and everything (Rebecca).

> we're in President Wilson which is the UN, one of the UN buildings. Um behind me we've got Rebecca and Ben and some of the Scottish and English people in with the, doing the formal presentations and I'm here waiting for Ben and Rebecca and the rest of us so that we can do the informal presentations (Chris).

> well um, most of the young people got to get their voices heard, every, every nation got to present their presentations, um yeah but I'd say the you know that was the main part of the day for me, I went in and I gave my voice across of what young people in Wales wanted (Chris).

What recommendations would you like to see the committee making?

The compulsory teaching of the UNCRC in PSE frameworks with training provided for teachers and the check of anti-bullying policies in all schools, working alongside with the Welsh Assembly Government. They'd be my main two priorities (Ben).

Linking with Policy Makers in Wales

Funky Dragon has always been very fortunate in its support from ministers and officials at the WAG. Jane Hutt – who was Minister for Children, Education, Lifelong Learning and Skills – has been a long time supporter of Funky Dragon. Throughout the process of the OROS project Funky Dragon members met Jane many times informing her both of the project's progress and the findings as they came out.

When published, a total of 66 recommendations had been made between both the children and the young people's reports. Jane Hutt had instructed officials to respond to them all in a report called *The Right Way Forward*. In May 2008, the minister met with the steering group to discuss each of Funky Dragon's recommendations at length and the subsequent WAG response. Due to the timing of the report some of the OROS recommendations such as bullying on school buses were immediately acted upon by WAG. On the same day, the steering group also met with the Children's Commissioner for Wales, Keith Towler, to discuss their findings.

Following this meeting the minister invited the young people to present their work at a Children and Young People's cabinet meeting a week after their return from Geneva. This was the first time young people had ever been invited to attend a WAG cabinet meeting.

Following presentation of their findings the young people were questioned by the First Minister and other cabinet members. Each of the Assembly Members commended Funky Dragon's work and listened intently to what the young people had to say.

Rapporteur Visit

In September 2008 the Children's Commissioner for Wales hosted Lucy Smith (a member of the CRC Committee and its rapporteur) for five days in Wales. The Commissioner had a very packed and comprehensive itinerary, which included both a meeting and a dinner with members of Funky Dragon. This was not the only time they met during the visit: members of Funky Dragon attended formal events at the National Assembly for Wales. When the three presenters met Lucy Smith in Geneva she had made clear her wish not just to see nice shiny offices, but that she was interested in the lives of children. With this in mind the Funky Dragon steering group met Lucy in 3Gs in Merthyr Tydfil. 3Gs is a youth project in the middle of the Gurnos social housing estate. A number of Funky Dragon members had been part of the project and lived on the estate. Merthyr and the Gurnos estate top Wales' areas of deprivation and related youth exclusion statistics. These include the highest rates of teenage pregnancy, unemployment and youth related crime in both Wales and the UK.

First on the itinerary was an informal meeting between Lucy Smith, the Children's Commissioner, Funky Dragon members and young people from the 3Gs project. During the meeting they discussed the findings of the OROS report and other issues of concern to the young people. Lucy described the reporting process and the constraints of the CRC concluding observations for a State Party. Next on the itinerary was a walk around the estate for Lucy Smith to see firsthand the young people's issues. In true Welsh fashion the skies opened and the rain poured down. The young people offered Lucy Smith the option of not going out in such terrible weather, but their solution was to borrow an umbrella and off they went. The evening's conclusion saw everybody relaxing over a pizza and the conversations continued until late into the night.

Concluding Observations

The CRC Committee published its Concluding Observations for the UK State Party in October 2008. There were 124 recommendations in total. The Grand Council looked at all of the Concluding Observations at a residential in April 2009 to decide which would impact on children and young people in Wales, and to start looking at what, if anything, Funky Dragon could do.

Due to the completion of their two-year term at Funky Dragon there remained only one steering group member who gave a presentation to the Grand Council on the process of reporting. Throughout the Our Rights, Our Story project, filming had been taking place to record the process. This was edited by staff and the DVD was shown to the young people.

As well as the two Funky Dragon reports submitted to the CRC Committee, other reports submitted from Wales that contributed to the development of the Concluding Observations were:

- NGO Report; *Stop, Look and Listen*, 2007
- UK Children's Commissioners Report, 2008
- UK State Party Report and Welsh Assembly Government's list of priorities, 2007

The UNCRC Monitoring Group, of which Funky Dragon was a member, reviewed the Concluding Observations to draw together an action plan for the following five years.

Outcomes of the Project

The project facilitated many outcomes that had not initially been anticipated. These included not only the reports that were sent to the CRC but also networking opportunities with contact with the NGOs throughout Wales and the UK, and the Children's Commissioner, participation of children and young people at a policy level with meetings with Welsh Assembly members and ministers, through to promotion of participation and the UNCRC. It would have been difficult to envisage such an impact at the outset but it was all achieved through the process of researching the reports. These are summarised below.

Reporting process:

- two reports were produced for the CRC Committee that were driven by young people, with a joint executive summary;
- participation of a young people's delegation at the pre-sessional meeting of the CRC Committee (June 2008);
- meetings with the WAG Children and Young People's cabinet to discuss findings which have since continued regularly as part of Funky Dragon's committed links with ministers;
- meeting with the Children Commissioner for Wales (May 2008);
- meeting with Jane Hutt, Minister for Children, Education, Lifelong Learning and Skills (May 2008);
- production of *The Right Way Forward* response by the Welsh Assembly to the *Our Rights, Our Story* and *Why Do People's Ages Go Up Not Down?* reports.

Promotion of participation rights in general:

- two launch events held in North and South Wales simultaneously promoting the reporting process and Funky Dragon (December 2006);
- dissemination of information whilst workshops and the national survey was being carried out, informing children and young people of the CRC;
- production of DVDs;
- translation of the CRC into Welsh.

Networking:

- contact with NGOs throughout Wales and the UK;
- contact with the Children's Commissioner for Wales;
- contact with other young people led organisations throughout the UK;
- contact with schools, organisations and hard to reach groups;
- contact with individual and groups of children and young people;
- contact with policy makers;
- contact with ministers and officials at the WAG.

Participation of children and young people at a policy level:

- debates and discussions between young people and Assembly members and ministers.

Conclusion

The aim of the Our Rights, Our Story project was to give young people from Funky Dragon the opportunity to lead, develop and write a report to inform the CRC Committee how children and young people in Wales can access their rights. The lack of research experience from the young people, and the staff, meant that they worked together in developing their knowledge and resulted in the staff and young people working together in a participatory way, learning together along the way.

As the choice of traditional research methods was less likely to have been initiated by the staff, the project could be deemed as 'child initiated' on Hart's (1992) Ladder of Participation. This is reinforced by the way that the initial visit made by young people from Funky Dragon in 2002 resulted in them stating how young people should be involved from the outset of a process, rather than an afterthought. In terms of the roles of adults working within Hart's participation framework, an understanding of the definition of participation is crucial. CRC Article 12 added focus for the child to 'be heard' and 'consulted on decision making'. The project's aims and outputs were achieved and the steering group's level of satisfaction evidenced in their evaluation. Its intended outcomes were to provide a benchmark and to influence improvements for young people in Wales. Since the publication of both reports, the WAG has published *Priorities for Wales* (WAG and Wales UNCRC Monitoring Group 2009) which sets out policy priorities for children and young people; responding to the CRC Committee's Concluding Observations to the UK State Party. In addition to this, the CRC Committee has acknowledged OROS as an exemplary practice in reporting and has asked for the report to be made available to all States Parties, through its own communication routes.

Next Steps

In November 2009, the opportunity to form a steering group for the next round of reporting to the UN was offered to the new Grand Council members including those that joined at the annual general meeting earlier in July. A number of young people took up the challenge even though they are unlikely to see the final report as the next deadline is currently January 2013; although this may change depending on the Committee. Due to the experience gathered by the staff throughout the previous process and the feedback from the OROS steering group, the next reporting process is likely to be quite different. Resources will differ, support staff knowledge and understanding in the field has grown and expectations of the organisation, in policy making arenas, have been established. OROS has provided benchmarking information as a starting point. These skills and experiences can also be transferred to other research/reporting projects.

One thing that will remain is the underlying ethos that the project will be led and directed by the young people and they will have the ultimate responsibility for directing the work and scope of the project. The children's element will remain separate from the young people's report and it is hoped that further funding can be secured to ensure it reaches its goal of producing a report for next time.

References

Alderson, P. and Morrow, V. 2004. *Ethics, Social Research and Consulting with Children and Young People*. Barkingside: Barnardo's.

Croke, R. and Crowley, A. 2007. *Stop, Look, Listen: The Road to Realising Children's Rights in Wales*. Cardiff: Wales Programme of Save the Children. Available at: http://www.savethechildren.org.uk/en/wales.htm [accessed 21 September 2010].

Dynamix. 2002. *Participation: Spice it Up!* Cardiff: Save the Children Fund.

Funky Dragon. 2006. *Our Rights Our Story: Information Pack*. Funky Dragon. Available at: http://www.funkydragon.org/en/fe/page.asp?n1=1437&n2=2108 &n3=1557 [accessed 21 September 2010].

——. 2007. *Our Rights, Our Story*. Funky Dragon. Available at: http://www. funkydragon.org/en/fe/page.asp?n1=1437&n2=2108 [accessed 21 September 2010].

——. 2007. *Why Do People's Ages Go Up, Not Down?* Funky Dragon. Available at: http://www.funkydragon.org/en/fe/page.asp?n1=1437&n2=2108 [accessed 21 September 2010].

—— (dir). 2006. *Our Rights, Our Story*. (DVD). Unit 15.

—— (dir). 2009. *The Our Rights Our Story Report Presentation to the United Nations*. (DVD). Funky Dragon.

Hart, R. 1992. *Children's Participation: From Tokenism to Citizenship*. Florence: UNICEF International Child Development Centre.

Kellett, M. 2005. *How to Develop Children as Researchers: A Step by Step Guide to the Research Process*. London: Sage.

MacNaughton, G. and Smith, K. 2005. Transforming research ethics: the choices and challenges of researching with children, in A. Farrell (ed.), *Ethical Research with Children*. Berkshire: Open University Press, pp. 112–23.

Tyebkhan, G. 2003. Declaration of Helsinki: the ethical cornerstone of human clinical research. *Indian Journal of Dermatology, Venereology and Leprology*, 69, 245–7. Available at: http://www.ijdvl.com/text.asp?2003/69/3/245/1013 [accessed 21 September 2010].

Walsh, K. 2005. Researching sensitive issues, in A. Farrell (ed.), *Ethical Research with Children*. Berkshire: Open University Press, pp. 68–80.

Welsh Assembly Government. 2008. *The Right Way Forward: The Welsh Assembly Government's Response to the Funky Dragon 'Our Rights, Our Story' Report and 'Why Do People's Ages Go Up, Not Down?' Report*. Cardiff: Welsh Assembly Government. Available at: http://www.funkydragon.org/en/fe/page. asp?n1=1437&n2=2108 [accessed 21 September 2010].

Welsh Assembly Government working in partnership with the Wales UNCRC Monitoring Group. 2009. *Priorities for Wales*. Cardiff: Welsh Assembly Government. Available at: http://www.funkydragon.org/en/fe/page. asp?n1=1437&n2=2108 [accessed 6 October 2009].

Index